GENDER AND ELECTIONS

Fifth Edition

The fifth edition of *Gender and Elections* offers a systematic, lively, multifaceted account of the role of gender in the electoral process through the 2020 elections. This timely, yet enduring, volume strikes a balance between highlighting the most important developments for women as voters and candidates in the 2020 elections and providing a more long-term, in-depth analysis of the ways in which gender has helped shape the contours and outcomes of electoral politics in the United States. Individual chapters demonstrate the importance of gender in understanding and interpreting presidential elections, voter participation and turnout, voting choices, congressional elections, the participation of African American women, the support of political parties and women's organizations, candidate communications with voters, and state elections. Without question, *Gender and Elections* is the most comprehensive, reliable, and trustworthy resource on the role of gender in electoral politics.

Susan J. Carroll is professor emerita at Rutgers University. Formerly a senior scholar at the Center for American Women and Politics, the Eagleton Institute of Politics, Rutgers University, she is coauthor of *A Seat at the Table: Congresswomen's Perspectives on Why Their Presence Matters* (2018, with Kelly Dittmar and Kira Sanbonmatsu) and *More Women Can Run: Gender and Pathways to State Legislatures* (2013, with Kira Sanbonmatsu).

Richard L. Fox is professor of political science at Loyola Marymount University. His research examines how gender affects voting behavior, state executive elections, congressional elections, and political ambition. Most recently he is coauthor of *Women, Men & US Politics: Ten Big Questions* (2017) and *It Still Takes a Candidate: Why Women Don't Run for Office* (Cambridge University Press, 2010), with Jennifer Lawless, and author of *Running from Office: Why Young Americans are Turned Off to Politics* (2015).

Kelly Dittmar is associate professor of political science at Rutgers-Camden and scholar and Director of Research at the Center for American Women and Politics, the Eagleton Institute of Politics, Rutgers University. Her research focuses on gender and American political institutions. She is the coauthor of *A Seat at the Table: Congresswomen's Perspectives on Why Their Presence Matters* (2018, with Kira Sanbonmatsu and Susan J. Carroll) and author of *Navigating Gendered Terrain: Stereotypes and Strategy in Political Campaigns* (2015).

Gender and Elections

SHAPING THE FUTURE OF AMERICAN POLITICS

Fifth Edition

Edited by

Susan J. Carroll
Rutgers University

Richard L. Fox
Loyola Marymount University, California

Kelly Dittmar
Rutgers University

CAMBRIDGE
UNIVERSITY PRESS

CAMBRIDGE
UNIVERSITY PRESS

University Printing House, Cambridge CB2 8BS, United Kingdom

One Liberty Plaza, 20th Floor, New York, NY 10006, USA

477 Williamstown Road, Port Melbourne, VIC 3207, Australia

314–321, 3rd Floor, Plot 3, Splendor Forum, Jasola District Centre, New Delhi – 110025, India

103 Penang Road, #05–06/07, Visioncrest Commercial, Singapore 238467

Cambridge University Press is part of the University of Cambridge.

It furthers the University's mission by disseminating knowledge in the pursuit of
education, learning, and research at the highest international levels of excellence.

www.cambridge.org
Information on this title: www.cambridge.org/highereducation/isbn/9781316511473
DOI: 10.1017/9781009052818

© Cambridge University Press 2006, 2010, 2014, 2018, 2022

First published 2006
Second edition published 2010
Third edition published 2014
Fourth edition published 2018
Reprinted 2018
Fifth edition published 2022

A catalogue record for this publication is available from the British Library.

Library of Congress Cataloging-in-Publication Data
Names: Carroll, Susan J., 1950- editor. | Fox, Richard Logan, editor. | Dittmar, Kelly,
1984– editor.
Title: Gender and elections : shaping the future of American politics / edited by Susan J.
Carroll, Rutgers University, Richard L. Fox, Loyola Marymount University, California,
Kelly Dittmar, Rutgers University.
Description: Fifth edition. | Cambridge, United Kingdom ; New York, NY : Cambridge
University Press, 2022. | Includes bibliographical references and index.
Identifiers: LCCN 2021034457 (print) | LCCN 2021034458 (ebook) | ISBN 9781316511473
(hardback) | ISBN 9781009055925 (paperback) | ISBN 9781009052818 (ebook)
Subjects: LCSH: Women – Political activity – United States. | Elections – United States. |
Voting – United States | Women political candidates – United States. | Sex role – Political
aspects – United States.
Classification: LCC HQ1236.5.U6 G444 2022 (print) | LCC HQ1236.5.U6 (ebook) | DDC
320.082/0973–dc23
LC record available at https://lccn.loc.gov/2021034457
LC ebook record available at https://lccn.loc.gov/2021034458

ISBN 978-1-316-51147-3 Hardback
ISBN 978-1-009-05592-5 Paperback

Additional resources at www.cambridge.org/carroll-fox-dittmar

Contents

Figures

Tables

Text Boxes

Contributors

Amy N. Benner is a Ph.D. candidate in the Department of Political Science at Rutgers University – New Brunswick. She also serves as the Public Leadership Education Network (PLEN) Coordinator for Douglass Residential College and is a graduate student research assistant at the Center for American Women and Politics. Her research interests include women's political participation, barriers to representation, campaign finance, and political psychology. She has coauthored research that focuses on the experiences of first-time women candidates and political contests that feature women running against women. Recent published work includes "Women and Campaigns: Generational Change, Growing Activism," featured in the fourth edition of *Campaigns on the Cutting Edge* (2021), coauthored with Dr. Susan A. MacManus.

Dianne Bystrom is director emerita of the Carrie Chapman Catt Center for Women and Politics at Iowa State University. She is a contributor to twenty-five books – most recently as coeditor of *Women in the American Political System: An Encyclopedia of Women as Voters, Candidates, and Office Holders* (2019) and *An Unprecedented Election: Media, Communication and the Electorate in the 2016 Campaign* (2018) – and has published journal articles on the media coverage and campaign communication of women political candidates, the Iowa caucuses, and youth voters.

Susan J. Carroll is professor emerita at Rutgers University. Formerly a senior scholar at the Center for American Women and Politics, the Eagleton Institute of Politics, Rutgers University, she is coauthor of *A Seat at the Table: Congresswomen's Perspectives on Why Their Presence Matters* (2018, with Kelly Dittmar and Kira Sanbonmatsu) and *More Women Can Run: Gender and Pathways to State Legislatures* (2013, with Kira Sanbonmatsu).

Earlier books include *Women as Candidates in American Politics* (2nd edn., 1994), *Women and American Politics: New Questions, New Directions* (2003), and *The Impact of Women in Public Office* (2001). Carroll also has published numerous journal articles and book chapters focusing on women candidates, voters, elected officials, and political appointees in the United States.

Rosalyn Cooperman is a professor of political science at the University of Mary Washington. Since 2004, she has served as principal investigator for the Convention Delegate Study, a survey of Democratic and Republican party delegates. Her research focuses on the role that political parties and women's campaign finance networks play in supporting women candidates. Her articles have appeared in journals such as the *American Political Science Review*, *Journal of Politics*, and *Party Politics*. She is presently working on a project that evaluates women's service in the Virginia General Assembly.

Kelly Dittmar is an associate professor of political science at Rutgers-Camden and scholar and Director of Research at the Center for American Women and Politics (CAWP), the Eagleton Institute of Politics, Rutgers University. Her research focuses on gender and American political institutions. She is the coauthor of *A Seat at the Table: Congresswomen's Perspectives on Why Their Presence Matters* (2018, with Kira Sanbonmatsu and Susan J. Carroll) and author of *Navigating Gendered Terrain: Stereotypes and Strategy in Political Campaigns* (2015). At CAWP, Dittmar manages national research projects, helps to develop and implement CAWP's research agenda, and contributes to CAWP reports, publications, and analyses.

Richard L. Fox is a professor of political science at Loyola Marymount University. His research examines how gender affects voting behavior, state executive elections, congressional elections, and political ambition. The coauthor of *Women, Men & US Politics: Ten Big Questions* (2017), his other books include *Running from Office: Why Young Americans Are Turned Off to Politics* (2015) and *It Still Takes a Candidate: Why Women Don't Run for Office* (Cambridge University Press, 2010). His articles have appeared in the *Journal of Politics*, *American Journal of Political Science*, *American Political Science Review*, *Political Psychology*, *PS*, *Women & Politics*, *Political Research Quarterly*, and *Public Administration Review*.

Susan A. MacManus is distinguished university professor emerita at the University of South Florida. She is the author of *Florida's Minority Trailblazers:*

The Men and Women Who Changed the Face of Florida Government (2017), *Targeting Senior Voters: Campaign Outreach to Elders and Others with Special Needs* (2000), and *Young v. Old: Generational Combat in the 21st Century* (1996); coauthor with Charles S. Bullock III, Jeremy D. Mayer, and Mark J. Rozell of *The South and the Transformation of US Politics* (2019), with Aubrey Jewett, Thomas R. Dye, and David J. Bonanza of *Politics in Florida* (5th edn., 2019), and with Thomas R. Dye of *Politics in States and Communities* (15th edn., 2015). MacManus was the long-time political analyst for WFLA-TV (Tampa's NBC affiliate), more recently for WFTS-TV (Tampa's ABC affiliate). She chaired the Florida Elections Commission from 1999 to 2001.

Celeste Montoya is an associate professor in women and gender studies and political science at the University of Colorado – Boulder. Her research focuses on gender and race in American and European politics. She has written extensively on intersectionality as it pertains to social movements, public policy, and political representation, and is the author of *From Global to Grassroots: The European Union, Transnational Advocacy, and Combating Violence against Women* (2013) and coeditor of *Gendered Mobilizations and Intersectional Challenges* (2019).

Melanye T. Price is inaugural director of the Ruth J. Simmons Center for Race and Justice and an endowed professor of political science at Prairie View A&M University, her alma mater. She is the author of two books: *The Race Whisperer: Barack Obama and the Political Uses of Race* (2016) and *Dreaming Blackness: Black Nationalism and African American Public Opinion* (2009). Price completed her Ph.D. in political science at The Ohio State University. A regular contributor to the *New York Times'* Opinion section, she has also been a political commentator for MSNBC, CNN, *Ms. Magazine*, *Elle Magazine*, and National Public Radio.

Anna Sampaio is professor of ethnic studies and political science, and chair of the ethnic studies department at Santa Clara University, with specializations in immigration, Latina/o/x politics, race and gender politics, intersectionality, and transnationalism. She is the author of *Terrorizing Latina/o Immigrants: Race, Gender, and Immigration Politics in the Age of Security* (2015), which won the 2016 American Political Science Association award for Best New Book in Latina/o/x Politics. She is currently coeditor of the Intersectionality book series at Temple University Press (with Julia Jordan-Zachery and Celeste Montoya) as well as coeditor of *Transnational Latino/a Communities: Politics, Processes, and Cultures* (2002, with Carlos

Vélez-Ibáñez). Her research has appeared in a wide range of research-centered and public-facing settings, including the *International Feminist Journal of Politics*, *Latino Decisions*, *NACLA*, *New Political Science*, *Politics Groups and Identities*, *Political Research Quarterly*, *PS: Political Science and Politics*, *The Gender Policy Report* and the *Washington Post*. Her current book project, *Latina Political Participation and Activism in the US*, examines the history of Latina political engagement in the United States, with particular attention to the experiences of Mexican American, Puerto Rican, and Cuban American activists in the nineteenth and twentieth centuries.

Kira Sanbonmatsu is professor of political science and senior scholar at the Center for American Women and Politics, the Eagleton Institute of Politics, Rutgers University. She is the coauthor (with Kelly Dittmar and Susan J. Carroll) of *A Seat at the Table: Congresswomen's Perspectives on Why their Presence Matters* (2018) and the coauthor (with Susan J. Carroll) of *More Women Can Run: Gender and Pathways to the State Legislatures* (2013). She is also the author of *Where Women Run: Gender and Party in the American States* (2006) and *Democrats, Republicans, and the Politics of Women's Place* (2002). Sanbonmatsu's research interests include gender, race/ethnicity, parties, elections, public opinion, and state politics. Her research has appeared in journals such as *Political Research Quarterly* and *Politics, Groups and Identities*.

Wendy G. Smooth is an associate professor in the departments of women's gender and sexuality studies and political science at The Ohio State University and is associate dean for diversity, equity, and inclusion and chief diversity officer for the college of arts and sciences. Her research focuses on the impact of gender and race in state legislatures, and Smooth's research on women of color in American politics appears in journals such as *Politics & Gender; Politics, Groups and Identities*, and *Journal of Women, Politics and Policy*.

Maria Wilson is a doctoral candidate in the political science department at Rutgers University. She holds a BA in political science from the University of New Mexico. Her research focuses on the structural and institutional barriers women face when running for office, with a particular focus on childcare and welfare policies. She is also currently a research assistant for the Eagleton Institute's Center for Youth Political Participation.

Acknowledgments

This volume had its origins in a series of three roundtable panels at professional meetings in 2002 and 2003 focusing on how women fared in the 2002 elections. Several of the contributors to this book were participants on those roundtables. As we gathered at these professional meetings, we began to talk among ourselves about a major frustration we faced in teaching courses on women and politics, campaigns and elections, and American politics. We all had difficulty finding suitable, up-to-date materials on women candidates, the gender gap, and other facets of women's involvement in elections, and certainly none of us had been able to find a text focused specifically on gender and elections that we could use. We felt the literature was in great need of a recurring and reliable source that would first be published immediately following a presidential election and then updated every four years so that it remained current.

At some point in our discussions, we all looked at one another and collectively asked, "As the academic experts in this field, aren't we the ones to take on this project? Why don't we produce a volume suitable for classroom use that would also be a resource for scholars, journalists, and practitioners?" In that moment *Gender and Elections* was born. We are enormously grateful to Barbara Burrell for organizing the first of our roundtable panels and thus identifying and pulling together the initial core of contributors to this volume.

We produced the first volume of *Gender and Elections* in the immediate aftermath of the 2004 presidential election and updated and expanded the volume in the second, third, and fourth editions following the elections of 2008, 2012, and 2016, respectively. Gratified by the positive response the book has received over the years, we are pleased to provide this fifth edition, which includes up-to-date information through the 2020 elections as well as some new chapters and contributors to reflect the changing times. We hope to continue to revise and publish new editions following future presidential elections.

This book would not have been possible without the assistance of the Center for American Women and Politics (CAWP) at Rutgers University and its various staff members. In particular, Debbie Walsh, director of CAWP, has embraced and encouraged this project and been supportive in numerous ways. Gilda Morales and Chelsea Hill have been invaluable in providing information about women and politics, and several contributors have relied on data they compiled over the years for CAWP.

As we approached the 2020 elections and a possible fifth edition, Sue and Richard knew the volume would need to undergo some significant changes, given the path-breaking developments taking place for women candidates in presidential politics, the increased mobilization of women as voters and activists following the 2016 elections, and the academic retirements of some key contributors. Fortunately, Kelly Dittmar graciously agreed to come on board as a coeditor to bring fresh eyes to the project. We reluctantly said goodbye to a couple of long-term contributors, Barbara Burrell and Georgia Duerst-Lahti, whom we cannot thank enough for all they have meant to this collective endeavor over the years. Although we are sad to lose Georgia and Barbara, we are very pleased to welcome a number of new contributors – Amy N. Benner, Rosalyn Cooperman, Celeste Montoya, Melanye T. Price, and Maria Wilson – all of whom bring renewed energy, scholarly expertise, and fresh perspectives to this edition.

Finally, we would like to thank Sara Doskow, senior editor, and Maggie Jeffers, development editor, who greatly assisted in helping bring the fifth edition to completion. We also are grateful to Robert Dreesen, our editor for the third and fourth editions, and Ed Parsons, our editor on the first two editions, for their support for this project over the years.

SUSAN J. CARROLL, RICHARD L. FOX, AND KELLY DITTMAR

Introduction

Gender and Electoral Politics in the Twenty-First Century

President Joe Biden gave his first address to Congress on April 28, 2021. He stood at the center of the US House rostrum, with two women seated behind him: Vice President Kamala Harris and House Speaker Nancy Pelosi. Biden began his speech by recognizing the historic moment of which he was part: "Madam Speaker, Madam Vice President. No president has ever said those words from this podium." He added, "And it's about time." Biden was right. Never before 2021 had a woman served as vice president (and thus president of the Senate), nor had the first and only woman Speaker of the House – Nancy Pelosi – sat next to another woman during a presidential address to Congress. But it is the full picture of that moment, including Biden's position at the podium as yet another white, male president of the United States, that captures the complexities of gender in the US elections in the early decades of the twenty-first century.

Specifically, that historic moment was the result of two elections that preceded Biden's 2021 address. The mobilization among Democrats, and Democratic women even more specifically, following the 2016 election continued through the 2018 midterm elections, where Democrats regained the majority in the US House of Representatives and returned the Speaker's gavel to Nancy Pelosi (D-CA), who had become the first woman Speaker of the House in 2007 and had served as Speaker until the Democrats lost the majority in 2011. The Democrats' success in the 2018 House elections can be credited to women since women voters turned out at high rates for Democratic candidates and women candidates won the majority of House seats that flipped from Republican to Democratic.

The momentum of election 2018, fueled in part by opposition to President Donald Trump, continued through election 2020. A record number of women waged candidacies for the Democratic presidential

1

nomination, including then Senator Kamala Harris (D-CA), as well as candidacies for congressional offices. Women voters and activists continued to play key roles in electoral strategy, mobilization, and outcomes. But women's continued and growing power in electoral politics did not yield gender parity. Despite the record number of women who campaigned to be president, the 2020 general election pitted two white men against each other, as it had in every other presidential election before 2008. Joe Biden's selection of Kamala Harris as his running mate demonstrated progress; she not only became the first woman but also the first Black and first South Asian person to be vice president. However, her selection would have been unexceptional if equality in representation was something expected in presidential politics.

At the same time that gender and racial progress was being made at the top of the ticket with Harris' nomination and ultimate victory, the incumbent president, Donald Trump, was doubling down on a campaign strategy that sought to mine racial resentment and reinforce masculinity as the standard by which fitness for office is measured. Trump's policy decisions from the start of his first term targeted racial and ethnic minorities – from the Muslim ban to stark immigration restrictions and family separation policies. His reluctance to denounce white supremacy after a 2017 rally of white nationalists in Charlottesville was seen again on a presidential debate stage in fall 2020. As the nation engaged in a reckoning on racial justice after the murder of George Floyd, an unarmed Black man killed by police, Trump called protesters "thugs" and described organizations like Black Lives Matter as "domestic terrorists." In attempts to win over suburban white women voters, he assured them that he would keep their neighborhoods safe by quelling racial justice protests and pushing back against policies that would further racially integrate their communities. When Harris joined the Democratic ticket, Trump's team shifted their attacks to her, leveraging gender and racial stereotypes to position her as "radical," dangerous, and "nasty."

Throughout all of this, Trump continued to use masculine rhetoric and imagery to establish his dominance, positioning himself as a "tough guy" who would rely on force and attack his opponents as weak and feminine. In the other major crisis confronting the country during election 2020, the COVID-19 pandemic, Trump's embrace of masculine dominance translated into a rejection of science and a conflation – which outlasted his presidency – of mitigating pandemic risk with showing weakness and surrendering personal freedom. Trump's gender and racial politics serve as a reminder that gender is an electoral force navigated by men as well as women, and that the gender dynamics of electoral politics do not occur in isolation from other influential forces, such as race. Finally, despite his loss, Trump's insistence and his supporters' continued belief that the election was stolen well after results were certified demonstrate that his brand of politics, and the gender and racial beliefs that it reflects, remains widely influential in the United States, and may continue to influence the future of our elections.

While Republicans lost the presidency in election 2020, they achieved success in federal and state legislative elections. In the US House, the Democratic majority narrowed significantly. Republican women were responsible for some of that narrowing, running for and winning House seats at record numbers and flipping more seats from Democrat to Republican than their male counterparts. The gains for Republican women officeholders in the House and in state legislatures serve as an important reminder that reaching gender parity in American politics will require progress on both sides of the aisle. These gains also demonstrate that women candidates and officeholders are not monolithic in their beliefs and priorities or even in how they perceive and navigate gender. When Joe Biden stood in front of the 117th Congress in April 2021, he addressed a US Congress with more women members than ever before. But the women who sat behind Biden were markedly different in their political perspectives than many of the women and men to whom he was making a case for legislative actions.

The 2020 elections showed that gender remains a visible and important influence in US politics. This volume analyzes various aspects of electoral politics, explaining how underlying gender dynamics are critical to shaping the contours and the outcomes of elections in the United States. No interpretation of American elections can be complete without an understanding of the growing role of women as political actors and the multiple ways that gender enters into and affects contemporary electoral politics.

THE GENDERED NATURE OF ELECTIONS

Elections in the United States are deeply gendered in several ways. Most obviously, men dominate the electoral playing field. Twenty-six of the thirty-two major party candidates who vied for the Democratic and Republican nominations for president in 2020 were men. Similarly, men constituted the vast majority of candidates for governor and Congress in 2020. Most behind-the-scenes campaign strategists and consultants – the pollsters, media experts, fundraising advisers, and those who develop campaign messages – are also men. Further, most of the best-known network news reporters and anchors charged with telling the story of the 2020 election and previous elections (e.g. David Muir, Lester Holt, Tucker Carlson, and Anderson Cooper) were men. Women are making strides in the world of broadcast news, with Fox News' Laura Ingram and MSNBC's Rachel Maddow becoming leading voices. But a 2019 study from the Women's Media Center found that only one-third of news directors at local television stations were women; and that less than 20 percent of guest op-eds in the most circulated major newspapers were penned by women. Women made up roughly one-third of the workforce at Facebook, even though women are more likely than men to be users.[1] Further, the leading voices in political talk radio, to whom millions of Americans listen every week, are men such as Rush Limbaugh (prior to his death in 2021), Sean Hannity, Dave Ramsey, and Mark Levin. And the majority of those contributing the largest sums of money to candidates and parties, perhaps the most essential ingredient in American politics, are men.[2]

Beyond the continued dominance of men in politics, gendered language permeates our political landscape. Politics and elections are most often described in terms of analogies and metaphors drawn from the traditionally masculine domains of war and sports. Contests for office are often referred to by reporters and political pundits as battles requiring the necessary strategy to harm, damage, or even destroy the opponent. The inner sanctums of presidential campaigns where core strategic advisers convene are called "war rooms." Candidates attack their opponents. They raise money for their war chests. The most attention in presidential races is focused on critical battleground states. In the increasingly uncertain global environment, candidates across the country have touted their toughness in wanting to hunt down and kill terrorists or stand up to China and Russia.

Along with the language of war, sports language is also prevalent in campaigns and in media coverage of campaigns. Considerable attention is devoted to which candidate is ahead or behind in the horse race. Similarly, commentators talk about how campaigns are rounding the bend, entering the stretch drive, or in the final lap. Although language drawn from the racetrack is common, so, too, is language drawn from boxing, baseball,

---

[1] The Status of Women in the US Media 2019, Women's Media Center, 2019, https://tools
    .womensmediacenter.com/page/-/WMCStatusofWomeninUSMedia2019.pdf
[2] Donor Demographics: Gender, Open Secrets, 2021, www.opensecrets.org/elections-overview/
    donor-demographics

football, and other sports. Coverage of political debates often focuses on whether one of the candidates has scored a knockout punch or inflicted any pain. When a candidate becomes aggressive, he or she is described as taking the gloves off. Candidates running for elective office frequently talk about making a comeback, scoring a victory, or being in the early innings of a campaign. When a campaign is in trouble, the candidate may need to throw a Hail Mary pass. An unexpected occurrence is labeled a "curve ball."

So prevalent is the language of war and sports in our political discourse that even those who wish to increase women's political involvement employ it. For example, to provide more opportunities for women to enter politics, advocates frequently argue that we need to level the playing field.

As the language used to analyze politics suggests, our expectations about the qualities, appearance, and behavior of candidates are also highly gendered. We want our leaders to be tough, dominant, and assertive – qualities much more associated with masculinity than femininity in American culture. In the current political context, a military background, especially with combat experience, is still considered desirable for a candidate. However, despite the election of several women veterans to Congress in recent years, military credentials continue to be more common for male than female candidates. Because the American public has seen few women among generals or top military officials, the idea of a female commander in chief or a female leader promising to fight the terrorists or the Russians remains a contradiction to many.

Masculine demands on candidates and officeholders have proven harder for women to negotiate. Women must walk a fine line in meeting masculine expectations while still displaying their femininity. Two areas that have proved particularly challenging for women have been in how they physically present themselves (e.g. dress, athleticism) and how they navigate parental roles, although recent elections have demonstrated some progress for women. Many women have moved away from the singular and professional uniform (e.g. Hillary Clinton's pantsuits) that has long been recommended to women to avoid attention to appearance. In fact, vice-presidential candidate Kamala Harris was celebrated by many when she wore Converse tennis shoes on the campaign trail. Nevertheless, Harris still *did* receive more attention for her shoe selection, as well as her appearance in general, than her male counterparts. Women candidates have also embraced their roles as mothers in more complex ways, not hiding their children for fear that voters will perceive a conflict between motherhood and officeholding, but instead leveraging motherhood as a motivator and credential for public service. Again, gendered standards have not gone away, with men still less likely to face scrutiny of the "balance" between their personal and professional lives. But these points of evolution indicate some shifts in the ways in which our elections are gendered.

Finally, elections in the United States are gendered in the strategies that candidates employ in reaching out to the general public. Candidates, both men and women, strategize about how to present themselves to voters of the same and opposite sexes. Pollsters and campaign consultants routinely try to figure out what issues or themes will appeal specifically to women or to men. Increasingly, candidates and their strategists are segmenting voters on the basis of their gender and other demographics. Specially devised appeals are directed at young women, working-class men, senior women, single women, married women, suburban women, white men, and Black women, to name only some of the targeted groups.

In short, when we look at the people, the language, the expectations, and the strategies of contemporary politics, we see that gender plays an important role in elections in the United States. Even when it is not explicitly acknowledged, it often operates in the background, affecting our assumptions about who legitimate political actors are and how they should behave. And often in the US, the effects of gender are inextricably intertwined with the effects of race and ethnicity. It is not surprising, for example, that the first nonwhite person elected to the presidency was a man or that the first female major party nominee was white.

This is not to say, however, that the role of gender has been constant over time. Rather, we regard gender as malleable, manifesting itself differently at various times and in different contexts in the electoral process. In women's candidacies for elective office, for example, there has been obvious change. As recently as twenty-five years ago, a woman seeking high-level office almost anywhere in the United States was an anomaly, and she might have faced overt hostility. Clearly, the electoral environment is much more hospitable now. Over the years, slowly but steadily, more and more women have entered the electoral arena at all levels. Hillary Clinton's nearly successful presidential run, coupled with Donald Trump's victory, while viewed by many as a setback to women in politics, actually motivated a significant number of Democratic women to consider running for elective office. Organizations promoting the election of more women reported a dramatic increase in the number of women interested in seeking elective office since the 2016 elections.[3] And though the race was ultimately won by an older white man, the 2020 presidential elections saw a record six women, all Democrats, run for president – Senator Kirsten Gillibrand of New York, Senator Elizabeth Warren of Massachusetts, Senator Amy Klobuchar of Minnesota, Senator Kamala Harris of California, Representative Tulsi Gabbard of Hawaii, and author Marianne Williamson.

Although there are important differences between women and men in the aggregate, there are also significant differences among women. The role of gender is neither constant over time nor independent of the influences of race, ethnicity, sexuality, social class, and even age/generation. Rather, these categories are mutually constitutive, and thus, for example, the experiences of an African American woman in politics are likely to differ from the experiences of a white woman, and the perspectives of a Latina millennial might vary from those of her senior citizen grandmother. The diversity among women was evident in the 2020 election, with young women favoring Bernie Sanders over any of the six women running for president in Democratic primary elections, Black women forming the bedrock of support for presidential candidate Joe Biden in critical states like South Carolina and Georgia, and white women of differing education levels voting for different general election candidates.

POLITICAL REPRESENTATION AND SIMPLE JUSTICE: WHY GENDER MATTERS IN ELECTORAL POLITICS

Beyond the reality that gender is an underlying factor that shapes the contours of contemporary elections, it is important to examine and monitor the role of gender in the electoral process because of concerns about justice and the quality of political representation. The United States lags far behind many other nations in the number of women serving in its national legislature. In 2021, with only 27 percent of members of Congress being women, the United States ranked number 66 among countries throughout the world for the proportion of women serving in its national parliament or legislature.[4] In 2021, women served as governors in only eight of the fifty states, and only 30.6 percent of all state legislators across

---

[3] Charlotte Alter, A Year Ago, They Marched. Now a Record Number of Women Are Running for Office, *Time*, January 18, 2018, https://time.com/5107499/record-number-of-women-are-running-for-office/

[4] Monthly Ranking of Women in National Parliaments, April 2021, Interparliamentary Union Parline, https://data.ipu.org/women-ranking?month=4&year=2021

the country were women, according to the Center for American Women and Politics (CAWP).[5]

Despite the relatively low proportion of women in positions of political leadership, women constitute a majority of the voters who elect these leaders. In the 2020 elections, for example, US Census figures showed that 82.2 million women reported voting, compared with 72.5 million men; thus, 9.7 million more women than men voted in those elections.[6] As a matter of simple justice, something seems fundamentally wrong with a democratic system where women are a majority of voters but remain dramatically underrepresented among elected political leaders. The fact that women constitute a majority of the electorate but only a minority of public officials is a sufficient reason, in and of itself, to pay attention to the underlying gender dynamics of US politics.

Beyond the issue of simple justice, however, are significant concerns over the quality of political representation in the United States. Beginning with a series of studies commissioned by CAWP in the 1980s, a great deal of empirical research indicates that women and men support and devote attention to somewhat different issues as public officials.[7] Although party differences are usually greater than gender differences,[8] at both national and state levels male and female legislators have been shown to have different policy priorities and preferences.[9] Female officeholders have reported feeling a special responsibility to act on behalf of women in two different studies of women in the US Congress.[10] More specifically, studies of members of the US House of Representatives have found that women have been more likely than men to support policies favoring gender equity, day-care programs, flextime in the workplace, legal and accessible

---

[5] Women in Elective Office 2021, Center for American Women and Politics (hereafter CAWP), 2021, https://cawp.rutgers.edu/women-elective-office-2021

[6] Gender Differences in Voter Turnout, CAWP, 2021, https://cawp.rutgers.edu/facts/voters/turnout

[7] Debra Dodson, ed., Gender and Policymaking: Studies of Women in Office, CAWP, 1991, https://cawp.rutgers.edu/gender-and-policymaking-studies-women-office

[8] Michele Swers, *Women in the Club: Gender and Policy Making in the Senate* (Chicago, IL: University of Chicago Press, 2013).

[9] Tracy Osborn, *How Women Represent Women: Political Parties, Gender, and Representation in the State Legislatures.* (New York: Oxford University Press, 2012); Jessica Gerrity, Tracy Osborn, and Jeanette Morehouse Mendez, Women and Representation: A Different View of the District?, *Politics & Gender* 3(2) (2007): 179–200.

[10] Kelly Dittmar, Kira Sanbonmatsu, and Susan J. Carroll, *A Seat at the Table: Congresswomen's Perspectives on Why Their Representation Matters* (New York: Oxford University Press, 2018); Susan J. Carroll, Representing Women: Congresswomen's Perceptions of Their Representational Roles, in *Women Transforming Congress*, ed. Cindy Simon Rosenthal (Norman, OK: University of Oklahoma Press, 2002).

abortion, minimum wage increases, and the extension of the food stamp program (now known as SNAP).[11] They have also been more likely to advocate for greater spending on women's economic initiatives and for efforts to address violence against women.[12] Congressional studies have also shown that women are more effective in securing federal funding and passing legislation, and that – on average – they propose *more* legislation than men.[13] They have also proven to be more responsive than men to their constituents, including to those with shared identities and on women's issues.[14] Similarly, several studies have found that women serving in state legislatures give priority to, introduce, and work on legislation related to women's rights, health care, education, and the welfare of families and children more often than men do, and that they are more responsive to women's groups.[15] Increased attention has been paid to the

---

[11] See, for example, Michele Swers, *The Difference Women Make: The Policy Impact of Women in Congress* (Chicago, IL: University of Chicago Press, 2002). See also Craig Volden, Alan E. Wiseman, and Dana E. Wittmer, Women's Issues and Their Fates in the US Congress, *Political Science Research and Methods* 6(4) (2016): 1–18.

[12] Corina Schulze and Jared Hurvitz, The Dynamics of Earmark Requests for the Women and Men of the US House of Representatives, *Journal of Women, Politics, & Policy* 37(1) (2016): 68–86.

[13] Jeffrey Lazarus and Amy Steigerwalt, *Gendered Vulnerability: How Women Work Harder to Stay in Office* (Ann Arbor, MI: University of Michigan Press, 2018); Craig Volden, Alan E. Wiseman, and Dana E. Wittmer, Why Are Women More Effective Members of Congress?, *American Journal of Political Science* 57(2) (2013): 326–41; Craig Volden and Alan E. Wiseman, Legislative Effectiveness in the United States Senate, *Journal of Politics* 80(2) (2018): 731–35; Sarah F. Anzia and Christopher R. Berry, The Jackie (and Jill) Robinson Effect: Why Do Congresswomen Outperform Congressmen?, *American Journal of Political Science* 55(3) (2011): 478–93; Carly Schmitt and Hanna K. Brant, Gender, Ambition, and Legislative Behavior in the US House, *Journal of Women, Politics, & Policy* 40(2) (2019): 286–308; Mary Layton Atkinson and Jason Harold Windett, Gender Stereotypes and the Policy Priorities of Women in Congress, *Political Behavior* 41 (2019): 769–89.

[14] Lazarus and Steigerwalt, *Gendered Vulnerability*; Daniel Butler, *Representing the Advantaged: How Politicians Reinforce Inequality* (New York: Cambridge University Press, 2014); Danielle M. Thomsen and Bailey K. Sanders, Gender Differences in Legislator Responsiveness, *Perspectives on Politics* 18(4) (2019): 1017–30; Kenneth Lowande, Melinda Ritchie, and Erinn Lauterbach, Descriptive and Substantive Representation in Congress: Evidence from 80,000 Congressional Inquiries, *American Journal of Political Science* 63(3) (2019): 644–59.

[15] See Osborn, *How Women Represent Women*; Susan J. Carroll, Representing Women: Women State Legislators as Agents of Policy-Related Change, in *The Impact of Women in Public Office*, ed. Susan J. Carroll (Bloomington, IN: Indiana University Press, 2001), pp.3–21; Sue Thomas, *How Women Legislate* (New York: Oxford University Press, 1994); Michael B. Berkman and Robert E. O'Connor, Women State Legislators Matter: Female Legislators and State Abortion Policy, *American Politics Quarterly* 21(1) (1993): 102–24; Lyn Kathlene, Uncovering the Political Impacts of Gender: An Exploratory Study, *Western Political Quarterly* 42 (1989): 397–421; and Elizabeth Weiner, Getting a High Heel in the Door: An

intersections of gender and race in shaping representational behavior at both the congressional and state legislative levels, with research demonstrating the important – and often distinct – impact of women of color in legislative institutions and showing how "policy leadership and substantive representation are raced-gendered."[16]

Beyond possible gender differences in policy priorities, women public officials exhibit leadership styles and ways of conducting business different from those of their male colleagues. A study of mayors found that women tend to adopt an approach to governing that emphasizes congeniality and cooperation, whereas men tend to emphasize hierarchy.[17] Similarly, a recent study of women members of Congress found that most of them believe they are more consensual and collaborative and more likely to work across party lines than their male colleagues.[18] Research on state legislators has also uncovered significant differences in the manner in which female and male committee chairs conduct themselves at hearings; women are more likely to act as facilitators, whereas men tend to use their power to control the direction of the hearings.[19] And recent work on women's caucuses demonstrates both the ways in which women collaborate in state legislatures and the constraints on gender-based organizing.[20] Women officials' propensity to conduct business in a manner that is more cooperative, communicative, inclusive,

Experiment on State Legislator Responsiveness to Women's Issue Lobbying, *Political Research Quarterly* online issue (2020): 1–15.

[16] Beth Reingold, Kerry L. Haynie, and Kristen Widner, *Race, Gender, and Political Representation: Toward a More Intersectional Approach* (New York: Oxford University Press, 2021), p. 18. See also Nadia Brown, *Sisters in the Statehouse* (New York: Oxford University Press, 2014); Michael G. Minta and Nadia Brown, Intersecting Interests: Gender, Race, and Congressional Attention to Women's Issues, *Du Bois Review: Social Science Research on Race* 11(2) (2014): 253–72; Byron D'Andrá Orey, Wendy Smooth, Kimberly S. Adams, and Kisha Harris-Clark, Race and Gender Matter: Refining Models of Legislative Policy Making in State Legislatures, *Journal of Women, Politics & Policy* 28(3–4) (2006): 97–119; Dittmar, Sanbonmatsu, and Carroll, *Seat at the Table*; and Lisa Garcia Bedolla, Katherine Tate, and Janelle Wong, Indelible Effects: The Impact of Women of Color in the US Congress, in *In Women and Elective Office: Past, Present, and Future*, ed. Sue Thomas and Clyde Wilcox, 3rd ed. (New York: Oxford University Press, 2014).

[17] Sue Tolleson Rinehart, Do Women Leaders Make a Difference? Substance, Style, and Perceptions, in *The Impact of Women in Public Office*, ed. Susan J. Carroll (Bloomington, IN: Indiana University Press, 2001), pp. 149–65.

[18] Dittmar, Sanbonmatsu, and Carroll, *Seat at the Table*.

[19] Lyn Kathlene, Alternative Views of Crime: Legislative Policy-Making in Gendered Terms. *Journal of Politics* 57 (1995): 696–723.

[20] Anna Mahoney, *Women Take Their Place in State Legislatures* (Philadelphia, PA: Temple University Press, 2018).

public, and based on coalition-building may well lead to policy outcomes that represent the input of a wider range of people and a greater diversity of perspectives.[21]

The presence of women among elected officials also helps to empower other women. Barbara Burrell captures this idea well when she writes: "Women in public office stand as symbols for other women, both enhancing their identification with the system and their ability to have influence within it. This subjective sense of being involved and heard for women, in general, alone makes the election of women to public office important."[22] Women officials are committed to ensuring that other women follow in their footsteps, and large majorities mentor other women and encourage them to run for office.[23]

Thus, attention to the role of gender in the electoral process, and more specifically to the presence of women among elected officials, is critically important because it has implications for improving the quality of political representation. Although Republican and Democratic women generally favor somewhat different solutions to public policy problems, nevertheless the election of larger numbers of women to office would likely lead to more legislation reflecting the greater priority women of both parties give to women's rights, the welfare of children and families, health care, and education. Further, the election of more women might lead to policies based on the input of a wider range of people and a greater diversity of perspectives. Finally, electing more women would most likely lead to enhanced political empowerment for other women.

ORGANIZATION OF THE BOOK

This volume utilizes a gendered lens to aid in the interpretation and understanding of contemporary elections in the United States. Contributors examine the ways that gender enters into and helps to shape elections for offices ranging from president to state legislator across the United States. As several chapters demonstrate, gender dynamics are important to the conduct and outcomes of presidential elections even though, to date, a

---

[21] See Cindy Simon Rosenthal, *How Women Lead* (New York: Oxford University Press, 1998).

[22] Barbara Burrell, *A Woman's Place Is in the House* (Ann Arbor, MI: University of Michigan Press, 1996), p.151.

[23] Debra L. Dodson and Susan J. Carroll, Reshaping the Agenda: Women in State Legislatures, Center for the American Women and Politics, CAWP, 1991, www.cawp .rutgers.edu/reshaping-agenda-women-state-legislatures

woman has not yet won the presidency. Gender also shapes both the ways candidates appeal to voters and the ways voters respond to candidates. Many women have run for Congress and for state offices; this volume analyzes the support they have received, the problems they have confronted, and the reasons that there are not more women candidates. Women of color face additional and distinctive challenges in electoral politics because of the interaction of their race or ethnicity and gender; this volume also contributes to an understanding of the status of women of color, particularly African American women and Latinas, and the electoral circumstances they encounter.

In Chapter 1, Melanye T. Price and Kelly Dittmar examine the gender, race, and intersectional dynamics of presidential politics, focusing specifically on the dominance of masculinity and whiteness at the highest level of American politics. After providing an overview of concepts key to understanding the presidency as a raced and gendered institution, they examine the evolution in understanding of and attentiveness to identity politics since 2008. They analyze how 2020 presidential and vice-presidential candidates navigated gender, race, and intersectional dynamics on the campaign trail, with evidence of both disruption and maintenance of white masculine dominance. Finally, in elaborating on Kamala Harris' selection and experience as the Democratic vice-presidential nominee, they illustrate barriers broken and hurdles that remain for women – and specifically a Black and South Asian woman – in presidential politics.

In Chapter 2, Kelly Dittmar examines the role of gender in presidential campaigns. She begins with the history of the pioneering women who have dared to step forward to seek the presidency or vice presidency. She then turns to the 2020 presidential campaigns of the record six women candidates who competed for the Democratic nomination. Dittmar analyzes the ways that gender stereotypes influenced the strategies employed by these candidates, media coverage of their campaigns, and public reactions to their candidacies. She argues that the 2020 presidential election revealed evidence of both persistence and disruption of gender stereotypes and gendered standards in presidential politics, providing insights into the hurdles that remain to electing the country's first woman president.

In Chapter 3, Celeste Montoya examines the role that gendered mobilization has played in US electoral politics, both historically and in the recent elections. She provides a conceptualization of gendered mobilization that emphasizes the importance of looking at the role that gender (often at the intersection of race and class) plays in a wide array of US social movements. She provides a historical overview that demonstrates the various ways in which gendered mobilizations have influenced the development of US democracy and the evolution of its electoral politics. Gendered mobilization has been a significant part of efforts to expand political participation and representation, as well as those to restrict it. It has shaped party platforms and electoral coalitions. The patterns of the past help explain the current political moment and what may be at stake.

In Chapter 4, Susan MacManus and Amy Benner focus on the record-breaking participation of women in nearly every facet of the historical 2020 election. They trace the evolution of passage of the Nineteenth Amendment, then detail the changing demographics of women voters – racial/ethnic diversity, generational shifts, sexuality and gender identities, partisan/ideological polarization – and their interrelationships. They describe how these changes generated new issues, activists, organizations, forms of activism, informational sources, and political mobilization techniques. They discuss how various women-centric organizations, including the media, registered and mobilized women to vote, and how the Biden and Trump campaigns used issues to micro-target different subgroups of women. The chapter ends with a review of how the COVID-19 pandemic prompted changes in the registration and voting processes which, along with women's activism, resulted in the highest voter turnout since 1900.

In Chapter 5, Susan Carroll examines voting differences between women and men in recent elections, with particular attention to the 2020 election. A gender gap in voting, with women more likely than men to support the Democratic candidate, has been evident in every presidential election since 1980 and in majorities of races at other levels of office. Carroll traces the history of the gender gap and documents its breadth and persistence. She examines the complicated question of what happens to the gender gap when one of the candidates in a race is a woman. Carroll reviews different explanations for gender gaps and identifies what we do and do not know about why women and men in the aggregate differ in their voting choices. She also analyzes the different strategies that candidates and campaigns have employed for dealing with the gender gap and appealing to women voters.

In Chapter 6, Anna Sampaio provides an intersectional analysis of Latinas' political participation in the 2020 election with particular attention to the impacts of race, gender, and the rise in political violence in a racialized campaign season on Latinas as candidates, voters, and political activists. She highlights the work of Latinas and other women of color elected to national office as they confront entrenched systems of race and gender inequality and attempt to legislate and lead in a political environment inflamed by misinformation and political polarization. She examines turnout and voting among Latinas and Latinos, changes in the Latina/o/x gender gap, and the roles that Latinas played as candidates, advisers, surrogates across parties and campaigns, and leaders within nonpartisan, community-based organizations key to addressing voter suppression and mobilizing Latina/o/x voters. She also compares the political engagement of Latina candidates in the historic 2018 midterms with the 2020 election season, paying attention to how both major political parties used race and gender and intersectionality to field candidates and gain leverage in competitive campaigns. The chapter concludes with an eye to obstacles and opportunities in the future of Latina politics and racial and gendered justice in the US.

In Chapter 7, Wendy Smooth traces African American women's participation in electoral politics as voters, political operatives, and candidates for public office. She chronicles African American women's steadfast voter participation since their first substantive opportunities to exercise the franchise following the passage of the Voting Rights Act of 1965, even outperforming other groups in voter turnout in recent elections. Smooth notes that in 2020 the nation's racial reckoning and social justice issues, along with the global COVID-19 pandemic, heightened attention to African American women's leadership as elected officials. Also, African American women mayors made national headlines navigating protests against police killings of unarmed African Americans while working to curtail the spread of the virus in their cities. This spotlight on African American women mayors, Smooth argues, was important for recognizing their executive leadership capabilities and potentially elevating future African American women as elected leaders. Similarly, African American women voting rights activists found themselves in the spotlight as they fought to protect challenges to voter access during the pandemic. Smooth argues that while attention to the contributions African American women make as political actors increased in 2020, there is still a long way to go to translate African American women's political activism and voting power into positions as elected officials.

In Chapter 8, Richard Fox analyzes the historical evolution of women running for seats in the US Congress. The fundamental question he addresses is why women continue to be so underrepresented in the congressional ranks. Fox examines the experiences of female and male candidates for Congress by comparing fundraising totals and vote totals through the 2020 elections. While acknowledging the historic number of women candidates in 2018 and 2020, his analysis also explores the subtler ways that gender dynamics manifest in the electoral arena, examining regional variation in the performance of women and men running for Congress, the difficulty of change in light of the incumbency advantage, and gender differences in political ambition to serve in the House or Senate. The chapter concludes with an assessment of the degree to which gender still plays an important role in congressional elections and the prospects for gender parity in the future.

In Chapter 9, Kira Sanbonmatsu and Maria Wilson turn to the often overlooked subject of gender in state elections. They examine the presence and performance of women who ran for the state legislatures and statewide executive offices in 2018 and 2020, analyze the reasons for the underrepresentation of women in these offices, and highlight changes in women's candidacies in recent years. They investigate the factors driving variation across states in women's officeholding, and assess the status of women of color and LGBTQ candidates. Understanding why women have not fared better in the states is critical to understanding women's status in electoral politics and their prospects for achieving higher office in the future.

In Chapter 10, Rosalyn Cooperman examines the role that political parties, women's organizations, and political action committees (PACs) play in the recruitment of women to run for federal office and support of women's candidacies. She examines the structures of the national Democratic and Republican parties and looks at how party organizations assist candidates to run for office. She assesses attitudes about women's political participation from Democratic and Republican party activists who influence who runs for office, and the issue positions they embrace. She looks at the strategies pursued by women's PACs, candidate training groups, and campaign finance networks to train and fund women candidates. Cooperman finds that the resources available to Democratic women candidates far exceed those available to their Republican counterparts, which holds implications for women as parties compete to capture or expand majority party status in Congress.

Finally, in Chapter 11, Dianne Bystrom examines three primary means used by political candidates to communicate with voters – television advertising, websites, and Twitter – with a consideration of the gender differences and similarities documented by research. These campaign communication channels became even more important in the 2020 election cycle, as the COVID-19 pandemic impacted the ability of political candidates to reach voters through in-person interactions. The chapter reviews the state of knowledge about how female and male candidates communicate through these channels and provides examples from the ten most competitive US Senate races featuring a woman candidate in the 2020 election cycle. These examples underscore some findings of previous research but also point to changes in how female candidates are choosing to present themselves in their campaign communication.

Collectively, the chapters provide an overview of the major ways that gender affects the contours and outcomes of contemporary elections. Our hope is that this volume will leave readers with a better understanding of how underlying gender dynamics shape the electoral process in the United States.

1 Gender, Race, and Presidential Politics: Assessing Institutional Change in 2020

When Kamala Harris took the stage on November 7, 2020, dressed in all white as a gesture to the suffragists who had worked so hard for this moment, she celebrated the breaking of "one of the most substantial barriers that exists in our country" through her election as the first woman, the first Black, and the first South Asian vice president of the United States. She reflected on the women who had paved the way to her victory and the message that her success would send to young people – that they should "dream with ambition, lead with conviction, and see yourself in a way that others might not see you." She highlighted her own mother's journey to America at age 19,

> I'm thinking about her and about the generations of women – Black Women, Asian, white, Latina, and Native American women through-out our nation's history who have paved the way for this moment tonight. Women who fought and sacrificed so much for equality, liberty, and justice for all … Tonight, I reflect on their struggle, their determination and the strength of their vision.[1]

On one of the most important stages in electoral politics, Harris not only embodied disruption of the dominance of white men in presidential politics but also gave voice to the women, and especially women of color, who have been overlooked in their work to create more equitable political institutions.

In this chapter, we make visible the gender, race, and intersectional dynamics of presidential politics that have been rendered invisible by the normalization of men, masculinity, and whiteness in our expectations of who and what is presidential. After providing an overview of the

---

[1] Kamala Harris, campaign victory speech, Wilmington, Delaware, November 7, 2019, www.washingtonpost.com/politics/2020/11/07/kamala-harris-victory-speech-transcript/

presidency as a raced and gendered institution, we point to the evolution of identity politics in presidential elections since 2008. We then analyze how 2020 presidential and vice-presidential candidates and voters navigated gender, race, and intersectional dynamics, with examples of both disruption and maintenance of white masculine dominance. In many ways, the 2020 election became a contest over the degree to which voters would accept and even promote transformation in the raced, gendered, and race-gendered foundations of presidential politics. Finally, in elaborating on Kamala Harris' selection and experience, we illustrate barriers that have been overcome and those that remain for women – and specifically Black and South Asian women – in presidential politics.

THE PRESIDENCY AS A GENDERED AND RACED INSTITUTION

The fact that all US presidents have been white and male is both an artifact of white supremacist patriarchy and an explanation for why Americans associate white men with fitness for leadership. Political scientist Sally Kenney describes the gendering of institutions as "the ways in which political institutions reflect, structure, and reinforce gendered patterns of power."[2] In other words, gender is a salient axis by which power within institutions is distributed and exercised. Gender is also evident in images, symbols, and language adopted within institutions, as was described in this volume's introduction. Finally, within gendered institutions, gender influences the behavior of and interactions between institutional actors. For example, presidents themselves face expectations of performing masculinity in ways that align with how inhabitants of the office have done the job before them; that said, presidents who navigate gender in ways different than their predecessors can change – instead of reinforce – the "gendered patterns of power" by suggesting a revaluation of traits, expertise, and leadership styles that are less strictly aligned with traditional ideas of masculinity and power.

Gender functions within institutions like the presidency in ways that are both parallel to and interactive with raced processes and practices that can either maintain or disrupt raced patterns of power. Like the role of gender within gendered institutions, racial norms, expectations, and often biases influence the allocation and exercise of power, the language and symbols upheld, and the actions of and interactions between those navigating raced

---

[2] Sally Kenney, New Research on Gendered Political Institutions, *Political Research Quarterly* 49(2) (1996): 445–66, at 455.

institutions. And, as scholars like Mary Hawkesworth have described, institutions are commonly raced-gendered, meaning that all of these forces are functioning simultaneously to influence how political institutions function and the distinct experiences of those who are seeking power and influence within them.[3] For nearly all of US history, the processes and practices in American political institutions have reinforced patterns of power that advantage masculinity and whiteness. Moreover, the privileging of masculinity and whiteness in presidential politics has benefited white men as candidates, officeholders, and voters and disadvantaged others.

Masculinity

Recognizing the presidency as a gendered institution reveals hurdles to women's presidential power. As Georgia Duerst-Lahti has written, "Masculinity is neither fixed nor uniform."[4] Scholars have relied on typologies of masculinity to better grasp the multiple forms in which it is privileged or expressed. Dominance masculinity prioritizes domination and control.[5] It is also categorized as authoritative and is linked to traits like aggression and decisiveness.[6] Expertise masculinity is tied to a mastery of fields or ideas and, relatedly, high levels of competence.[7] Masculinity has also been categorized as patriarchal – related to dominance, but in relation to women specifically – and toxic – which upholds norms of masculinity that are harmful to both men and women. Finally, instead of recognizing the full spectrum of gender power and expression, masculinity is often viewed and exercised in contrast to femininity; hence, proving masculinity means rejecting femininity and as a result rejecting women candidates.

Presidential campaigns represent a site of contestation over what is masculine and whether or not candidates uphold masculine credentials. Scholar Jackson Katz argues, "Presidential politics has long been the site of an ongoing cultural struggle over the meanings of American manhood."[8] The US presidency, wherein leaders have been characterized as heroes,

---

[3] Mary Hawkesworth, Congressional Enactments of Race-Gender: Toward a Theory of Raced-Gendered Institutions, *American Political Science Review* 97(4) (2003): 529–50.

[4] Georgia Duerst-Lahti, Presidential Elections: Gendered Space and the Case of 2012, in *Gender and Elections: Shaping the Future of American Politics*, ed. Susan J. Carroll and Richard L. Fox (New York: Cambridge University Press, 2012), p. 37.

[5] Ibid.

[6] Jackson Katz, *Man Enough? Donald Trump, Hillary Clinton, and the Politics of Presidential Masculinity* (Northampton, MA: Interlink Books, 2016), p. 30.

[7] Duerst-Lahti, Presidential Elections; R. W. Connell, *Masculinities*, 2nd ed. (Berkeley, CA: University of California Press, 2005).

[8] Katz, *Man Enough?*, p. 1.

protectors, and fathers of the nation, has been most aligned with dominance masculinity. Presidential campaign history is replete with examples of candidate efforts to prove their manhood in accordance with stereotypical expectations and apart from stereotypically feminine traits.[9] For example, candidates have used masculine imagery associated with force and war as evidence of their authoritative leadership. In an attempt to challenge attacks that he was weak on national defense and to position him as a credible commander in chief, 1988 Democratic nominee Michael Dukakis famously staged a photo-op standing in a battle tank. The strategy failed, but similar imagery has been adopted by other candidates to reinforce masculine – and thus presidential – bona fides. Trump's emphasis on masculine imagery, rhetoric, and performance in the 2016 election was especially overt and infiltrated all aspects of candidate presentation and campaign strategy. At campaign rallies across the country Trump encouraged his supporters to verbally and physically attack Black protesters.

Trump also leveraged emasculation of his opponents as a primary mode of attack. About Hillary Clinton, he reminded voters, "I just don't think she has a presidential look."[10] Trump described his Republican primary opponents as "little," "super low energy," "really weak," and, of one, "a frightened little puppy." Previous presidential contenders had been attacked for failing to meet masculine expectations and/or appearing too feminine. For example, after a newspaper published a forged letter and another item that painted him and his wife in negative lights, Democrat Ed Muskie spoke passionately to a crowd of reporters to call out the publishers. Some reports said he was crying, others did not. Regardless, Muskie recognized how it hurt his campaign. He said, "It changed people's minds about me, of what kind of guy I was. They were looking for a strong, steady man, and here I was, weak."[11] Other men were painted as vain or unathletic as evidence that they were not "man enough" for presidential office.

Donald Trump's election revealed a persistent preference for masculine leaders among some Americans, and an expectation of masculine leaders among most Americans. In a 2017 Pew Research Survey, 53 percent of respondents said that most people in our society look up to men who are

[9]   Ibid.
[10] Ashley Parker, Donald Trump Says Hillary Clinton Doesn't Have "a Presidential Look," *New York Times*, September 6, 2016, https://nyti.ms/3fkg3Ge
[11] Robert Mitchell, The Democrat Who Cried (Maybe) in New Hampshire and Lost the Presidential Nomination, *Washington Post*, February 9, 2020, www.washingtonpost.com/history/2020/02/09/new-hampshire-ed-muskie-tears-primary/

manly or masculine, while 32 percent said most people in society look up to women who are womanly or feminine.[12] While more Democrats than Republicans, and more women than men, report that society looks up to manly men, Republicans (78%) are much more likely than Democrats (49%) to report that doing so is a good thing.[13] This partisan difference in perceptions of gender and leadership is consistent with long-held associations between Democrats and femininity and Republicans and masculinity.[14] The same survey finds that Republican men are more likely than Democratic men to describe themselves as "very masculine" and that Republicans – men and women – are less likely to say it is a good thing for parents to encourage young boys to play with toys or participate in activities typically associated with girls, and to say society is *not* accepting enough when it comes to women taking on roles typically associated with men.[15] These beliefs, which indicate concern about disrupting established gender roles, are consistent with two additional findings from the 2019 American Values Survey conducted by the Public Religion Research Institute (PRRI). This found that 65 percent of Republicans compared to 26 percent of Democrats believe that society is becoming too soft and feminine.[16] Trump's supporters, surveyed in 2016, were even more likely to hold this belief, indicating that Trump's strategy of reinforcing masculinity was likely effective in both recognizing and addressing fears that masculinity itself – and the power associated with it – was becoming too fragile.[17]

Whiteness
Understanding the presidency as a raced institution means revealing the ways it privileges whiteness, which is often rendered invisible as a default racial identity. Naming and defining whiteness is a first step to recognizing

[12] Kim Parker, Juliana Menasce Horowitz, and Renee Stepler, On Gender Differences, No Consensus on Nature vs. Nurture, Pew Research Center, report dated December 5, 2017, www.pewresearch.org/social-trends/2017/12/05/on-gender-differences-no-consensus-on-nature-vs-nurture/

[13] Ibid.

[14] Nicholas J. G. Winter, Masculine Republicans and Feminine Democrats: Gender and Americans' Explicit and Implicit Images of the Political Parties, *Political Behavior* 32 (2010): 587–618.

[15] Parker, Horowitz, and Stepler, On Gender Differences.

[16] Fractured Nation: Widening Partisan Polarization and Key Issues in 2020 Presidential Elections, Public Religion Research Institute (hereafter PRRI), report dated October 20, 2019, https://bit.ly/3j8Ib0s

[17] Daniel Cox and Robert P. Jones, Two-Thirds of Trump Supporters Say Nation Needs a Leader Willing to Break the Rules, PRRI, April 7, 2016, www.prri.org/research/prri-atlantic-poll-republican-democratic-primary-trump-supporters/

how it functions within all institutions, including the presidency. The dominance of whiteness is evident since forty-five of forty-six presidents and forty-seven of forty-nine vice presidents have been white men (Vice President Charles Curtis, who served from 1929 to 1933, was Native American on his mother's side). It is also evident in the power dynamics within presidential politics that have deemed white people – primarily men, white cultural referents and practices, and white citizens' experiences and priorities as primary, "normal," and thus privileged in holding, exercising, and benefiting from presidential power.

Institutions dominated by whiteness have often masked racial differences and encouraged those who seek power within them to do the same. For example, scholars have cited Barack Obama's election as the first Black (and non-white) president as dependent, at least in part, on his "race-transcendent Black politics," which avoided direct racial appeals and employed a "deracialized" campaign strategy.[18] Melanye Price explains how Obama relied on "race-neutral themes or themes related to aspects of African American history that have become part of America's universal understanding of itself."[19] This attempt to transcend difference is a function of white dominance and may have appeased those concerned about its disruption through Obama's electoral advantage, but Price emphasizes it also "reinforces the existing racial order" where whiteness is privileged.[20] Moreover, while Obama was successful, this approach did not insulate him from race-based scrutiny and racism on the campaign trail and once in office.

The 2016 presidential election exposed how threats to white dominance fueled political behavior. Racial resentment, or believing that minorities seek special favors and denying the existence of racial discrimination and inequity, was a strong predictor of support for Donald Trump.[21] In rhetoric and strategy, Trump capitalized on and likely furthered those feelings among his supporters, fostering a perception of threat from racial minority groups. From launching his campaign by calling Mexicans immigrating to the United States rapists to continuing to demonize immigrants

---

[18] Valeria Sinclair-Chapman and Melanye Price, Black Politics, the 2008 Election, and the (Im)Possibility of Race Transcendence, *PS: Political Science & Politics* 41(4) (2008): 739–45.

[19] Melanye Price, *The Race Whisperer: Barack Obama and the Political Uses of Race*. New York: New York University Press, 2016), p. 18.

[20] Ibid.

[21] Brian F. Schaffner, Matthew Macwilliams, and Tatishe Nteta, Understanding White Polarization in the 2016 Vote for President: The Sobering Role of Racism and Sexism, *Political Science Quarterly* 133(1) (2018): 9–34.

of color and banning Muslim entry into the country, Trump earned significant support among white supremacists. By 2019, the PRRI found that Republicans were just as likely to view discrimination against whites as a problem as they were to problematize discrimination against Blacks.[22] Nearly two-thirds of Republicans reported that "immigrants are invading the country and changing American culture," compared to about one in five Democrats.[23] Fears of white fragility, parallel to concerns about masculine fragility that will be outlined below, appeared to fuel support for Trump in 2016 and 2020. In a Data for Progress survey in the weeks before Election Day 2020, more than 80 percent of respondents who strongly *disagreed* that white people have certain advantages because of the color of their skin intended to vote for Trump's reelection.[24]

Intersectionality

The dominance of whiteness and of masculinity in presidential politics cannot be viewed in isolation from each other. As Jackson Katz argues, the study of presidential masculinity "needs to incorporate a racialized understanding of gender, not to mention a gendered understanding of race."[25] This argument aligns with the fundamental claims of intersectionality, a theoretical framework developed by Black feminists to explain the experiences of Black women at the convergence of multiple systems of oppression.[26] As Wendy Smooth notes, intersectionality is "the assertion that social identity categories such as race, gender, class, sexuality, and ability are interconnected and operate simultaneously to produce experiences of both privilege and marginalization."[27] Applying an intersectional lens to our understanding of presidential politics means challenging single-axis approaches to understanding gendered and raced dynamics as discrete, and instead grappling with the ways in which these dynamics are interacting. It requires recognizing that while race and gender have always organized presidential power dynamics, they were rendered invisible

---

[22] PRRI, Fractured Nation.

[23] Ibid.

[24] Brian Schaffner, Twitter post, October 23, 2020, https://twitter.com/b_schaffner/status/1319748953781510149

[25] Katz, *Man Enough?*, p. 7.

[26] Kimberlé Crenshaw, Demarginalizing the Intersection of Race and Sex: A Black Feminist Critique of Antidiscrimination Doctrine, Feminist Theory, and Antiracist Politics, *University of Chicago Legal Forum* 1 (1989): 139–67.

[27] Wendy G. Smooth, Intersectionality From Theoretical Framework to Policy Intervention, in *Situating Intersectionality: Politics, Policy, and Power*, ed. Angelia R. Wilson (London: Palgrave Macmillan, 2013), p. 11.

based on the assumption that the race default was white and the gender default was male.[28] It is not until presidential candidates who are not white men wage viable challenges to these accepted defaults that race, gender, and intersectional dynamics become difficult to ignore.

The 2008 presidential election provides a notable demarcation in this recognition and definition of "identity politics" at the presidential level. In that year, the two most viable candidates for the Democratic nomination deviated from the presidential norm; a Black man (Barack Obama) and a white woman (Hillary Clinton) made claims to presidential power in ways that not only shifted the image of who could be presidential but also made visible the assumptions of white male dominance that had long persisted without significant interrogation. But simply making visible these power dynamics does not fully upend or disrupt them. As noted above, Obama's attempts to transcend race are tied to the recognition that his Blackness – and more broadly his "otherness" – was a hurdle to overcome in meeting voter expectations.

Obama also contended with the interaction of race and gender in his performance of masculinity. Whereas reinforcing dominant masculinity has worked to the advantage of white men, "assertions of Black male authority are viewed as problematic, threatening, and out of place."[29] Historically, Black masculinity has been caricatured as violent, hypersexual, and threatening, therefore justifying disproportionate surveillance, policing, and punishing Black men.[30] As a result, Obama was unable to navigate gender in the same way as white men. While still expected to prove his toughness and assertiveness, he had to do so without appearing angry or threatening. He found success in navigating this with an especially calm demeanor – illustrated by a nickname of "no drama Obama" – and distancing himself from more overt expressions of dominant masculinity. Of course, that approach was not without its penalties, especially as president. He was criticized as being weak, tentative, and even "soft" – all viewed as stereotypically feminine traits and counter to effective presidential leadership. *New York Times* columnist Maureen Dowd even nicknamed him "Obambi," an arguably emasculating moniker meant to emphasize timidity instead of the fearlessness expected of presidents. Moments of decisiveness and force – such as the assassination of terrorist

[28] Katz, *Man Enough?*, p. 7; Jane Junn, Making Room for Women of Color: Race and Gender Categories in the 2008 US Presidential Election, *Politics & Gender* 5(1) (2009): 105–10.
[29] Sinclair-Chapman and Price, Black Politics, 743.
[30] Herman Gray, Black Masculinity and Visual Culture, *Callaloo* 18(2) (1995): 401–05.

Osama bin Laden – helped undermine these characterizations, but his experiences as both candidate and officeholder reveal the ways in which race and gender interact to create distinct realities for presidential contenders. Moreover, they make clear that discussions of presidential masculinity had – at least until Obama's election – been centered on white masculinity without overt recognition of the racialized norms and constraints of masculine dominance.

In Chapter 2, Kelly Dittmar details how white masculine dominance has also forced women to confront incongruent expectations of their gender and presidential leadership, with additional challenges for women of color who are more easily positioned as threats to the status quo. These distinct gender dynamics were made especially visible by Hillary Clinton's 2008 presidential campaign, which was the first campaign waged by a woman to be perceived as viable. In preparation for the 2008 campaign, Clinton's chief campaign strategist warned that the United States was not ready for a "first mama" president, but would be open to "the first father being a woman." As a result, Clinton sought to emphasize her masculine credentials instead of challenging institutional dynamics that disadvantaged women and discounted stereotypically feminine traits, expertise, and experiences. From the very beginning, she presented herself as a tough-as-nails fighter who would never give up. Campaigning in Ohio, she told a crowd of supporters, "I'm here today because I want to let you know, I'm a fighter, a doer and a champion, and I will fight for you."[31] Governor Easley of North Carolina described Clinton as someone "who makes Rocky Balboa look like a pansy."[32] A union leader in Indiana even introduced her as a person with "testicular fortitude!"[33] She frequently reiterated that she was "not running as a woman," but instead emphasized her toughness, decisiveness, and leadership experience. In her campaign's efforts to prove her masculinity, Clinton combatted notions of white womanhood that characterized women as passive, fragile, and nice. But she also benefited from the privilege of her white womanhood in many ways, including perceptions of white women as less threatening – including to the status quo – than women or men of color.

---

[31] Rick Pearson, Hillary Clinton: "A Fighter, a Doer and a Champion," *Chicago Tribune*, March 2, 2008, www.chicagotribune.com/chinews-mtblog-2008-03-hillary_clinton_a_fighter_a_do-story.html

[32] Governor Mike Easley of North Carolina Endorses Hillary, YouTube, April 29, 2008, www.youtube.com/watch?v=zbqFEaP4Vow

[33] Fernando Suarez, From the Road: Union Boss Says Clinton Has "Testicular Fortitude," *CBS News*, April 30, 2008, www.cbsnews.com/blogs/2008/04/30/politics/fromtheroad/entry4059528.shtml

A frequent discussion stemming from 2008 was whether Obama's version of a Black male presidency or Clinton's version of a white woman presidency would win the day. Ultimately, Obama earned the nomination but neither presented an alternative version of race and gender in presidential politics. Instead, they made modest adjustments to prevailing norms of white male authoritative leadership. After Obama was inaugurated and started to govern, his ability to avoid raced and gendered stereotypes disappeared. Discussions of identity by subsequent presidential candidates were expected to be more overt and to reflect an understanding of and principal disagreement with current challenges to a more inclusive society.

In 2016, Clinton adopted a more evolved gender strategy by seeking to reassure voters that being a woman was not a detriment but a benefit. She told voters, "I'm not asking people to vote for me simply because I'm a woman. I'm asking people to vote for me on the merits. I think one of the merits is that I am a woman."[34] Clinton focused less on proving credentials of dominant masculinity and instead offered alternative credentials – those tied with women's lived experiences and stereotypically feminine traits and expertise. Her 2016 campaign featured fewer boxing gloves and emphasized strength in numbers ("Stronger Together") versus strength through force. She criticized the tough talk of her Republican counterparts, arguing, "Promising to carpet bomb until the desert glows doesn't make you sound strong, it makes you sound like you're in over your head. Bluster and bigotry are not credentials for becoming Commander-in-Chief." Taking advantage of the ability to position herself in contrast to Trump's hypermasculinity, she faced an electoral context – and an opponent – different than when she ran in the 2008 Democratic primary.[35]

As in 2008, Clinton navigated her 2016 presidential bid as a white woman, which brought with it distinct expectations and privileges. Clinton more overtly acknowledged that privilege in 2016 than she did eight years prior; for example, when she spoke at the Little Rock A.M.E. Zion Church in the wake of the death of Keith Lamont Scott at the hands of local police, she explained, "I'm a grandmother, and like every grandmother, I worry about the safety and security of my grandchildren, but

---

[34] Eric Bradner, Hillary Clinton: "One of the Merits Is I Am a Woman," *CNN*, July 23, 2015, www.cnn.com/2015/07/23/politics/hillary-clinton-gender-merits
[35] The Office of Hillary Rodham Clinton, Hillary Clinton Lays Out Comprehensive Plan to Bolster Homeland Security, press briefing, December 15, 2015, https://bit.ly/3yi1qel

my worries are not the same as Black grandmothers, who have different and deeper fears about the world that their grandchildren face."[36] While Clinton spent more time in 2016 discussing her own racial privilege than she did in 2008, the effects of her whiteness on both campaigns has been given minimal attention. In 2020, Kamala Harris' campaign for the Democratic nomination – alongside the campaigns of multiple white women – provided another point of evolution for understanding the interactive effects of race and gender in presidential campaigns, particularly for candidates.

Understanding the presidency as a raced and gendered institution characterized by the dominance of whiteness and masculinity does not mean accepting this reality as immutable. Instead, just as our beliefs of gender and race are not static, neither are the ways in which institutions distribute power along racial, gender, and intersectional lines. This is why revealing gender, race, and intersectional realities – and inequities – in institutions matters; making visible axes of marginalization and privilege leaves space for disrupting them. In presidential politics, that disruption can come from many sources, including voters, media, candidates, and officeholders. In the remainder of this chapter, we analyze the ways in which the 2020 presidential election disrupted white and masculine dominance and revealed both the persistence of white male privilege and strategies that capitalized on efforts for its preservation. The 2020 election makes clear that disrupting institutional power dynamics is difficult and that progress toward gender and racial equity within institutions is neither inevitable nor without backlash. Instead, the dynamism and interaction of these forces should be the focus of continued study and vigilance.

GENDER, RACE, AND THE 2020 ELECTION

Electoral Context

If the 2008 presidential election made visible the underlying gender and race dynamics of the presidency, the political context since has provided more opportunities for understanding and illustrating the complexity of how these axes of power shape not only candidate and officeholder behavior but also voter expectations. After eight years of a Black president, Trump capitalized upon feelings of racial resentment and backlash to gender evolution to wage a campaign promising a return to a bygone

---

[36] Josh Haskell, Clinton Says Her White Grandchildren Are Spared the Fearful Experiences Many Black Children Face, *ABC News*, October 2, 2016, https://abcn.ws/3zWYkN8

era. His campaign theme – "Make America Great Again" – signaled a return to conservative policies and "America first" priorities. Trump's rhetoric and strategy forced a response by his opponents – Democrats and Republicans – leading to even more overt discussions about racism and sexism in politics and beyond. Clinton's recognition of racial privilege in Little Rock was repeated in major urban areas as she made public appearances at Black churches with grieving Black mothers known as the Mothers of the Movement. While her attempts to expose and address these realities were not always successful, they, alongside the persistent efforts of activists and voters, brought new concepts and language into presidential politics. Specifically, Clinton used the language of intersectionality on the campaign trail, not only in acknowledging how race and gender shape her own experience and perspective, but also in advocating for policy analyses and approaches that are cognizant of intersecting forces of inequity.[37]

As this volume details, the outcome of the 2016 presidential election and Trump's subsequent policy changes mobilized Americans, many on the basis of gender, race, and intersectional identities. The largest mass protest of women occurred just one day after he was sworn into office, and racial justice activism that had increased under the Obama administration reached new heights under a president whose rhetoric and policies were more overtly hostile. Simultaneously, white nationalist groups grew under the Trump administration, up 55 percent from 2017 to 2019 according to the Southern Poverty Law Center.[38] That rise in activity was made especially visible in August 2017, when white nationalists gathered in Charlottesville, Virginia for the "Unite the Right" rally. The images of white men with torches chanting "White lives matter!" and "Jews will not replace us!" were combined with the horrific murder of a young woman when a white nationalist drove directly into a group of counter-protesters. Three days later, President Trump condemned "this egregious display of hatred, bigotry, and violence," but then told reporters, "You had some very bad people in that group [the white nationalists], but you also had people that were very fine people, on both sides."[39] These events, layered

---

[37] Claire Foran, Hillary Clinton's Intersectional Politics, *The Atlantic*, March 9, 2016, www.theatlantic.com/politics/archive/2016/03/hillary-clinton-intersectionality/472872/

[38] The Year in Hate and Extremism 2019, Southern Poverty Law Center report, 2020, www.splcenter.org/sites/default/files/yih_2020_final.pdf

[39] Angie Drobnic Holan. In Context: Donald Trump's "Very Fine People on Both Sides" Remarks, *Politifact*, April 26, 2019, www.politifact.com/article/2019/apr/26/context-trumps-very-fine-people-both-sides-remarks/

onto the policy changes and ongoing activism, ensured that efforts to preserve and promote greater gender and racial equity became a more prominent electoral issue. They became part of the 2018 midterm agendas upon which a record number of women and a more racially diverse pool of candidates were elected to office. And it was that specific comment by Trump that Joe Biden cites as his impetus to run for president. After hearing Trump's response, Biden said, in his presidential campaign launch video in April 2019, "I knew the threat to our nation was unlike any I'd ever seen in my lifetime." Biden's campaign theme became to "Restore the Soul of This Nation," and he viewed Charlottesville as evidence that it was being lost.

The racial tensions were amplified further by the Trump administration's family separation policy at the southern border, continued violence by police against Black and Brown Americans, debates over Confederate monuments, and a continued rise in domestic terror at the hands of white supremacists. The effects were evident across groups, with a specific racial reckoning among white liberals. In national surveys, white liberals were more likely than ever by the fall of 2018 to identify racial discrimination as the cause for racial inequality, to see the criminal justice system as biased against Black Americans, and to see the Confederate flag as a symbol of racism instead of southern pride.[40]

Happening simultaneously was a reckoning on gender imbalances in power across institutions and industries. From the backlash to Trump's "locker room talk" in the "Access Hollywood" tape to the Women's March, the country was paying greater attention to persistent gender inequities. The #MeToo movement, which took hold in the fall of 2017 alongside exposure of sexual harassment and assault at the hands of powerful men, made clear the abusive roots to those inequities. #MeToo conversations also revealed racial disparities among women, in exposure to abuse, being believed, and having access to remedy and accountability. Together, the racial and gender reckonings at play were nearly impossible for political leaders to ignore, whether in office or on the campaign trail in both 2018 and 2020.

In winter and spring 2020, as the coronavirus pandemic spread globally and began its strike on the United States, anti-Asian hate increased domestically, arguably spurred by President Trump and other leaders referring to the virus as the "China virus" or "kung flu." As infections and

---

[40] Asma Khalid, How White Liberals became Woke, Radically Changing Their Outlook on Race, *NPR*, October 1, 2019, https://n.pr/3zXwu3b

deaths spiked and the country was forced to shut down, the health and economic effects of the pandemic made clear the racial disparities that predated this moment; Black and Brown Americans were more likely to contract and die from COVID-19, and bore the brunt of resulting economic hardships. Then, in June 2020, the murder of George Floyd by police in Minneapolis – which was filmed and shared widely – reinvigorated racial justice protests and activism nationwide. Those protests also invoked the many other Black and Brown victims of police violence, including Breonna Taylor, who was murdered in her own home by police in March 2020. This moment gave renewed and increased attention to the #SayHerName campaign that had been launched by Kimberlé Crenshaw – who originated intersectionality theory – to make visible the Black *women* who were victims of police violence.

The confluence of these forces and events undoubtedly influenced the 2020 election, in terms of both how candidates engaged gender and race on the campaign trail and the motivations of voters. Added to this reality was the most gender and racially diverse pool of presidential candidates in US history, with six women – including two women of color – and five men of color competing for the Democratic nomination for president alongside seventeen white men. By August 2020, the selection of Kamala Harris – the first woman, the first South Asian, and the first Black person to be a vice-presidential nominee – only further amplified the attention to gender, race, and intersectional dynamics. The dominance of whiteness and masculinity in presidential politics could no longer be rendered invisible.

Maintaining Power Dynamics

How much did the 2020 election reveal persistent privileging of masculinity and whiteness? While not a comprehensive assessment, there is evidence that the balance of gender and racial power in presidential politics remains unleveled. First, after successfully tapping into racial resentment and sexism in 2016, Donald Trump adopted a largely similar – and especially brazen, compared to recent presidential contenders – approach to navigating these dynamics in his 2020 bid for reelection. His response to Charlottesville and defense of Confederate monuments demonstrated his hesitancy in fully denouncing white supremacist groups, individuals, and symbols. He also continued to employ rhetoric and attacks that othered racial minorities. In July 2019, Trump directed a Twitter attack on the freshman women of color House members collectively known as "The Squad," for criticizing his border policy. He said that the women (all but one of whom were born in the US), should "go back and help fix the totally broken and crime infested places from which they came." But it is the positive reaction of Republican voters to his tweet – more than the tweet itself – that explained why he continued to engage in white identity politics. A *USA Today*/Ipsos poll conducted soon after the tweet found that just 25 percent of Republicans, compared with 88 percent of Democrats, found Trump's attack "un-American." Moreover, only a minority of Republicans (45%) considered telling minorities to "go back where they came from" to be a racist statement.[41] Another survey showed a five-point bump in Trump's net approval among Republicans in the days after his tweet.[42]

Throughout Trump's first term, and even on the campaign trail, he boasted about the good he did for communities of color. He touted passage of the First Step Act in December 2018, bipartisan criminal justice reform legislation to address, among other things, the stark racial inequities in sentencing and incarceration. Trump also pointed to the economic growth during his tenure as bringing specific benefits to Black and Brown communities, though evidence tempers these claims. These achievements led Trump to assert multiple times during the campaign season that he had "done more for the Black community than any other president."[43] Trump's team sought to capitalize on these claims by attacking Joe Biden for his race record in targeted advertising and messaging to the Black community. In ads narrated by and featuring Black men, Trump's campaign stated that Biden "insulted millions" of Black Americans by assuming they would support him and that he "jailed us" due to his support for the 1994 Crime Bill. Two Black women surrogates for Trump – known as Diamond and Silk – went further by calling Joe Biden "Jim Crow Joe," arguing he had not done enough for the Black community in his nearly fifty years of public service and implying instead that he had done damage.

While these messages reflect an attempt to both reject and address racial inequity, they often conflicted with Trump's demonization of Black Lives Matter and protests for racial equity. As racial justice protests escalated, Trump called Black Lives Matter a "symbol of hate" and derided

---

[41] Chris Jackson and Mallory Newall, Views of Trump's Twitter Attack on Four Congresswomen Highly Partisan, Ipsos news release, July 17, 2019, www.ipsos.com/en-us/news-polls/trump-tweet-response-2019

[42] Chris Kahn, Republican Support for Trump Rises after Racially Charged Tweets: Reuters/Ipsos poll, Reuters, https://reut.rs/

[43] Dan Mangan, Trump Suggests Lincoln's Legacy Is "Questionable," Brags about His Own Work for Black Americans, *CNBC*, June 12, 2020, https://cnb.cx/3C4oiQx

protests as "riots" while reiterating his support for law enforcement. His continued calls to quell protests with force not only reinforced his expression of dominant masculinity but also mined racial divisions. Moreover, by the September 2020 presidential debate, he appeared unwilling to condemn white supremacist groups. Asked to directly condemn white supremacist group the Proud Boys, he waffled and, upon further prodding, said, "Proud Boys, stand back and stand by." He quickly added, "But I'll tell you what … somebody's got to do something about Antifa and the left because this is not a right-wing problem." Despite walking these comments back, many – including white supremacist groups – viewed Trump's response as a tacit endorsement of white supremacist groups and acceptance of their support.[44]

Trump and his team used racial justice protests to foster fear among white communities. At the Republican National Convention (RNC), a white couple from St. Louis who had made headlines for waving guns at racial justice protesters told viewers that Joe Biden would "abolish the suburbs," and warned, "Make no mistake: No matter where you live, your family will not be safe in the radical Democrats' America." They added, "It seems as if Democrats no longer view the government's job as protecting honest citizens from criminals, but rather protecting criminals from honest citizens."[45] Evoking fear allowed Trump to position himself as masculine protector.[46] Even before the RNC, Trump made thinly veiled claims that he would protect white suburban populations from the threat – both physical and economic – of racial integration. In July 2020, he affirmed that "people living their Suburban Lifestyle Dream" would "no longer be bothered or financially hurt by having low-income housing built in your neighborhood." Later in the campaign, as Susan Carroll details in Chapter 5, Trump assured "suburban housewives" that he was "getting [their] husbands back to work," relying on a model of masculine dominance and feminine dependence.

Consistent with 2016, Trump used nicknames as a tool of emasculation. He frequently referred to Democratic candidate Michael Bloomberg

[44] Craig Timberg and Elizabeth Dwoskin, Trump's Debate Comments Give an Online Boost to a Group Social Media Companies Have Long Struggled Against, *Washington Post*, September 30, 2020, www.washingtonpost.com/technology/2020/09/30/trump-debate-rightwing-celebration/

[45] Caitlin Oprysko, In Grievance-Filled Speech, St. Louis Couple Warn of Chaos in the Suburbs if Democrats Elected, *Politico*, August 24, 2019, www.politico.com/news/2020/08/24/mccloskey-convention-speech-guns-suburbs-401297

[46] Iris Marion Young, The Logic of Masculinist Protection: Reflections on the Current Security State, *Signs: Journal of Women in Culture and Society* 29(1) (2003): 1–25.

as "Mini Mike," evoking height as an indicator of masculine power. Trump used "Sleepy Joe" to characterize Democratic nominee Biden as weak and tired. He elaborated on Biden's physical weakness on the campaign trail, telling variants of the same story of how he could knock Biden down with a small push, saying that without even closing his fist, "Ding, he's gone."[47] Trump also criticized mask-wearing as effeminate. At a September 2020 rally, he asked about Biden, "Did you ever see a man who likes a mask as much as him?" He continued, "Because, you know what, it gives him a feeling of security. If I were a psychiatrist, I'd say, 'This guy's got some big issues.'"[48] Just days after mocking Biden again for mask-wearing at the first presidential debate, Trump was treated for COVID-19. Upon his release from the hospital, he made a show of unmasking on the White House balcony. In contrast, Biden told audiences that mask-wearing was patriotic. He explained, "It's not about being a tough guy. It's about doing your part."[49]

Like in 2016, other 2020 presidential candidates sometimes fell into the masculinity trap themselves, using emasculating language and attacks to discredit Trump or opponents. Elizabeth Warren joked about Michael Bloomberg's height, Kamala Harris called Trump a "small man," and Barack Obama – while stumping for Biden – mocked Trump by saying, "When *60 minutes* and Lesley Stahl are too tough for you, you ain't all that tough."[50] Biden also put out an ad in July 2020 with a strongly masculine tone. In "That's a President," voters are reminded that being president takes strength and courage while seeing images of Biden with (nearly all) male and military leaders. While women make a cameo when the ad touts Biden's compassion, the ad's masculinized tone – quite literally in music that mirrors that used in Ford truck commercials – adheres to norms that perpetuate instead of disrupt the alignment of political leadership with masculinity.

Unlike for Trump, these examples were rare among Democratic presidential candidates. In fact, Biden and his surrogates were more likely to

[47] Daniel Dale, Twitter post, November 1, 2020, 12:19 p.m., https://twitter.com/ddale8/status/1322951401358663683?lang=en

[48] Robert Mackey, Trump Is Hospitalized with Covid-19, Days after Mocking Biden for Wearing a Mask, *The Intercept*, October 2, 2020, https://theintercept.com/2020/10/02/trump-tests-positive-covid-48-hours-mocking-biden-wearing-mask/

[49] Jeff Mason and Trevor Hunnicutt, After Trump's COVID-19 Diagnosis, Biden Says Masks Not about Being a "Tough Guy," Reuters, October 2, 2020, https://reut.rs/3jesWCT

[50] Benhamin Fearnow, Obama Mocks Trump at Miami Biden Rally: "Florida Man Wouldn't Even Do This Stuff," *Newsweek*, October 24, 2020, https://bit.ly/3j6sF54

present alternative definitions of toughness less tied to dominant masculinity. For example, WWE champion Dave Bautista endorsed Biden in an October 2020 ad titled "That's Toughness" where he argued that toughness was not proven by bullying, but was instead shown in Biden's ability to unite people, work out disputes, and fight for Americans. Likewise, Obama said while stumping for Biden that it "used to be, being a man meant taking care of other people." Biden leaned into this identity throughout his campaign, sharing experiences of overcoming personal grief and seeking professional collaboration to elevate empathy, compassion, and compromise as presidential strengths more than aggression, force, or a *lack* of emotion.

The dominance of masculinity and whiteness in presidential politics is evident not only in candidate behavior but also in voter perceptions and candidate evaluations. In Chapter 2, Kelly Dittmar elaborates on how perceptions of electability were gendered in the 2020 presidential election, forcing women candidates to combat stronger doubts that they could be successful. Duerst-Lahti argues, "Presidential timber derives from the perception of others. That is, others must see a potential candidate as possessing it."[51] Election 2020 not only made clear the importance of electability among the candidate characteristics voters seek in selecting a presidential nominee, but also made clear how impossible it is to separate race, gender, and perceptions of electability, since the idea of electability is so deeply rooted in previous election outcomes. As many pointed out during the Democratic primary in particular, the electability myth is perpetuated if and when voters see attempts to disrupt white male privilege as too risky. Elizabeth Warren challenged Democratic primary voters to reject this by asking, "Are we gonna show up for people we [don't] actually believe in … because we are too afraid to do anything else?" Evidence from voter surveys indicated, to some extent, they were. Beyond fear, the resulting success of white men is not proof of their greater electability over women or candidates of color. Instead, it indicates the continued functioning of an institution in which power is both perceived and allocated along gender and racial lines. Media is also culpable in reinforcing these power imbalances. As Democratic candidate Julián Castro tweeted after Kamala Harris dropped out of the Democratic primary, "The media's flawed formula for 'electability' has pushed aside women and candidates of color." He added, "Our party's diversity is our strength," seeking to shift

---

[51] Duerst-Lahti, Presidential Elections, p. 32.

both the perceived and actual balance of gender, racial, and intersectional power at the presidential level.[52]

Disrupting Power Dynamics

The 2020 presidential election also revealed shifting power dynamics, especially in how Democratic candidates both experienced and navigated gender, race, and intersectional dynamics. First, Democratic presidential candidates spoke explicitly about and positioned themselves in contrast to, as candidate Pete Buttigieg phrased it, President Trump's "white guy identity politics" that "uses race to divide the working and middle class."[53] Julián Castro leveraged his own Latino identity to reject Trump's race politics. In an August 2019 ad titled "A Message to Donald Trump," he spoke directly to camera and to Trump: "You referred to countries as shitholes. You urged American congresswomen to 'go back to where they came from.' You called immigrants rapists. Innocent people were shot down because they look different from you. Because they look like me. They look like my family. Words have consequences. ¡Ya Basta!"[54] Democratic nominee Joe Biden rooted his decision to run in Trump's unwillingness to reject white supremacy and, in an October 2020 presidential debate, called Trump "one of the most racist presidents we've had in modern history."[55] Likewise, Biden's running mate – Kamala Harris – called out the Trump administration's denial of racial inequality and bias in the vice-presidential debate. Directly to Vice President Pence, she said, "Yes, Joe Biden and I recognize that implicit bias does exist, Mr. Vice President, contrary to what you may believe."[56]

Harris' use of "implicit bias" was one of many examples of presidential candidates both addressing and being asked about concepts not commonly raised in presidential elections. From "systemic racism" to "intersectionality," candidates were expected to be versed in axes of inequity. They were also proactive in affirming language and worldviews that

---

[52] Julián Castro, Twitter post, December 3, 2019, 10:09 p.m., https://twitter.com/juliancastro/status/1202062440348966914?lang=en

[53] Alexandra Jaffe, "Buttigieg to Democrats: Don't Get Bogged Down Zinging Trump," *Associated Press*, April 17, 2019, https://apnews.com/article/cbadc3cbc75548378ce22b5f4e24db04

[54] Julián Castro, "A Message to Donald Trump," YouTube, August 13, 2019, www.youtube.com/watch?v=0mjA1xGwX-8

[55] Transcript of presidential debate at Belmont University, Nashville, Texas, October 22, 2020, Commission on Presidential Debates (hereafter CPD) (website), www.debates.org/voter-education/debate-transcripts/october-22-2020-debate-transcript/

[56] Transcript of vice presidential debate at the University of Utah, Salt Lake City, Utah, October 7, 2020, CPD, https://bit.ly/2ViJS2Z

disrupted gender and racial norms. For example, Julián Castro made
news for asking an activist to share their preferred pronouns, demonstrating both a respect for nonbinary communities as well as an evolved
understanding of gender identity and expression. White candidates were
also more likely than ever to address their racial privilege. In one of the
few clips that caught fire from her campaign, Democratic presidential
contender Kirsten Gillibrand responded to a white Ohio voter who asked
about "so-called white privilege." Gillibrand distinguished the suffering of
the white working class from that caused by "institutional racism,"
explaining,

> Institutional racism is real. It doesn't take away your pain or suffering.
> It's just a different issue. Your suffering is just as important as a Black
> or Brown person's suffering but to fix the problems that are happening
> in a Black community you need far more transformational efforts that
> target for real racism that exists every day. ... A white woman like me
> who is a senator and running for president of the United States has to
> lift up their voice just as much as I would lift up yours. That's all it
> means.[57]

Elizabeth Warren also discussed her racial privilege, telling an audience in
February 2020, "I get it. I am not a woman of color. ... I have the privilege
of never having been slammed into the wall by a police officer." But, like
Gillibrand, she vowed to be aware of that privilege as a political leader;
"But I tell you this," she continued, "I listen to people who have. I listen
and I say when I am president of the United States that's not going to happen to human beings."[58] The election was marked by acknowledgments
of racial positioning and pledges to consider racial equity in policy and
decision-making. Meanwhile, a similar coming to terms with gender was
also underway.

In 2020, white male candidates, perhaps for the first time, were asked
to address their race and gender privilege as potential liabilities to their
presidential bids instead of assuming they were electoral advantages.
Asked by reporters whether being a white man would be a disadvantage
in the Democratic primary, Beto O'Rourke responded, "I would never
begin by saying it's a disadvantage at all. As a white man who has had

---

[57] Catherine Kim, A White Woman from Ohio Asked Gillibrand about White Privilege. Her
Answer Was Spot On, *Vox*, July 12, 2019, https://bit.ly/3zVLu1J

[58] Sarah Taylor, Warren Tells Minority Voters Her White Privilege Prevented Her from
Police Abuse: "I Am Not a Woman of Color," Blaze Media, February 25, 2020, www
.theblaze.com/news/warren-tells-minority-voters-her-white-privilege-prevented-her-
from-police-abuse

privileges that others could not depend on or take for granted, I've clearly had advantages over the course of my life."[59] That self-awareness is notable and important for challenging institutional power dynamics. As Pete Buttigieg explained in an April 2019 interview, "Any white candidate needs to show a level of consciousness around issues like white privilege." Asked whether he had experienced white privilege himself, Buttigieg said, "Part of privilege is not being very conscious of it, right?"[60] Democratic presidential candidate and governor Jay Inslee elaborated on the need for not only consciousness but also humility in navigating political power as a white man. When asked why he would be the best candidate to heal the racial divide in the country, Inslee responded,

> I approach this question with humility because I have not experienced what many Americans have. I've never been a Black teenager pulled over in a white neighborhood. I've never been a woman talked over in a meeting. I've never been an LGBTQ member subject to a slur. And so I have believed I have an added responsibility, a double responsibility, to deal with racial disparity.[61]

Simply questioning – in mainstream political coverage – the ways in which privilege might affect candidates' capacity for presidential leadership was important, as well as rare in past elections. It also opened the door for women candidates and candidates of color to more overtly discuss their identities and experiences as values-added. Still, measuring whether presidential power dynamics have shifted requires more than a change in rhetoric. As Rashad Robinson, executive director of Color of Change, said during the election, "I don't need you simply talking about these issues. I need you using your power to act on them."[62] That could come in candidates outlining policy agendas, which many did, or be demonstrated by past actions. Moving from rhetoric to action is also best measured by continuing these conversations as the Biden–Harris administration does its work.

Kamala Harris notably centered her distinct experience as a multiracial girl in the first Democratic primary debate. After asserting that "the

[59] Hunter Woodall, O'Rourke: Being White Male Doesn't Put Me at Disadvantage, *Associated Press*, March 17, 2019, https://apnews.com/article/6c5781673cf64a8ab01832778fbd743a

[60] Errin Haines Whack, White Presidential Hopefuls Navigate Questions of White Privilege, *Associated Press*, April 24, 2019, https://bit.ly/37hrAlv

[61] Eugene Scott, Jay Inslee's Insightful Comments on White Privilege and Discrimination, *Washington Post*, March 12, 2019, https://wapo.st/2Vmiscv

[62] Whack, White Presidential Hopefuls.

issue of race is still not being talked about truthfully and honestly," she described, "Growing up, my sister and I had to deal with the neighbor who told us her parents [said she] couldn't play with us because we were Black."[63] She also directed criticism to Biden for not only boasting about working with segregationist senators but also for opposing busing policies to integrate public schools. Just over a week before the debate, Cory Booker, another Black senator running for the Democratic nomination, issued a statement condemning Biden's comments about the civility with which he worked with segregationist senators and joking about one senator calling him "boy." Booker said, "Vice President Biden's relationships with proud segregationists are not the model for how we make America a safer and more inclusive place for black people, and for everyone."[64] Booker called on Biden to apologize and later reported having a "constructive" conversation where he was able to explain the hurt that these comments caused.[65] These examples demonstrate both the importance of racial diversity among presidential candidates, as well as the increased attention to candidates' race records.

In addition to explaining his relationship with segregationists and his opposition to busing, Biden was repeatedly called upon to explain his vote for the 1994 Crime Bill, which contributed to the mass incarceration of Black men. He also faced backlash for telling hosts of *The Breakfast Club* in May 2020, "If you have a problem figuring out whether you're for me or Trump, then you ain't Black." While he walked back his comment, it heightened fears about Biden's racial awareness and sincerity, given his legislative record. Airing these critiques and concerns was both essential and justified, according to Kimberlé Crenshaw. She wrote in August 2019, "Voters who are activated to battle tooth-and-nail against the resurrection of our white supremacist past have every reason to press candidates for evidence that their failing marks on some of the most consequential issues affecting race and gender justice won't be repeated."[66] In the same article, Crenshaw questioned Biden's record on gender, particularly the mistreatment of Anita Hill in the 1991 confirmation hearing for Supreme Court

63 Time Staff, transcript of Democratic presidential debate, June 27, 2019, https://time .com/5616518/2020-democratic-debate-night-2-transcript/

64 Scott Detrow, Democrats Blast Biden for Recalling "Civil" Relationships with Segregationists, *NPR*, June 19, 2019, https://n.pr/3C6ZMhW

65 Orion Rummier, Booker Blasts Biden for Praising His "Civility" with Senate Segregationists, Axios, June 19, 2019, https://bit.ly/3rKHP3X

66 Kimberlé Crenshaw, The Destructive Politics of White Amnesia, *New Republic*, August 6, 2019, https://newrepublic.com/article/154605/joe-biden-destructive-politics-white-amnesia

Justice Clarence Thomas. Hill was subject to ridicule, humiliation, badgering, and abuse from the white male Judiciary Committee as she testified about the sexual harassment she experienced with Thomas. Biden, the Judiciary Committee chair, expressed his regret for how Hill was treated, but stopped short of apologizing. Biden also faced allegations of making women uncomfortable by invading their personal space and was forced to issue a response. In an April 2019 video, he apologized and said, "The boundaries of protecting personal space have been reset. I get it … I'll be much more mindful. That's my responsibility and I'll meet it."

Biden was not the only Democratic candidate asked to address their records. Michael Bloomberg's presidential campaign was derailed in large part due to this scrutiny. In February 2020, Bloomberg faced combined attacks of fostering a hostile workplace for women at Bloomberg LP as well as promoting racial profiling through his "stop-and-frisk" policy as mayor of New York. At the February 2020 Democratic debate, he was attacked by multiple opponents for his race record, and Elizabeth Warren levied an especially effective attack on his unwillingness to release former women employees from nondisclosure agreements. She made her case not only on the basis of character but also by challenging viewers and voters to think differently about what we deem as disqualifying in presidential leaders. Within the first few minutes of the debate, Warren said,

> I'd like to talk about who we're running against. A billionaire who calls women fat broads and horse-faced lesbians. And no, I'm not talking about Donald Trump, I'm talking about Mayor Bloomberg. Democrats are not going to win if we have a nominee who has a history of hiding his tax returns, of harassing women and of supporting racist policies like redlining and stop-and-frisk.[67]

Warren was not, however, without her own racial issues. Specifically, she launched her campaign in the shadow of an arguably botched attempt to respond to claims that she had previously identified as Native American for professional gain. In October 2018, Warren took a DNA test to show her Native American ancestry, leading to even more criticism of conflating DNA with heritage. Pete Buttigieg faced particular scrutiny for how he, as mayor of South Bend, handled a police shooting of a Black resident in June 2019. As former prosecutors, both Kamala Harris and Amy Klobuchar were subject to criticism for the ways in which they upheld a

---

[67] Transcript of Democratic presidential debate, February 20, 2020, *NBC News*, www .nbcnews.com/politics/2020-election/full-transcript-ninth-democratic-debate-las-vegas-n1139546

discriminatory criminal justice system. These were not the only records scrutinized, but they illustrate the attention and value placed on presidential candidates' ability to both understand and promote gender and racial equity. They demonstrate greater accountability for past behavior that perpetuated inequity or bias and brought these issues to broader public audiences for debate ahead of primary and general elections.

Kamala Harris

One of the clearest sites for disruption of presidential power dynamics came in the nomination and election of the first woman, first South Asian, and first Black vice president of the United States: Kamala Harris. When Harris formally accepted the vice-presidential nomination in August 2020, she explained, "That I am here tonight is a testament to the dedication of generations before me," noting her debt to many, including Shirley Chisholm, the first Black congresswoman and the first Black woman to wage a major-party bid for president. Reflecting on her 1972 campaign, Chisholm explained, "I ran because someone had to do it first," adding, "In this country everybody is supposed to be able to run for president, but that's never really been true."[68] Many of the challenges that contributed to her primary defeat persisted through 2003, when the next Black woman presidential candidate competed for a major-party nomination. Senator Carol Moseley-Braun left the 2004 primary before voting started despite her hope that "Americans are prepared to think outside the box and elect a person who is female and African American."[69] Harris' faith in the American people "to know that we will never be burdened by the assumptions of who can do what based on who historically has done it" may have been similarly unfounded, as she also ended her run before the primaries began. But these women helped to soften the ground for Harris' eventual nomination and success at the presidential level.

Harris was also preceded by two major-party women vice-presidential nominees: Democrat Geraldine Ferraro in 1984 and Republican Sarah Palin in 2008. Both women exposed gender biases in presidential politics. While distinct electoral contexts meant that their bids provided little road-mapping for Harris, there were some similarities with Ferraro's nomination thirty-six years prior. Feminist organizations sought to leverage the power of women's votes and affinity for the Democratic Party to pressure

[68] Shirley Chisholm, *The Good Fight* (New York: HarperCollins, 1973), p. 3.
[69] Paula D. McClain, Niambi M. Carter, and Michael C. Brady, Gender and Black Presidential Politics: From Chisholm to Moseley Braun, *Journal of Women, Politics, and Policy* 27(1–2) (2005): 51–68.

the nominee in 1984 to select a woman running mate.[70] They were successful, even if the ticket was not. In 2020, the idea of a woman running mate was perhaps less exceptional. In fact, most of the male Democratic candidates were asked about their intentions to select a woman running mate if they won the nomination; their responses ranged from definitive commitments to suggestions that it would be hard to imagine *not* selecting a woman.[71] But once it became clear that the Democratic nomination would go to one of two white men (Biden or Senator Bernie Sanders), the pressure to select a woman grew. Like in 1984, women's groups mobilized to make very public demands.

In early March 2020, a coalition of women's organizations – including Women's March, Planned Parenthood Action Fund, UltraViolet, NARAL Pro-Choice America, SuperMajority, EMILY's List, She the People, Care in Action, #VOTEPROCHOICE, and National Women's Law Center Action Fund – published an open letter to presidential candidates, in which they asked them to do the following: (1) appoint women (with shared values of justice and equality) to at least half of all presidential appointments; (2) select a woman running mate; and (3) ensure racial, religious, and gender identity representation for all presidential appointments.[72] Less than a week later, Biden and Sanders were asked on the debate stage if they would commit to selecting a woman running mate. While Sanders hedged a bit by saying, "In all likelihood, I will," Biden said, "I commit I will in fact pick a woman to be vice president."[73] Once it was evident that Biden would secure the nomination, additional pressure came from women's organizations to select a Black woman. An April 2020 open letter from Sisters Lead, Sisters Vote made clear, "It is a fact that the road to the White House is powered by Black women."[74] They were right. Black women were the most reliable group – voting at the highest rates and at the highest percentage of support – in the successful Obama coalition. Biden also relied on strong support from Black women to win the nomination. In

[70] Susan Carroll, The Gender Gap as a Tool for Women's Political Empowerment: The Formative Years, 1980–84, in *The Legacy of Second-Wave Feminism in American Politics*, ed. Angie Maxwell and Todd Shields (London: Palgrave Macmillan, 2018).

[71] Eliza Relman and Kate Taylor, Howard Schultz Won't Commit to a Female Vice Presidential Running Mate. Here Are the Other Male Candidates Who Have, *Business Insider*, March 22, 2019, https://bit.ly/3iiUHeE

[72] Women Setting the Agenda, open letter, March 2020, https://bit.ly/3fkpSUI

[73] Transcript of Democratic presidential debate, March 15, 2020, *CNN*, http://transcripts.cnn.com/TRANSCRIPTS/2003/15/se.03.html

[74] Sisters Lead Sisters Vote, open letter, April 24, 2020, https://actionnetwork.org/petitions/black-women-leaders-letter-to-support-black-women-for-vp/

this letter and follow-up meetings and lobbying, Black women leaders demanded a return on the investment that they had not only placed in Biden himself, but in the Democratic Party for decades.

As racial justice protests increased nationwide, Democratic voters agreed that it was important for Biden to choose a woman of color running mate; a *USA Today*/Suffolk University survey in late June 2020 found that 72 percent of Democrats agreed, including 75 percent of white Democrats and 60 percent of Black Democrats.[75] At the same time, Klobuchar withdrew her name from consideration and said, "I truly believe that this is a historic moment for our country. ... And I think the right thing to do right now ... is to put a woman of color on the ticket."[76] After Biden named Harris as his running mate, 60 percent of Americans – including 87 percent of Democrats and 37 percent of Republicans – viewed it as a "major milestone," and women viewed Harris more favorably than they viewed Biden.[77] And, according to a fall 2020 PRRI survey, Black women were most likely, followed by college-educated white women, to say that selecting a Black woman running mate was a good decision for Biden.[78]

When Biden announced Harris' nomination, he also pointed to the attacks – rooted in sexism and racism – that were likely to come. He reminded viewers that Trump had already been calling Harris "nasty" and "mean" and asked, "Is anyone surprised Donald Trump has a problem with a strong woman ... ?" Importantly, Biden added, "We know more is to come. ... Kamala Harris has had your back, and now we have to have her back."[79] Outside groups were already mobilized, anticipating the bias she would confront, especially from the media. On August 6, 2020, TIME'S UP Now and a coalition of women's organizations issued a letter to news media that stated, "We believe it is your job to not just pay attention to [gender and racial] stereotypes, but to actively work to be anti-racist and anti-sexist in your coverage (ie: equal) ... As much as you have

[75] Susan Page and Sarah Elbeshbishi, Exclusive USA TODAY Poll: Biden Widens His Lead, but Trump Keeps Edge on Enthusiasm, *USA Today*, June 30, 2020, https://bit.ly/3fgzRug

[76] Ed O'Keefe and Bo Erickson, Amy Klobuchar Withdraws from Vice Presidential Consideration, Says Joe Biden Should Pick a Woman of Color, *CBS News*, June 19, 2020, www.cbsnews.com/news/amy-klobuchar-withdraws-joe-biden-vice-president-consideration/

[77] Chris Kahn, Exclusive: Harris Could Help Biden with Women, Young Voters, Maybe Some Republicans Too – Reuters/Ipsos Poll, Reuters, August 12, 2020, https://reut.rs/3ieKoYU

[78] Dueling Realities: Amid Multiple Crises, Trump and Biden Supporters See Different Priorities and Futures for the Nation, PRRI, October 19, 2020, https://bit.ly/3rZsTPH

[79] Transcript of Joe Biden's speech announcing running mate Kamala Harris, August 12, 2020, Rev.com, https://bit.ly/3C1Deiu

the public's trust, you also have great power. We urge you to use it wisely."[80] They warned that they would be monitoring unfair coverage, as they did for the duration of the campaign via an initiative called #WeHaveHerBack. These overt acknowledgments and rejections of racist and sexist coverage – from the presidential nominee, outside organizations, and others – marked an important shift in making visible forces in presidential politics that have long served to disadvantage those who challenge the dominance of masculinity and whiteness.

As expected, Harris was subject to racist and sexist attacks. Even before she was selected as the Democratic vice-presidential nominee, attention to her past relationship with former San Francisco mayor Willie Brown led to characterizations – so common to women – that her political advancement was due to a sexual relationship. Crude hashtags like #HeelsUpHarris circulated online, and President Trump played into this trope when he told a New Hampshire audience, "I don't want to see a woman president get into that position the way she'd do it."[81] Upon Harris' selection, Sarah Palin told Fox News' Tucker Carlson that she would not have "prostituted" herself and her positions to get better coverage, as she implied Harris had.[82] Whether intentional or not, these characterizations and this language play into tropes that Black women use sexual power to manipulate and deceive. Finally, Harris was subject to another form of objectification during the vice-presidential debate, when Google trends showed a spike in people searching for "Senator Kamala Harris" alongside "nude," "bathing suit," and "bikini."[83]

Harris' gender and race were also leveraged by opponents to position her as radical, dangerous, and threatening, characterizations made simpler because of her direct challenge to the white, male status quo. Immediately, Republican National Committee (RNC) chair Ronna McDaniel said, "Kamala Harris' extreme positions … show that the left-wing mob is controlling Biden's candidacy, just like they would control

[80] Open letter, August 6, 2020, Time's Up, https://timesupnow.org/work/we-have-her-back/we-have-her-back-letter/

[81] Libby Cathey, Trump Mocks Harris' Name, Says Having Her as President Would be an "Insult" to Country, *ABC News*, September 9, 2020, https://abcnews.go.com/Politics/trump-mocks-harris-president-insult-country/story?id=72901540

[82] Kathleen Gray and Andy Newman, On Fox News, Palin Used a Sexist Smear to Suggest Harris Betrayed Her Convictions, *New York Times*, August 20, 2020, https://nyti.ms/3rNlin4

[83] Kashmira Gander, Kamala Harris "Nude" Google Searches after Debate Speak Volumes about Women in Politics, *Newsweek*, October 8, 2020, www.newsweek.com/kamala-harris-nude-google-searches-debate-women-politics-1537461

him as president."[84] RNC emails called her a "radical leftist" who will "destroy America" and Trump campaign advertisements argued she wanted to confiscate citizens' guns by force and "give cop killers a pass." Conservative news outlets latched on to claims that Harris was really in charge, further evidence that they believed her to be a more mobilizing opponent than Biden. Trump called Harris a "monster" and latched onto the idea that electing Biden would lead to a Harris presidency. At a late October 2020 rally, he told a crowd of supporters, "We're not going to have a socialist president, especially a female socialist president," adding, "We're not going to put up with it."[85]

Trump also fueled racist and unfounded rumors that Harris was ineligible to be vice president, telling reporters after her selection, "I heard it today she doesn't even meet the requirements."[86] These doubts – echoing Trump's "birther" claims against Obama – dominated online misinformation campaigns through Election Day.[87] Another strategy for "othering" Harris was to mispronounce her name. Republican leaders and Trump surrogates employed this tactic, with Senator David Perdue referring to her as "Kamala-mala-mala."

Attempts to highlight Harris' racial identities as distinct from the white norm stood in contrast to the scrutiny over the authenticity of her Black and South Asian identities. Both as a presidential and vice-presidential candidate, Harris' multiracial roots, upbringing, and ties to the Black and South Asian community were interrogated in ways that candidates' whiteness is not. Candidate Harris neither ignored nor emphasized her identities. She grounded her candidacy in her familial roots, acknowledged that she would – as a "first" – face doubt about her electability, and drew upon her personal experience with racial discrimination and segregation in one of the most notable moments of her primary campaign. At times, she leaned into cultural reference points as evidence and reminders of her connection to Black and South Asian communities – speaking at Howard University (her alma mater) immediately after announcing her candidacy, dancing with Black drumlines at a historically Black college,

[84] RNC Statement on Biden's Radical VP Pick, press release, Republican National Committee, August 11, 2020, https://gop.com/rnc-statement-on-bidens-radical-vp-pickoh-ne

[85] Lydia O'Connor, Trump Balks at Idea of a "Female Socialist President," *Huffington Post*, October 23, 2020, https://bit.ly/3yjAXwU

[86] Mara Liasson, Trump Questions Harris' Eligibility to be the Vice Presidential Candidate, *NPR*, August 13, 2020, https://bit.ly/3yjAXwU

[87] Amanda Seitz, Harris Target of More Misinformation than Pence, Data Shows, *Associated Press*, October 29, 2020, https://bit.ly/3j6uE9w

touting membership in the Black sorority Alpha Kappa Alpha, and cooking masala dosa with Indian American actress Mindy Kaling. At the same time, however, she told the *Washington Post* she felt no need to explain her identity, especially her multiracial identities. "I am who I am. I'm good with it," she said, adding, "You might need to figure it out, but I'm fine with it."[88]

Upon her selection as Biden's running mate, Harris' intersectional identity became more central, reflecting the Biden campaign's hope to show their embrace of diversity, as well as Harris' likely expanded opportunity to talk about identity as the vice-presidential – instead of presidential – contender. From her first speeches, where she celebrated the Black women trailblazers, to her targeted outreach to women, Black, and South Asian communities, Harris' vice-presidential candidacy departed from Obama's "race transcendent" politics. Harris led the campaign's "Sister to Sister" voter engagement program to target Black women and sought to reassure the Black community that a Biden–Harris administration would not take their votes for granted. On the eve of Election Day, Harris penned an open letter in *Essence* magazine, telling Black women, "We need you," and noting, "Joe and I can't do this alone – and we're grateful that Black women across the country have had our backs."[89] The campaign portrayed Harris' history-making candidacy as a sign of their commitment to institutional change. While symbolic appeals are sometimes met with skepticism and mixed effects, previous scholarship demonstrates the positive effects of descriptive representation on Black women's political efficacy.[90] Similarly, a survey of Indian Americans revealed Harris' candidacy increased their enthusiasm for the Democratic presidential ticket and close to 50 percent of respondents said her selection increased their likelihood of voting on Election Day.[91]

Voters and advocates raised valid concerns that Harris' selection would be a proxy for commitment to gender and racial equity *without* substantive

[88] Kevin Sullivan, "I Am Who I Am": Kamala Harris, Daughter of Indian and Jamaican Immigrants, Defines Herself Simply as "American," *Washington Post*, February 2, 2019, https://wapo.st/3zYKZ6V

[89] Kamala Harris, "I'm Grateful That Black Women Have Had My Back," Essence, November 2, 2020, www.essence.com/feature/kamala-harris-election-2020-black-women/

[90] Christopher Stout and Katherine Tate, The 2008 Presidential Election, Political Efficacy, and Group Empowerment, *Politics, Groups, and Identities* 1(2) (2013): 143–63.

[91] Sumitra Badrinathan, Devesh Kapur, and Milan Vaishnav, How Will Indian Americans Vote? Results from the 2020 Indian American Attitudes Survey, Carnegie Endowment for International Peace, October 14, 2020, https://bit.ly/2Vdb2Zh

policy outcomes once in office. These concerns were amplified by some of the campaigns' outreach efforts to Black communities that relied on stereotypical imagery.[92] Substantive messaging from both Biden and Harris that utilized language of racial and gender justice activism to reflect both awareness of and commitment to shifting the power dynamics were likely more effective. Harris made this shift toward visibility and recognition explicit in her first post-election address, saying, "I want to speak directly to the Black women in our country. Thank you. You are too often overlooked and yet are asked time and again to step up and be the backbone of our democracy. We could not have done this without you."[93]

Holding the Biden–Harris administration accountable to these statements and commitments continues to be the work of many communities working to advance racial and gender equity.

CONCLUSION

In his 2016 book, Jackson Katz concludes by noting the "ultimate irony" of presidential politics: "It will be necessary for a woman to win the election and go to work in the Oval Office for us to see just how crucial the presidency has always been in the symbolic architecture of men's cultural dominance."[94] That full realization of masculine dominance may very well require the election of a woman president, but recent elections have made significant progress to this end without a woman winner. Hillary Clinton's ability to situate herself as a viable candidate in 2008 and her near victory in 2016 unsettled the gendered foundations of the presidency, calling into question expectations about a woman's capacity to win and the path she would need to take to be successful. Likewise, Barack Obama's 2008 victory revealed and disrupted the raced foundations of presidential politics, but certainly did not fully upend them. Election 2020 built on this progress to further transform the raced, gendered, and race-gendered foundations of presidential politics. In both the election of a Black and South Asian woman vice president and the navigation of gender, race, and intersectional dynamics by the most diverse field of presidential contenders ever, the 2020 election went a long way toward

92 Camille D. Burge, Julian J. Wamble, and Chryl N. Laird, Missing the Mark? An Exploration of Targeted Campaign Advertising's Effect on Black Political Engagement, *Politics, Groups, and Identities* 8(2) (2020): 423–37.
93 Transcript of Kamala Harris' victory speech, November 7, 2020, *Washington Post*, www .washingtonpost.com/politics/2020/11/07/kamala-harris-victory-speech-transcript/
94 Katz, *Man Enough?*, p. 273.

exposing and disrupting institutional norms and practices that have upheld inequities in privilege along gender and racial lines. This has left open opportunities for further change in not only who has power but also how that power is distributed and won. But as this chapter also reveals, the dominance of whiteness and masculinity has not been fully upended, and partisan differences reveal disparities in investment or divestment in these forces as a strategy for winning or holding presidential power. Making these forces – both historically and at present – visible is key to considering the paths forward to institutional disruption that will create more equitable conditions for all candidates who seek presidential office, as well as hold presidential candidates and officeholders accountable in understanding and addressing the inequities experienced by voters upon whom they rely to win.

2 Women as Presidential and Vice-Presidential Contenders: History Made and History Deferred

On March 5, 2020, US Senator Elizabeth Warren dropped out of the Democratic presidential primary contest, marking the departure of the last viable woman in the race. That evening, she spoke to MSNBC host Rachel Maddow, who prompted Warren by noting that her loss "feels a little bit like a death knell in terms of the prospects of having a woman for president in our lifetimes." Warren quickly rebuked that conclusion, arguing, "This cannot be the right answer. … It doesn't mean it's not going to happen." She elaborated: "Look, here's how I see this. You get in this fight, you know when you go into it there were multiple people who just said, this will be part of the problem. But you get in the fight because you just got to keep beating at it until you finally break the thing."[1] The "thing" to which Warren refers here is the highest, hardest glass ceiling in American politics: the United States presidency. For 233 years, that glass ceiling has remained unshattered, despite the many cracks that have come from women who waged presidential campaigns. But women have, in Warren's words, stayed in the fight. In 2016, that led to the first-ever woman major-party nominee for president who went on to win the national popular vote. In 2020, a record six women ran for the Democratic presidential nomination and, while none won the nomination, one – US Senator Kamala Harris – became just the third woman, and first woman of color, vice-presidential nominee. She was sworn in as the first woman, the first Black person, and the first South Asian person to ever be vice president of the United States on January 20, 2021.

Women's resilience in presidential politics is mirrored by the persistence of stereotypes of gender and candidacy that have acted as hurdles to

---

[1] Elizabeth Warren interview transcript, *The Rachel Maddow Show*, March 5, 2020, www.msnbc.com/transcripts/rachel-maddow-show/2020-03-05-msna1338256

electing the first woman president. For decades, research in political science and psychology has revealed an incongruity between stereotypes of gender and the presidency for women; the traits and expertise valued most in our political candidates and leaders, especially executives, are those most often associated with masculinity and men.[2] As noted by Melanye Price and Kelly Dittmar in Chapter 1, the dominance of masculinity in the US presidency is not just upheld in images or occupants of the office, but is maintained by voters and media who associate political power with meeting masculine credentials, and by candidates who adhere to these standards by which presidential timber is measured. But women are not only held to masculinized standards of presidential leadership; they are also held to higher standards than their male counterparts when it comes to proving they are qualified, likable, and electable.

This chapter begins with a history of women as presidential and vice-presidential candidates. I then turn to the 2020 presidential election, analyzing the ways that gender stereotypes influenced the strategies employed by major-party candidates, the media's coverage of their campaigns, and public reactions to their candidacies. Candidate strategy, media coverage, voter evaluations, and electoral outcomes in the most recent presidential election reveal evidence of both maintenance and disruption of gender stereotypes and gendered standards in presidential politics. Together, they provide insights into why a woman president remains an aspiration instead of a reality in twenty-first-century America.

HISTORY OF WOMEN CANDIDATES FOR PRESIDENT AND VICE PRESIDENT

While the nation's topmost executive posts – the presidency and the vice presidency – remain male preserves, a handful of women dared to put themselves forward as candidates for these offices prior to 2020. These women trailblazers slowly chipped away at the gender role expectations that have traditionally relegated women to the East Wing instead of the West Wing of the White House.

---

[2] Alice H. Eagly and Steven J. Karau, Role Congruity Theory of Prejudice Toward Female Leaders, *Psychological Review* 109(3) (2002): 573–98; Leonie Huddy and Nayda Terkildsen, The Consequences of Gender Stereotypes for Women Candidates at Different Levels and Types of Offices, *Political Research Quarterly* 46(3) (1993): 503–25; Shirley M. Rosenwasser and Norma Dean, Gender Role and Political Office: Effects of Perceived Masculinity/ Femininity of Candidate and Political Office, *Psychology of Women Quarterly* 13(1) (1989): 77–85.

Two women became candidates for the presidency in the nineteenth century, even before they could cast ballots themselves. Both Victoria Woodhull in 1872 and Belva Lockwood in 1884 were nominated as presidential candidates by a group of reformers identifying themselves as the Equal Rights Party. Woodhull, a newspaper publisher and the first woman stockbroker, was only 33 years old when she was nominated, too young to meet the constitutionally mandated age requirement of 35 for the presidency, and as an advocate of free love, Woodhull spent Election Day in jail on charges that she had sent obscene materials through the mail.[3] Unlike Woodhull, who made no real effort to convince voters to support her, Lockwood actively campaigned for the presidency, despite public mockery and even criticism from her fellow suffragists. As the first woman to practice law in front of the US Supreme Court, Lockwood knew what it felt like to stand alone and did so again in a second presidential bid in 1888.

Before the next female candidate claimed a space on the presidential ballot, three women had been considered for vice-presidential slots. Nellie Tayloe Ross of Wyoming, a true pioneer as the nation's first female governor, won thirty-one votes for the vice-presidential nomination on the first ballot at the Democratic convention in 1928. Twenty-four years later, in 1952, two Democratic women – India Edwards and Sarah B. Hughes – were considered for the vice-presidential nomination, but both withdrew their names before convention balloting began.

In 1964, Republican Senator Margaret Chase Smith of Maine became the first female candidate to have her name placed in nomination for president at a major-party convention, winning twenty-seven delegate votes from three states. Eight years later, in 1972, Congresswoman Shirley Chisholm of New York, the first Black woman elected to Congress, became the first woman and the first Black person to have her name placed in nomination for the presidency at a Democratic National Convention, winning 151.95 delegate votes. At the same convention, Frances (Sissy) Farenthold, a former Texas state legislator, won more than 400 votes for the vice-presidential slot, finishing second.[4]

Smith and Chisholm, like their predecessors Woodhull and Lockwood a century earlier, recognized the improbability of their nominations, measuring success in other terms. Smith prioritized normalizing the image

---

[3] Jo Freeman, *We Will Be Heard: Women's Struggles for Political Power in the United States* (Lanham, MD: Rowman & Littlefield, 2008).

[4] Women Presidential and Vice Presidential Candidates, Center for American Women and Politics (hereafter CAWP), n.d., https://cawp.rutgers.edu/levels_of_office/women-presidential-and-vice-presidential-candidates-selected-list

of a woman running for executive office, and Chisholm sought to pave the way for women after her, proving that "it can be done."[5]

Despite the presence of women on some minor party ballots, no woman was nominated to a major party's presidential ticket until 1984, when New York Congresswoman Geraldine Ferraro was chosen as presidential nominee Walter Mondale's Democratic running mate. Her candidacy was shaded by questions surrounding her gender, from whether she was schooled enough in military and foreign policy to how she should dress and interact with presidential nominee Mondale. Much attention, too, was paid to her husband, a trend that continued with female candidates who came after her.

While the defeat of the Mondale–Ferraro ticket in 1984 disappointed voters looking to make history, many supporters of women in politics had their hopes renewed in 1987 as they watched Congresswoman Patricia Schroeder of Colorado prepare to make a presidential bid. Despite the fact that Schroeder raised more money than any woman candidate in US history, she was not able to raise enough. Her decision, long before the first primary, not to become an official candidate resulted in tears from her supporters and Schroeder herself. Those tears, considered unacceptable for a woman candidate, made national news and provoked public debate about gender traits and presidential politics.

In 1999, two-time presidential cabinet member Elizabeth Dole established an exploratory committee and mounted a six-month campaign for the Republican nomination for president, taking the next step toward putting a woman in the White House. Although Dole consistently came in second in public opinion polls, behind only George W. Bush, and benefited from name recognition, popularity, and political connections, many people doubted that she could win. Even her husband, Senator Bob Dole, who had been the Republican nominee for president in the previous election, expressed reservations about her campaign, telling a *New York Times* reporter that "he wanted to give money to a rival candidate [McCain] who was fighting for much of her support. He conceded that Mrs. Dole's operation had had growing pains, was slow to raise money early and was only beginning to hit its stride. And while Mr. Dole was hopeful, he allowed that he was by no means certain she would even stay in the race."[6] In mid-October, five months after Bob Dole's comments and a few

---

[5] Shirley Chisholm, *The Good Fight* (New York: HarperCollins, 1973).

[6] Richard L. Berke, As Political Spouse, Bob Dole Strays from Campaign Script, *New York Times*, May 17, 1999, www.nytimes.com/1999/05/17/us/as-political-spouse-bob-dole-strays-from-campaign-script.html?pagewanted=all&src=pm

months before the first primary, Elizabeth Dole withdrew from the race for the Republican nomination.

In 2003, Carol Moseley Braun, the first Black woman to serve in the US Senate and a former ambassador to New Zealand, was the only woman among ten candidates who competed for the Democratic presidential nomination. Her appearance in six televised debates among the Democratic hopefuls helped to disrupt the white, masculine image of presidential contenders so strongly embedded in the American psyche. Although major women's groups endorsed her, Moseley Braun dropped out of the race in January 2004, shortly before the first primaries and caucuses.

Standing on the shoulders of the pioneering women who came before her, former US Senator and First Lady Hillary Clinton launched a campaign in 2008 that moved women presidential candidates from novelty to viability. Holding the front-runner position throughout her first year of campaigning for the Democratic nomination, Clinton blazed a new trail, crossing the country with a motto of "making history" and exciting voters – especially women of all ages, for whom the prospect of a woman president became real. Many observers thought her background, political clout, and wide coalition of supporters made her nomination inevitable. Historians and analysts will, for decades, look back at her campaign to see what shifted the narrative from almost certain winner to underdog. Poor campaign management and strategy, perceptions of her status as a Washington insider, her vote in favor of the Iraq War, the role of her husband Bill Clinton, the altered primary season calendar, and the phenomenon of her major opponent, Senator Barack Obama, were among the many possible reasons for Clinton's downslide in polls and, later, in the Democratic primaries. Despite winning nine of the last sixteen primaries and caucuses and nearly 18 million votes nationwide, Hillary Clinton conceded the Democratic nomination on June 7, 2008.

Nearly three months later, John McCain announced his choice of Alaska Governor Sarah Palin as the Republican candidate for vice president. Motivated by hopes of curbing Obama's momentum, McCain's strategy proved successful, as Palin quickly became the focus of news media and water-cooler conversation. Palin was an unexpected candidate, novel for her outsider identity, her colloquial candor, and – for many – her gender. However, much of that attention turned negative as Palin's personal life and questions of preparedness plagued the Republican ticket, made worse by her stumbles with major media interviews. By the end of the 2008 presidential campaign, few voters seemed indifferent toward Palin; her supporters were as passionate in their enthusiasm for her as her detractors were in their criticism. Sarah Palin emerged from the 2008 election as one of the most fascinating women on the political scene, making history as only the second woman (after Ferraro) on a major-party presidential ticket and stirring speculation that she might compete for the top spot on the ballot in upcoming elections.

Palin did not translate her vice-presidential candidacy into a presidential run. Instead, another favorite of strong conservatives – Minnesota Congresswoman Michele Bachmann – officially announced her candidacy for the Republican nomination for president on June 27, 2011. However, as the field of candidates narrowed by half by January 2012, Bachmann was among the candidates edged out due to waning popularity, campaign missteps and disorganization, and insufficient resources.

Four years later, Hillary Clinton and Carly Fiorina competed for major-party nominations, marking the 2016 election as the first presidential election with women running in Democratic and Republican party primaries. Republican candidate Carly Fiorina, a former CEO of Hewlett-Packard (HP) and well known for being the first woman to head up a Fortune 20 company, entered the 2016 presidential race on May 4, 2015. After finishing seventh in the second primary contest in New Hampshire in February 2016, she ended her presidential bid.

Hillary Clinton announced her second presidential candidacy on April 12, 2015. She entered the race, as in 2008, as the strong front-runner, successfully clearing most of the field before even confirming her bid. While five other candidates entered the Democratic primary race, it was only Vermont Senator Bernie Sanders who challenged Clinton beyond the first caucus votes cast in Iowa. Sanders proved to be a formidable opponent, capturing the support of young people and progressives who sought the antiestablishment "revolution" he promised. Despite significant wins in populous states like Colorado, Michigan, Minnesota, and Washington, Sanders failed to best Clinton in either the popular vote or delegate count. By June 2016, Clinton had a 389-vote lead in pledged delegates and a twelve-point lead in the popular vote in primary states. Sanders did not concede the nomination until the Democratic National Convention vote in July 2016, where Clinton's delegate lead grew to just under 1,000.

On July 28, 2016 Hillary Clinton became the first woman to ever be nominated as a major-party candidate for US president. In accepting the nomination, she noted the importance of this milestone: "Standing here as my mother's daughter, and my daughter's mother, I'm so happy this day has come. Happy for grandmothers and little girls and everyone in between. Happy for boys and men, too – because when any barrier falls in America, for anyone, it clears the way for everyone. When there are no ceilings, the sky's the limit." Clinton's emphasis on inclusivity over individual achievement was reflected in her campaign's theme: "Stronger Together." In embracing that theme, she created a stark contrast with the campaign of her Republican opponent, Donald Trump, who had emerged victorious from a field of seventeen contenders by capitalizing on race, class, and ideological divides.

From July through November, Clinton and Trump engaged in a general election campaign notable for its negativity, unpredictability, and peculiarity. While Clinton maintained a fairly steady lead in national polls and electoral vote predictions, she was dogged by a persistent focus on her use of a personal email server while she was secretary of state. Investigation and public releases of her emails, in addition to the leak of emails of her top advisor John Podesta – later found to be part of a Russian hacking operation – dominated news coverage and created continued problems for her campaign. Clinton's opponent was tied to even more scandal, from questions about his financial dealings and business ethics to myriad accusations and examples of his misogynistic rhetoric and treatment of women. In October, when the 2005 "Access Hollywood" tape of Donald Trump was released, in which he bragged about his ability to "grab women by the pussy" without penalty, even some of Trump's prominent supporters wavered in their willingness to back his candidacy. However, even after more than ten women made public their experiences of sexual harassment or assault by Trump in the days after the video release, it was a renewed focus on Clinton's emails – thanks to a letter by FBI director James Comey – that shifted attention away from Trump's criminal behavior. With one week remaining in the campaign, Trump had restored much of the support he had lost immediately after the video release, while Clinton's support appeared to wane. These trends turned out to be stronger than nearly anyone – including the Trump campaign – anticipated on Election Day, when Donald Trump beat Hillary Clinton in multiple key swing states that she had been expected to win. In an unexpected result of an extraordinary campaign, Donald Trump won the Electoral College vote by seventy-seven votes to become the forty-fifth president of the United States. Importantly, however, Hillary Clinton won the popular vote by nearly 3 million votes, besting every white male presidential candidate in US history to that date, including Trump.

In her concession speech on the morning of November 9, 2016, Clinton recognized the disappointment that many of her supporters, especially women, felt. She said, "I know we have still not shattered that highest and hardest glass ceiling, but some day someone will and hopefully sooner than we might think right now." Clinton is one among the class of women who have run for president that have blazed paths, opened doors, and challenged established gender stereotypes and gender role expectations. They set the stage for the women presidential and vice-presidential contenders in 2020 to turn Clinton's concession hope into reality.

2020 ELECTION

Clinton's 2016 defeat – and Trump's success – did not yield a drop in women's political engagement, candidacies, or success. In fact, the 2018 midterm elections set records for women's candidacies, nominations, and wins across levels of office. While these successes were concentrated among Democratic women, they led to record levels of women's political representation in Congress and state legislatures nationwide.[7] It was in this context that six women launched their candidacies for the 2020 Democratic presidential nomination. They joined a field of twenty-eight Democrats who launched campaigns eager to run against Donald Trump, an incumbent with low approval ratings and already mobilized opposition in the electorate. The presence of multiple women candidates made clear the diversity among women – in paths to office, lived experiences and perspectives, ideology, policy agendas and priorities, and political strategy. That clarity contributed to the disruption of monolithic conceptions of what it means to be a woman presidential candidate, forcing voters and media to accept the same diversity among women that they had long allowed – and even expected – from men.

Massachusetts Senator Elizabeth Warren became the first woman to enter the Democratic primary contest for president when she launched an exploratory committee on December 31, 2018. She sought a lane to the nomination between the most progressive candidate – Senator Bernie Sanders – and the more centrist Democrats, including former Vice President Joe Biden. Warren drew upon her own upbringing and decades of work fighting corruption and inequity in America's economic systems to lay out her plan to "rebuild America's middle class." Before being elected to the US Senate for the first time in 2012, Warren served as chair

---

[7] Kelly Dittmar, Unfinished Business: Women Running in 2018 and Beyond, CAWP, 2019, https://womenrun.rutgers.edu/

of the Congressional Oversight Panel for the Troubled Asset Relief Program – the government's response to the 2008 economic recession. She was instrumental in the creation of the Consumer Financial Protection Bureau, an agency that was meant to promote the same corporate accountability that Warren had lobbied for as a bankruptcy law expert, author, and consumer advocate. Most of Warren's advocacy came during her more than thirty years as a law professor, a career she pursued after first spending some time as an elementary school teacher.

Warren's presidential campaign had early challenges, including missteps and criticism surrounding her past claims of Native American ancestry. But by early summer 2019, the media and insider narratives were that she was a serious contender and a particular threat to Bernie Sanders due to their overlapping appeal to progressive voters. She waged a policy-heavy campaign, embraced a grassroots fundraising strategy, and touted direct contact with voters – including taking over 100,000 selfies with supporters – as key to her campaign. Her campaign theme "Dream Big. Fight Hard" was paired with "Persist," a slogan capitalizing on the support she received – especially from women – after being silenced and scolded on the Senate floor by Republican majority leader Mitch McConnell in 2017. Apart from the "Persist" theme, Warren was less overt than some other women candidates in gender-based messaging until later in her campaign. However, one of the most circulated set of images of candidate Warren were those where she made "pinkie swears" with young girls, urging them to remember that she was running for president "because that's what girls do."

Warren fared well in Democratic primary debates and had few notable blunders leading into the first-in-the nation caucuses in Iowa. Still, while Warren's poll numbers increased through the fall of 2019, she continued to fare better as voters' *second* – instead of first – choice for Democratic nominee. She was reluctant to go negative against her opponents – including Sanders – but shifted messaging in the final weeks before the Iowa caucuses to focus more explicitly on her electability and her ability to unite Democratic voters against Donald Trump. Warren came in third place in the Iowa caucuses, falling behind Sanders and South Bend, Indiana mayor Pete Buttigieg. She did not meet the threshold for earning primary delegate votes again until Super Tuesday – March 3, 2020. But that day also marked her third-place finish in her home state of Massachusetts, behind Sanders and Biden. While she outlasted most of the other women in the race, Warren dropped out of the Democratic primary contest on March 5, 2020. By the end of her campaign, she had won sixty-three primary delegates and about 7.7 percent of the Democratic primary vote nationwide.

New York Senator Kirsten Gillibrand became the second woman to enter the Democratic presidential primary election on January 15, 2019. Gillibrand centered gender in her campaign from its first days, listing her role as "mom" as primary in her announcement video, touting her record of advocacy on women's rights, and describing her campaign as embracing a "women plus" platform.[8] Gillibrand, who was appointed to the US Senate in January 2009, began her career in elected office as representative from New York's 20th congressional district to the US House from 2007 to 2009. Prior to that, she was a private and public sector attorney with experience at the Department of Housing and Urban Development and the US Court of Appeals' Second Circuit.

While Gillibrand touted her success in promoting governmental transparency and accountability and standing up for 9/11 first responders, among other things, her message was especially focused on her commitment to gender equity and her record of taking on Donald Trump. In a June 2019 speech to Iowa voters, Gillibrand – the only woman candidate with school-aged children – said, "Imagine what we could achieve with a working mother in the White House instead of a misogynist."[9] Despite efforts to capitalize on the energy and activism of women in the #MeToo era, Gillibrand's campaign struggled to catch fire. She suffered from weak fundraising, which some attributed to fallout from her public call for Senator Al Franken to resign due to allegations of sexual harassment in 2017. Gillibrand's poll numbers were consistently low, making it difficult for her to earn significant media attention, and a dearth of home-state endorsements further added to a narrative that her campaign was unlikely to succeed.

After learning that she did not qualify for the third Democratic presidential primary debate scheduled for September 2019, Gillibrand ended her bid for the nomination. In her departure video, she sought to define the legacy of her campaign, asserting, "We have taken on the fights others wouldn't. We've led the fights that we can't afford to lose for women and families – and moved the entire field along with us." Gillibrand was unapologetic in her approach, concluding, "We have put the civil rights of

---

[8] Lisa Lerer and Shane Goldmacher, Kirsten Gillibrand's Unabashedly Feminist Campaign, *New York Times*, February 12, 2019, www.nytimes.com/2019/02/12/us/politics/kirsten-gillibrand-president-feminist.html

[9] Kirsten Gillibrand, speech at Iowa Democrats Hall of Fame celebration, Cedar Rapids, Iowa, June 9, 2019.

women front and center, and never backed down when it comes to valuing them."[10]

California Senator Kamala Harris became the third woman to announce her bid for the Democratic presidential nomination on January 21, 2019. Her announcement video emphasized the urgency of the moment, arguing that the country's key values – truth, justice, decency, equality, freedom, and democracy – were all on the line in the 2020 election. At her first rally in her hometown of Oakland, California, she introduced herself as the best candidate to prosecute the case against Donald Trump. Tying her roles as an elected prosecutor to her commitment as a presidential candidate, Harris explained, "I'm running to be president, of the people, by the people, and for all people." In that first speech and throughout her presidential campaign, Harris shared her family's story – noting she was the child of a South Asian mother and Jamaican father who were active in the fight for civil rights. She also acknowledged the doubts that would inevitably be raised about her capacity to win. In Oakland, she said, "We know what the doubters will say. It's the same thing they've always said. They'll say it's not your time. They'll say wait your turn. They'll say the odds are long. They'll say it can't be done. But America's story has always been written by people who can see what can be unburdened by what has been."[11] Harris was accustomed to proving the doubters wrong. She had become the first woman and the first Black person elected as district attorney of San Francisco in 2003. In 2010, she became the first woman elected as California's attorney general. And in 2016, Harris was elected to the US Senate as just the second Black woman to ever serve in that body.

These doubts, despite Harris' optimism, did prove to burden her campaign. But her campaign's struggles were not only tied to skepticism that she – as a Black and South Asian woman – could win the presidency. Harris also struggled to put forth a clear and consistent message and policy agenda to voters. She was cautious in taking positions on issues without conducting further research – touting this as evidence of a good executive – and was not easily categorized in any one ideological lane. Another common critique of Harris was that her prosecutorial past was inconsistent with progressive calls for criminal justice reform. In contrast, one of

---

[10] Kirsten Gillibrand, Twitter post, August 28, 2019, 5:35 p.m., https://twitter.com/SenGillibrand

[11] Kamala Harris, campaign speech, Oakland, California, January 27, 2019, www.c-span.org/video/?457212-1/california-senator-kamala-harris-launches-presidential-campaign-oakland

Harris' most successful moments in the campaign was when she challenged Biden on his race record in the first Democratic presidential primary debate on June 27, 2019. Harris shared her own experience as a child who had been bused in efforts to desegregate California schools, calling out Biden's history of opposing busing. Her campaign leveraged the moment in messaging and outreach and saw a significant, but short-lived bump in poll numbers. While Harris' direct nod to her own racial identity and experience in that debate seemed to resonate with primary voters, it was not central to her messaging throughout the campaign. Asked in a May 2019 interview with *The Atlantic* why she was not more explicit about the historic nature of her candidacy, she replied, "There are certain self-evident truths."[12]

By August, as she struggled to advance in the polls, Harris shifted time and money to Iowa, and offered a closing message that more directly targeted Donald Trump. Her final ad, "The Antidote to Trump," describes her as, "in every possible way, … the anti-Trump." But Harris did not stay in the race to see if that message was effective enough to win over Iowa voters. She dropped out of the Democratic primary race on December 3, 2019, citing her struggle to raise the money she needed to compete.

On December 4, 2019, the day after Harris suspended her campaign, *Rolling Stone*'s Jamil Smith wrote, "I would wager that the image of [Harris], the third black woman to run for president as a member of a major party, will not be forgotten anytime soon," adding "She didn't shatter that proverbial ceiling, but it is more fragile today."[13] Smith was right. Just nine months later, Harris was tapped by Democratic nominee Joe Biden as his running mate. She was elected vice president three months later, shattering another ceiling in presidential politics and making the highest, hardest glass ceiling even *more* fragile than Smith had characterized less than a year before. As Biden's running mate, Harris brought energy and enthusiasm to a challenging campaign for Biden amidst a pandemic and among those disappointed that the Democratic nominee was a septuagenarian white man. She also centered her own story, highlighted her history-making past and potential, and leveraged her identities more clearly than in the primary election as a value-added to her public service

---

[12] Edward-Isaac Dovere, Kamala Harris Is the Jan Brady of the 2020 Race, *The Atlantic*, May 16, 2019, www.theatlantic.com/politics/archive/2019/05/kamala-harris-tries-breakthrough-2020-race/589546/

[13] Jamil Smith, Kamala Harris Mattered, and Still Does, *Rolling Stone*, December 4, 2019, www.rollingstone.com/politics/political-commentary/kamala-harris-race-gender-2020-democratic-primary-922279/

and the Biden–Harris administration. Upon accepting the nomination as vice president on August 20, 2020, Harris acknowledged, "That I am here tonight is a testament to the dedication of generations before me. Women and men who believed so fiercely in the promise of equality, liberty, and justice for all."[14]

Minnesota Senator Amy Klobuchar memorably launched her presidential campaign on February 20, 2019. Standing outside during a snowstorm in Minneapolis, Minnesota, Klobuchar positioned herself as a Midwesterner with working-class roots and the "grit" necessary to take on Donald Trump. She described her campaign as "home-grown" and promised to "lead from the heart," emphasizing her capacity for bipartisanship, pragmatism, and getting things done. Klobuchar often pointed to her record in the US Senate, where she had served since 2007, as evidence that she would make good on these promises as president.

Before becoming a US Senator, Klobuchar had served as Hennepin County attorney for close to a decade, leaving her with a prosecutorial record that likely served as more of a hindrance than a help in the 2020 Democratic primary. This was most evident in the final month of her presidential campaign, when newly revealed information about a case she prosecuted raised questions about the murder conviction of a 16-year-old Black boy. Klobuchar's campaign challenges began much earlier, though. In the weeks leading up to her announcement, she was dogged with news reports that she was abusive of her congressional staff. The coverage of that story continued for weeks beyond her snow-filled launch. As the campaign gained better footing, Klobuchar led with her qualifications and record of both legislative and electoral success. She touted her role as a mother as motivating her public service, and frequently celebrated the potential election of a woman president, but was careful to return to qualifications apart from her gender. In a February 2020 CNN town hall, for example, she said, "I know it would be cool to be the first woman president, … but I think that the story that we tell and the campaign that we run has to be more than about that."[15]

Klobuchar never reached the top tier of Democratic primary candidates in fundraising or poll numbers, but she was able to stay in the race due to solid debate performances, a clear and consistent message, and

[14] Kamala Harris, acceptance speech at the Democratic National Convention, Wilmington, Delaware, August 20, 2020, www.cnn.com/2020/08/19/politics/kamala-harris-speech-transcript/index.html

[15] CNN Town Hall with Senator Amy Klobuchar, February 18, 2020, http://transcripts.cnn.com/TRANSCRIPTS/2002/18/se.03.html

forging a more centrist – and in her characterization, pragmatic – lane than her more progressive colleagues. She, with Warren, earned the endorsement of the *New York Times* editorial board in January 2020, ahead of the first primary caucuses. While she had hoped that her Midwest roots would yield success in Iowa, she earned just one pledged delegate in the Iowa caucuses, coming in fifth place. Her rebound to a third-place finish in the next primary in New Hampshire provided a surge of much-needed campaign funds, but also proved to be the campaign's last gasp. Klobuchar failed to meet the threshold for delegates in South Carolina and Nevada primaries, evidence of her continued struggle to attract voters of color, and dropped out of the race on the eve of Super Tuesday to endorse Joe Biden. She ended her bid after winning a total of seven primary delegates and 1.4 percent of the Democratic primary vote. Klobuchar's decision to endorse Biden led to much speculation that she sought to be his running mate, but by June 2020 she publicly withdrew from consideration for the role, stating, "I think the right thing to do right now, and I told this to Vice President Biden, is to put a woman of color on the ticket as the next vice president of our country."[16]

Hawaii Congresswoman Tulsi Gabbard made her presidential candidacy public during a January 11, 2019 interview with CNN's Van Jones, but did not formally launch her campaign until February 2, 2019. Gabbard – who served in the US House from Hawaii's 2nd congressional district from 2013 to 2021 – focused her campaign on promoting peace by opposing what she described as "regime change wars." Gabbard leveraged her own experience as an combat veteran, including service in the Iraq War and membership of the Hawaii National Guard, to make the case for nomination. At her launch rally, she said, "I will bring this soldier's principles to the White House, restoring the values of dignity, honor and respect to the presidency and above all else, love for our people and love for our country."[17]

Gabbard had political success at a young age and was the youngest of all of the women running for president in 2020. She was elected to the Hawaii House of Representatives at age 21, and served on the Honolulu

[16] Ed O'Keefe and Bo Erickson, Amy Klobuchar Withdraws from Vice Presidential Consideration, Says Joe Biden Should Pick a Woman of Color, *CBS News*, June 19, 2020, www.cbsnews.com/news/amy-klobuchar-withdraws-joe-biden-vice-president-consideration/

[17] Tulsi Gabbard, campaign launch speech, Honolulu, Hawaii, February 2, 2020, https://medium.com/@TulsiGabbard/i-will-bring-a-soldiers-heart-to-the-white-house-restoring-integrity-honor-and-respect-fc8b21e21574

City Council before becoming the first Hindu person to serve in Congress in 2013. Between January and February 2019, news outlets reported on Gabbard's ties to Hindu nationalists, her previous work for an anti-gay group, and her refusal to denounce Syria's President Bashar Assad – who she had controversially met with in 2017 – as a US adversary or war criminal. As the primary season continued, the little coverage Gabbard received came from these stories as well as questions about her ties to a religious group called Science of Identity and her support among right-wing extremists. In the July 2019 Democratic presidential primary debate, she earned media and voter attention for attacking Harris' record as a prosecutor. While that moment garnered attention and may have caused headaches for Harris – who was already contending with her prosecutorial past – it did not yield a significant boost in support for Gabbard's campaign. Gabbard fell short of eligibility for Democratic primary debates after November 2019. By the end of the primary, she had earned less than 1 percent of all Democratic primary votes. On March 19, 2020, Gabbard announced she was dropping out of the race and endorsing Joe Biden.

Gabbard's message of peace was often paired with the supposition that there was "no force more powerful than love." Likewise, Marianne Williamson – who announced her presidential candidacy on January 28, 2019 – embraced a campaign slogan of "turning love into a political force." A famous author, lecturer, entrepreneur, and activist, Williamson came to her presidential campaign with little political experience. Apart from a failed 2014 bid for the US House in California, her fame had come as a spiritual thought leader who authored many best-selling books and had a national following. Williamson described being called to run for president to address the division sowed by Donald Trump. Her campaign website featured this message: "Our task is to generate a massive wave of energy, fueled and navigated by we the people, so powerful as to override all threats to our democracy. Where fear has been harnessed for political purposes, our task is to harness love."[18] Williamson's message of love was backed by an especially progressive policy agenda that included plans for – among many other things – reparations, combating poverty, advocating for children, Native American justice, and racial reconciliation and healing.

Despite her ambitious goals, Williamson struggled to be taken seriously as a presidential contender. She received very little media coverage, often being left out of candidate profiles – including a *Vogue* magazine

---

[18]   Marianne Williamson 2020, https://marianne2020.com/issues

profile and photo shoot of the five other women running for president in March 2019. After garnering some attention in the first two Democratic debates, media focus turned negative as stories emerged that drew on her past comments to paint her as anti-science. She failed to reach eligibility for the third primary debate and decided to leave the race before the first caucus votes were cast. On January 10, 2020, Williamson shared a message with supporters that acknowledged her goal in the contest was to "take every possible opportunity to share our message." She added, "The primaries might be tightly contested among the top contenders, and I don't want to get in the way of a progressive candidate winning any of them." About six weeks later, Williamson endorsed Bernie Sanders.

After over fourteen months of campaigning, each of the record six women who waged campaigns for the 2020 Democratic presidential nomination had left the race, along with many of their male colleagues. *New York Times* reporter Lisa Lerer reflected on the turn from the record-setting success of Democratic women in election 2018 to the impending result of the 2020 Democratic primary, writing in early March 2020, "In the end, the pink wave carried two white men ashore."[19] By June 5, 2020, Joe Biden had secured the votes he would need to win the Democratic nomination against Bernie Sanders, ensuring a general election between two white men in their seventies against each other and that 2020 would not be the year that the United States elected its first woman president.

GENDER STEREOTYPES AND GENDERED STANDARDS IN THE 2020 PRESIDENTIAL ELECTION

As noted by Melanye Price and Kelly Dittmar in Chapter 1, gender and race dynamics earned heightened saliency and visibility in election 2020; these were undeniably influential within the political, economic, and social contexts within which the campaign was contested, and were underlined and accentuated by presidential candidates' rhetoric, agendas, and behaviors. Neither race nor gender was the singular or isolated cause of a candidate's victory or defeat in 2020, but both are key pieces of the complex puzzle of presidential politics.

In the remainder of this chapter, I evaluate the ways in which candidate gender shaped how women presidential contenders navigated the cam-

---

[19] Lisa Lerer, Was It Always Going to Be the Last Men Standing?, *New York Times*, March 5, 2020, www.nytimes.com/2020/03/05/us/politics/women-voters-democratic-candidates.html

paign as well as how they were evaluated along four key axes: electability, experience and qualifications, strength and toughness, and likability and emotion.

Electability

A Gallup poll in 1937 found that just 33 percent of Americans would vote for a qualified woman for president. By 2019 a strong majority – 94 percent of Americans – told Gallup they would vote for a qualified woman for president.[20] The apparent willingness to cast a ballot for a generic woman candidate must be reconciled with the very real women candidates campaigning for the presidency, as well as the distinct political environments in which they run. Prior to Hillary Clinton's 2008 candidacy, women were rarely – if ever – seen as viable contenders for the presidency. Clinton changed that in 2016 when she not only won the Democratic nomination but won more votes than any other presidential candidate ever had, including her opponent. But while her 2016 achievement challenged doubts of a woman's ability to win, her defeat at the hands of the electoral college and her experience of gender-based challenges en route to that outcome also caused some to view selecting another woman as too risky a bet in 2020. This tension in interpreting recent electoral outcomes as bellwethers for the 2020 presidential election was heightened by the success of Democratic women in subpresidential elections in 2018. As Neera Tanden, former president of the Center for American Progress and adviser to Clinton, told the *New York Times* in January 2019, "On one hand, women are leading the resistance and deserve representation. But on the other side, there's a fear that if misogyny beat Clinton, it can beat other women."[21] These considerations fueled the electability debate of the 2020 presidential election.

Just under a year before the first caucus votes were cast, Democratic primary voters signaled that defeating Donald Trump was a key motivator to their voting behavior. In February 2019, for example, 40 percent of Democratic primary voters said they preferred a presidential candidate "with the best chance to defeat Donald Trump" to one who "comes closest

---

[20]   Clare Malone, From 1937 to Hillary Clinton, How Americans Have Felt about a Woman President, *FiveThirtyEight*, June 9, 2016, http://fivethirtyeight.com/features/from-1937-to-hillary-clinton-how-americans-have-felt-about-a-female-president/; Justin McCarthy, Less Than Half in US Would Vote for a Socialist for President, *Gallup*, May 9, 2019, https://news.gallup.com/poll/254120/less-half-vote-socialist-president.aspx

[21]   Lisa Lerer and Susan Chira, Democrats Puzzle over Whether a Woman Will Beat Trump, *New York Times*, January 5, 2019, www.nytimes.com/2019/01/05/us/politics/women-candidates-president-2020.html

to [their] views on issues."[22] While the majority of primary voters (56%) were still motivated by issue alignment, the gap narrowed significantly from previous elections; when *NBC News/Wall Street Journal* asked the same question in July 2015, just 20 percent of Democratic primary voters reported electability as more important to their vote choice.[23]

There is both quantitative and qualitative evidence that electability concerns were gendered in the 2020 presidential election. A June 2019 survey for Data for Progress showed that Joe Biden benefited most when voters considered general election success in their primary vote choice. When respondents were told they could use a "magic wand" to allow their preferred candidate to bypass the general election and win presidential office, Elizabeth Warren was the top choice among Democratic primary voters.[24] That finding held through January 2020 and aligned with more direct evidence that voters rated Biden as most electable and harbored concerns that the country was not ready for a woman president.[25] In a February 2020 *Morning Consult* poll, for example, about two-thirds of those surveyed perceived the belief that the United States was not ready for a woman president as an obstacle to women presidential contenders.[26] For women of color, perceptions of electability hurdles were only amplified by the dominance of whiteness in presidential election history, as detailed by Melanye Price and Kelly Dittmar in Chapter 1.

These concerns, which were slightly stronger among women voters, cannot be wholly separated from what happened in 2016. At an April 2019 CNN town hall, Elizabeth Warren was asked directly what she would do to prevent from being "Hillary-ed," a term that cued the concern that Clinton's gender was a hindrance to her presidential success.[27] While discussing the causes of Hillary Clinton's 2016 defeat at a January 2020

22 Nathaniel Rakich and Dhrumil Mehta, Democrats Care More about Winning Than Usual, *FiveThirtyEight*, March 8, 2019, https://fivethirtyeight.com/features/democrats-care-more-about-winning-than-usual/

23 Ibid.

24 Data for Progress and YouGov Blue, Pre- and Post-Debate Survey, open memorandum, July 2019, www.filesforprogress.org/datasets/pre_post_debate/FIRSTDEBATE_MEMO.pdf

25 Mark White, Ambivalent Support, Part 2: Supporting a Non-Preferred Candidate, Data for Progress, February 3, 2020, www.dataforprogress.org/blog/2020/2/3/ambivalent-support-part-2-supporting-a-non-preferred-candidate

26 Morning Consult, National Tracking Poll, February 4–5, 2020, https://ots.nbcwpshield.com/wp-content/uploads/2019/09/LX-Morning-Consult-Gender-Crosstabs.pdf

27 Tara Golshan, At a CNN Town Hall, Elizabeth Warren Had to Explain Why She, a Woman, is Electable. Twice, *Vox*, April 22, 2020, www.vox.com/2019/4/22/18511866/cnn-townhall-elizabeth-warren-hillary-clinton-trump

town hall in Iowa, Biden tapped into similar fears. He explained that Clinton suffered from unfair sexist attacks and assured the audience, "That is not going to happen to me."[28] Though he denied them publicly, Bernie Sanders reportedly harbored his own doubts that a woman candidate could defeat Donald Trump in 2020. After this story leaked days before the Iowa caucuses, Elizabeth Warren confirmed that Sanders had expressed this doubt to her at a private dinner in December 2018.

It is within this context that women candidates for president were forced to wage two campaigns at once. First, like their male counterparts, they made a case that they were the candidates with the best qualifications, positions, and plans to be president. That case included drawing contrasts with the incumbent officeholder and explaining why they would be the best candidate to compete against him. But women, unlike most men in the race, also waged secondary – and concurrent – campaigns to prove not that they could win against Donald Trump but that they could win *at all*. In waging these "concurrent campaigns of belief," women candidates in 2020 revealed a persistent gender hurdle in the path to the presidency.[29]

Whether in response to their opponents or to voters, the women candidates waged these concurrent campaigns to rebut electability doubts. In an interview with *BuzzFeed*, Kamala Harris said, "I am actually surprised about this whole electability conversation," adding, "I shouldn't be, because it's not new to me. But I have to tell you, I have sometimes said to my team, is this really a thing? Like I know it is, but is it *really* a thing?"[30] Despite her surprise, Harris integrated a direct response into her campaign stump speeches from day one, discussing her record of being the first – first woman, first person of color – in various political offices and emphasizing her faith in the American people "to see what can be, unburdened by what has been." While campaigning in Iowa in spring 2019, Kirsten Gillibrand spoke plainly: "To the pundit class who still says, 'Can a woman win?' Yes, of course we can."[31]

[28] Amanda Terkel, Joe Biden Said Hillary Clinton Faced Sexism, But "That's Not Going to Happen with Me," *Huffington Post*, January 3, 2020, www.huffpost.com/entry/joe-biden-sexism_n_5e0f6d5ec5b6b5a713b982cc

[29] Political strategist Priyanka Mantha used this term in an interview with the author.

[30] Molly Hensley-Clancy, Why Kamala Harris Uses Female Pronouns When She Talks about the Presidency, *BuzzFeed*, October 2, 2019, www.buzzfeednews.com/article/mollyhensleyclancy/kamala-harris-electability

[31] Lisa Lerer, It's a Question No One Says They Want to Ask. But the Women Running for President Keep Hearing It, *New York Times*, July 3, 2019, www.nytimes.com/2019/07/03/us/politics/women-presidential-candidates-2020.html

Women candidates also used more subtle strategies to normalize the idea of a woman president, like using feminine pronouns when referencing the next president.[32] When asked about electability challenges in the early months of the Democratic primary, Elizabeth Warren was quick to pivot away from the topic. But the continued chatter and survey evidence of its effects – especially on her campaign – appear to have shaped her campaign's electability messaging in the months leading up to the Iowa caucuses. The campaign adopted "Win with Warren" as a major slogan and argued not only that a woman *could* defeat Trump, but that women were actually best situated to succeed. In January 2020, the Warren campaign released at least four advertisements that centered on her electability, including one featuring an elderly white man who voted for Trump in 2016. In "She Can Win," the man tells Iowans, "To people who say that a woman can't win, I say 'Nonsense.' I believe a woman can beat Trump and I believe Elizabeth is that woman."

By the time Democrats met for the January 14, 2020 debate in Iowa, Warren was more direct than ever. "This question about whether or not a woman can be president has been raised, and it's time for us to attack it head-on," she said. She went on to explain that while the men on the debate stage had collectively lost ten elections, the women on the stage – Warren and Klobuchar – were undefeated in their political campaigns. Klobuchar backed up this message, reiterating, "When you look at what I have done, I have won every race, every place, every time."[33] Warren's winning message also relied on the electoral records of women in the 2018 election. Online and during her stump speeches, Warren reminded voters that women had outperformed men in competitive elections across the country since Donald Trump was elected.[34] This strategy reflects what Kamala Harris described as the most effective response to electability concerns. Asked by the Associated Press how she deals with those who doubt her ability to win, Harris said, "You win."[35] In these and other examples,

---

[32] Jessica Bennett, She's the Next President. Wait, Did You Read That Right?, *New York Times*, January 24, 2020, www.nytimes.com/2020/01/24/us/politics/woman-president-she-her.html

[33] Emily Stewart, Elizabeth Warren and Amy Klobuchar Are Their Own Evidence That Women Can Win, *Vox*, January 14, 2020, www.vox.com/policy-and-politics/2020/1/14/21066598/women-electability-elizabeth-warren-amy-klobuchar-debate

[34] Elizabeth Warren, Twitter post, February 3, 2020, 5:38 p.m., https://twitter.com/ewarren/status/1224462313127927809

[35] Errin Haines Whack, Kamala Harris on Race and Electability in 2020, *Associated Press News*, July 8, 2019, https://apnews.com/38025aad29de43e08cdc2a7fef940e17

the 2020 Democratic primary revealed that the opportunity costs of waging a concurrent campaign of belief are real, whether calculated in the time spent discussing electability, the energy spent rebutting doubts, or even the financial costs of conveying one's capacity for success in campaign advertising.

The social construction of electability was especially evident in election 2020, and it was deeply tied – to the detriment of women, candidates of color, and more specifically women of color – to what has been in US presidential politics instead of what could be. It was also raised strategically by those benefiting from this construction to tap into perceived risk. In his final message to voters before the Iowa caucuses, Joe Biden released an advertisement titled "Threat" that explained, "Every day he is president, Donald Trump poses a threat to America and the world. We have to beat him. Joe Biden is the strongest candidate to do it." While Biden was unsuccessful in Iowa, his message ultimately resonated with Democratic voters despite the best efforts of women candidates to debunk the myth that their nomination was any riskier than the selection of another white man.

Experience and Qualifications

Viewed as apart from the norm of male and masculine officeholders, women are assumed to be less qualified than men to hold public office, even when they have more experience and stronger credentials. Research reveals that the penalty for voter perceptions of candidate incompetence is greater for women than men candidates.[36] This is consistent with findings from political practitioners, who report that women candidates need to prove themselves while their male colleagues face fewer questions of credibility to lead.[37] It is no surprise, then, that research finds women candidates and officeholders are more qualified than their male counterparts on multiple measures of political experience – an indication that women who run for office know that they need to accumulate more credentials to be perceived as equally qualified to male candidates.[38]

Amy Klobuchar relied heavily on her record of achievement to make her case for the presidency. She detailed decades of experience in public service as preparing her for this role. She also called out the *inexperience* of

---

[36] Tessa Ditonto, A High Bar or a Double Standard? Gender, Competence, and Information in Political Campaigns. *Political Behavior* 39(2) (2017): 301–25.

[37] Kelly Dittmar, *Navigating Gendered Terrain: Stereotypes and Strategy in Political Campaigns* (Philadelphia, PA: Temple University Press, 2015).

[38] Sarah Fulton and Kostanca Dhima, The Gendered Politics of Congressional Elections, *Political Behavior* (2020), doi.org/10.1007/s11109-020-09604-7

at least one of her white, male opponents as evidence that women are held to higher standards in proving their experience and qualifications for elective office. In response to questions about gender and Pete Buttigieg's rising popularity in June 2019, Klobuchar said about the women in the race, "Could we be running with less experience than we had? I don't think so," adding, "I don't think people would take us seriously."[39]

The lack of media attention and voter support received by the less-experienced women candidates – Tulsi Gabbard and Marianne Williamson – in contrast to similarly experienced men provides some support for her argument. Both Buttigieg and Beto O'Rourke, who each had comparable public service experience to Gabbard, garnered cover stories in major magazines in April 2019 – Buttigieg in *New York Magazine* and Beto O'Rourke in *Vanity Fair* – as at least one indicator that they were being taken more seriously than similarly or more qualified women counterparts.

Elizabeth Warren appeared aware of these different standards and engaged in a strategy that made it near impossible to question her qualifications for the job. In a June 2019 profile of Warren, *GQ Magazine* described her as an "overachiever" and explained, "Warren has managed to kick-start her own momentum by grinding it out – out-policy-proposing, out-tweet-thread-explaining, and out-hustling every other contender in the race." Writer Mari Ayehara added, "In other words, she's running like a woman."[40] Warren's campaign embraced the slogan "I have a plan for that," as it produced at least eighty detailed policy proposals in the fourteen months of her candidacy. This approach was meant, in part, to contrast the lack of clarity in research-supported policy making during the Trump administration. It also made it harder to discount Warren's qualifications for presidential officeholding.

Despite the robustness of her agenda and approach, Warren still faced scrutiny that she was not ready for the job. Throughout the fall of 2019, Buttigieg attacked Warren for lacking specificity in her health care plan. On the October 2019 debate stage, he said, "Your signature, senator, is to have a plan for everything – except this."[41] Buttigieg was not alone in

[39] Nick Corasaniti, Pete Buttigieg vs. Amy Klobuchar: An Abridged History of Midwestern Iciness, *New York Times*, February 25, 2020, www.nytimes.com/2020/02/25/us/politics/pete-buttigieg-amy-klobuchar-debate.html

[40] Mari Ayehara, Elizabeth Warren Is Running Like a Woman, *GQ Magazine*, June 14, 2019, www.gq.com/story/elizabeth-warren-running-like-a-woman

[41] Thomas Kaplan, Elizabeth Warren and Pete Buttigieg Clash at Debate, *New York Times*, October 15, 2019, www.nytimes.com/2019/10/15/us/politics/medicare-for-all-elizabeth-warren.html

pushing Warren for more specifics on her health care plan – which she provided soon after, but the contrast between his criticism and his own approach is notable. In the three months between launching an exploratory committee and officially announcing his candidacy for president, Buttigieg offered little in the way of a policy platform. When pushed on this in April 2019, Buttigieg told the *New York Times* that he did not believe the Democratic race would hinge on "who has the most elegant policy design," and argued it would be "inauthentic" to make too many detailed promises.[42] While his campaign did go on to provide more detail on his own policy agenda, Buttigieg's demand for specificity from Warren both signaled a standard to which he did not hold himself and evidenced a possible downside to Warren's content-heavy strategy: in distinguishing herself as the most prepared candidate, the completeness of that preparation became a site for contention that others who never claimed the same level of preparedness had to address.

Kamala Harris' experience and qualifications – particularly as a district attorney and attorney general – also proved to be double-edged in their influence on her presidential candidacy. From the first day of her campaign, Harris led with her prosecutorial experience as evidence that she would be best to prosecute the case against Donald Trump. With the slogan "For the People," she reminded voters of the work she did to fight on behalf of the citizens of San Francisco and California, as she would do for the American people as president. Emphasizing this resumé was key to proving her credentials for higher office according to research that demonstrates the additional scrutiny of candidates from identity groups that have been persistently underrepresented in political leadership. But it was this resumé that also created political problems for Harris in a Democratic primary where progressive voters raised concerns that she represented an unjust criminal justice system instead of crediting her efforts to reform it from the inside. Harris' identity as a Black woman working within a system that has disproportionately punished Black people likely heightened criticism, as was evident in the different degree of attention her prosecutorial past received in comparison to Klobuchar, who also started her political career as a prosecutor and evaded sustained criticism of her resume until late in the campaign. Harris' experience demonstrates that demands for more qualified women candidates are

---

[42] Alexander Burns, Pete Buttigieg's Focus: Storytelling First. Policy Details Later, *New York Times*, April 14, 2019, www.nytimes.com/2019/04/14/us/politics/pete-buttigieg-2020-writing-message.html

laden with more particular expectations for *which* qualifications women should meet to prove themselves as best fit for presidential office.

Strength and Toughness

Perceptions that presidential candidates are qualified are not only tied to experience but also to candidates' capacity to meet stereotypical credentials for the job. One of those credentials is being tough enough to take command and handle the emotional demands of being president. Presidential candidates have historically been expected to demonstrate toughness and strength in addressing military, national security, and foreign affairs to prove their capacity to be commander in chief. Voters have worried that women lack experience and expertise in these areas. As recently as 2018, Pew found that 35 percent of respondents believed men in politics are better than women at dealing with national security and defense issues; just 6 percent reported that women were better suited than men at handling these issues.[43] Women candidates have also faced concerns that they will be too "soft" in dealing with US enemies. For example, Geraldine Ferraro, when she was the Democratic nominee for vice president in 1984, was asked on *Meet the Press* if she would be able, if necessary, to push the button to launch nuclear weapons. No man seeking the presidency or vice presidency had ever been asked a similar question on national television. As a result, women candidates have historically taken steps to prove their national defense bona fides and combat perceptions of weakness in taking on any perceived or real enemies of the United States.

Interestingly, while Trump reinforced toughness as a masculine standard by which he measured presidential fitness, his unpopularity – particularly among Democrats – may have created more space for challenging stereotypically masculine displays of toughness as essential to presidential contenders in 2020. This evolution is not only beneficial for women, as toughness remains a trait more commonly associated with masculinity and men, but it appears strategically smart for Democrats – at least in the Trump era. Nearly a year after Trump took office, Pew found that 48 percent of Democrats (compared to 20 percent of Republicans) said that it was a bad thing that society looks up to masculine or manly men.[44] Democrats'

---

[43] Juliana Menasce Horowitz, Ruth Igielnik, and Kim Parker, Women and Leadership 2018, Pew Research Center, September 20, 2018, www.pewresearch.org/social-trends/2018/09/20/women-and-leadership-2018/

[44] Kim Parker, Juliana Menasce Horowitz, and Renee Stepler, On Gender Differences, No Consensus on Nature vs. Nurture, Pew Research Center, December 5, 2017, www.pewresearch.org/social-trends/2017/12/05/americans-see-society-placing-more-of-a-premium-on-masculinity-than-on-femininity/

skepticism of tough guy presidents may have shaped the presidential campaigns of both women and men in 2020. For example, while Biden launched his presidential campaign noting he was ready to go to battle, his was a "battle for the soul of this nation," not one that would be fought with brute force. Biden's approach was responsive to critiques that Trump's brand of toughness and strength was dangerous domestically and abroad.

Still, women presidential candidates in 2020 were not immune from the pressures to prove toughness or strength. In a July 2018 Pew poll, 36 percent of respondents argued that the perception that "women aren't tough enough for politics" is a major or minor reason there are not more women in high political offices.[45] And recent research shows that women of both parties who present themselves as tough and assertive benefit in voter evaluations that they are knowledgeable and strong leaders.[46] Women candidates made some effort to prove these credentials in the presidential campaign. For example, they were especially likely to use the word "fight" in their announcement speeches, embracing this rhetoric more than their male counterparts, for whom toughness is more likely assumed.[47] Kirsten Gillibrand repeatedly committed to "fighting like hell" on issues, most notably against abortion restrictions. Elizabeth Warren used the same rhetoric, integrating her commitment to "fight hard" into all aspects of her campaign and often concluding remarks and interviews – and even her campaign – by reminding her supporters to "stay in the fight." Amy Klobuchar's fight was cued in her emphasis on the "grit" she brings to political leadership.

But the fights in which these women engaged were neither physical feats nor fueled by militarization or police force. And their toughness credentials came from stories of persistence and resilience instead of direct combat. Like Clinton did in 2016, multiple women candidates in 2020 shared stories of navigating discrimination in their personal and professional lives as evidence that they are accustomed to overcoming challenges and as evidence of strength of character. For Warren, that included facing pregnancy discrimination as a school teacher. For Harris, that included facing racial discrimination as a young child through adulthood. This approach is consistent with findings from research that distinguish

[45]   Horowitz, Igielnik, and Parker, Women and Leadership 2018.
[46]   Nichole Bauer, The Effects of Counterstereotypic Gender Strategies on Candidate Evaluations, *Political Psychology* 38(2) (2017): 279–95.
[47]   Ezra Klein, Twitter post, April 16, 2019, 12:29 p.m., https://twitter.com/ezraklein/

between toughness and strength in analyzing effective strategies for women candidates, arguing that strength is more directly tied to personal character, can be decoupled from toughness, and has surpassed toughness in traits most important to voters.[48] While this research was not conducted at the presidential level, it suggests that women candidates can meet credentials of toughness or strength in less stereotypically masculine ways.

Their fights were also for targeted, and sometimes under-addressed, causes, including gender and racial equity. A clear example of this came at the February 19, 2020 Democratic debate, when Warren began the night by calling for voters to deem accusations and evidence of sexual harassment and misogyny from Michael Bloomberg and at his companies as disqualifying for presidential leadership. Responses to her attack, which many credit with derailing Bloomberg's campaign, were mixed. Many praised Warren's display of strength and principles. Massachusetts Congresswoman Ayanna Pressley, a Warren supporter, explained, "She is a fighter. When she was on that debate stage fighting, I didn't see her attacking anyone. She was holding people accountable. In that moment, as a survivor of sexual violence, I thank her for defending survivor's justice." But Warren's fight that night also elicited criticism more typical of the gender backlash that women candidates have historically sought to avoid. One source of that backlash was against her problematization of bad behavior that has long been overlooked in presidential politics – specifically, the mistreatment of women. Another source of backlash, however, was the counter-stereotypic style she employed. Despite demands on presidential candidates to appear strong, tough, and assertive, that assertiveness by women is still more likely to be negatively received by individuals who perceive it as a violation of feminine norms of niceness and likability.

Likability and Emotion

Boston Globe columnist Scot Lehigh tweeted about Warren's debate performance: "Elizabeth Warren ups Bernie in attacking Bloomberg. Tough, tough, tough – and well-designed. But is it too aggressive?"[49] *Washington Post* columnist Jennifer Rubin thought so, tweeting, "Mean and angry

---

[48] Turning Point: The Changing Landscape for Women Candidates, Governors Guidebook Series, Barbara Lee Family Foundation, 2011, www.barbaraleefoundation.org/wp-content/uploads/Turning-Point.pdf

[49] Scot Lehigh, Twitter post, February 19, 2020, 9:06 p.m., https://twitter.com/GlobeScotLehigh/

Warren is not a good look."[50] Despite evidence of progress, this example shows that communicating toughness and strength can still be particularly tricky for women candidates, who risk being accused of emasculation, or labeled as "aggressive," "bitchy," or "cold" when they seek to appear strong and assertive. As he did in 2016, Donald Trump again sought to capitalize on these different gender standards in 2020 by amplifying concerns about Warren's assertive style. He said of Warren soon after the February 2020 debate, "She's not dumb, but she's just so damn mean."[51] A week later, after Warren dropped out of the Democratic primary, he elaborated, "She is a very mean person and people don't like her. People don't want that. They like a person like me that isn't mean."[52]

In each of these attacks, opponents and critics mine a vein of particular vulnerability to women candidates. Specifically, a 2012 study by the Barbara Lee Family Foundation found that evaluations of women's qualifications for office are tied to perceptions of their likability in a way they are not for men. In other words, men can earn voters' support while being unlikable, while women must simultaneously demonstrate they are likable *and* qualified. Failing to succeed in meeting either expectation can undermine a woman's candidacy, creating an additional burden on women's campaigns to strike a balance between masculine and feminine behavior, between toughness and niceness, in a way that meets stereotypical expectations of gender and candidacy or at least reduces the backlash to stereotype disruption.

The early months of election 2020 revealed that likability would remain a source of gender-based challenge for women presidential candidates. On the same day that Elizabeth Warren announced her campaign in 2018, *Politico* posted a profile that characterized "an unmistakable challenge" for her campaign: "How does Warren avoid a Clinton redux – written off as too unlikable before her campaign gets off the ground?"[53] Kirsten Gillibrand also faced the likability question on day one of her campaign, as a reporter asked if she considered the fact that "a lot of people see you

[50] Jennifer Rubin, Twitter post, February 19, 2020, 9:27 p.m., https://twitter.com/ JRubinBlogger/
[51] Brett Samuels, Trump Surveys South Carolina Supporters on Preferred Democratic Opponent, *The Hill*, February 28, 2020, https://thehill.com/homenews/campaign/ 485249-trump-surveys-south-carolina-supporters-on-preferred-democratic-opponent
[52] Aaron Rupar, Twitter post, March 6, 2020, 9:42 p.m., https://twitter.com/atrupar/
[53] Natasha Korecki, Warren Battles the Ghosts of Hillary, *Politico*, December 31, 2018, www .politico.com/story/2018/12/31/elizabeth-warren-hillary-clinton-1077008

as pretty likable" as a "selling point" for her campaign.[54] Amy Klobuchar was profiled as unlikable before her campaign even launched, as multiple reports emerged about her abusive treatment of congressional staff. But hitting the likability sweet spot again proved elusive for women running for president. For example, in February 2019, *Politico* – the same outlet that raised likability as a necessary credential for women candidates in December – criticized Kamala Harris as potentially *too* likable, reporting, "She's connecting with audiences – sometimes to a fault."[55] More optimistically, however, scrutiny of and backlash to this double standard came from a variety of sources, including supporters, journalists, commentators, and candidates themselves. The heightened unwillingness to accept gender biases as expected or normal, as well as the increased time spent in pointing them out, evidence the possibility for institutional change.

Concerns about Klobuchar's behavior evoked another gendered challenge directly related to likability: that women are too emotional for political leadership. This concern – at least applied to women's political leadership across levels of office – has declined significantly in the past three decades; according to the 2018 General Social Survey, just 13 percent of Americans say that men are better suited emotionally for politics than women.[56] But that persistence of doubt, even among a minority of the population, can be cued by political commentary and critiques of women candidates. Besides Klobuchar, both Harris and Warren faced attacks of being too angry. For Harris, accusations of being angry or "nasty," as President Trump called her, evoked a particular trope of "angry Black women" meant to discount righteous anger, arouse fear, and contribute to a candidate's dehumanization. While anger has not been used in the same way for white women, opponents – particularly Joe Biden and Pete Buttigieg – painted Warren's passion as anger in an attempt to discredit her criticism of their records and policy positions.[57] Again,

[54] Jenna Johnson, On Day One, Kirsten Gillibrand Faces the "Likable" Question, *Washington Post*, January 16, 2019, www.washingtonpost.com/politics/on-day-one-kirsten-gillibrand-faces-the-likable-question/2019/01/16/568cb58c-1922-11e9-9ebf-c5fed1b7a081_story.html

[55] Christopher Cadelago, Kamala Harris' Big Question Mark, *Politico*, February 28, 2019, www.politico.com/story/2019/02/28/kamala-harris-policies-1192919

[56] Associated Press and NORC, Women in Politics, the Workplace, and Family Life, issue brief, March 2018, https://apnorc.org/wp-content/uploads/2020/02/APNORC_GSS_gender_equality_2019.pdf

[57] Gregory Krieg and Eric Bradner, Elizabeth Warren Responds to "Angry" Charge: "I Am Angry and I Own It," *CNN*, November 9, 2019, www.cnn.com/2019/11/08/politics/elizabeth-warren-joe-biden-sexism-charges/index.html

Warren was quick to respond via campaign channels. In a fundraising email with the subject line "I am angry and I own it," she wrote: "Over and over we are told that women are not allowed to be angry. It makes us unattractive to powerful men who want us to be quiet." Warren continued to "own" her anger throughout the election, incorporating this message into her stump speech and campaign messaging.[58]

While Warren was bold in her response to these accusations, she was aware of the line women walk in expressing emotion in pursuit of political leadership. This awareness was especially evident from both Warren and Klobuchar at a December 2019 Democratic debate. When all candidates were given the opportunity to either ask forgiveness of or offer a gift to someone on stage, Warren and Klobuchar – the only women on stage – were the only candidates to ask for forgiveness. They both asked for forgiveness for the same traits for which women are disproportionately punished. Warren said, "I know that sometimes I get really worked up, and sometimes I get a little hot," adding, "I don't really mean to."[59] Warren explained that her anger was rooted in passion to fight for people in great need of a champion, providing a vocal justification for counterstereotypic behavior that could otherwise be used against her. Klobuchar offered a similar justification for getting "worked up," explaining, "It's because I believe it so much in my heart that we have to bring people with us and not shut them out."[60] Though subtle, these comments could have caused some viewers to consider the bias with which they evaluate women's expression of emotion. But they were still framed as pleas for forgiveness for the same passion that is perceived as a positive attribute of political men.

CONCLUSION

Women candidates for the top executive offices in the United States navigate several obstacles and challenges that their male counterparts do not confront. Men who seek the presidency or vice presidency do not have to continually prove themselves qualified for office. They are far less likely to face the double binds placed on women to be tough but likable, experienced but authentic, and bold but modest. The 2020 election also

[58] Elizabeth Warren, Twitter post, February 25, 2020. 6:31 p.m., https://twitter.com/ewarren/status/1232448067997249536

[59] Maggie Astor, The 2020 Democrats Were Told to Give a Gift or Ask Forgiveness, Guess What the Women Chose, *New York Times*, December 20, 2019, www.nytimes.com/2019/12/20/us/politics/klobuchar-warren-democratic-debate.html

[60] Ibid.

highlighted an especially stubborn obstacle to electing a woman president: doubts that she can win. Whether the electability concerns that the women candidates faced in 2020 were heightened due to the loss of a woman nominee four years prior or were simply more salient because of voters' sense of urgency to unseat the incumbent, perceptions that a woman is less capable of presidential success are dangerous in their ability to ensure that women are not given the opportunity to be successful.

Despite illustrating these challenges, the 2020 election also offers evidence of progress. Not only did a record number of women compete for a major party nomination, but they continued the disruption caused by women who have been willing to contest the nation's highest office. From offering new models to meet stereotypically masculine credentials to embracing the electoral advantages of being women, they chipped away at long-held images and expectations of the presidency. They directly challenged sexist attacks and rejected the electability myth that put them at an electoral disadvantage. Apart from the women themselves, media, commentators, and even some men in the race reflected more critically on the gender biases that have been persistent in presidential elections. And, finally, while women were unable to dismantle the highest, hardest glass ceiling in American politics in 2020, Kamala Harris shattered another in becoming the first woman vice president of the United States. Together, these points of progress contributed to the disruption necessary to clear the path for a future woman president.

3 Gendered Mobilization and Elections: The Intersectional Politics of Protest

On January 21, 2017, the day after the inauguration of Donald J. Trump, the world witnessed the largest single-day protest in US history. The 2017 Women's March spread not only across the United States but also worldwide. From major metropolitan areas to small rural towns, the streets filled, accented by pink knitted hats. In Washington, DC, the day started with a rally headlined by Angela Davis, Gloria Steinem, Janet Mock, and other prominent activists from an array of social justice movements (e.g. feminist, racial justice, LGBTQ, immigration, environmental, and labor). A panoply of signs reflected the varied motivations of marchers. Some expressing gendered outrage at Trump directly, twisting his own rhetoric and misdeeds to articulate resistance: "Our rights are not up for grabs," "This pussy grabs back," and "Nasty Women make (her)story." Others addressed the many issues thought to be threatened by a candidate whose campaign was fraught with racist rhetoric about Muslims and Mexicans and an administration poised to undo decades of progressive policy. The protest was peaceful, even as the numbers swelled beyond what the march organizers or the city planners could ever have imagined. Women made up the highest percentage of marchers, but all genders and ethnoracial groups were represented. While people showed up for different reasons, and with an array of emotions, the mood was largely of joyous resistance, even if only to temporarily hold at bay the fear of what was to come.

Fast forward to January 6, 2021, the day that Joe Biden was scheduled to become the certified winner of the 2020 presidential election. As members of Congress gathered in the Capital, so too did crowds of Trump supporters at the Save America Rally and March for Trump. Trump, joined on stage by some of his fiercest allies (Roger Stone, Rudy Giuliani, and John Eastman), repeated false allegations challenging the results of the presidential election and firing up the crowd:

They rigged the election. They rigged it like they've never rigged an election before.

We will never give up, we will never concede. It doesn't happen.

When you catch somebody in a fraud, you're allowed to go by very different rules.

And we fight. We fight like hell. And if you don't fight like hell, you're not going to have a country anymore.[1]

The event was planned by a coalition that included several right-wing women's organizations, but the crowds that day were mainly composed of white men, dotted with both camouflage and red "Make America Great Again" hats and shirts. In the middle of a global pandemic that had cost hundreds of thousands of lives in the US and millions worldwide, participants were mostly unmasked and some of them armed. They responded to Trump enthusiastically, with chants of "Fight for Trump! Fight for Trump!" Soon after he ended his speech, violence broke out as protesters broke through the barricades and forced their way into the capitol building, breaking down doors and shattering windows. Congress was forced to adjourn and take shelter. Other buildings were evacuated as two pipe bombs were found at the headquarters of the Democratic and Republican national committees. Across the country, similar protests were taking place, with a demonstration in the Oregon capitol in Salem also turning violent. It would not be until that evening that rioters were pushed back and the session of Congress resumed. During the insurrection, five people were killed and numerous were injured.

There are many important comparisons and contrasts to be made between these two mobilizations. While both events were planned by women and prompted by the outcome of a recent presidential election, they are a part of two very different and oppositional social movement trajectories that have shaped US politics, one focused on challenging gendered and racial power structures and the other seeking to uphold them. Both have profound implications for elections and the future of democracy.

This chapter explores the relationship between social movements and elections, with an emphasis on the role that both gender and race play. It is an intersectional analysis that provides important insights into why and how some groups have mobilized and to what effect. The chapter is organized as follows: first, I provide an introduction to the intersectional study

---

[1] Brian Naylor, Read Trump's Jan. 6 Speech, A Key Part of Impeachment Trial, *NPR*, February 10, 2021, www.npr.org/2021/02/10/966396848/read-trumps-jan-6-speech-a-key-part-of-impeachment-trial

of gendered mobilizations and an overview of the relationship between social movements and elections. Next, I provide a historical overview of race-gendered mobilizations and their interaction with US elections, including the role they have played in democratizing them and the impact they have had on parties and their electoral coalitions. Then, I return to contemporary politics and the role that race-gendered mobilizations continue to play in US elections.

GENDERED MOBILIZATION

Within the gender and politics literature, much attention is given to feminist mobilizations. This is with good reason. Feminist movements have been a key means of increasing women's representation both descriptively (securing women's right to vote and legitimizing women's political participation and leadership) and substantively (getting important gendered issues on the political agenda). Feminist movements, however, are only one specific type of gendered mobilization. Scholars have made important distinctions between "women's movements," "feminist movements," and "women in movement."[2] Each is an important component of gendered mobilization, but with markedly different focus and impact. Women's movements are a subset of movements that are "characterized by the primacy of women's gendered experiences, women's issues, and women's leadership and decision making."[3] Here, how a movement defines itself and articulates issues are specific to women, developed and organized by them with reference to their gender identity. Women's movements might encompass some feminist movements, but they might also encompass other movements where women are mobilizing as women and using that gender identity in various ways that are not directed at women's rights. This includes conservative women's movements. A third and overlapping form of gendered mobilization is "women in movement," which focuses on women's participation that extends to movements not organized around gender in any explicit manner and/or where men may even dominate leadership and decision-making roles. Women have been a part of other movements that do not emphasize gender, but nevertheless may have an important (and gendered) impact on their lives. Figure 3.1 shows the relationship between these three

[2] Karen Beckwith, The Comparative Study of Women's Movements, in *The Oxford Handbook of Gender and Politics*, ed. Georgina Waylen, Karen Celis, Johanna Kantola, and S. Laurel Weldon (New York: Oxford University Press, 2013).
[3] Ibid.

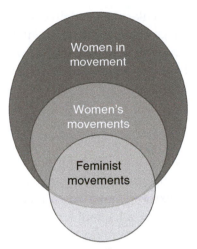

Figure 3.1 Women in movement, women's movements, and feminist movements.

forms of mobilization in terms of potential overlap, but also in regard to extension beyond.

These categories provide a useful but partial typology of gendered mobilization. They do not include every possible type of gendered mobilization and rigid adherence may even obscure important forms of gendered mobilization. A more expansive understanding of gendered mobilization would include movements in which other gender identities are central to mobilization, such as the men's movements or transgender movements (the latter of which may also fit within or overlap with the various categories being discussed above). You might also apply a gendered analysis to any movement. Are there any gendered patterns in who is participating, in the leadership structures, in the way that issues are prioritized, addressed, or framed?

It is also important to recognize that gender may not be the only relevant characteristic of a mobilization. An intersectional analysis – one that examines how gender intersects with race, class, sexuality, and other axes of identity – provides a more thorough analysis of gendered mobilization. It is a better means of highlighting the experiences of those at the intersection of multiple marginalities, such as women of color, working-class women, queer or trans women, disabled women, and so on. Such groups have often mobilized between or across movements, engaging in multi-issue organizing or work on several political fronts that may or may not put gender at the center, but that have a gendered impact nonetheless.[4]

Intersectional analysis can also show how a particular group might experience oppression on one dimension and privilege along another. An intersectional approach helps to uncover the challenges of working across difference in a single movement. It also helps to explain how women might end up in diametrically opposed movements.

SOCIAL MOVEMENTS AND ELECTIONS

Social movements are often framed as separate from electoral politics. Whereas an institutional mechanism for change is offered by electoral politics, social movements are often seen as extra-institutional, a means of creating change when institutions fail to provide adequate representation. There is, however, a "fuzzy and permeable boundary" that exists between institutionalized and noninstitutionalized politics, with social movements serving less as an alternative to electoral politics, and more as a complementary and intertwined mode of political action.[5] The ebb and flow of movements can shift electoral politics, and electoral politics can shift the ebb and flow of movements.

Political scientists have found several prominent linkages between social movements and elections.[6] First, social movements play a pivotal role in the creation, expansion, and maintenance of democracies, including the United States. Under the original Constitution, only white men aged 21 and older who owned land could vote. The abolition movement to end slavery, the women's suffrage movement, and various civil rights movements have worked toward expanding US democracy to include people of all gender, ethnoracial, and socioeconomic groups. This includes the expansion of voting rights as well as the subsequent mobilization of new electorates. Social movements can even produce new leaders in the

---

[4] Maylei Blackwell, *Chicana Power! Contested Histories of Feminism in the Chicano Movement* (Austin, TX: University of Texas Press, 2011); Celeste Montoya and Mariana Galvez Seminario, Guerreras y Puentes: The Theory and Praxis of Latina(x) Activism, *Politics, Groups, and Identities* (2020), doi.org/10.1080/2/21565503.2020.1821233

[5] Jack A. Goldstone, "More Social Movements or Fewer? Beyond Political Opportunity Structures to Relational Fields." *Theory and Society* 33(3–4) (2004): 333–65; Doug McAdam and Sidney Tarrow, Social Movements and Elections: Toward a Broader Understanding of the Political Context of Contention, in *Future of Social Movement Research: Dynamics, Mechanisms, and Processes*, ed. Jacqueline van Stekenlenburg, Conny Roggeband, and Bert Klandermans (Minneapolis, MN: University of Minnesota Press, 2013).

[6] Michael Heaney, Elections and Social Movements, in the Wiley-Blackwell *Encyclopedia of Social and Political Movements* online edn., 2013, doi.org/10.1002/9780470674871; Doug McAdam and Sidney Tarrow, Ballots and Barricades: On the Reciprocal Relationship between Elections and Social Movements, *Perspective on Politics* 8(2) (2010): 529–42.

electoral arena, as activists from marginalized groups seek institutional modes of change by running for office.

Another important link is between social movements and political parties. Parties and social movements have an important but uneasy symbiotic relationship. Parties are important targets for social movements because they can get concerns on the political agenda and are key to translating movement demands into policy changes. Social movements are important to parties because they can mobilize the electorate, providing a competitive advantage to political parties when they mobilize new or key constituencies.[7] At the same time, there is the possibility of hostility between the two as they compete for resources and over the priority and framing of issues. Social movement actors are often critical of parties for their perceived role in upholding the status quo. Parties can be critical of social movements, particularly when they see them as disrupting their policy agenda and potentially destabilizing the electoral coalitions necessary to keep them in power.

During cycles of protest – a time period in which social movement activity is expansive in its geographic scale; the number, size, and diversity of social groups participating; and the prevalence of disruptive and confrontational activity – social movements can substantially change the electoral landscape. In the United States, the success or failure of the two major parties depends on their ability to appeal to a wide swath of voters and mobilize an electoral coalition large enough to secure a plurality, if not a majority of votes. Mass movements can destabilize these coalitions. They put on the agenda new issues that challenge party platforms and mobilize different constituencies. This can polarize parties internally or from each other, and can even trigger significant party realignments.

Shifts in electoral regimes can also have significant and long-term impacts on the prospects for social movements, which is why groups may mobilize proactively for or against candidates that they see as helping or hurting their interests.[8] Social movements might also mobilize reactively, after the election. When the outcome of an election is seen as threatening the interests of the group, this may prompt mobilization as resistance. A favorable outcome might also serve to mobilize. If groups perceive a new administration as opening up political opportunities, they may see this as precisely the time to mobilize. More favorable election outcomes might

[7] Mildred A. Schwartz, Interactions between Social Movements and US Political Parties, *Party Politics* 16(5) (2010): 587–607.

[8] Kathleen M. Blee and Ashley Currier, How Local Social Movement Groups Handle a Presidential Election, *Qualitative Sociology* 29(3) (2006): 261–80.

also serve to demobilize movements. It may diminish the sense of urgency for some participants or coalition members.

An administration can also shape the mobilizing prospects of a group by easing or increasing restrictions or in the authorization of force. For example, many people noted the difference in the relative lack of police or national guard presence on January 6, when a primarily white group of protesters was expected, in comparison to other mobilizations by and for people of color, where law enforcement has responded in greater numbers and use of force. Although the First Amendment protects freedom of speech and assembly, government officials have been given a large degree of latitude in regulating and policing protest.

The interactions between race-gendered social movements and elections are a key component of US political history. The next two sections provide an overview of this history, setting the necessary context for understanding contemporary politics.

RACE-GENDERED MOBILIZATION IN US HISTORY

Race-gendered mobilization has played an important role in expanding US democracy, not only via the more recognized forms of women's and feminist movements but also by women who have fought for full citizenship rights through a diverse array of racial justice movements. Race-gendered mobilization has also been part of the powerful backlash and counter-mobilizations aimed at restricting access and maintaining inequality. This section examines two ways in which race-gendered mobilizations have profoundly impacted US electoral politics. First, it looks at efforts to establish citizenship rights. Here we start with the Nineteenth Amendment, expanding the traditional narrative of women's suffrage by using intersectional analysis that links it to mobilizations for and against racial suffrage and citizenship rights more broadly. The second focus is on the role that race-gendered mobilization played in the mid-twentieth-century movements that reshaped the political parties and their electoral coalitions.

Race-Gendered Mobilization within and beyond the Women's Suffrage Movement

One of the most celebrated gendered mobilizations in US history is the women's suffrage movement. In 2020, the US celebrated the hundredth anniversary of the Nineteenth Amendment establishing women's formal voting rights. This anniversary, however, did not hold the same meaning for all women. For some, this was not the defining moment or movement for establishing voting rights. An intersectional analysis that looks at gender and race both complicates and broadens the narrative. First, it helps to highlight the racial divisions within and surrounding the movement. Second, it examines gendered mobilization that occurred within various racial justice movements, some of which continued to be necessary long after formal voting rights were established. Finally, it examines gendered mobilization as a part of racial backlash.

Race and the Suffrage Movement

The women's suffrage movement was a decades-long fight. It started with an overlap and tenuous alliance with the abolition movement seeking to end slavery. Some of the earliest supporters of women's suffrage began their political journey as abolitionists. The first women's rights convention held at Seneca Falls, New York, in 1848 was organized by such women, including Elizabeth Cady Stanton and Lucretia Mott. The esteemed abolitionist Frederick Douglass spoke, as one of the few men and the only African American in attendance.

One of the first major divisions between the two movements occurred as the Fifteenth Amendment was being debated, passed, and ratified in 1870. It was one of the three Civil War amendments designed to ensure equality for African Americans after emancipation. The Fifteenth Amendment prohibited denying the right to vote on account of race, color, or previous condition of servitude. That women were not included caused a rift within the abolitionist movement, leading to the disbanding of the American Equal Rights Association as well as the emergence of two rival suffrage organizations. The American Woman Suffrage Association led by Lucy Stone supported the Fifteenth Amendment, seeing it as a step in the right direction. The National Woman Suffrage Association, led by Susan B. Anthony and Elizabeth Cady Stanton, vehemently opposed it for its exclusion of women. This split marked a shift by some from an antebellum suffrage ideology that "emphasized a common victimhood" between women and those adopting a postbellum suffrage ideology that "stressed white women's racial-cultural superiority to newly enfranchised male constituencies – not just black men, but also naturalized immigrant men."[9] This type of racist ideology was reflected in the following statement by Elizabeth Cady Stanton: "Think of Patrick and Sambo and Hans and Yung

---

[9] Louise Michele Newman, *White Women's Rights: The Racial Origins of Feminism in the United States* (New York: Oxford University Press, 1999).

Tung who do not know the difference between a Monarchy and Republic, who never read the Declaration of Independence or Webster's spelling book, making laws for Lydia Marie Child, Lucretia Mott or Fanny Kimble."[10]

When the two organizations merged in 1890, a relentless focus on the Nineteenth Amendment yielded exclusionary strategies to maintain an alliance with women's suffragist organizations in the South, many of whom did not allow Black members. This included leveraging racist rhetoric, such as justifying votes for white women as a means of maintaining white electoral power, as well as a reluctance to allow Black women to participate in public events. For example, Alice Paul – a leading white suffragist who later established the National Woman's Party and its fight for a constitutional amendment to enfranchise women – begrudgingly allowed the members of Black sorority Delta Sigma Theta to participate in the 1913 national suffrage parade, but only at the end of the parade, behind the men's section. Some accounts tell of sorority members, such as prominent journalist and activist Ida B. Wells, slipping away from their segregated sections to march with the white women of their geographic delegations.

Women of Color Mobilizing on Multiple Fronts

Despite the discrimination that they faced within the women's suffrage movement, women of color were still an important part of it. They were also mobilizing on other political fronts aimed at establishing political rights and justice for their communities. Black women were strong supporters of women's suffrage, something they pursued alongside other issues important to their own organizations. The National Association of Colored Women, which was formed in 1896, included among its membership prominent suffragists such as Harriet Tubman, Mary Church Terrell, and Ida B. Wells. It was a part of the outgrowth of the Black women's club movement, which addressed issues similar to those addressed in white women's clubs (suffrage, education, health, etc.), but also racial uplift and efforts to combat racism, including lynching.

Native, Mexican, and Asian American women were also engaged in the struggle for suffrage, often alongside broader struggles for citizenship rights and protections that were less focused on gender. The 1848 Treaty of Guadalupe-Hidalgo – ending the Mexican-American War and redrawing

---

[10]   Ann D. Gordon, *The Selected Papers of Elizabeth Cady Stanton and Susan B. Anthony*, vol. II, *Against an Aristocracy of Sex* (New Brunswick, NJ: Rutgers University Press, 2000).

the borders of the Southwest – promised but did not deliver full citizenship rights to the new Mexican Americans on the US side of the border. The 1882 Chinese Exclusion Act halted Chinese immigration and prohibited those already living in the United States from becoming citizens. Native American tribes were subjected to different treaties, some of which granted some voting rights, but for the most part Native Americans were involuntarily treated as wards and excluded from democratic participation, granted neither sovereignty nor full citizenship rights.

Like Black women, these women fought for women's suffrage alongside ethnoracial citizenship rights. Jovár Idar, much like Ida B. Wells, was a journalist who spoke out against the lynchings used to terrorize the Mexican American community in Texas. She wrote about racism but also supported women's suffrage and encouraged women to vote, founding and becoming the first president of La Liga Femenil Mexicaista (The League of Mexican Women) in 1911. In California and New Mexico, women like Maria Guadalupe Evangeline de Lopez and Adelina "Nina" Otero-Warren translated suffrage pamphlets and speeches into Spanish to reach Mexican American women. Mabel Ping-Hua Lee, a Chinese immigrant from Guangzhou, wrote essays on feminism and women's rights to vote. She notably rode on horseback in the 1912 New York City suffrage parade, even knowing she would not have access to the franchise given the restrictions of the Chinese Exclusion Act. Marie Louise Bottineau Baldwin, a North Dakota Turtle Mountain Chippewa, participated in suffrage events (like the 1913 parade and as part of the delegation to speak to Woodrow Wilson in 1914), as a part of her lifelong fight for Native American rights.

While women of color played an important role in securing the Nineteenth Amendment, their fight for the right to vote was far from over. They would mobilize again as part of the civil rights movement decades later, as well as a century later in the context of contemporary elections.

The Mobilization of White Womanhood in Racial Backlash

Not all women were mobilizing on behalf of expanding political rights. The gendered racial tension within the suffrage movement occurred alongside and in tandem with the wave of nationalistic white supremacist organizing that swept the rural South after the Civil War. For a short while after the Civil War amendments were passed, newly enfranchised Black men gained a voice in government for the first time in US history, not only by voting but also by running for office. Black political (and economic) power expanded dramatically, with more than 1,500 Black men holding public office in the South. This period was short-lived. As the federal government withdrew troops, a white backlash was mobilized to usher in the Jim Crow era of racial violence and oppression. An even bigger wave of white supremacist organizing emerged in the 1920s influenced by the spread of anti-Black racism following the postwar migration of Blacks from the South to the North and an increase in nationalistic anti-immigration sentiment fueled by World War I propaganda and a rise in religious and political fundamentalism.[11] This wave spread well beyond the South, extending all the way to the West Coast and to the northernmost states.

White women were a vital part of these movements, including those that had been working to expand democracy via the Nineteenth Amendment. Kathleen Blee argues that a particularly intriguing aspect of the 1920s Women of the KKK (Ku Klux Klan) was that while some Klanswomen sought to uphold both gender and racial hierarchies, others developed a complex ideology that carried gender equality into their struggle against Blacks, Jews, Catholics, labor radicals, socialists, Mormons, and immigrants.[12] While women were rarely involved in the violence or vigilantism perpetrated by the men, they helped in legitimizing organizations, planning events to mobilize the political base, and leading political assaults (often via boycotts and whispering campaigns) against businesses owned by people of color, political officials of color, and those who supported racial equality.

Mobilized white backlash successfully impeded the ability of people of color to participate in elections in many parts of the country. Poll taxes, literacy tests, grandfather clauses, as well as voter intimidation and violence were used against Black, Mexican, Asian, and Native Americans in the South and the West. In the northern cities, poll watchers targeted immigrants (often relying on racial and ethnic cues), demanding proof of citizenship. Gendered violence was a part of the intimidation; sexual assault was used against women of color and accusations of rape (against white women) were used to justify violence against men of color. It was not until the rise of the civil rights movement of the mid-twentieth century that groups were able to effectively push for federal protections.

[11] Kathleen M. Blee, *Understanding Racist Activism: Theory, Methods and Research* (New York: Routledge, 2017).

[12] Kathleen M. Blee, Women in the 1920s' Ku Klux Klan Movement, in *US Women in Struggle: A Feminist Studies Anthology*, ed. Claire Goldberg Moses and Heidi I. Hartmann (Urbana, IL: University of Illinois Press, 1995), pp. 89–109.

Race-Gendered Mobilization and Party Realignment

After the Nineteenth Amendment, the movement for women's rights entered a period of abeyance that would continue until the 1960s brought forth a new wave of feminist mobilization. This is not to say that gender mobilization (or the fight for women's rights) stopped, but rather that the women who were mobilizing were often doing so on other political fronts. Two of the most influential movements of the mid twentieth century were the labor movement and the civil rights movement. Race-gendered mobilization was an important part of these movements, playing a role in the overlapping cycles of protest with each other and with the women's liberation movement. All three movements played an important role in reshaping the political parties. At the start of the twentieth century, the Republican Party was seen as more supportive of gender and racial equality, taking a liberal democratic approach of supporting individual rights. It was under their leadership and support that the Thirteenth, Fourteenth, Fifteenth, and Nineteenth Amendments were added to the Constitution. In contemporary elections, it is the Democratic Party that is often seen as more favorable to gender and racial equality – something that is reflected in party platforms and partisan voting gaps. The next section looks at the realignments that took place and the role that race-gendered (and classed) mobilization played throughout.

Post-Suffrage to New Deal Era

The racial alignment of the Democratic and Republican Parties at the start of the twentieth century was shaped in the post–Civil War era. (Northern) Republicans played a vital role in establishing the formal constitutional rights to racial equality. Black men registered to vote, most identifying with the Republican Party. The ability of Black men to fully participate in elections, however, was short-lived. In southern states like Louisiana, Black registration rates went from almost 100 percent to the single digits, where they would remain until the civil rights movement began.[13] White elites transformed the South into a one-party racial autocracy and the "Solid South" became the electoral cornerstone of the national Democratic Party. As discussed in the previous section, women were included among both the oppressors and the oppressed.

---

[13] Luke Keele, William Cubbison, and Ismail White, Suppressing Black Votes: A Historical Case Study of Voting Restrictions in Louisiana, *American Political Science Review* 115(2) (2021): 694–700.

After the Nineteenth Amendment was passed, women were slow to enter the electorate and did not constitute a distinct or influential voting bloc. While some women continued to work for women's rights and in other movements, the mass movement dissipated. Both parties worked to incorporate (primarily white) women voters, but gender was not a particularly salient dimension of party platforms or identification. There is some evidence to suggest that early women voters favored the Republican Party.[14] It had been a Republican Congress that passed the Nineteenth Amendment, which may have garnered the favor of suffragists, many of whom were middle-class Protestant white women. Those identities were also directly associated with Republican identification and access to the resources that increased likelihood of voter turnout. Geography also played a factor, with (primarily white) women more likely to support Democrats in Democratic-leaning states (the Solid South) and Republicans in Republican-leaning states (the North and West).

The first racial partisan shift occurred in the New Deal Era of the 1930s. The Great Depression and the labor movement made class a particularly salient dimension of partisan politics. Democratic President Franklin D. Roosevelt's economic policies helped create a northern, liberal, labor wing of the Democratic Party. African Americans in the North, many of whom were a part of the working class, started to move to the Democratic Party. Roosevelt's economic policies were also well liked in the poverty-stricken South. While Roosevelt had expressed pro-civil rights ideas, he retained southern support by mostly staying silent on issues of race. The New Deal provided disproportionate socioeconomic relief. For example, the government subsidized the mass production of subdivisions with racial covenants while refusing to insure mortgages in neighborhoods that were predominantly Black (a practice called "redlining"). This effectively mandated segregation and contributed to contemporary patterns in discriminatory policing and education inequality.

The party positions on gender reflected some of the socioeconomic and ideological divisions that were emerging in feminism. Democrats adopted the positions of working-class socialist feminists, which included women of color, in the labor movement. They advocated for protectionist labor policies aimed at improving the working conditions for women and children employed in factories. While women faced discrimination within

---

[14] Christina Wolbrecht and Kevin J. Corder, *A Century of Votes for Women* (New York: Cambridge University Press, 2020).

the larger labor movement, they mobilized in their own unions, such as the International Ladies' Garment Workers' Union, and demonstrated their worth as union allies. These protectionist policies were at odds with the liberal feminist anti-discrimination approach to equal employment rights, a position supported by the Republicans, who were the first to add the Equal Rights Amendment (ERA) to their party platform in 1940. The ERA had been first introduced by Alice Paul in 1923, and originally stated "Men and women shall have equal rights throughout the United States and every place subject to its jurisdiction." Paul rewrote it in 1943, to better reflect the language in both the Fifteenth and Nineteenth Amendments, as "Equality of rights under the law shall not be denied or abridged by the United States or by any state on account of sex." The Democrats added this to their platform in 1944. In 1950 and 1953 the ERA was passed – with greater support by Republicans – in the US Senate, with a provision that allowed special protections for women. It was blocked, however, in the US House by (Southern) Democrats.

The Civil Rights Era

The second major partisan shift started in the context of the Black civil rights movement, which began in the 1940s and continued into the 1960s. This movement addressed a range of issues related to racial injustice, including the ongoing challenges to voting rights. Although rarely in the spotlight, Black women's organizations and women in Black churches were an important part of this mobilizing effort. They helped organize and run voter drives. Later, other women of color would play a similarly vital role in mobilizing their communities in the Chicano, Asian American, and American Indian movements.

Initially, Republicans were the more receptive, albeit sometime reluctant, supporters of civil rights. The Republican Eisenhower administration worked to desegregate the armed forces, the federal bureaucracy, and the schools; they sent troops into southern states to enforce the Supreme Court's ruling in *Brown v. The Board of Education* when southern whites mobilized to obstruct it. They initiated and helped pass the Civil Rights Act of 1957, which included a number of important provisions protecting voting rights and established the Civil Rights Division of the Justice Department. But the movement was also gaining support from Democrats who now faced a fracturing electoral coalition. Democratic President John F. Kennedy won the presidency with the New Deal/labor coalition of Black and southern white voters. Like Roosevelt, Kennedy initially tried to balance the demands of both, but before his death had started to develop a proactive civil rights agenda. Even knowing the partisan consequences, his successor Lyndon B. Johnson (a Texan) continued this agenda. It was in his reelection in 1964 that some white southerners cast their first votes for the Republican Party.

The 1960s were turbulent. The civil rights movement had gained momentum, but it faced violent backlash in the South. During the Freedom Summer of 1964, Black women marched alongside men, and were not spared the violence. Police often used tear gas and billy clubs on the participants of peaceful marches. One of the most powerful testimonies in Congress for the Voting Rights Act of 1965 came from Fannie Lou Hamer, a key organizer in the Mississippi Freedom Summer. In her testimony, she spoke of the beating and sexualized abuse she experienced at the hands of Winona police after she was arrested for attending a voter registration workshop.

As the Democratic Party was moving to take more progressive stances on racial equality, the Republican Party started moving in the opposite direction, influenced by a different movement. A white southern segregationist movement seeking to uphold racial hierarchy, once again inspired a national backlash. This included white women, who mobilized as mothers against the desegregation of the schools.[15] George Wallace, governor of Alabama and a staunch segregationist, ran against Johnson in the 1964 Democratic primary, with some success not only in the South but also among the white working class in the industrial North. He left the Democratic Party, running as a third-party candidate in the 1968 presidential election. The Republican Party, fearing that Wallace might split the conservative vote and seeing an opportunity in the destabilization of the Democratic electoral coalition, began to pursue a "Southern Strategy" that reversed previous positions supporting racial equality and instead relied on "targeting white southerners who felt alienated from, angry at, and resentful of the policies that granted equality."[16] This included courting both those who held explicitly racist positions as well as the white southern moderates who might have accepted an abstract notion of equality but objected to federal efforts to achieve it. The party accomplished this through subtle racial coding or "dog whistle" politics. This strategy helped secure a presidential victory for Republican Richard

---

[15] Elizabeth Gillespie McRae, *Mothers of Massive Resistance: White Women and the Politics of White Supremacy* (New York: Oxford University Press, 2018).

[16] Angie Maxwell and Todd Shields, *The Long Southern Strategy: How Chasing White Votes in the South Changed American Politics* (New York: Oxford University Press, 2021).

Nixon – once a supporter of civil rights – in 1968, and charted a new course for the party.

Women's Liberation

The third movement reshaping the parties focused on gender. The feminist movement was politically diverse, with multiple wings representing very different understandings and approaches to gender equality. There was a liberal wing, focused on anti-discrimination laws and working within the institutions, and there was the more radical women's liberation wing, focused on a larger societal transformation. Women were also mobilized, within and outside of the movement, on issues of racial, sexual, and class equality, which sometimes became a source of contention within the movement. Front and center on the liberal policy front were employment discrimination and the Equal Rights Amendment. The more radical wing took on abortion and gender violence.

The shifting coalitions caused by the racial realignment had important implications for women's rights. The movement of white southerners, many of whom held traditional and socially conservative policy preferences, into the Republican Party and the movement of moderate northerners into the Democratic Party started to influence party positions on gender. Women's rights became linked to race in various ways, as feminists sought to add sex to civil rights legislation that Democrats increasingly backed. The Republicans, however, continued to support women's rights until a growing movement of conservative (mostly white) women gave them reason not to.

As with the civil rights movement, the feminist movement inspired a powerful backlash. The STOP ERA ("Stop Taking Our Privileges") campaign was the start of an influential movement of socially conservative women that helped justify a change in course for Republicans who had previously been supportive of the amendment. It was led by Phyllis Schlafly, a conservative attorney, author, and activist. Schlafly argued that the ERA would take away women's gender privileges such as "dependent wife" benefits and alimony, end separate bathrooms, and subject women to the draft. The movement – made up of mostly white, Evangelical women from the middle and upper classes – gained grassroots support and momentum, spreading in the suburbs and rural areas through church organizations and Bible study groups. The movement claimed to be defending the real rights of women – the right to be in the home as a wife and mother – and used traditional gender symbolism through the campaign (i.e. lobbying legislators with home-made pies, bread, and jam).

They drew heavily from conceptualizations of traditional (white) mother-hood, casting aspersions on those not falling within its parameters (the unmarried, single moms, gay women, and women of color), who they conflated with feminists and feminism. Anti-feminism, like white back-lash, was aimed at preserving a particular way of life, one imbued with intersecting social hierarchies. When feminists planned the 1977 National Women's Conference in Houston, Schlafly organized a pro-life, pro-family rally and counterconference.

Phyllis Schlafly's approach became part of a "Long Southern Strategy," with the GOP adopting the demonization of feminism and working to court (white) women voters on the basis of religion and family values.[17] It was institutionalized into party platforms in the 1980s, as the social conservative wing of the Republican Party grew in strength.[18] After forty years of support, the Republican Party removed the ERA from its platform and started adopting socially conservative platforms that were increas-ingly hostile to women's rights (and LGBT rights) and more supportive of traditional gender hierarchies. Although not all Republican women were explicitly antagonistic toward women's rights, they were not supportive of them either.[19] The agnostic laissez-faire approach of those who were both economic conservatives and social moderates posed little opposition to those hostile to feminism.

As we have seen, an intersectional approach to gendered mobilization helps to uncover all the different ways that women were mobilizing and how that varied mobilization overlapped and interacted to reshape the political parties. In the next section, we take a look at the role that race-gendered mobilization plays in contemporary elections.

RACE-GENDERED MOBILIZATIONS AND CONTEMPORARY ELECTIONS

In the new millennium, the oppositional trajectories of race-gendered mobilization have continued. Scholars have argued that the election of Trump helped prompt a new cycle of protest, starting with the 2017 Women's March.[20] This section provides an overview of the various

---

[17] Ibid.

[18] Christina Wolbrecht, *The Politics of Women's Rights: Parties, Positions, and Change* (Princeton, NJ: Princeton University Press, 2000).

[19] Ronnee Schreiber, *Righting Women: Conservative Women and American Politics* (New York: Oxford University Press, 2008).

[20] David S. Meyer and Sidney Tarrow, *The Resistance: The Dawn of the Anti-Trump Opposition Movement* (New York: Oxford University Press, 2018).

movements participating in this period of heightened protest. It looks at the dynamics of the contemporary progressive and conservative movements and their interaction with elections. This includes an examination of the ongoing battle for voting rights. While voter suppression never went away entirely, there has been a resurgence of restrictive policies within the last decade. The mobilization on both sides of this battle shaped the 2020 presidential election and is still playing out in its aftermath. The patterns emerging are not unlike those of the past, and will determine the future path of US democracy.

Race-Gendered Mobilization on the Left

The 2017 Women's March was a reactive mobilization, intended to demonstrate resistance to the election of Donald J. Trump and the threat he was perceived to represent. What started as a call for a women's march on social media – initially drawing on a mostly white, elite liberal feminist movement – transformed into a broader-based, intersectional march that became what is believed to be one of the largest single-day protests in US history.[21] More than just a women's march, the massive scale of this event was achieved by drawing on an array of existing activist networks as well as mobilizing people (of all ages) to participate in protest activity for the first time.

Part of the success of this mobilization should be attributed to the multiracial team of women community activists who chaired the Washington, DC march: Carmen Perez, Linda Sarsour, Tamika Mallory, and Bob Bland. They were recruited in response to the criticism levied against the initial framing of the event in the viral Facebook invite for the "Million Woman March." The original organizers, a group of primarily white women, were criticized for appropriating the name of an event that had been organized by Black women in 1997. Activists from communities of color questioned whether white women had the authority to lead such a movement, given that 53 percent of white women had voted for Trump in 2016. Furthermore, groups questioned the framing of a march around women specifically, given that the Trump administration represented a threat to so many other groups, including queer communities and communities of color.

The new leadership worked to reframe the march in more intersectional terms. Its "unity principles," created with the input of more than

---

21 Marie Berry and Erica Chenoweth, Who Made the Women's March, in *The Resistance: The Dawn of the Anti-Trump Opposition Movement*, ed. David S. Meyer and Sidney Tarrow (New York: Oxford University Press, 2018), 75–89.

twenty leaders from various movements, included traditional feminist commitments such as reproductive rights and gender violence, but also included LGBTQ rights, worker rights, civil rights, disability rights, immigrant rights, and environmental justice. The outreach was also intentionally intersectional. It drew on two streams of social justice activism: a more institutional stream that included the larger and more established progressive and feminist organizations, for example NOW, Planned Parenthood, CODEPINK, ACLU, AFL-CIO, and the National Union of Healthcare Workers; and a younger grassroots stream of activism, including online groups and networks, such as Occupy, Black Lives Matter (BLM), immigrant justice, Indigenous rights, and climate action.

This younger grassroots stream is notable for a number of reasons. First, it represents a new and diverse generation of activists, one that reflects the growing racial (and gender/sexual) diversity of the population. These activists bring with them a different model of activism, one that is more decentralized and democratized. This "leaderful" approach allowed for better representation of women, people of color, and LGBTQ activists than had previous generations of leftist organizing. Second, it is a group frustrated with party politics. This included animus toward what is perceived as the moderate tendencies of the Democratic Party. Many of these movements mobilized under the Obama administration, a period of ostensibly more open political opportunities for progressive mobilizing but also one of policy disappointment. The youth-led Dreamers' movement grew out of the 2006 immigration rights protests under Bush, but continued mobilization throughout the Obama administration, both to push for the promised policy reform but also to protest the increased level of mass deportations. The Occupy Wall Street movement began in 2011 and addressed growing economic inequality and corporate influence in politics. It criticized the bailout of banks and corporations over the distribution of public resources. BLM, addressing policy brutality and racially motivated violence against Black people, began on social media in 2013 after the acquittal of George Zimmerman in the shooting death of Black teenager Trayvon Martin. The protests against the Dakota Access Pipeline, and its threat to water sources on and near the Standing Rock Indian Reservation, started in the spring of 2016, raising the intersecting issues of Indigenous and environmental rights. These movements were all critical of Obama, but their participants also understood the increased threat of a Trump administration.

The Women's March tipped off a renewed cycle of protest and provided a coalitional focal point for "The Resistance." The Women's March organization continued to work after January 2017, holding subsequent marches in 2018 and in 2019. Beyond that, much of their work was aimed at participating in and endorsing the events organized by the broad array of partners they had amassed in the original march. Many of the movements that predated the Trump administration continued their work, albeit with a renewed sense of urgency and sometimes with a broader array of support as they tapped into the expanding networks of oppositional activists. New mobilizations emerged as well, such as the #MeToo movement addressing sexual violence and harassment and the youth-led March for Our Lives, working for gun reform after a mass school shooting in Florida.

Some of the mobilizing energy of "The Resistance" turned to electoral politics, with the first impact seen in the 2018 election. A unified Republican government meant that much of the agenda feared by protesters was being realized, parts of it with great speed and devastating results. The 2018 midterm elections were unprecedented in a number of ways. Fifty-three percent of eligible voting-age citizens voted, up almost twelve percentage points from 2014 and the highest midterm turnout in four decades.[22] This included increases in turnout among youth (+ 16%), Asian Americans (+ 13%), Hispanics (+ 13%), and African Americans (11%), and contributed to a record-breaking number of women (127), people of color (116), and LGBTQ (10) members of Congress. Thirteen of the thirty-six nonincumbent women elected to the US House were women of color – all Democrats. Some of the candidates came – if not directly then indirectly – from the contemporary movements. Most notable, perhaps, was the election to the House of "the Squad": Alexandria Ocasio-Cortez, Ayanna Pressley, Rashida Tlaib, and Ilhan Omar. The four Democratic women of color are young, unapologetic progressives who were quick to chastise not only the Trump administration and Republicans but also Democratic leadership. They ran grassroots campaigns and have maintained their activist approach while in office, participating in direct action and utilizing social media repertoires of action.

Race-Gendered Mobilization on the (Far) Right

While the Trump administration was perceived as a threat by some, to others it was received as an opening for political opportunities. The mobilization on January 6, 2021 to reject Trump's defeat also had deeper roots.

---

[22] US Census Bureau, Current Population Survey, Voting and Registration Supplement, www.census.gov/programs-surveys/cps.html

It connected various streams of right and far-right movements, some of which had arisen in resistance to the Obama administration and were legitimized and emboldened under Trump. Like the Women's March, the Save America rally was, in part, initiated by a group of white women, albeit a group with very different politics and coalition partners. Kylie Jane Kremer, the executive director of Women for America First, filed the permit for the event. Her organization was joined by two other right-wing women's organizations, Phyllis Schlafly Eagles and Moms for America. Also a part of the event were two influential right-wing organizations, the Tea Party Patriots (cofounded by Tea Party movement activists Jenny Beth Martin, Amy Kremer, and Mark Meckler) and Turning Point Action (a student-oriented organization led by Charlie Kirk).

One of the most important movements shaping Trump support in 2016 and again in 2020 was the Tea Party. It first mobilized in 2009, after the inauguration of Barack Obama, the first Black US president who had been elected by a multiracial coalition (with record levels of Black turnout). While the Obama administration was an important target of the Tea Party, so was the Republican Party. They criticized it for its moderation, with frustration aimed at the "compassionate conservativism" espoused by former Republican President George W. Bush. The Tea Party was disproportionately white and often focused on the racially coded framing of issues that had been used in the past. Central among these was a staunch anti-immigration stance with an emphasis on national security. These issues would become the focus of the Freedom Caucus – a group formed by Republicans, in Congress in 2015, many of whom were ideologically aligned with the Tea Party movement and were elected in 2012 after successfully challenging moderate Republican incumbents.

Women played an important part in the Tea Party. Whereas the party's rhetoric often served to reify racial and class inequalities, their approach to gender was more complicated. As with earlier iterations of the conservative movement, Tea Party women drew on motherhood and pro-family frames in their activism, arguing big government was harmful to American families and promoted women's dependence on government rather than empowerment.[23] Participation in the movement itself became a form of political empowerment for these women, some taking on important

---

[23] Melissa M. Deckman, *Tea Party Women: Mama Grizzlies, Grassroots Leaders, and the Changing Face of America* (New York: New York University Press, 2016).

leadership roles and even entering the electoral realm as political candidates.[24] Tea Party activists used pro-women and even pro-feminist rhetoric to support their conservative positions, including that of gun rights and restrictive immigration policies. The resonance and power of this type of gendered activism, and the growing importance of the Tea Party, were perhaps best foretold by the nomination of "Mama Grizzly" Sarah Palin as the vice-presidential candidate in 2008. Her nomination was seen as a strategic move by Republican presidential nominee John McCain (who had traditionally been considered more of a moderate) to appeal to the far right contingent, but also as a possible appeal to moderate white women, who had supported Hillary Clinton but were disillusioned by her loss to Obama.

Although Obama ultimately won the election, so did many Tea Party candidates at national and state levels. The Tea Party movement would become the growing right wing of the party and its members – voters and officeholders – the key supporters of the Trump campaign, where the racialization became less coded and more blatant. The Trump campaign in 2016 drew heavily from this wing of the party. Throughout his campaign, Trump praised the Tea Party and spoke directly and explicitly to their concerns, particularly in regard to immigration and national security. In the speech announcing his candidacy, he promised to suspend immigration from certain parts of the world. Using right-wing race-gendered strategies, he stated that "Radical Islam is anti-woman, anti-gay and anti-American" and that Mexicans were "bringing drugs, they're bringing crime. They're rapists … "[25]

The Trump presidency reenergized the various elements of the Tea Party movement, who embraced "Trumpism," mobilizing on the president's behalf and in his defense against the protests of "The Resistance." Furthermore, the president emboldened far-right extremist groups. Throughout his campaign and presidency, Trump signaled his support, circulating their ideas and materials, refusing to disavow them, and even going so far as to remove government resources designated for investing and combating right-wing extremism. A series of well-publicized rallies were held, bringing together self-identified members of white nationalist

[24]   Meghan A. Burke, *Race, Gender, and Class in the Tea Party: What the Movement Reflects about Mainstream Ideologies* (London: Lexington Books, 2015).
[25]   Full Text: Donald Trump Announces a Presidential Bid, *Washington Post*, June 16, 2015, www.washingtonpost.com/news/post-politics/wp/2015/06/16/full-text-donald-trump-announces-a-presidential-bid/

groups and militias. The first was a night-time rally held in Charlottesville, Virginia, on August 11, 2017 to protest the city's plans to remove the statue of Confederate General Robert E. Lee. The spectacle included pro-testers, many of them young white men, carrying torches and chanting "Jews will not replace us!" The Unite the Right Rally was held the next day. Participants carried flags and wore clothing with the symbols of the Tea Party, the Confederacy, neo-Nazis, and the KKK. That day, a rally participant deliberately drove his car into a crowd of counter-protesters, killing a young woman and injuring nineteen others. Trump responded initially with statements commenting on the "violence on many sides" and later that there were "very fine people on both sides."[26] It would be one of the many times he signaled his favoring of white supremacist groups. This event, and Trump's response to it, also had electoral implica-tions, as detailed by Melanye Price and Kelly Dittmar in Chapter 1. Joe Biden pointed to this as the moment he decided to run for president, and racial justice movement advocates sought to hold him accountable to promises that he would "restore the soul of the nation" by addressing the scourge of white supremacy.

The Contemporary Battle for Voting Rights

Even with the Voting Rights Act of 1965, voter suppression has never gone away and has in fact seen a resurgence in the United States, particu-larly in the past decade. Starting after the 2010 midterm election – which ushered in a red wave of Republicans into many statehouses – states began passing restrictive voting laws shown to disproportionately impact voters of color.[27] Republicans justified this as a necessary move to prevent voter fraud, which is an extremely rare occurrence. They began framing voting as a privilege rather than a right. While many of these new restrict-ive laws were challenged, a particularly devastating blow against voting rights occurred with the 2013 Supreme Court 5–4 decision in *Shelby County v. Holder.* The conservative majority ruled to remove a provision of the act that provided federal oversight of new laws passed in states with histories of voter discrimination. This effectively returned power to the

---

[26] Ayesha Rascoe, A Year after Charlottesville, Not Much Has Changed for Trump, *NPR,* August 11, 2018, www.npr.org/2018/08/11/637665414/a-year-after-charlottesville-not-much-has-changed-for-trump

[27] Election 2016: Voting Laws by the Numbers, Brennan Center for Justice, expert brief, September 28, 2016, www.brennancenter.org/our-work/research-reports/election-2016-restrictive-voting-laws-numbers

states, making it easier for them to pass and implement discriminatory laws before they could be challenged.

The 2016 election was the first presidential election after *Shelby*. Fourteen states had new restrictive voting laws in place for the first time, in addition to the six that had already done so after 2010. Included among these were several notable swing states where Donald Trump won: Wisconsin, Ohio, Virginia, Georgia, Florida, and Arizona. In addition to restrictive voting laws, many of these states engaged in other questionable practices, such as removing voters from registration lists (voter purges) and limiting the places and times where voters can cast their votes. According to the Brennan Center, approximately 33 million voters were purged nationwide between 2014 and 2018, a significant increase from previous years and at a rate 40 percent higher in jurisdictions that had previously been subject to preclearance. The reduction of polling opportunities increased burdensome waiting times, particularly in communities of color.

PANDEMICS, PROTESTS, AND THE 2020 ELECTION

The 2020 election was unprecedented on a number of fronts. The United States, like the rest of the world, was dealing with the ravages of the COVID-19 pandemic. The Trump administration was slow and limited in its response, and the health and economic costs were disproportionately felt by communities of color. The summer of 2020 and the months leading up to the election were characterized by high levels of protest activity, with clashes between the two polarized movements in the streets and in political institutions.

On the left were the Black Lives Matter protests. The recorded killing of George Floyd by a Minneapolis police officer on May 25th, two months after the death of Breonna Taylor, who was fatally shot in her apartment by Louisville police, inspired another record-breaking mobilization that peaked on June 6, 2020, when nearly a half a million people tuned out in nearly 550 locations across the United States.[28] In the months of protests, it is estimated that anywhere from 15 to 26 million people participated, potentially making this the largest movement in US history. The scale demonstrated a significant shift in the movement and in public perception, which was now more favorable to it than in the past.

---

[28] Larry Buchanan, Quoctrumg Buid, and Jugal K. Patel, Black Lives Matter May Be the Largest Movement in US History, *New York Times*, July 3, 2020, www.nytimes.com/interactive/2020/07/03/us/george-floyd-protests-crowd-size.html

Mobilization on the right was often in the form of counter-protest. From Georgia to Oregon, violent clashes broke out between BLM protesters and far-right groups, such as the Proud Boys. These protests made it on to the presidential debate stage. When Trump was asked by Fox News correspondent Chris Wallace if he was ready to denounce the violence of the white supremacist and militia groups at these protests, he notably responded, "Proud Boys, stand back and stand by." Right-wing protest was also a major part of the anti-lockdown protests, which included mainstream Republicans, far-right groups, and armed militia members. The FBI arrested thirteen men linked to a militia group for plotting to kidnap Gretchen Whitmer, the governor of Michigan.

All these protests may have played an important role in mobilizing voters. Social movement scholars have shown the protests can greatly increase turnout at the polls by increasing the salience of political issues and motivating participation. Social movement organizations also play a more direct role in registering voters and getting them to the polls. Not only do they work to facilitate voter enthusiasm and a sense of urgency, but they are a vital means of helping voters navigate restrictive voting laws and practices. This was the case in 2018 and in 2020 – when voters not only had to navigate voter suppression but also the pandemic. Voter turnout in 2020 was record-breaking. Two-thirds of eligible US voters cast ballots. This included increased turnout by Black, Latinx, Asian, and Native Americans in places with long histories of voter suppression. Most notable were Arizona and Georgia, two states that ultimately flipped from red to blue in presidential vote choice. While much attention was given to particular groups and leaders in the light of these successes in the weeks subsequent to the election, this extraordinary mobilization effort should be attributed to the vast multiracial coalition of local and national organizations. Gendered mobilization, in its expansive and intersectional understanding, was an important component of this. Women of color played a vital role in leading the initiative.

The most visible leader was Stacey Abrams, but she was joined by an extensive network of women of color activists. After losing the 2018 Georgia gubernatorial race to then Secretary of State Brian Kemp in a questionable election characterized by large voter purges, among other voter suppression tactics, Stacey Abrams started Fair Fight, a national voting rights organization rooted in Georgia. But she had started her voter mobilization effort much earlier. At the end of 2013, then Georgia House minority leader Abrams started the New Georgia Project focused on registering minority voters across the state for the 2014 midterm elections.

Fair Fight (led by Lauren Groh-Wargo) and the New Georgia Project (led by Nsé Ufot) worked alongside numerous other organizations founded and/or led by (primarily Black) women of color in registering and mobilizing voters for both the November presidential election and the January runoff election that gave the US Senate to the Democrats. This includes Georgia organizations like the Georgia STAND-UP led by Deborah Scott, The People's Agenda led by Helen Butler, Pro Georgia led by Tamieka Atkins, and the Georgia Latino Alliance for Human Rights led by Adelina Nichols. They worked with other national organizations also led by women of color: Black Voters Matter founded by LaTosha Brown and currently led by Wendy Sherman, the National Coalition on Black Civic Participation led by Melanie Campbell, and Mijente – a Latinx organization led by Marisa Franco.

In Arizona, mobilization efforts had also started long before the 2020 election. In 2010, a movement of mostly youth and immigrants began to emerge to fight against the restrictive anti-immigrant measures. Some of these youth leaders, who were Latinx and queer, later helped to facilitate a coalition with LGBTQ groups working to fight the same-sex marriage ban.[29] A progressive network continued to grow and mobilize. By the 2016 election, that network was able to secure several notable local victories, including a Democratic majority in the Phoenix City Council, the defeat of Maricopa Sheriff Joe Arpaio, and the recall of anti-immigration leader Russell Pearce. Like in Georgia, the coalition that ended up flipping the state was a multiracial one full of women leaders and activists, including a number of Latinas and Native American women. This includes Arizona organizations such as Poder in Action, led by Viri Hernandez; environmental and social justice organization Chispa, led by Laura Jimena Dent; Our Voice, Our Vote Arizona, codirected by Cymone Bolding; and the Native Vote Election Protection Project, part of the Indian Legal Clinic at Arizona State University College of Law, coordinated by Patty Ferguson Bohnee. It also included national organizations like Four Directions Vote, directed by Barb and Donna Semans, and Voto Latino, led by Maria Teresa Kumar.

These coalitions did what many thought was impossible: they achieved record levels of turnout among hard-to-mobilize groups during one of the worst moments in contemporary US history and against all odds achieved Democratic victories in two voter-suppressed red-leaning states.

---

[29] See Erin Mayo-Adams, *Queer Alliances: How Power Shapes Political Movement Formations* (Stanford, CA: Stanford University Press, 2020).

A NEW ADMINISTRATION AND PROSPECTS FOR CHANGE

While the Trump administration played a significant role in motivating and shaping this most recent cycle of protest, does the new Biden administration signal its end? At the time of writing this is hard to ascertain. On the left, even though "The Resistance" had roots in larger ongoing movements, the perceived urgency to mobilize may be greatly reduced for certain segments of the movement. At the same time, the Democrats generally and Joe Biden in particular have signaled a return to moderate politics with an emphasis on bipartisanship. There will still be a need for progressive mobilizing, both within and outside of institutions. Some of the newest members of Congress, including Missouri Democratic Representative Cori Bush – a nurse, pastor, and BLM activist representing St. Louis – have strong activist roots and are bringing those protest politics into Congress.

On the right, the political opportunities provided by the Trump administration may be diminishing, particularly for far-right groups. There is, however, no indication that the movement will be dissipating; rather, it is gearing up for resistance. The Stop the Steal mobilizations continue, with many Trump and right-wing loyalists in Congress and in local office. In the spring of 2020, a new record-breaking wave of voter suppression legislation was introduced.

The race-gendered mobilization on both sides is causing fractures within and placing pressure on the major political parties in ways that have significant implications for future elections. Currently, there are no clear indications of a realignment or the direction that might take. The United States is in a precarious moment in its democratic history, with movements on one side mobilizing to expand and protect political participation and those on the other looking to restrict it. An intersectional analysis of social movements helps to highlight the role that gender and race have and continue to play in US elections.

4 Voter Participation and Turnout: More Diverse Electorate, New Forms of Activism, Record Turnout

The 2020 election will always be remembered for the tumultuous context in which it occurred – a pandemic, rising unemployment, social and racial justice protests. But from a women's participation perspective, it was a record-breaking election in every way – registration, turnout, activism, and electoral successes at every level. The breakthroughs in 2020 were quite fitting because they coincided with the 100th anniversary of passage of the Nineteenth Amendment to the US Constitution (1920), guaranteeing the right of women to vote.

The Centennial Women's Suffrage celebration greatly elevated awareness of the many women of color who had played major roles in the women's suffrage fight but were largely excluded from historical accounts of the movement. The ostracism put a spotlight on the country's rapidly changing demographics, notably the nation's growing racial/ethnic diversity, generational shifts, sexuality and gender identities, partisan/ideological polarization – and their interrelationships. Greater awareness of the more diverse women's electorate begat new issues, activists, organizations, forms of activism, informational sources, and political mobilization techniques.

In this chapter, we present a brief history of women's suffrage, examine the changing demographics and party identifications of women voters, and highlight the major events that increased their activism in 2020. We also discuss how the Biden and Trump campaigns targeted subgroups of women by focusing on major issues of importance to them, detail how various women-centric organizations registered and mobilized women to vote, and highlight the changing media landscape and women's roles in it. The chapter ends with a review of how the pandemic prompted changes in the registration and voting processes which, along with women's activism, resulted in the highest voter turnout since 1900, with women yet again turning out at a higher rate than men.

A BRIEF HISTORY OF WOMEN'S SUFFRAGE

The notion of women's voting rights began at the nation's birth (see Text Box 4.1) when women like Abigail Adams urged men writing the Declaration of Independence to include women: "If particular care and attention is not paid to the ladies, we are determined to foment a rebellion, and will not hold ourselves bound by any laws in which we have no voice or representation." Was she ever right!

TEXT BOX 4.1 The History of the Women's Vote

Today, every US citizen who is 18 years of age by Election Day and meets state residency requirements is eligible to cast a ballot. However, women, African Americans, Native Americans, and members of certain religious groups were not allowed to vote during the early years of the country's history. In 1787, the US Constitution granted each state government the power to determine who could vote. Individual states wrote their own suffrage laws. Early voting qualifications required that an eligible voter be a white man, 21 years of age, Protestant, and a landowner. Many citizens who recognized the importance of the right to vote led the suffrage movement.

One Hundred Years Toward the Women's Vote

Compiled by E. Susan Barber

1776

Abigail Adams writes to her husband, John, at the Continental Congress in Philadelphia, asking that he and the other men – who are at work on the Declaration of Independence – "Remember the Ladies." The Declaration's wording specifies that "all men are created equal."

1848

The first women's rights convention in the United States is held in Seneca Falls, New York. Many participants sign the "Declaration of Sentiments and Resolutions," which outlines the main issues and goals for the emerging women's movement. Thereafter, women's rights meetings are held on a regular basis.

1861–65

The American Civil War disrupts suffrage activity as women, North and South, divert their energies to "war work." The war, however, serves as training ground, as women gain important organizational and occupational skills they will later use in postwar organizational activity.

1866

Elizabeth Cady Stanton and Susan B. Anthony form the American Equal Rights Association, an organization for white and Black women and men dedicated to the goal of universal suffrage.

1868

The Fourteenth Amendment is ratified. It extends to all citizens the protections of the Constitution against unjust state laws. This amendment is the first to define citizens and voters as "male."

1870

The Fifteenth Amendment enfranchises Black men.

1870–75

Several women – including Virginia Louisa Minor, Victoria Woodhull, and Myra Bradwell – attempt to use the Fourteenth Amendment in the courts to secure the vote (Minor and Woodhull) and the right to practice law (Bradwell). All are unsuccessful.

1872

Susan B. Anthony is arrested and brought to trial in Rochester, New York, for attempting to vote for Ulysses S. Grant in the presidential election. At the same time, Sojourner Truth appears at a polling booth in Grand Rapids, Michigan, demanding a ballot; she is turned away.

1874

The Woman's Christian Temperance Union (WCTU) is founded by Annie Wittenmyer. With Frances Willard at its head (1876), the WCTU becomes an important force in the struggle for women's suffrage. Not surprisingly, one of the most vehement opponents of women's enfranchisement is the liquor lobby, which fears women might use the franchise to prohibit the sale of liquor.

1878

The Woman Suffrage Amendment is introduced in the US Congress. (The wording is unchanged in 1919 when the amendment finally passes both houses.)

(continued)

TEXT BOX 4.1 (*continued*)

1890

Wyoming becomes the first women's suffrage state on its admission to the Union. Rival suffrage groups merge to form the National American Woman Suffrage Association (NAWSA).

1893

Colorado becomes the first state to adopt a state amendment enfranchising women.

1896

Mary Church Terrell, Ida B. Wells-Barnett, Margaret Murray Washington, Fanny Jackson Coppin, Frances Ellen Watkins Harper, Charlotte Forten Grimke, and the former slave Harriet Tubman meet in Washington, DC, to form the National Association of Colored Women (NACW).

1903

Mary Dreier, Rheta Childe Dorr, Leonora O'Reilly, and others form the Women's Trade Union League of New York, an organization of middle- and working-class women dedicated to unionization for working women and to women's suffrage. This group later becomes the nucleus of the International Ladies' Garment Workers' Union (ILGWU).

1911

The National Association Opposed to Woman Suffrage (NAOWS) is organized. Led by Mrs. Arthur Dodge, its members include wealthy, influential women and some Catholic clergymen – including Cardinal Gibbons, who, in 1916, sends an address to NAOWS's convention in Washington, DC. In addition to the distillers and brewers, who work largely behind the scenes, the "antis" also draw support from urban political machines, southern congressmen, and corporate capitalists – like railroad magnates and meat-packers – who support the "antis" by contributing to their war chests.

1912

Theodore Roosevelt's Progressive (Bull Moose/Republican) Party becomes the first national political party to adopt a women's suffrage plank.

1913

Alice Paul and Lucy Burns organize the Congressional Union, later known as the National Woman's Party (1916). Borrowing the tactics of the radical, militant Women's Social and Political Union in England, members of the Woman's Party participate in hunger strikes, picket the White House, and engage in other forms of civil disobedience to publicize the suffrage cause.

1914

The National Federation of Women's Clubs – which by this time includes more than 2 million white women and women of color throughout the United States – formally endorses the suffrage campaign.

1916

Jeannette Rankin of Montana becomes the first woman elected to represent her state in the US House of Representatives.

August 26, 1920

The Nineteenth Amendment is ratified. Its victory accomplished, NAWSA ceases to exist, but its organization becomes the nucleus of the League of Women Voters.

Source: Adapted from *Election Focus 2004* 1(8), April 14, 2004, https://bit .ly/3ixaA18

WOMEN'S CHANGING DEMOGRAPHICS: AN OVERVIEW

The heavy focus on the 100th anniversary of passage of the Nineteenth Amendment prompted analysts to draw some parallels between the 1920 and 2020 elections.

> The echoes of a century ago are everywhere today. The year 1920 was also an election year; and in the years leading up to it, the streets were filled with protesters (who honed the tools activists use today), while a pandemic [the Spanish flu] ravaged the globe, nearly upending the women's suffrage movement itself.[1]

However, the demographic composition of the voting age population (VAP) in 2020 was vastly different from that in 1920. In fact, it is constantly

[1] Prouix, Natalie, Lesson of the Day: "The Complex History of the Women's Suffrage Movement," *New York Times*, September 17, 2020, https://nyti.ms/3ylImvt

in flux and differs from state to state, even from one community to another. Over the past decade alone, noticeable changes have occurred in the composition of women in the United States. Rapid changes in women's racial/ethnic, age, education, and party affiliation makeup help explain shifts in their levels of political involvement and civic engagement, and in the nation's power dynamics.[2]

Race/Ethnicity

Non-Hispanic white women, once the dominant share of the electorate, have become a smaller share as women of color have gained as a consequence of the increased racial diversity among younger generations (see Table 4.1). Black women are the largest portion of the nonwhite VAP, although in several states and among Gen Z and Millennials, Hispanics have surpassed them. Asian Americans, Native Americans, bi- and multiracial women make up smaller, but growing, shares.

From a campaign perspective, use of broad racial/ethnic categories (such as Hispanic, Asian) mask significant cultural, socioeconomic, political, even language differences that are critical to effectively microtargeting messages to individual voters. (In Florida, for example, Puerto

TABLE 4.1 Among eligible voters, women in younger generations are more diverse

Generation	% of total voting age population	White (%)	Black (%)	Hispanic (%)	Asian (%)	Other (%)
Gen Z	9.4	55.8	14.0	20.9	5.3	4.0
Millennial	26.2	59.7	15.0	16.8	5.3	3.2
Gen X	24.6	63.8	13.9	13.7	6.2	2.4
Baby Boomer	29.4	73.2	11.8	8.7	4.6	1.7
Silent Gen and older	10.4	78.7	8.8	7.0	4.2	1.3
Total	100.0	66.3	12.7	13.4	5.2	2.4

Notes: Birth years: Gen Z (after 1996); Millennial (1981–96); Gen X (1965–80); Baby Boomer (1946–64); Silent Gen and older (before 1928–45). Whites, Blacks, and Asians are single-race non-Hispanic only. "Other races" are non-Hispanic only and include people who identify with multiple races. Hispanics are of any race.
Source: Author's analysis of November 2020 monthly Current Population Survey (IPUMS).

[2] Safinia, Marjan, Celebrating Female Trailblazers for Women's Suffrage Centennial, *PBS News Hour Weekend*, June 28, 2020, www.pbs.org/newshour/show/celebrating-female-trailblazers-for-womens-suffrage-centennial

Ricans vote differently than Cuban or Venezuelan Americans, Vietnamese differently than Indian Americans.) In 2020, one-size-fits-all approaches were tossed aside and replaced with more distinct targeting by heritage (country of origin). As we will discuss later in this chapter, women's organizations pushed for more involvement by specific groups of women of color, often different in their age and educational backgrounds.

Generation (Age)

The emergence of Millennials (born 1981–96) and Gen Z (born after 1996) in the electorate focused a lot of attention on an emerging generational (and political) divide. The two younger generations made up nearly 40 percent of the eligible voting population (37%) in 2020. Women in these two youngest generations are much more likely to be racially/ethnically diverse than Baby Boomers or older (born before 1965). Women of color make up a larger share of eligible young voters in the more racially diverse southern and western states (see Figure 4.1). Nearly half of these

Among Eligible Voters, Share of Gen Z and Millennial Women Who Are Women of Color ...
Less than 15%　15–24%　25–34%　35–49%　50% or greater

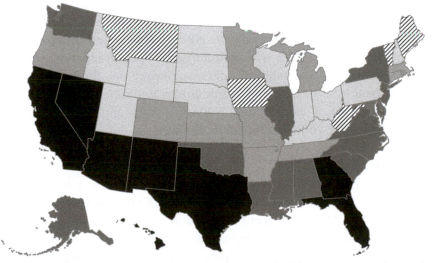

Figure 4.1 Women of color were a larger share of eligible young voters in southern, western states, 2020.
Note: Map shows the share of Gen Z and Millennial women who are Hispanic or any non-Hispanic racial identity except non-Hispanic, single-race white in the eligible voter population.
Source: Author's analysis of November 2020 monthly Current Population Survey (IPUMS).

younger generations identify as a racial or ethnic minority. In contrast, three-fourths of Boomers and older are white.

This generational shift played out in a number of ways, but particularly in how each campaign could deliver their get-out-the-vote messages; for older voters, it was easy – TV or Facebook. But for the younger, more racially and politically diverse women, it was more challenging than ever in 2020 – Snapchat? Instagram? Twitter? TikTok? Podcasts? Blogs? Memes? Social media networks? Campaigns often miscalculated how best to engage these young, issue-oriented generations by overrelying on traditional media – television and radio – that younger generations are less likely to turn to for political information.[3]

Education

By 2020, the sharp increase in the educational achievements of young women had become obvious. A much larger proportion were going to college, graduating, and becoming politically active. Educational level became a good predictor of partisan voting patterns, particularly among white women. A slightly larger share of those with college degrees voted Democrat in 2020 than in 2016, but a wide divide remained in support for Republican candidates between those with and without a college degree.

Among women of color, there was a clear generational difference in educational levels that translated into higher levels of participation in the political arena. Younger women were going to college and graduating at a far greater rate than their male counterparts. Upon graduation, some of these women became political activists, community organizers giving voice to issues confronting their communities, and candidates running for office. There was a sharp uptick in Black women and other women of color running for and winning political office.[4]

Party Affiliation

In general, older women are more strongly partisan than the younger generations, a growing share of whom are identifying themselves as independents. In 2020, 37 percent of Millennial women registered voters across the country described themselves as independents, 36 percent as Democrats, and 22 percent as Republicans. By contrast, among Boomers,

---

[3] Amy Mitchell, Mark Jurkowitz, J. Baxter Oliphant, and Elisa Shearer, Americans Who Mainly Get Their News on Social Media Are Less Engaged, Less Knowledgeable, Pew Research Center, July 30, 2020, https://pewrsr.ch/3IiQlWF

[4] Results: Women Candidates in the 2020 Election, Center for American Women and Politics (hereafter CAWP), November 4, 2020, https://bit.ly/3jfxEAl

39 percent were Democrats, 32 percent Republicans, and 26 percent independents.[5] Younger women are increasingly identifying themselves as independents, although they lean more Democratic in their voting patterns. But the generational differences made reaching younger voters more difficult because they are driven more by issues and individual candidates than by party alone.

Connections between party and race/ethnicity are strong. Women of color, especially Blacks, are more heavily Democrats than Republicans. So, too, are Latinas and Asians, although a larger share are independents, most notably relatively recent arrivals from other countries or territories.

In summary, the changing composition and complexities of women of voting age in 2020 made it much more challenging to register, engage, and mobilize women to vote than even four years prior, when Republican Donald J. Trump Jr. was elected president. Further complicating engagement was the fact that the number of competitive battleground states had grown since 2016 and an unprecedented number of major events and movements constantly forced campaigns to redirect their efforts and messages.

EVENTS THAT MOBILIZED WOMEN TO VOTE

Women's activism and engagement extended far beyond the voting booth in the 2020 election cycle, driven by multiple events, many of which had occurred over the previous four years. Women organized and mobilized around issues of racial justice, reproductive rights, sexual assault, gun violence, access to quality health care, equal pay, voting rights, environmental justice, immigration reform, and affordable childcare. Significantly, all these concerns were exacerbated by the onset of the COVID-19 pandemic early in 2020, which left women, especially women of color, in greater peril than their male counterparts.

The Women's March

On election night 2016, many women across the country were stunned at the loss of the country's first woman major party presidential nominee, Hillary Rodham Clinton, to political novice Donald J. Trump. But rather than dwell in angst, women immediately began to organize what would become the largest single-day protest in American history. Eleven weeks

---

[5] In Changing US Electorate, Race and Education Remain Stark Dividing Lines, Pew Research Center, 2020, https://pewrsr.ch/3iitdpd

after that unforgettable night, the Women's March on Washington occurred in cities around the globe. Millions of women objected to the vitriol that spewed from the Trump campaign during the previous election cycle, which largely targeted women, racial minorities, and immigrants. Additionally, they protested Trump's campaign promises, like the rollback of their reproductive rights, the wall along the Mexican border, and the repeal of the Affordable Care Act.

MeToo Movement

Later in 2017, the global proliferation of the MeToo movement amplified concerns of sexual harassment and assault against women at home and in the workplace. MeToo was founded more than a decade earlier by Black civil rights activist Tarana Burke in an effort to bring together women from marginalized communities who disproportionately are victims of sexual violence. After the tweet that went viral by actress Alyssa Milano, the hashtag #MeToo reached women around the globe. Women shared their own personal stories of sexual assault, and subsequently mobilized to enact change in their own communities and workplaces.

Notably, MeToo continued to exert its influence in the 2020 election cycle. President Trump's tenure in office was filled with allegations of past sexual assault, including high-profile court cases such as journalist E. Jean Carroll's accusation of rape by Trump and CBS CEO Les Moonves. Trump's presidential campaign took notice, especially after the president suffered a drop in support among women, particularly suburban mothers that had helped propel him to victory in 2016. Many women were undoubtedly mortified when the president acknowledged hush money payoffs to porn star Stormy Daniels and Playboy model Karen McDougal.

Allegations of Reprehensible Behavior

In July 2018, the president nominated Judge Brett Kavanaugh to the nation's highest court. Shortly afterward, Dr. Christine Blasey Ford came forward with accusations of prior sexual assault by Kavanaugh in the summer of 1982. In response, angry crowds of women stormed the nation's capital in protest at Kavanaugh's nomination, gathering at Capitol Hill and on the steps of the Supreme Court. Some even cornered lawmakers like Senator Jeff Flake (R-AZ) in an elevator. Maria Gallagher, a sexual assault survivor, exclaimed, "Look at me and tell me that it doesn't matter what happened to me."[6]

---

[6] Doug Stanglin and Caroline Simon, "Rise Up, Women!": Angry Crowds Flood Capitol Hill to Protest Brett Kavanaugh Nomination, *USA Today*, September 28, 2018, https://bit.ly/2VoxKh4

But President Trump was not the only candidate accused of past shameful behavior during the 2020 election. Democratic presidential hopefuls suffered the wrath of women during the primary election, especially former New York City Mayor Mike Bloomberg. Former Vice President Joe Biden also had to deal with his own MeToo moments. During his Senate tenure, his antagonistic treatment of Anita Hill during the Clarence Thomas confirmation hearings in 1991 resurfaced, along with concerns about his overly "friendly" treatment of women colleagues.

Immigration Policies

The Trump administration's policy of separating undocumented migrant families at the Mexican border came under fire by women voters prior to the 2020 election. Horrific images of children in cages, many left crying out for their mothers, sparked protests across the country. Former First Lady Laura Bush wrote in a *Washington Post* op-ed column that the policy "is cruel. It is immoral. And it breaks my heart."[7] Other demonstrations included installations of cages with mannequins displayed on streets in major cities like New York. Organizations like the League of Women Voters called for investigations and hearings into the policy's enforcement. Other groups, like RAICES (Refugee and Immigrant Center for Education and Legal Services, a Texas nonprofit), ran social media campaigns to bring attention to the issue, which included the hashtags #DontLookAway and #NoKidsInCages.

Yet, the crisis along the border also brought a different set of issues, especially for conservative women. They were worried about the security measures, particularly when it came to issues of human and child sex trafficking. Additionally, they were troubled by the smuggling of illegal drugs and weapons, which potentially could result in violent crimes in their own communities across the country.

Murders of Black Americans by Police

The deaths of many Black Americans at the hands of armed vigilantes and police officers rallied women around concerns related to racial justice. The murders of Ahmaud Arbery, George Floyd, Tony McDade, Breonna Taylor, and several others led to massive numbers of protests and marches, which erupted across the country in the summer of 2020. Many of these protests were led by organizations like Black Lives Matter (BLM), a movement founded and led by Black women, as well as the Movement for Black Lives, a coalition of more than fifty groups.

---

[7] Laura Bush, Opinion: Separating Children from Their Parents at the Border "Breaks My Heart," *Washington Post*, June 17, 2018, https://wapo.st/3jfxWHr

Alongside the BLM marches and protests, the African American Policy Forum (AAPF) #SayHerName campaign sought to highlight the names of Black women who were missing from the conversation centered on racial injustice and police brutality. The deaths of a few Black women, like Sandra Bland and Breonna Taylor, who died at the hands of the police, garnered national attention. Yet, many Black women, like Kayla Moore and Michelle Cusseaux (both of whom had mental health issues), were largely ignored.

According to an AAPF founder, Kimberlé Crenshaw, literally saying the names of murdered Black women would prompt learning of their stories. The #SayHerName campaign gained prominence during the Women's National Basketball Association's 2020 season. Many players spoke out over social media, and wore T-shirts and jerseys displaying the logo "Say Her Name." The Atlanta Dream, co-owned by Senator Kelly Loeffler (R-GA), openly campaigned for Loeffler's opponent the Rev. Raphael Warnock (D) during the 2020 election cycle and called for Loeffler to sell her stake in the team when she proclaimed an anti-BLM position.

Included in the growing national spotlight were transwomen, particularly transwomen of color. In addition to alarming rates of attacks and murder, discriminatory practices by the media and others drew attention. Among these practices was the *misgendering* of trans persons – that is, using terms related to how they identified before their transition. During BLM protests, slogans of #TransLivesMatter appeared amongst the crowds of protesters and on social media platforms.

In 2017, Senator Heidi Heitkamp (D), the first woman elected to the US Senate from North Dakota (2013–19), embraced the #NotInvisible campaign, which seeks to raise awareness of the epidemic of missing and murdered Indigenous women. According to the campaign, 84 percent of Native American women have faced some kind of violence throughout their lifetime. Senator Heitkamp also introduced a bill to improve law enforcement cooperation in contending with the issue.

Vice-Presidential Nomination

During the Democratic primary in the spring of 2020, candidate Joe Biden promised he would nominate a woman as his running mate. Once he had been officially selected as the Democratic Party's presidential nominee, women fervently began to lobby the Biden campaign with names of women they believed would make an ideal vice-presidential candidate. Some of these women included former 2020 presidential hopefuls like Senator Elizabeth Warren (MA) and Senator Amy Klobuchar (MN).

Others called for a woman of color on the Democratic ticket. Black women, in particular, demanded that they be rewarded for their legacy of organizing and mobilizing voters for the Democratic Party. Finally, in August 2020, Biden announced Senator Kamala Harris (CA) as the official vice-presidential nominee. She would be the first Black woman and the first Southeast Asian woman to be nominated for vice president by any major political party.

Death of Justice Ruth Bader Ginsberg

The death of Supreme Court Justice Ruth Bader Ginsberg in September 2020 mobilized women across the country. Over the course of her tenure on the US Supreme Court, she became a liberal icon because of her history of dissent, especially on cases involving gender discrimination and voting rights, as well as her support of access to reproductive health care (including abortion). Although the GOP pushed through Trump nominee Amy Coney Barrett to replace Ginsberg in record time, women across the country took note. The threat of a conservative bench opposed to reproductive rights and health care alongside other forms of gender and racial discrimination were significant motivators for more liberal women as they headed to the polls.

For conservative women who had long wanted a conservative-majority US Supreme Court, the nomination and confirmation of conservative pro-life Amy Coney Barrett as Ginsberg's replacement was an equally powerful motivator to turn out to vote for Trump.

COVID-19 Pandemic

Although the pandemic undoubtedly impacted every American during 2020, women more keenly felt its effects. The coronavirus only exacerbated existing problems of gender discrimination for women voters. Mothers were more likely to quit their jobs, as they were forced to watch over their kids homebound due to school closings. Many had no access to reliable or affordable childcare options, and even lost their employer-sponsored health care coverage once they left their jobs.

Women were also more likely to be on the front lines of the pandemic. Many were employed as teachers, nurses and health care aides, grocery store workers and retail associates. Women of color, in particular, were overrepresented among frontline workers.

Notably, COVID-19 also disproportionately impacted women in Black, Latino, LGBTQ+, and Native/Indigenous communities in other ways. All these communities had suffered even before the pandemic, particularly when it came to health care, housing and food insecurity, and pay inequity. Since being hit by the coronavirus, these communities were hammered with infections and suffered more losses of life.

All these events provided ample political opportunities for candidates, campaigns, and organizations to register and mobilize women voters ahead of the 2020 election.

HOW AND WHO MOBILIZED WOMEN VOTERS

Candidates, political parties, and organizations all took note of the significant role women voters had to play in the upcoming 2020 election. Importantly, women voters are far from being a monolithic voting bloc. Thus, it became crucial to target subgroups of women by the very issues they deemed important going into the voting booth.

Both Republicans and Democrats identified suburban women as a critical swing vote for the 2020 cycle. Yet both parties needed to be able to effectively target women from all demographic groups if they expected to be victorious on Election Day. This included targeted messaging on key issues like racial discrimination, immigration reform, gendered violence, access to affordable health care, along with the economy and safety.

President Trump and the GOP

President Trump's reelection campaign knew early on they would have to win back women voters, especially white suburban women that crossed party lines to support Democrats in the 2018 midterms. Although GOP women predominantly supported Trump in 2016,[8] many were turned off by his less-than-presidential rhetoric and behavior, in addition to his nonstop tweeting.[9] Furthermore, they were less than supportive of his handling on issues related to the COVID-19 pandemic and the racial justice protests that engulfed the country in the summer of 2020.[10] Others were not convinced that his economic policies had benefited them during his administration.[11]

---

[8] According to CNN's analysis of the 2016 national presidential exit poll, 88 percent of Republican women voted for Donald Trump for president; see www.cnn.com/election/2016/results/exit-polls

[9] Michael Scherer and Josh Dawsey, As Trump Slumps, His Campaign Fixes on a Target: Women, *Washington Post*, June 22, 2020, https://wapo.st/3xnM2M2

[10] Kendall Karson, "A Push Against Donald Trump": Why Some Older Women Are Turning Away from the President, *ABC News*, June 5, 2020, https://abcnews.go.com/Politics/push-donald-trump-older-women-turning-president/story?id=71067257

[11] William Galston, New Polling: Eroding Support from White Working-Class Women Threatens Trump's Reelection, Brookings, June 3, 2020, https://brook.gs/3C95CiT

Yet, one key strategy to target women by the GOP was to amplify the gains they made in Trump's economy. Republicans believed that women were likely to have benefited from job creation that resulted from the delivery of promised tax cuts and the removal of federal regulations. Trump also tried to directly appeal to suburban women by proclaiming he was the law and order candidate. At a rally in Johnsonville, Pennsylvania, Trump was quoted as saying, "[C]an I ask you to do me a favor, suburban women? Will you please like me? Please. Please. I saved your damn neighborhood, OK?"[12]

The Republican Party also suggested that the Trump campaign stick to traditional GOP talking points. This messaging included a strong national defense and border security, protection of Second Amendment rights and religious freedom, as well as implementing pro-life policies and securing pro-life judges. They also framed Democrats, especially members of "The Squad," which included four women of color, in Congress as socialists. More so, they argued that Democrats sided with the "angry, violent mobs" that appeared alongside BLM protests.

In order to directly engage GOP women, the Trump campaign kicked off a "Women for Trump" bus tour and featured many prominent Republican women at campaign events. This included Trump family members, like daughters Ivanka and Tiffany Trump, as well as women who were key players in his administration, namely senior advisor Kellyanne Conway and White House Press Secretary Kaleigh McEnany. The campaign also featured Republican National Committee chair Ronna McDaniel and former Florida attorney general Pam Bondi. At these events, women were encouraged to show their unwavering support for Trump, and more importantly, bring their friends.

Former VP Joseph Biden and the Democrats

Although Biden and the Democrats had an advantage when it came to the sheer number of women registered voters, it was critical that they acknowledge the diversity among women within their party, and more importantly, how issues differentially impacted them, in order to mobilize them to go to the polls. This meant being able to communicate messages that effectively targeted women of all racial and ethnic backgrounds, generations, and sexual orientations. All these subgroups of women were

[12] Meredith Conroy, Amelia Thomson-DeVeaux, and Erin Cassese, Why Trump Is Losing White Suburban Women, *FiveThirtyEight*, October 20, 2020, https://fivethirtyeight.com/features/why-trump-is-losing-white-suburban-women/

impacted by things like pay inequity, access to health care and childcare, education reform, and the COVID-19 pandemic, but they were affected in significantly different ways.

For Black women, Democrats needed not only to acknowledge their ability (both past and present) to organize and mobilize voters to turn out at the polls, but also to promise to enact policies that would directly uplift their communities. Democrats needed targeted messaging on how they would solve issues of systemic racism and inequality in policing and the criminal justice system. Racial discrimination in health care was a prominent concern, as Black women face maternal mortality rates of two to three times that of white women. They also needed to emphasize the protection and expansion of voting rights, as Black women have been on the front lines of that fight for generations.

For Latina voters, Democrats had to think about expansion. Stephanie Valenzuela of EquisLabs stated that Latinas "will not just turn out to vote themselves, but that they will organize and engage others around them to go and vote as well."[13] One significant concern for Latinas was the economy, as they were more likely to be unemployed compared to any other demographic group leading up to the election. They were also significantly concerned about issues related to access to health care, food and housing insecurity, and immigration reform.

Younger generations, which failed to show up for Hillary Clinton in 2016, were a prime target. But with college campuses resembling ghost towns during the COVID-19 pandemic, it became more difficult to reach Millennials and Gen Z women voters with traditional outreach methods. Yet, Democrats still needed to target younger women with messages on issues like student loan reform, climate change, racial justice, access to reproductive health care, as well as job creation and gender-based violence.[14]

The LGBTQ+ community looked poised to vote against Trump. After all, the Trump administration had previously promoted policies that discriminated against the LGBTQ+ population in health care, housing, and public accommodations. Furthermore, it had withdrawn protections for

---

[13] Daisy Contreras, The Key to Winning the Latino Vote in 2020? Latinas, *The World*, May 25, 2020, www.pri.org/stories/2020-05-25/key-winning-latino-vote-2020-latinas

[14] The Top Issues that Drove Youth to the Polls, Center on Information and Research on Civic Learning and Engagement, November 6, 2020, https://bit.ly/3ijjA9T; Courtney Connley, "The 19th Amendment Means Everything": 5 First-Time Voters on 100 Years of Women's Suffrage and the 2020 Election, *CNBC*, August 18, 2020, www.cnbc.com/2020/08/18/5-first-time-women-voters-on-the-19th-amendment-and-2020-election.html

transgender youth in schools and banned transgender soldiers from serving in the military. In recent years, dozens of transgender and gender nonconfirming persons had been murdered across the nation, many of whom were Black transwomen. But would the trans community trust the Democrats? The Biden campaign needed to not only acknowledge the community's specific issues but also to devise policies that would address all their concerns.

Organizations that Mobilized Women Voters to the Polls

As pundits and politicos projected that the "women's vote" would be the key decider of the 2020 election season, organizations of all sorts doubled down to mobilize this diverse group of voters. Women's organizations that had been established as key actors in previous election cycles still played a critical role in 2020, whereas nascent groups popped up to fill the gaps in mobilizing specific subgroups of women to the polls. Although not specifically targeting women voters, several social movement and voting rights organizations – many of which were founded and led by women – also put their hats in the 2020 ring.

While organizations get much of the credit for advancing political and social movements, it is important to realize that they do not spring up wholly formed. Often it is an individual – in this case, an individual woman – who gets an idea for forming an organization and then uses her confidence, courage, and energy to lead an organization to fulfill its purpose.

Republican Women's Groups These are usually organized at a local level and focus their energies on traditional GOTV efforts like door-to-door canvassing in their own communities. Such organizations included the National Federation of Republican Women, which has many local and state chapters in addition to the national organization, as well as the Independent Women's Forum, which is designed to engage and educate women about policies. Other organizations that typically focus on promoting GOP women candidates also stepped up to help mobilize Republican voters. Included here are the Susan B. Anthony List, a group that canvassed traditionally Democratic homes with anti-abortion messaging, and Maggie's List, which also runs GOTV programs.

Young Republican women voters were involved with established organizations like Young Republicans, Young Americans for Freedom (YAF), as well as College Republicans and the Network of Enlightened Women (NeW) on college campuses. Gen Z conservatives took to social media platforms to engage with young conservative voters. Included here are The MAGA Girls, Tik Tok House, Conservative Teen Girl on Instagram, and the use of the hashtag #TeensforTrump.

Democratic Women's Groups On the other side was an array of well-established Democratic-leaning organizations. Among them was EMILY's List, which traditionally funds Democratic pro-choice women for office. In 2020, they reinstituted the Women Vote! campaign (originally founded in 1995), which was designed to educate women voters on issues important to them and their families. NARAL, a pro-choice group, ran a campaign that specifically targeted suburban women voters, a voting bloc considered a toss-up going into the 2020 election. Other prominent Democratic-leaning groups included Planned Parenthood and the Women's March, which also targeted women in efforts to turn them out to the polls.

Key players in mobilizing the women's vote for Democrats were unions, particularly two of the country's largest teachers' unions, the National Education Association and the American Federation of Teachers. In addition, the Service Employees International Union, which represents many of the frontline workers across the country, ran a campaign to target "infrequent" voters of color to show up for Joe Biden in the closing days of the election.

Supermajority In April 2019, a team of high-profile community organizers like Alicia Garza, Cecile Richards, and Ai-jen Poo launched the "Supercharge: Women All In" campaign to mobilize millions of women in the 2020 election cycle.[15] This newly formed, member-based organization set up events that featured prominent Democratic women like former presidential nominee Hillary Clinton and Senator Elizabeth Warren (MA). Organizers sent millions of text messages, made thousands of phone calls, and wrote letters to women to emphasize the importance of voting. Women's organizations that were partners in these events included TIME'S Up Now and Ultraviolet, in addition to Swing Left, a progressive group founded after the election of Donald Trump in 2016.

Nonpartisan Women's Groups Well-established women's groups like the League of Women Voters and the National Organization for Women (NOW) swung into action. Several organizations were designed to mobilize

---

[15] Supermajority Announces "Supercharge: Women All In," a National Campaign to Mobilize Millions of Women for the 2020 Election, September 2, 2020, Supermajority. com, https://bit.ly/3A48EmK

specific subgroups of women. She the People, which hosted the first ever presidential forum dedicated to issues affecting women of color, focused on mobilizing Black, Latina, Asian, and other racial minority women. Other organizations used a generational approach. IGNITE ran a campaign called #IGNITEtheVote, which focused on turning out new voters to the polls. Groups like Rock the Vote and Get Out the Vote also targeted young adults.

Black Women's Groups There was no shortage of organizations that focused on mobilizing Black women to the polls in 2020. This included prominent Black women's sororities of the Divine Nine like Alpha Kappa Alpha, Delta Sigma Theta, Zeta Phi Beta, and Sigma Gamma Rho. Democratic VP nominee Kamala Harris, a member of Alpha Kappa Alpha Sorority, attended events like the "Sister to Sister" voter engagement program. Higher Heights, an organization dedicated to help elect Black women to political office and advance a progressive political agenda, established a #BlackWomenVote campaign. Other organizations that focused on Black women included Sisters Lead Sisters Vote, Black Girls Vote, and Own Your Vote (founded by Oprah Winfrey).

Importantly, many of these groups worked alongside other organizations to mobilize Black voters across the country. This included voting rights organizations founded and/or led by Black women, including Fair Fight (Stacey Abrams), When We All Vote (Michelle Obama, Janelle Monae), Electoral Justice Voter Fund (Jessica Byrd, Rukia Lumumba, and Kayle Reed) and Black Voters Matter (LaTosha Brown). Black Church PAC, cofounded by Bishop Leah Daughtry, sought to organize faith leaders to assist in mobilizing voters across the country.[16] Many of these groups also helped organize events to mobilize Black women voters, including the Black Women's Agenda, a virtual voting rights town hall.

Latinx Community Groups like Poder Latinx, Latino Victory, and Voces de la Frontera all dedicated their efforts to registering and mobilizing Latinx voters. Mi Familia Vota specifically targeted new and young voters. Other voting organizations were founded and/or led by Latinas, including Voto Latino (Maria Teresa Kumar, founding president) and Mijente (Marisa Franco).

---

[16] Erin Delmore, "Collaborate, Don't Duplicate": How Black Women's Groups Helped Deliver the Election to Biden, Harris, *NBC News*, January 19, 2021, https://bit .ly/3A48EmK

Asian American Groups Asian American and Pacific Islander (AAPI) organizations like APIA Vote understood how important voter outreach was in the 2020 election cycle. In particular, they knew how important AAPI women were as messengers in their own communities. They were joined by the Asian American Organizing Project, which was dedicated to mobilizing young voters. Many of these organizations were operating in specific geographic areas. For instance, VietLead and SEAMAAC were active in Pennsylvania, a key battleground in the 2020 election.

LGBTQ+ This community took cues from groups that focused on policy issues important to them, including organizations like The Trevor Project, GLAAD, and GLSEN. The Human Rights Campaign (HRC) attempted to register and mobilize voters across the country in efforts to elect pro-equality candidates, including Democrat Joe Biden. LGBTQ+ Voter Fund was designed to provide resources to groups organizing in LGBTQ+ communities. Specifically, their efforts were to either establish groups or strengthen the current efforts of existing organizations to elect leaders that would endeavor to protect and expand rights for the LGBTQ+ population.

DIVERSE MEDIA LANDSCAPE CHALLENGING TO CAMPAIGNS

The media landscape had become more diverse by 2020 – a multiplicity of print, electronic (TV, radio), and social media sources of information and communication. The biggest challenge in reaching voters was to determine which sources they relied on and trusted the most for their political news. Without such knowledge, mobilization efforts were destined to miss the mark. *Micro-targeting is only as effective as getting the right message to the potential voters using their preferred communication mechanism.*

Women were quite diverse in the sources they relied upon for political election news: local TV (66%), social media (58%), network TV (57%), print (55%), cable TV (51%), radio (48%), and news websites or apps (39%).[17] In general, younger Americans turned more to social media and news websites and apps than older voters, who depended more on traditional sources (print, TV).

Gender, race/ethnicity, and education were intertwined with media source preferences. For example, women were much more likely than

[17]   Amy Mitchell, Mark Jurkowitz, J. Baxter Oliphant, and Elisa Shearer, Demographics of Americans Who Get Most of Their Political News from Social Media, Pew Research Center, July 30, 2020, https://pewrsr.ch/3C7f2eE

men to cite network TV (CBS, ABC, CBS) as major sources. In cable TV news, Fox News viewers were predominantly white, while nearly half of CNN viewers were nonwhite.[18] Blacks relied more on local and cable TV, Hispanics on social media. Those with more education turned to NPR and the *New York Times*.

Social Media: Growing Importance, Greater Mistrust

Social media use increased significantly over 2016, much of it a consequence of the pandemic. In 2020, campaigns and candidates had to be more strategic than ever in reaching potential supporters via social media – and not just those sites that users perceived as providing political news. Overall, the share of women users of seven popular social media platforms was Facebook (75%), YouTube (68%), Instagram (43%), Pinterest (42%), SnapChat (24%), LinkedIn (24%), and Twitter (21%).[19] Facebook was more popular with older users; Instagram, Twitter, SnapChat with younger users; LinkedIn, Pinterest, and YouTube with college graduates and those with higher incomes. TikTok, not included in many social media rankings, took off like a rocket in 2020, becoming the go-to social media source for Gen Zers. Blacks and Hispanics were more likely than whites to use social media platforms as venues for political engagement and social activism.

Engaging with voters heavily reliant on social media was difficult. The intersections between gender, age, race/ethnicity, and party differed from person to person, as did interest in politics. Cross-posting messages on multiple networks became the answer for how to reach different voters in the shortest amount of time, although there was no guarantee the message would be received in the same way due to the different user profiles populating various platforms. Attention-grabbing messages were difficult to craft; nontraditional often worked best. The heavily sought-after younger voter was also the most adept at ignoring messages delivered via social media.

As the campaign progressed, social media users became more critical of political content on their social media platforms. More than half (55%) said they were "worn out" by the number of political posts they encountered and preferred that social media companies prohibit political ads on

[18] Elizabeth Grieco, Americans' Main Sources for Political News Vary by Party and Age, Pew Research Center, FactTank, April 1, 2020, https://pewrsr.ch/2WDf8dA

[19] Jenn Chen, Social Media Demographics to Inform Your Brand's Strategy in 2020, Sprout blog, August 4, 2020, https://bit.ly/3Ak9oUB

their platforms.[20] Distrust was highest of Facebook (59%), Twitter (48%), Instagram (42%), and YouTube (36%); it was less so on Reddit (24%) and LinkedIn (18%).[21] Social-media-reliant individuals were found to be less engaged, less knowledgeable about politics, and more vulnerable to misinformation, but more trusting of it. Campaigns never let these potential supporters get out of sight. To reach low-information women in their midst, voter advocacy groups and campaigns turned to women activists and media professionals.

Women Play Vital Roles in Media Use, Message Transmission

With women as the key target, campaigns recognized the vital importance of having women figure out how to target, message, and reach other women in a way that would sway them to vote for candidate X. Likewise, on the heels of the #MeToo and #BLM movements, various media outlets were pressed to have more women as vital parts of their campaign coverage team(s). Numerous studies documented the underrepresentation of women among media professionals.[22]

Consequently, women played a bigger role in media campaign coverage in 2020 – as producers, anchors, reporters, commentators, talk show hosts, columnists, podcasters, and bloggers. For the first time ever, all three major broadcast networks (ABC, NBC, CBS) put female executive producers in charge of their morning shows – designed to appeal to women viewers. Virtually all the major TV news programs (network, public TV, and cable) had females covering politics. These women varied in age, ranging from late twenties to early seventies, with a majority in their forties. Women of color were high-priority hires, reflective of their growing share of the voting age population and demands for greater representation by activists. New news outlets were created by women and major print and social media outlets hired and promoted more women executives, political reporters, and columnists in response to criticism of the too-long underrepresentation of women.

[20] Monica Anderson and Brooke Auxier, 55% of US Social Media Users Say They Are "Worn Out" By Political Posts and Discussions. Pew Research Center, FactTank, August 19, 2020, https://pewrsr.ch/3ynKAL8

[21] Mark Jurkowitz and Amy Mitchell, An Oasis of Bipartisanship: Republicans and Democrats Distrust Social Media Sites for Political and Election News, Pew Research Center, January 29, 2020, https://pewrsr.ch/3fmsZM4

[22] Simge Andi, Meera Selva, and Rasmus Kleis Nielsen, Women and Leadership in the News Media 2020: Evidence from Ten Markets, Reuters Institute for the Study of Journalism, University of Oxford, March 8, 2020, https://reutersinstitute.politics.ox.ac.uk/women-and-leadership-news-media-2020-evidence-ten-markets

The growing successes of women running for office and the record number of women running for president forced political parties and major TV networks to include more women as debate moderators and analysts. Six women of color served as Democratic primary debate moderators or co-moderators – Gayle King (CBS), Kristen Welker (NBC), Linsey Davis (ABC), Vanessa Hauc (Telemundo), Amna Nawaz, and Yamiche Alcindor (PBS). The nonpartisan Commission on Presidential Debates tapped Welker to moderate the second of two presidential debates between Trump and Biden. Susan Page, *USA Today*'s Washington Bureau chief, moderated the vice-presidential debate between Mike Pence and Kamala Harris. Gender diversity was omnipresent among speakers and videos shown at both parties' political conventions.

Young women activists gained clout by creating new blogs, podcasts, and videos for posting on social media. News sources targeted to women of color – The 19th*, Prism, TheGrio, and others – elevated the name recognition of women candidates, generated donors, highlighted key issues, and mobilized supporters.

Women's creativity was on display. Conservative women on college campuses created websites and blogs to give greater voice to their presence, issue priorities, and candidate preferences. A weekly podcast called *In the Thick*, hosted by Maria Hinojosa and Julio Ricardo Varela for Futuro Media Group, gave listeners discussions of racial and identity politics. *Pod Is a Woman*, created by three women (Alejandra Campoverdi, Darienne Page, and Johanna Maska) from the Obama administration, focused on interviewing key women political players. *The Brown Girls Guide to Politics*, a show on the Wonder Media Network hosted by A'shanti Gholar, was promoted as a place "to meet some truly remarkable BIPOC (Black, Indigenous People of Color) women running for office."[23] And there were many more examples of women creating new media spaces to rally women to register and vote.

Visuals – videos, infographics, and memes – were more powerful than ever, particularly with the increase in live streaming and cellphone-generated footage readily shared. In the words of one campaign consultant: "The benefit of posting visual content is that it's prime for sharing which in turn gets your campaign account in front of more voters. In turn, you set yourself up for fresh followers who can learn about your

---

[23] Eliana Dockterman, The Best Politics Podcasts to Help You Make Sense of the 2020 Election, *Time*, November 6, 2020, https://time.com/5883606/best-political-podcasts-2020/

platform and what you stand for. *Think of such sharing as a sort of digital word of mouth"* (author's emphasis).[24]

Within campaigns, more women ascended to high-level positions charged with every facet of getting out the vote for their party's presidential candidate. In campaign 2020, there were many more examples of women's heavy influence on ad construction, placement, and defense than in the past. There was greater recognition of the vital need for a more effective micro-targeted, woman-to-woman approach to messaging and communicating in the middle of a pandemic, when in-person contact was limited. Always, the primary goal was to convince women to vote ... and for their candidate.

PANDEMIC PROMPTS CHANGES IN ELECTORAL PROCESSES

Efforts to get out the vote were different in 2020, as states changed their electoral processes (registration and voting) in response to the pandemic, although not without great post-election controversy in some battleground states. Interest was intense in registering new voters from the two youngest and most diverse generations (Gen Zers and Millennials).

Registration Drives: Political and Civic Groups, Celebrities, Plus Businesses

The expected down-to-the-wire race between incumbent President Donald Trump and challenger former Vice President Joe Biden and their respective supporters made registering voters a high priority. Each wanted to expand their base by registering new voters, getting others to change party affiliations, and helping voters who had moved to update their addresses.

Multiple groups, partisan and nonpartisan, put a lot of time and money into registration efforts. Women were heavily involved in every registration-focused organization, from traditional groups like the League of Women Voters and Rock the Vote to Voto Latino, She the People, and NextGen America. It was not just political and civic groups that were engaged in efforts to register and engage women; women's sports leagues and star athletes, musicians, celebrities, and filmmakers were also involved.

---

[24] Brent Barnhart, Social Media and Politics: 10 Best Practices for Campaigns to Know, Sprout blog, August 4, 2020, https://sproutsocial.com/insights/social-media-for-political-campaigns/

A new twist in 2020 was the involvement of businesses, including media firms, in voter registration. Many decided that encouraging customers to register and vote was a good business practice – a great way to promote their brand. Firms showcasing women in their advertising outreach included Gap (Stand United), Patagonia, ViacomCBS and the Ad Council (Vote For Your Life), Foot Locker (footlocker.com/vote), Under Armour (Run to Vote), The CW (#CWVoterReady), CBS's *The Late Show with Stephen Colbert* (BetterKnowABallot.com), and TBS's *Full Frontal with Samantha Bee* ("I Know What You Did Last Election"), among others. Almost all pushed links to registration portals and how-to-vote information.

There was no escaping efforts to get individuals to register and vote in 2020. They were nonstop and saturated every facet of a potential supporter's life. Amanda Mull, a young health writer for *The Atlantic*, detailed her personal experiences.

> I have recently been reminded, asked, or commanded to vote approximately 6 million times. These nudges have come from the people and places I'd expect – candidates, local officials, civic and political organizations – but also, more so than in any other election year I remember, from the places I wouldn't. Uber, Nike, Postmates, the ticket service AXS, the New York Mets, and the fast-casual restaurant chain Dig have all reminded me to check my voter registration, at least once in the past two weeks. Others, including Amazon and the home-decor retailer Lulu and Georgia, have nestled links to voting information in their usual marketing emails. Seemingly every time I open Facebook or Instagram, I am greeted by a notification about the importance of voting.[25]

Registration Rolls Grow; Process Easier

The number of Americans registered to vote in 2020 was estimated to be considerably higher (215 million or more) than the 211 million registered in 2018.[26] It is almost impossible to get a precise number because each state is responsible for managing its own voter rolls and people are constantly registering, moving to another state, and dying. Duplicate registrations may occur when a voter moves from one location to another

[25] Amanda Mull, Why Is Uber Begging Me to Vote?, *The Atlantic*, September 29, 2020, www.theatlantic.com/health/archive/2020/09/brands-are-marketing-right-vote/616532/

[26] Jude Joffee-Block, Posts Falsely Claim There Are Only 133 Million Registered Voters in the US, Associated Press, December 29, 2020, https://apnews.com/article/fact-checking-afs:Content:9889123447

and voter rolls have not been updated. The bottom line, however, is that more Americans registered to vote in 2020 as processes for registering improved and were made more user-friendly. The aggressive registration outreach efforts by women activists played a big part as well. According to US Census data, 74 percent of all women were registered; for men, 71 percent.[27]

Ways to Register A person can register in one of three ways – in person, by mail, or online. Registering to vote became much more convenient in 2020 as more states permitted *online registration* – up from thirty-two in 2016 to forty-one in 2020. States vary in the documentation, especially signatures and proof of residency, needed to prove eligibility when registering online. Younger voters are more likely to register online than others, prompting voter outreach groups to reach them in that way. Overall, in states permitting online registration, 11 percent chose that method to register, but among those age 18–24 it was over one in five (21%).[28]

Voto Latino, a digital organization devoted to registering young Latino voters in 2020, found that targeted online video ads ahead of voter registration deadlines in Florida, Texas, and Arizona reminding Latinos of impending deadlines and leaving action in their hands were effective. In Arizona, the script was: "Monday is the voter registration deadline in Arizona. This means that to vote in the presidential election, you have until this Monday to make sure you're registered to vote. Registering to vote is quick, easy, and important. But you only have until Monday to get it done."[29]

Placing it on multiple platforms – traditional and nontraditional – resulted in nearly 65,000 new voter registrants in just five days in the three states. Ameer Patel, Voto Latino's director of data and analytics, observed that "if you get someone to search, they will register" if you get the message to them in a timely fashion on a platform they frequent.[30]

Deadlines for Registering Most states require citizens to register in advance of an election, usually eight to thirty days. But by 2020, twenty-one

---

[27] United States Census Bureau, Voting and Registration in the Election of November 2020, table 13, https://bit.ly/2VxRYVW

[28] United States Census Bureau, Voting and Registration in the Election of November 2020, table 12, https://bit.ly/2VxRYVW

[29] Adam Wollner, How One Group Pushed Young Latino Voters to Register: Letting Them Google How to Do It, *Miami Herald*, February 16, 2021, www.mcclatchydc.com/news/politics-government/article249211345.html

[30] Ibid.

states plus the District of Columbia permitted citizens to register and vote on Election Day – referred to as same-day registration (SDR). Voter advocacy groups have long been pushing for states to allow SDR, arguing that it would increase voter participation. Critics say it increases the likelihood of fraud – ineligible or double-registered voters casting a ballot – particularly in high-growth states. One state, North Dakota, does not even require voters to register. An eligible voter there may vote in an election by simply providing acceptable identification.

Automatic Voter Registration (AVR) The National Voter Registration Act of 1993, or "motor voter" law, directed states to give citizens an opportunity to register to vote when applying for or renewing a driver's license at a Department of Motor Vehicles office. A citizen's relevant information from that process is then electronically transmitted to election officials, who verify voter eligibility (citizenship, age, and residency). The same act requires any state office providing public assistance or operating state-funded programs serving individuals with disabilities to offer them the opportunity to register. The citizen must be given the option of opting out. Most states give that option at the point of contact with government agencies; two states ask for opt-outs later in the process.

The number of states that have adopted AVR increased from six in 2016 to fifteen plus the District of Colombia in 2020. A study by the Brennan Center for Justice found that where AVR was put in place, the number of registrants significantly increased. Opponents' major concern about AVR is whether ineligible persons are filtered out, specifically non-citizens who in some states can get identification cards, like a driver's license, legally.

Voting Procedures Altered; Partisan Divide Emerges over Vote by Mail

Prior to 2020, the number of voters choosing to vote in person on Election Day had been declining in many states. More were choosing to vote either by mail or in person at an early voting site (where authorized by state law), mostly out of convenience. The spread of the coronavirus, with no vaccine approved by Election Day and social distancing rules in place, forced many states to modify election procedures and administration. Democrats and the Biden campaign heavily pushed for voters to vote by mail. The Trump campaign repeatedly attacked voting by mail as wrought with fraud, and pushed supporters to vote in person, either early or on Election Day.

"We have to make it easier for everybody to be able to vote, particularly if we are still basically in the kind of lockdown circumstances we are in now … . But that takes a lot of money, and it's going to require us to provide money for states and *insist they provide mail-in ballots.*" (Joe Biden; author's emphasis)[31]

"They send 80 million ballots out. Where are they going? Who are they sending them to? Are they sending them to certain areas and not other areas? Are they sending them to Democrat areas? These are all controlled by Democrat governors, like your politically motivated governor … . They should make people – if you register, if you want a solicited ballot, that's where you ask for it. You have to sign papers. You get it 'cause you can't be there. That's one thing. When they send [automatically] 80 million ballots to people, they have no idea where they're going." (Donald Trump at a rally in Minden, Nevada)[32]

States vary in *how* a voter receives a mail ballot. Five states conduct elections entirely by mail (Colorado, Hawaii, Oregon, Utah, and Washington), and every registered voter automatically receives a ballot. Some states *automatically* send each registrant *an application* for a mail ballot, while others require a voter to *request* a ballot. States also differ in whether a voter must give a *reason* for voting absentee. Some have "no-excuse" absentee voting, while others require voters to give an excuse for why they would not be able to vote in person (early voting or Election Day). A growing number of states allow voters to track the status of their absentee ballot and to "cure" mistakes on it, such as failing to sign the envelope, to make it valid.

Ballotpedia reported that thirty-nine states made at least one voting procedure change for the 2020 general election. Some were permanent, others temporary. Nothing got more attention, or generated more debate, than voting by mail (absentee).

Thirty-six states made a change(s) to their absentee/mail-in voting procedures in 2020.[33] *Automatically* sending mail ballots (five states) or applications for them (ten states) to all registered voters were the most controversial, mostly due to concerns about fraud. The most common,

---

[31] Bill Barrow, Biden Backs Mail Vote, Says Trump's Opposition "Un-American," Associated Press, April 23, 2020, https://apnews.com/article/6cf3ca7d5a174f2f381636cb4706f505

[32] Donald Trump, Minden, Nevada Rally Speech Transcript September 12, Rev.com, September 12, 2020, www.rev.com/blog/transcripts/donald-trump-minden-nevada-rally-speech-transcript-september-12

[33] Changes to Election Dates, Procedures, and Administration in Response to the Coronavirus (COVID-19) Pandemic, 2020, Ballotpedia, November 2020, https://bit.ly/3CBdR7F

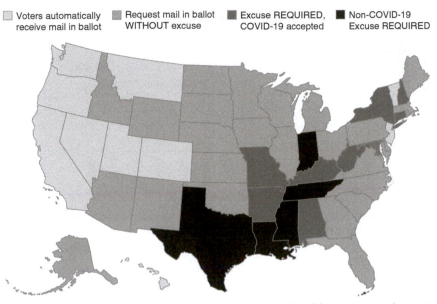

Voters automatically receive mail in ballot • Request mail in ballot WITHOUT excuse • Excuse REQUIRED, COVID-19 accepted • Non-COVID-19 Excuse REQUIRED

Figure 4.2 Vote-by-mail procedures varied across the fifty states in the 2020 election.
Source: Compiled from 2020 data reported by Ballotpedia, National Conference of State Legislatures, and ABC News.

and largely noncontroversial, changes were related to "excuse" policies; some states eliminated them altogether, others allowed COVID-related concerns as an excuse (see Figure 4.2).

VOTER TURNOUT: HIGHER THAN 2016 IN ALL FIFTY STATES

Turnout in 2020 was the highest since 1900. Nearly 155 million Americans voted – 17 million more than in 2016. The voter turnout *rate* skyrocketed from 56 percent in 2016 to 67 percent in 2020 – the highest in 120 years.[34]

Turnout rate is defined as the percentage of the nation's *eligible voting-age population* (18 and older, minus noncitizens and ineligible felons) who voted. The turnout rate for women in 2020 was higher than for men – a pattern that began in 1980 (see Figure 4.3). Before then, men's turnout rate exceeded that of women. In 2016, women's turnout rate was 63 percent compared to men's 59 percent.[35] Nearly 10 million more women than men voted. In 2020, the turnout rate for women was 68 percent

[34] United States Census Bureau, Voting and Registration in the Election of November 2020, April 2021, table 13, https://bit.ly/2VxRYVW
[35] Gender Differences in Voter Turnout, Center for American Women and Politics (hereafter CAWP), 2021, https://cawp.rutgers.edu/facts/voters/turnout#GGN

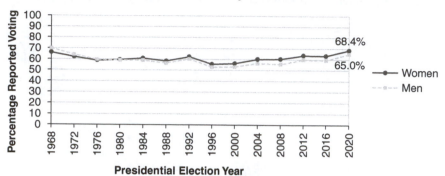

Figure 4.3 Self-reported voter turnout rate by gender shows women slightly more likely than men to vote in 2020.
Source: United States Census Bureau, Voting and Registration in the Election of November 2020, 2021.

compared to men's 65 percent, with 9.6 million more women than men voting (see Figure 4.3).[36]

Voter turnout was higher in every state than in 2016. In fact, it was a record-shattering year for voter participation. What's more, women were a driving force at every stage of the election.

Major Reasons for Spike in Turnout

Why this spike in turnout? The epic battle between incumbent President Donald Trump and challenger Joe Biden was fueled by high levels of partisan polarization – voters either loved (Republicans) or despised (Democrats) President Trump. As in the 2018 midterm election where turnout was the highest in any midterm since 1912, Trump was a big motivation for voters to go to the polls in droves.

A huge percentage of Americans closely followed the 2020 election and a record share (83%) of registered voters said it really mattered who won the presidential contest.[37] When voters feel their vote makes a difference, they are more likely to cast a ballot. For that reason, turnout was particularly high in the competitive battleground states where projections predicted a tight race going down to the wire.

36 United States Census Bureau, Voting and Registration in the Election of November 2020, table 13.
37 Carroll Doherty, Jocelyn Kiley, Nida Asheer, and Calvin Jordan, Election 2020: Voters Are Highly Engaged, But Nearly Half Expect to Have Difficulties Voting, Pew Research Center, August 13, 2020, www.pewresearch.org/politics/2020/08/13/views-of-the-2020-campaign-and-voting-in-november/

The pandemic prompted many states to make it easier and more convenient to vote in response to requests from election officials, voter advocacy groups, and voters themselves. Expanding when and how it could be done, and safely, also resulted in higher voter turnout rates.

Finally, scholars and practitioners alike agreed that massive mobilization (get out the vote) efforts by a multiplicity of grassroots organizations (new and established) drove this sharp increase in turnout even in the middle of a pandemic. This chapter has highlighted the successes of many women-centric organizations in their efforts to increase women's participation in Election 2020.

Women's Turnout Rate Patterns Similar to 2016

The turnout rate again was higher among women than men. *Nationally*, women turned out at a higher rate than men, white and Black women at higher rates than other women of color, older women (especially Baby Boomers) more than younger women, and women with higher levels of education at a higher rate than those with lesser formal education. These *turnout patterns varied somewhat by state* due to differences in their demographic and political composition.

What held true at both levels was that women candidates and advocacy groups – Democrat and Republican – played key roles in increasing women's interest in and motivations for voting. The Census Bureau's post-election analysis of who reported voting found that women made up 53 percent and men 47 percent of all voters.[38]

Expansion of When and How to Vote Drives up Women's Participation

Making it easier to vote without fear of coming in contact with a COVID-19 carrier at a congested polling place on Election Day increased the proportion of Americans voting by mail and voting early at locations with social distancing-enabling facilities. A number of states made it easier to vote by mail, extended times when one could vote early in person, and/or created sites where voters could drop off their ballot or put it in a drop box to avoid any contact.

Even before Election Day, estimates were that at least three-quarters of all registered voters would be eligible to receive a ballot in the mail and that more voters would choose to vote by mail than did so in 2016. That

---

[38] United States Census Bureau, Voting and Registration in the Election of November 2020, table 13.

is exactly what happened. Overall, 43 percent voted by mail, 30 percent in person on Election Day, and 26 percent in person before Election Day. Slightly more women than men voted by mail (44% vs. 41%).[39]

More voters choosing to cast their ballot by mail increased turnout rates. A Pew Research Center analysis found that seven of the ten states where turnout rose the most in 2020 conducted their vote for president entirely or mostly by mail. Six had adopted all-mail voting since 2016 either permanently (Utah and Hawaii) or for the 2020 elections only (California, New Jersey, Vermont, and most of Montana).[40]

An analysis of voting in several battleground states found that women were much more likely to vote early (by mail or in person) than men. The woman director of political strategy at the Way to Win organization was stunned at the increase over 2016: "The numbers are insane. I've been working in politics in Texas, Nevada, Florida, nationally and nobody has ever seen numbers like these ... I think this election is a referendum and people are not willing to not speak up."[41]

Partisan patterns in the choice of how to vote – Republicans (in person), Democrats (by mail) were quite evident and as predicted. A month ahead of the election, a Pew Research Center poll found that when asked whether ballots sent by mail would be delivered in time to be counted, 67 percent of Biden supporters were confident they would, but only 33 percent of Trump supporters. And when queried whether in-person polling places would be run safely without spreading the coronavirus, 91 percent of Trump supporters said yes but only 70 percent of Biden supporters.[42]

Higher Turnout of Women Helped Flip Five States from Red to Blue

In spite of record turnout, a state's partisan leanings predicted the *outcome* of the election in all but five states: "Neither the tumultuous presidency of Donald Trump nor an influx of more than 20 million new voters made

[39] United States Census Bureau, Voting and Registration in the Election of November 2020, April 2021, table 14, https://bit.ly/2VxRYVW

[40] Drew DeSilver, Turnout Soared in 2020 as Nearly Two-Thirds of Eligible US Voters Cast Ballots for President, Pew Research Center, FactTank, January 28, 2021, https://pewrsr.ch/3AfxeBd

[41] Mariel Padilla, More Women Than Men Are Voting Early in Key Battleground States, *The 19th*, November 2020, www.elle.com/culture/career-politics/a34549594/women-driving-2020-election/

[42] Carroll Doherty, Jocelyn Kiley, Nida Asheer, and Calvin Jordan, Deep Divisions in Views of the Election Process – and Whether It Will Be Clear Who Won, Pew Research Center, October 14, 2020, https://pewrsr.ch/3C7694U

any real dent in the partisan stalemate; state-by-state voting patterns in Trump's narrow defeat almost exactly replicated those in his narrow victory in 2016."[43] Except for a few battleground states, the red states (Republican) stayed red and the blue states (Democrat) blue. In the states that flipped from Trump to Biden in 2020 – Michigan, Wisconsin, Pennsylvania, Georgia, and Arizona – changes in the turnout rates and/or a larger number of votes for Biden among women helped him flip the state and win the presidency.[44] Women's share of all voters increased in Georgia, Michigan, and Arizona. According to exit polls, Biden got a higher percentage of the women's vote than did Hillary Clinton in 2016 in Michigan (+ 4%), Wisconsin (+ 3%), and Arizona (+ 2%). Black women played a big part in Georgia and Michigan and in the heavily populated urban areas of Pennsylvania. In Arizona, it was Latinas and Native Americans. In Wisconsin, young and college-educated whites, suburban women, and Black women.

Biden's winning coalition nationally was described by some as resembling that of former President Barack Obama: "African Americans, women, college-educated professionals, seniors … along with anti-Trump Republicans and working class white men."[45] Missing from that description but very much a big part of Biden's coalition were Latinos, Asian Americans, Native Americans, LGBTQ+ persons, along with the rising younger generations (Gen Z and Millennials) of voters, a larger share of whom are women and multiracial.

Without question, women's participation in election 2020 made a difference in who was elected at every level – national, state, and local. Women also rewrote history with their trailblazing activism and record-breaking turnout.

REFLECTIONS

The story of women's participation in various facets of election 2020, particularly the presidential election, is one of collective action on the part of grassroots organizations, some new, others long established. "A coalition

[43] Larry M. Bartels, Trench Warfare: The 2020 Election in Historical Perspective, Vanderbilt Project on Unity and American Democracy, Vanderbilt University, February 9, 2021, www.vanderbilt.edu/unity/2021/02/09/trench-warfare/

[44] William H. Frey, Exit Polls Show Both Familiar and New Voting Blocs Sealed Biden's Win, Brookings, November 12, 2020, https://brook.gs/3iihlnj

[45] Trevor Hunnicutt, James Oliphant, Joseph Ax, and Jarrett Renshaw, Biden's Winning Strategy: Flip Rust Belt Trump States and Hold on Tight, Reuters, November 7, 2020, https://reut.rs/3jcO2l9

of labor rights, immigrant rights, Latino, Latina, Latinx, African Americans, Asian Americans, Native Americans … as well as LGBTQ+ organizations"[46] worked to elect Joe Biden and Kamala Harris. Putting together such a coalition was more successful in some areas than others … but in terms of how it is done nowhere is more interesting, going forward, than Georgia.

In discussing how Georgia became the Deep South's first state to flip from Republican to Democrat in decades, two prominent Black women cofounders of Fair Fight Action, Stacey Abrams and Lauren Groh-Wargo, pointed to building "registration, turnout, engagement and support from every community – Black, white, Latino, Native American, Asian-American." Their advice on how to successfully build political clout is to pay close attention to changing demographic numbers and rely on "an authentic, multiracial, multiethnic, multigenerational and truly statewide coalition" to provide "moral clarity."[47] *It takes time* and *"must not be centered on one election or one leader,"* they affirmed.

The question we are left with post 2020 is whether the record-breaking levels of participation by women of all political persuasions will be repeated in subsequent election cycles. After all, it took more than a century to achieve the high turnout we saw in 2020. While there are few signs that deep partisan divides will dissipate anytime soon, allowing individuals to have different opinions and make different choices are central to a democracy.

Just as there was diversity of opinion among women with regard to passage of the Nineteenth Amendment, there will continue to be diversity among women in their political preferences in the years ahead … and women's voices will continue to grow louder as more are elected to offices at every level, including the presidency.

---

[46] Alex Bell and Ashley Valenzuela, The 2020 Presidential Election Saw Historic Numbers for Voter Turnout, *23ABC News* (ABC), Bakersfield, California, January 18, 2021, www.turnto23.com/news/politics/the-2020-presidential-election-saw-historic-numbers-for-voter-turnout

[47] Stacey Abrams and Lauren Groh-Wargo, Stacey Abrams and Lauren Groh-Wargo: How to Turn Your Red State Blue, *New York Times*, February 11, 2021, www.nytimes.com/2021/02/11/opinion/stacey-abrams-georgia-election.html

5 Voting Choices: The Importance of Women Voters and the Gender Gap

Women voters have received special attention from the presidential candidates in recent elections primarily because of differences between women and men in their political preferences, a phenomenon commonly referred to as the gender gap. Statistically, a gender gap can be defined as the difference between the proportion of women and the proportion of men who support a particular politician, party, or policy position. In the 2020 presidential election, the winning candidate, Democrat Joe Biden, received 57 percent of women's votes, compared with 45 percent of men's, resulting in a gender gap of twelve percentage points.[1]

A gender gap in voting has been evident in every general election for president since 1980. In each of the last eleven presidential elections, a greater proportion of women than men voted for the Democratic candidate. For example, in 2012, when Democrat Barack Obama was reelected, 55 percent of women, compared with only 45 percent of men, cast their votes for him, resulting in a gender gap of ten percentage points. In 2016, 54 percent of women, but only 41 percent of men, cast their votes for the Democratic candidate, Hillary Clinton, who lost the presidential election despite winning a majority of women's votes.[2]

Prior to the 1980 election, it was widely believed that women and men took similar positions on most issues, had similar political preferences, and voted in much the same ways. In other words, the assumption before 1980 was that gender did not matter much in voting. Today the assumption is exactly the opposite – that gender does matter in politics. Women and men, in the aggregate, express different positions on many

---

[1] The Gender Gap, Center for American Women and Politics (hereafter CAWP), fact sheet, 2021, https://cawp.rutgers.edu/sites/default/files/resources/ggpresvote.pdf
[2] Ibid.

issues and tend to vary in their party identification and support for political candidates. The gender gap is now viewed as an enduring part of the
political landscape, and candidates, parties, and politicians must pay specific attention to women voters if they want to win elections.

Nevertheless, even though women in the aggregate vote differently
than men, women voters are not monolithic and do not all share the
same political preferences. Political divisions and differences are apparent
among women, especially among women of different races and ethnicities, ages, educational levels, and marital statuses. These differences
among women have perhaps never been more apparent than they were
in the 2020 elections, when various subgroups of women voters played
critical roles in helping determine the outcome of the presidential election.

This chapter begins with an overview of the role that women voters
and the gender gap played in the 2020 presidential election. It then traces
the origins of and explores possible explanations for the gender gap. It
also examines the strategies candidates have employed in attempting to
appeal to women voters.

WOMEN VOTERS AND THE 2020 PRESIDENTIAL ELECTION

The election of Donald Trump as president in 2016 was followed by a high
level of activism on the part of women. Hundreds of thousands of women
participated in the Women's March on January 21, 2017, in Washington,
DC and in cities across the country in reaction to the election of Donald
Trump and in support of women's rights and other progressive policies.
This was followed by the emergence of the #MeToo movement, focused
on sexual abuse and sexual harassment of women, which gained widespread attention and momentum in the fall of 2017 with the revelation of
numerous accusations against movie producer Harvey Weinstein.
Although #MeToo has not focused exclusively on politics and politicians,
a major goal of this movement has been explicitly political: to change the
laws pertaining to sexual harassment and assault. Women also joined
other protests against Trump administration policies in large numbers,
including protests against the so-called Muslim Ban, prohibiting the
admission into the United States of refugees and visitors from certain
Islamic countries.

The heightened politization and activism among American women
evident in the activities of these movements were also very much evident
in the 2018 elections. Women across the country were mobilized to run

for office in record numbers, especially on the Democratic side. More women than ever before ran for governor, Congress, and seats in state legislatures throughout the country. And more women were elected to office than in previous years. As a result of the 2018 elections, record numbers of women served in Congress and state legislatures heading into the 2020 election cycle.

Heightened activism also was evident as women went to the polls to vote in 2018. Women turned out to vote in record numbers; 65.3 million reported voting in 2018 compared with 49.2 million in 2014, the most recent nonpresidential election year. And women voted in higher proportions than men, with 55.0 percent of women casting ballots in 2018 compared with 51.8 percent of men.[3]

Women overall voted much more heavily Democratic in 2018 than did men. For example, 59 percent of women, compared with 47 percent of men, cast their ballots for Democratic congressional candidates according to the national exit poll conducted by Edison Research. Support for Democratic candidates was particularly strong among women of color, with 92 percent of Black women and 73 percent of Latinas voting for Democratic candidates for the US House of Representatives. Because of the large overall difference between women and men in their support for Democratic candidates, women were credited with propelling the Democratic takeover of the House of Representatives in the 2018 elections as well as the victories of numerous Democratic candidates for other offices across the country.[4]

As a result of this increased activism among women between 2016 and 2020 as movement participants, candidates, and voters, many observers expected to see both high levels of turnout among women voters in the 2020 elections and a larger-than-usual gender gap, with women voting for Democrat Joe Biden (and against Republican Donald Trump) in much greater proportions than men. Of course, observers had also expected the historic nature of Hillary Clinton's candidacy and the offensive nature of some of Donald Trump's behavior during the 2016 presidential election to lead to big differences in the voting behavior of women and men in that election, and yet women's overall preference for the Democratic candidate was not sufficient to propel Clinton to victory. Because Donald Trump

---

[3] Gender Differences in Voter Turnout, CAWP, 2021, https://cawp.rutgers.edu/facts/voters/turnout

[4] Women Voters Propel Democratic Takeover of US House of Representatives; Large Gender Gaps Apparent in Most 2018 Senate and Gubernatorial Races, CAWP, press release, November 8, 2018, press-release-women-voters-2018_0.pdf (rutgers.edu)

was the Republican candidate in both 2016 and 2020 and because the 2016 election helped to establish expectations for what to expect in 2020, a brief review of the gender dynamics of the 2016 presidential election helps set the stage for understanding what happened with women voters in 2020.

In the 2016 election Hillary Clinton highlighted her gender and attempted to use it to her strategic advantage, especially with women voters. From the outset, the campaign emphasized the historic nature of Clinton's candidacy – that she would, if elected, be the first woman to serve as president of the United States. The short video she released in April 2015, announcing her candidacy and depicting "Everyday Americans" in need of a champion, featured women who were white, Black, Latina, and Asian American, young, middle-aged, and elderly in a variety of roles and settings. She frequently appeared during her campaign with African American mothers who had lost children as a result of gun violence. She often made reference to being a grandmother and talked about how the birth of her granddaughter made her more concerned about the world that her granddaughter and her granddaughter's generation would inherit. Clinton spoke repeatedly about her history of advocacy on behalf of women and girls. On the campaign trail, she frequently noted that as president she would fight for policies such as equal pay, paid family leave, women's reproductive rights, affordable childcare, an increase in the minimum wage, and measures to counter violence against women that would help all or specific subgroups of women.

In contrast to Clinton, Donald Trump's 2016 campaign did little to try to win over women voters beyond those who supported him because they were Republicans, because they strongly disliked Hillary Clinton, or because they found his positions on issues such as immigration, trade, terrorism, and health care appealing. At the urging of his daughter, Ivanka, Trump did hold one press conference in September 2016 where he announced proposals for six weeks of paid maternity leave (in contrast to family leave favored by the Democrats) and a tax deduction for childcare expenses. But beyond this press conference, he devoted little attention to such issues in his campaign.

In fact, most of the media coverage related to Trump and women during his 2016 campaign focused not on his policy proposals, but rather on his behavior. Throughout his career before becoming a candidate, Trump made numerous offensive comments about women, but the offensive comments were not limited to Trump's past. Rather, during the campaign itself, Trump continued to insult women, for example referring to

Hillary Clinton as a "nasty woman" in the third general election debate and claiming that Megyn Kelly, a Fox News anchor and moderator of one of the Republican primary debates, had blood "coming out of her wherever."[5]

Of course, Trump received the most attention in October 2016 with the release of the "Access Hollywood" audiotape where he bragged about forcing himself on women: "I'm automatically attracted to beautiful [women]. I just start kissing them … I don't even wait. And when you're a star, they let you do it. You can do anything … Grab 'em by the pussy. You can do anything."[6] The release of this tape provoked a national uproar that many observers thought would cost Trump the election. While Trump's comments did stimulate a nationwide discussion about sexual assault, they did not prevent a Trump victory. Rather, millions of women and men across the country decided that Trump's treatment of women was not sufficiently problematic to override the other reasons they had for voting for him.

In the end, despite her attempts to maximize her support among women voters, Hillary Clinton lost the 2016 general election to Donald Trump. Many factors contributed to her loss, but she did not lose because women failed to support her, as some media outlets mistakenly suggested at the time. A majority, 54 percent, of women voted for her over Trump, according to the 2016 Edison Research Exit Poll, and Clinton would have been elected president if men, a majority of whom supported Trump, had voted for her in the same proportion as women did. Nevertheless, Clinton – a female candidate who actively sought the support of women voters – did not win women by as large a margin as some observers thought she would.

For a Democratic presidential candidate to defeat Donald Trump in 2020, the candidate would likely have to fare even better with women voters than Hillary Clinton had. That was one of the challenges facing Democrat Joe Biden as he embarked on his 2020 presidential campaign. Clearly, Biden could not appeal to women voters on the basis of being a woman, as Hillary Clinton did. However, he did start with an advantage over Donald Trump in that more women in the electorate are Democrats than Republicans. A Pew Research Center report issued in June 2020 found that 39 percent of female registered voters identified as Democrats

5 Philip Rucker, Trump Says Fox's Megyn Kelly Had "Blood Coming Out of Her Wherever," *Washington Post*, August 8, 2015, https://wapo.st/37mgmMz
6 Transcript: Donald Trump's Taped Comments about Women, *New York Times*, October 8, 2016, www.nytimes.com/2016/10/08/us/donald-trump-tape-transcript.html

compared with 28 percent who considered themselves Republicans. The remaining chunk of women voters, an additional 30 percent, considered themselves independents.[7] Thus, the challenge that Biden faced in trying to exceed the support Hillary Clinton received from women voters in 2016 was twofold. On the one hand, Biden had to mobilize as many women in the Democratic base as he could; he had to maximize turnout among women who were registered Democrats. On the other hand, he also had to win the votes of a majority of independents who were not as strongly committed to the Democratic Party.

Black women are a key group of voters within the Democratic base. They vote heavily Democratic, and in Joe Biden's case their support was perhaps even more critical than usual. Biden's 2020 presidential campaign emphasized several issues of major concern to African American women. For example, Biden pledged to attack systemic racism and promote racial justice. In fact, he claimed that the white supremacist march in Charlottesville, Virginia, in 2017, and Trump's comment suggesting that there were "some very fine people on both sides" of the march, motivated him to run for president. Biden chose an African American woman, Kamala Harris, as his running mate, and pledged to put the first Black woman on the Supreme Court. And unlike Donald Trump, who downplayed the COVID-19 pandemic that disproportionately affected Black communities, Biden proclaimed that addressing the pandemic would be a top priority of his administration.

Donald Trump's campaign also made some attempts to attract Black voters, especially Black men, where they saw greater possibilities for success. Trump took credit for the First Step Act that made long overdue reforms in the criminal justice system, claimed that Blacks had the lowest unemployment rate ever under his administration, and touted his support of federal funding for historically Black colleges and universities (HBCUs). But Trump also repeatedly took positions and engaged in behaviors that were likely to offend many Black voters. For example, he denounced Black Lives Matter, criticized Black female members of Congress and other prominent Black public figures, and put forth the highly questionable claim that he had done more for African Americans than any other president except for Abraham Lincoln.

In the end, Trump failed to make significant gains in Black support while Black voters, especially women, proved critical to Biden's victory.

---

[7] In Changing US Electorate, Race and Education Remain Stark Dividing Lines, Pew Research Center, June 2, 2020, https://pewrsr.ch/3jqxZAn

As Vice President–Elect Kamala Harris tweeted less than a week after the election: "I want to speak directly to the Black women in our country. Thank you. You are too often overlooked, and yet are asked time and again to step up and be the backbone of our democracy. We could not have done this without you."[8]

In fact, it is not far-fetched to suggest that Joe Biden would never have won the Democratic primaries and become the Democratic candidate without the strong and unwavering support of African American women. Joe Biden did not fare well in Iowa and New Hampshire, the first two states to select delegates to the Democratic national convention, finishing fourth among all Democratic candidates in the Iowa caucuses and fifth in the New Hampshire primary. Both states are overwhelmingly white, unlike South Carolina, the third state to select delegates, which has a large Black population. In fact, according to Edison Research, 56 percent of voters in the 2020 South Carolina Democratic primary were Black, and 61 percent of them chose Joe Biden. The next closest candidate was Bernie Sanders, with 17 percent of the Black vote.[9] Biden's victory there basically turned his flagging campaign around, and as he continued to win primary victories in southern states with sizable Black populations, he became the Democratic front-runner.

Black voters continued to support Biden throughout the Democratic primaries and in his general election campaign against Republican Donald Trump. Reports suggested that Blacks turned out to support him in record numbers. In his acceptance speech after being declared winner of the presidential race in November 2020, Biden acknowledged the critical report he received from Black voters, declaring, "And especially for those moments when this campaign was at its lowest – the African American community stood up again for me. They always have my back, and I'll have yours."[10]

Although a large majority of Black men as well as Black women supported Joe Biden's candidacy, Black women turned out to vote at higher rates than Black men,[11] and their level of support for Biden was even

[8] Kamala Harris, Twitter feed, November 9, 2020, quoted in Suzette Hackney, Black Voters Steer America toward Moral Clarity in Presidential Race, *USA Today*, November 12, 2020, https://bit.ly/3yCBhak

[9] Sarah Dutton, The South Carolina Primary: A Quick Look at Black Voters, Edison Research, blog feature, March 2, 2020, www.edisonresearch.com/the-south-carolina-primary-a-quick-look-at-black-voters/

[10] Transcript of President-Elect Joe Biden's Victory Speech, November 7, 2020, Associated Press, https://bit.ly/3irT0LM

[11] Gender Differences in Voter Turnout, CAWP, 2021.

greater than the strong support exhibited by Black men. According to the Edison Research exit poll, an overwhelming 90 percent of Black women voted for Biden in the general election compared with 79 percent of Black men.[12] Moreover, as suggested by Susan MacManus and Amy Benner in Chapter 4 of this volume, Black women such as Stacey Abrams often took the lead in efforts to register new voters and to get voters to turn out on Biden's behalf. As a result, although Black voters overall played a very important role in Biden's election to the presidency, Black women voters were especially critical.

Like Black women, a sizable majority of Latinas – 69 percent according to the Edison Research exit poll and 73 percent according to Latino Decisions' American Election Eve Poll – also voted for Biden.[13] As Anna Sampaio details in Chapter 6, in certain states where the Latino population is concentrated, Latinas were a critical component of the winning coalition for Joe Biden.

In contrast to Latinas and Black women, white women, a majority of whom have backed the Republican candidate in every recent presidential election, cast a majority of their votes nationwide, 55 percent, for Donald Trump. Even the most pro-Democratic age group of white female voters, 18- to 29-year-olds, broke for Trump. White women among the under 30 age group cast 53 percent of their votes for Trump and 44 percent for Biden.

Although a majority of white women voters supported Trump, white women were divided in their preferences along educational lines. A majority of white women with college degrees, 54 percent, voted for Biden. In contrast, a majority of white women who were not college graduates, 63 percent, cast their ballots for Trump. Traditionally, well-educated white women and men have tended to vote more Republican than Democrat, but in recent elections white voters with college degrees have been moving in a Democratic direction. The 2020 election seems to have continued the trend with Biden winning a slightly higher proportion of the votes of white women college graduates than Clinton did in 2016 (54 percent versus 51 percent).

On the flipside, white voters who are not college graduates have become more Republican in their voting patterns in recent elections. And Donald Trump received large majorities of their votes, with 63 percent of

[12]   CNN, 2020 Exit Polls, https://edition.cnn.com/election/2020/exit-polls/president/national-results. All poll results in the paragraphs that follow are from this exit poll unless otherwise noted.

[13]   Latino Decisions, American Election Eve Poll 2020, https://electioneve2020.com/poll/#/en/demographics/latino/

white women and 70 percent of white men without college degrees casting ballots for him. White women and men without college degrees were among the subgroups of voters who most strongly supported Trump.

The Trump campaign also hoped to win the votes of women who lived in the suburbs in 2020. Presidential campaigns have often targeted suburban women because as a group they are viewed as swing voters who do not consistently vote Democratic or Republican but who can be persuaded to support one party or the other depending on the candidates and the context of the election. In the 2016 election, Trump actually won suburban voters (women and men combined) over Clinton by a margin of 49 percent to 45 percent. In contrast, Democrats fared well with suburban voters in the 2018 nonpresidential elections; an overwhelming majority of the US House seats picked up by Democrats in that election were in suburban districts.

While both Democratic and Republican presidential campaigns in 2020 attempted to appeal to women swing voters in suburban areas, Trump had his own distinctive way of appealing to them. In Pennsylvania, Trump pleaded with suburban women to support him based on his ending of an anti-segregation fair housing policy enacted by the Obama administration: "Suburban women, they should like me more than anybody here tonight because I ended deregulation that destroyed your neighborhood. I ended the regulation that brought crime to the suburbs … So can I ask you to do me a favor? Suburban women, will you please like me? I saved your d— neighborhood."[14]

In Michigan a couple of weeks later, Trump tried out some other appeals:

> Because women, suburban or otherwise, they want security … They want safety. They want law and order. They have to have law and order, and we're gonna do great. And I love women, and I can't help it. They're the greatest. I love them much more than the men. Much more than the men. So I'm saving suburbia. I'm getting your kids back to school, get your kids back to school.[15]

He followed these comments up with a pledge that he was getting the women's husbands back to work. This was despite the fact that more women than men had lost jobs during the pandemic. As many commentators

---

[14] Trump quoted in Colby Itkowitz et al., Trump Begs for Suburban Women's Support While Biden Appeals to Older Voters, *Washington Post*, October 13, 2020.

[15] Trump quoted in Philip Bump, With a Week Left, Trump Modifies His Pitch to Suburban Women, *Washington Post*, October 27, 2020.

observed, Trump's comments seemed to be a throwback to an earlier era in the mid-twentieth century when the suburbs were less diverse, women were far less likely to work outside the home, and racial segregation was far too common.

Not surprisingly, Trump did not fare particularly well in winning the votes of women who live in the suburbs. He won 43 percent of their votes compared with Biden's 56 percent according to the Edison Research exit poll.

In the end Joe Biden became president in part because he was successful in winning a larger percentage of women's votes than did Hillary Clinton in 2016. Biden won 57 percent of women's votes compared to the 54 percent that Clinton won. Nine of every ten Black women supported Biden, and all indicators suggest that they turned out to vote in higher numbers in 2020 than in 2016. About seven of every ten Latina voters cast a ballot for Biden, contributing significantly to his victories in states such as Arizona, California, New Mexico, Nevada, and Colorado. He carried women in suburbs across the country, and in key states like Pennsylvania and Georgia, the votes of suburban women, in all their diversity, were critical. Finally, while a majority of white women supported Trump, Biden fared better with white women who both were and were not college grads than did Hillary Clinton in 2016. A majority of college-educated women supported the Democratic candidate in both the 2016 and 2020 elections, but Biden received 54 percent of their votes compared with the 51 percent Clinton received. And while white women without college degrees went overwhelmingly for Trump in both elections, Biden was able to attract slightly more, 36 percent, in 2020 than Clinton had won, 34 percent, in 2016.

Thus, a diversity of women – Black women, Latinas, women in the suburbs, white women who were college graduates, and even a sliver of white women who were not college graduates – contributed to his victory. Together they managed to give Joe Biden the largest gender gap, according to the Edison Research exit polls, that any president has ever received with 57 percent of women, compared with only 45 percent of men, voting for Biden for a gender gap of twelve percentage points.

THE ORIGINS OF THE GENDER GAP

In Chapter 4 of this volume, Susan MacManus and Amy Benner describe the suffrage movement that led to the addition of the Nineteenth Amendment to the Constitution in 1920, granting women the right to vote. Over the course of the several decades that it took to win the right to vote, suffragists used a variety of arguments to win support from different segments of the all-male electorate and political structure. Some approaches stressed fundamental similarities between women and men and demanded the vote for women as a matter of simple justice. Suffragists observed that women were human beings just as men were, and therefore women, like men, were created equal and had an inalienable right to political equality and thus the vote.

However, suffragists also used arguments that focused on how women were different from men and would use their votes to help make the world a better place. Suffragists claimed that women's experiences, especially their experiences as mothers and caregivers, gave them special values and perspectives that would be readily apparent in their voting decisions. They argued that women would use their votes to stop wars, promote peace, clean up government, ban the sale of liquor, and bring justice to a corrupt world.

The use of such arguments led some people to eagerly anticipate and others to greatly fear the consequences of women's enfranchisement. Many observers at the time expected women to go to the polls in large numbers and thought that their distinctive impact on politics would be immediately apparent. However, the right to vote, in and of itself, proved insufficient to bring about a distinctive women's vote. Rather, a women's vote would emerge only decades later after other changes in society and women's perceptions of themselves took place. In the elections immediately following women's enfranchisement in 1920, women voted in much lower numbers than men, and there were few signs that women were voting much differently than men or using their votes to express a distinctive perspective.

As the decades passed after 1920, it seemed that the women's vote, feared by some and longed for by others, would never materialize. However, by the early 1980s, a sufficient number of women finally achieved the social and psychological independence necessary to bring about a divergence in the voting patterns of women and men. In the decades since 1980, the women's vote promised by the suffragists has finally arrived, although with underlying issues and dynamics somewhat different from those anticipated during the suffrage era.

In the decades between 1920 and 1980, the vast majority of women, especially white women,[16] remained economically dependent on men, not necessarily by choice but because society offered them few options. As

---

[16] This account applies largely to white women who constituted a large majority of women in the United States throughout these decades. The situation for African American women and other women of color was somewhat different. African American women

a result, women's political interests were intertwined with, even insepa-
rable from, the political interests of men, and for the most part women did
not make political decisions that differed from those made by men.
However, since the 1960s and 1970s, women's dependence on men has
begun to unravel, and as this unraveling has taken place, women have
started making political choices that are more independent of men's
wishes and interests.

At least three critical developments over the past several decades have
contributed to the increased independence of women from men and have
made possible the emergence of gender differences in voting choices. The
first is the fact that, for a variety of reasons including higher divorce rates
and longer life spans, more women are living apart from men, often heading households on their own. The second development is that more
women have achieved professional and managerial positions that, even
when they live with men, provide them with sufficient incomes to support themselves and allow them a substantial degree of financial independence from men. The third critical development is the contemporary
women's movement, which began with the founding of the National
Organization for Women (NOW) in 1966 and the development of wom-
en's liberation groups around the country in 1967 and 1968. Although
even today a majority of women in American society do not call themselves feminists, the women's movement has changed the way most
women in the United States see themselves and their life options. Most
women now recognize that they have concerns and interests that are not
always identical to those of the men in their lives, and they are aware that
these concerns can be relevant to their political choices.

Brief glimpses of gender differences in voting had been apparent from
time to time before 1980. For example, women were slightly more likely
than men to vote for Dwight Eisenhower, the victorious Republican candidate, in the 1952 and 1956 elections. However, these pre-1980 gender
differences in voting were not persistent, nor were they accompanied by
consistent gender differences in evaluations of presidential performance,
party identification, or voting for offices other than president. A textbook
on public opinion commonly used in political science courses, published
just before the 1980 election, reflected the conventional thinking about

were less likely than white women to be economically dependent on men because they
more often worked outside the home (although usually in low-paying jobs). However,
the political interests of African American women and men still were generally
intertwined because society offered limited options for African Americans of either
gender.

gender differences at that time. This 324-page book devoted only half a page to women and gender, concluding, "Differences in the political attitudes of men and women are so slight that they deserve only brief mention ... In political attitudes and voting, people are seldom different because of their sex."[17]

Even though women had achieved a substantial degree of independence from men and their attitudes about themselves were changing throughout the 1970s, it was not until 1980 that a political candidate came along who could crystallize political differences between women and men into a gender gap. Governor Ronald Reagan, the Republican who was elected president in 1980 and reelected in 1984, proved to be the catalyst for the gender gap. In contrast to the 1976 presidential campaign, where most positions taken by the Republican and Democratic candidates were not starkly different, the 1980 presidential campaign presented voters with clear alternatives. Reagan offered policy proposals that contrasted sharply with the policies of then-incumbent President Jimmy Carter. Reagan promised to cut back on the size of the federal government, greatly reduce government spending, increase the strength of the US military, and get tough with the Soviet Union. When offered such clear-cut alternatives, women and men expressed different preferences. Although Reagan defeated Carter in 1980 and was elected president, he received notably less support from women than from men. Exit polls conducted by the major television networks on Election Day showed that women were between six and nine percentage points less likely than men to vote for Reagan. For example, an exit poll conducted jointly by CBS and the *New York Times* showed that only 46 percent of women, compared with 54 percent of men, voted for Reagan, resulting in a gender gap of eight percentage points. Clearly, women were less attracted to the candidacy and policies of Reagan than men were. (Alternatively, looking at the gender gap from the flip side, the polls showed that the policies and candidacy of Reagan resonated more with men than with women.)

Many commentators in the early 1980s thought that this gender gap in presidential voting might be short-lived and would disappear in subsequent presidential elections, much like earlier glimpses of gender differences (e.g. those in the presidential elections of the 1950s), but this time the gender gap was here to stay. As Table 5.1 shows, in every presidential election since 1980, differences have been apparent in the proportions of

[17] Robert S. Erikson, Norman R. Luttbeg, and Kent L. Tedin, *American Public Opinion: Its Origins, Content, and Impact,* 2nd ed. (New York: John Wiley, 1980), p. 186.

TABLE 5.1 A gender gap in voting has been evident in every presidential election since 1980

Election year	Winning presidential candidate	Women voting for winner (%)	Men voting for winner (%)	Gender gap (in percentage points)
2020	Joe Biden (D)	57	45	12
2016	Donald Trump (R)	41	52	11
2012	Barack Obama (D)	55	45	10
2008	Barack Obama (D)	56	49	7
2004	George W. Bush (R)	48	55	7
2000	George W. Bush (R)	44	54	10
1996	Bill Clinton (D)	55	44	11
1992	Bill Clinton (D)	45	41	4
1988	George H. W. Bush (R)	50	57	7
1984	Ronald Reagan (R)	56	62	6
1980	Ronald Reagan (R)	47	55	8

Source: Data are from exit polls conducted by CBS/*New York Times*, 1980, 1984, 1988; Voter News Service, 1992, 1996, 2000; Edison Media Research and Mitofsky International, 2004, 2008; Edison Research 2012, 2016, 2020.

women and men who voted for the winning candidate, ranging from a low of four percentage points in 1992 to a high of twelve percentage points in 2020. In each of these elections, women have been more likely than men to support the Democratic candidate for president.

If the suffragists who had worked so hard to achieve voting rights for women could return today to see the results of their efforts, they would surely say, "I told you so." It may have taken sixty years to arrive, but the women's vote that the suffragists anticipated is now clearly evident and has been influencing the dynamics of presidential elections for four decades.

THE BREADTH AND PERSISTENCE OF THE GENDER GAP

The gender gap has become an enduring feature of American politics, evident across a wide variety of political attitudes, preferences, and behaviors. Since 1980, the gender gap has been apparent not only in voting in presidential elections but also in voting at other levels of office, in party identification, and in the performance ratings of various presidents.

Gender Gap in Races below the Presidential Level

The exit polls conducted on each Election Day have asked voters not only about their selections in the presidential contest but also about their choices in US House, US Senate, and gubernatorial elections. In every election since 1982, women have been more likely than men to vote for Democrats in races for the US House of Representatives. For example, according to the 2020 exit poll conducted by Edison Research, a majority (57%) of women, but only a minority (45%) of men voted for the Democratic candidate for Congress in their district, resulting in a gender gap of twelve percentage points.[18]

Gender gaps also have been evident in a large majority of recent races for US Senate and gubernatorial seats. Thirty-three of the 100 seats in the US Senate were up for election in 2020, and twelve of the fifty states elected governors. Exit poll data indicate that women and men had significantly different candidate preferences in most of these races. In eleven of the sixteen US Senate races where exit polls were conducted by Edison Research, gender gaps ranging from six to fifteen percentage points were evident. (Similarly, in the two US Senate runoff elections in Georgia held on January 5, 2021, Democratic candidates Jon Ossoff and Raphael Warnock won with gender gaps of nine and seven percentage points, respectively.) In all four of the gubernatorial races where exit polls were conducted on Election Day 2020, there were gender gaps of six to eighteen percentage points. In each of the US Senate and gubernatorial elections in which a notable gender gap was present, women were more likely than men to vote for the Democratic candidate.[19]

Gender Gap in Party Identification

Women not only are more likely than men to vote for Democratic candidates, but also are more likely than men to identify with the Democratic Party. Some observers have argued that the gender gap in voting is the result of changes in men's, not women's, political behavior, and the data on party identification offer strong evidence in support of this view. In the 1970s, both women and men were more likely to identify as Democrat than Republicans, and no significant gender gap in party identification was apparent. However, that pattern changed beginning in the early 1980s, following the election of Ronald Reagan. Men shifted in the direction of the Republican Party, becoming more likely to identify as

---

[18] CNN, 2020 Exit Polls.
[19] Ibid.

Republicans and less likely to identify as Democrats than they had been in the 1970s. In contrast, women's party identification remained more stable, showing less dramatic changes since the 1970s. Women were more likely to identify as Democrats than as Republicans in the 1970s, and they remained more likely to be Democrats in 2016.

Although the gender gap in party identification apparently seems to have been initiated by changes among men, this does not mean that the gap is the result of men's behavior alone; the behavior of women was also critical. Prior to 1980, when shifts occurred in the political environment, women and men generally responded similarly. But with the increasing independence of women from men, the politics of the 1980s produced a different result. When men chose to shift their party identification, women chose not to follow them.

A gender gap in party identification is very much evident in the current political context. When asked whether they think of themselves as Democrats, Republicans, or independents, more women than men consider themselves Democrats. For example, the Pew Research Center reported in June 2020 that female registered voters were much more likely to call themselves Democrats than Republicans, with 39 percent of women identifying as Democrats and only 28 percent as Republicans. In contrast, male registered voters were more likely to identify as Republicans than Democrats by a margin of 31 percent to 26 percent. A sizable chunk of women (30%) and men (39%) considered themselves to be independents, but among these independents, a larger proportion of women than men leaned toward the Democratic Party. In total, 56 percent of women, compared with 42 percent of men, identified with or leaned toward the Democratic Party, a gender gap of fourteen percentage points.[20]

While women are more likely than men to consider themselves Democrats, demographic characteristics other than gender also affect the extent to which women identify with the two parties. The same Pew study found sizable differences among women based on age, education, and race and ethnicity.[21] Millennial women (ages 18–35) were more Democratic and less Republican than women in any other age group. Women with undergraduate or postgraduate degrees were more Democratic than women with less education. And women of color

[20] In Changing US Electorate, Race and Education Remain Stark Dividing Lines, Pew Research Center, June 2, 2020, https://pewrsr.ch/3jqxZAn

[21] Ruth Igielnik, Men and Women in the US Continue to Differ in Voter Turnout Rate, Party Identification, Pew Research Center, August 18, 2020, https://pewrsr.ch/2X0nYCl

(African American, Latina, and Asian American) were much more Democratic than white women; in fact, white women split about evenly in their identification between the Democratic and Republican parties.

However, while women of different demographic groups varied in their party identification, women across all demographic categories were more likely than the men who shared the same characteristics to be Democrats. While 60 percent of millennial women identified with or leaned toward the Democratic Party, this was true for only 48 percent of millennial men. Similarly, 65 percent of women with college degrees identified as Democrats, compared with only 48 percent of their male counterparts.

Among Blacks, 87 percent of women compared with 77 percent of men considered themselves Democrats. Among Latinos, 67 percent of women and 58 percent of men identified with the Democratic Party. Among whites, 48 percent of women and 35 percent of men leaned toward or identified as Democrats. Thus, although Blacks and Latinos are much more heavily Democratic than whites, gender differences are apparent within all three groups.

Gender Gap in Presidential Performance Ratings

Just as a gender gap has been evident in party identification, a gender gap has also been apparent in evaluations of the performance of presidents who have served since 1980. On surveys conducted throughout the year, the Gallup poll asks whether people approve or disapprove of the way the incumbent is handling his job as president. Some presidents have had higher approval ratings than others, and the ratings for each president have varied across his tenure in office. But regardless of the president or his level of popularity, women have consistently ranked the performance of Democratic presidents higher and Republican presidents lower than men.

For example, at the time of his first inauguration in January 2009, support for Democratic President Barack Obama was very high; Gallup found that 69 percent of women, compared with 64 percent of men, approved of Obama's performance as president, a gender gap of five percentage points. Throughout Obama's two terms in office, his popularity varied, dipping as far as the lower 40 percent range, but women consistently gave him more favorable job performance ratings than did men. Obama ended his second term in office with fairly strong approval ratings and a gender gap similar in size to the gap when he was first inaugurated; 63 percent of women and 56 percent of men approved of his performance in office in mid-January 2017, a gender gap of seven percentage points.[22]

Similarly, Republican President Donald Trump entered the presidency with a gender gap in his approval rating. Trump's 45 percent approval rating at the time of his inauguration in January 2017 was the lowest of any president in the history of polling. While 48 percent of men approved of his performance, only 42 percent of women did so, a gender gap of six percentage points.[23] Trump's performance rating and gender gap remained fairly consistent across his four years in office, with his overall approval rating never surpassing 49 percent. Trump left office in January 2021 with the lowest level of voter approval throughout his term, 34 percent. Only 30 percent of women, compared with 39 percent of men, rated his performance favorably for a gender gap of nine percentage points.[24]

Democratic President Joe Biden entered the presidency in January 2021 with an approval rating of 57 percent, considerably higher than that for outgoing President Trump. President Biden's eleven-percentage-point gender gap in approval was also slightly larger than Trump's. Biden received favorable ratings from 63 percent of women compared with 52 percent of men.[25]

Gender gaps were apparent in the performance ratings of earlier presidents as well. Women have been more critical than men of every Republican president and more approving of every Democratic president who has served since 1980. Thus, women were less likely than men to approve of the way Republicans Ronald Reagan, George H. W. Bush, and George W. Bush handled their jobs as president, but more likely than men to evaluate favorably Democrat Bill Clinton's performance.

THE GENDER GAP AND WOMEN CANDIDATES

As other chapters in this volume document, the number of women running for public office has increased over the past several decades. Every election year, women are among the candidates who run for the US House,

[22] Obama Weekly Job Approval by Demographic Groups, Gallup, www.gallup.com/poll/121199/obama-weekly-job-approval-demographic-groups.aspx

[23] Lydia Saad, Trump Sets New Low Point for Inaugural Approval Rating, Gallup, January 23, 2017, https://news.gallup.com/poll/202811/trump-sets-new-low-point-inaugural-approval-rating.aspx

[24] Jeffrey M. Jones, Last Trump Job Approval 34%; Average Is Record-Low 41%, Gallup, January 18, 2021, https://news.gallup.com/poll/328637/last-trump-job-approval-average-record-low.aspx

[25] Jeffrey M. Jones, Biden Begins Term with 57% Job Approval, Gallup, February 4, 2021, https://news.gallup.com/poll/329348/biden-begins-term-job-approval.aspx

US Senate, and governor. What happens to the gender gap in the general election when one (or both) of the candidates for one of these offices is a woman?

Unfortunately, there is no straightforward, easy answer to this question. It depends on whether the woman candidate is a Democrat or a Republican, and if she is a Republican, how moderate or conservative she is. The answer may also depend on the state or district in which she runs and the larger context of the election.

Years ago, voter prejudice may have been a major problem for the few women who were brave enough to seek public office. However, bias against women candidates has declined significantly. Since 1937, pollsters have asked voters whether they would be willing to vote for a "qualified" woman for president. In 1937, only about one-third of voters said that they would vote for a woman. In contrast, by the beginning of the twenty-first century, about nine of every ten Americans reported that they would vote for a woman for the nation's highest office (although there is some evidence that this high level of support dipped for a while in the aftermath of the attack on the World Trade Center in 2001).[26] Thus, voter prejudice against women candidates, even for the most powerful office in the United States, has declined considerably, although it has not disappeared completely.

But if there are still some voters predisposed to vote against women, there are also voters predisposed to cast affirmative votes for women candidates. Moreover, research has shown that women are more likely than men to be inclined to support women candidates.[27] This predisposition on the part of some voters to vote for or against a woman candidate, all other things being equal, becomes an additional factor that can alter the size of the gender gap when women run for office. While there is a clear consensus among scholars that partisanship exerts the strongest influence on vote choice, the gender of the candidate may also make a difference in some circumstances.

In general, women candidates who are Democrats tend to have gender gaps (with women voters more likely than men to vote for them) that are similar in size to or sometimes larger than those for male Democratic candidates. In contrast, women candidates who are Republicans tend to have gender gaps (with women voters more likely than men to vote

[26] Jennifer L. Lawless, Women, War, and Winning Elections: Gender Stereotyping in the Post-September 11th Era, *Political Research Quarterly* 53(3) (2004): 479–90.
[27] Kira Sanbonmatsu, Gender Stereotypes and Vote Choice, *American Journal of Political Science* 46 (2002): 20–34.

against them) that are similar in size to or sometimes smaller than those for male Republican candidates. An analysis of US House races in three elections in the early 1990s found that the gender gap was, on average, greater in races where the Democratic candidate was a woman candidate than in races where a Democratic man ran against a Republican man. Similarly, on average, the gender gap was smaller in races where the Republican candidate was a woman than in races where a Republican man ran against a Democratic man.[28] However, in recent years as the political parties have become more polarized and partisan considerations have come to matter more and more in vote choice, considerations such as the candidate's gender have likely had less influence.

Although seven women were elected to the US Senate in 2020, exit polling was conducted in only four of their races. Table 5.2 presents the proportions of votes from women and men that each of the four victorious women received in these races. Three of the women defeated men of the opposing party; the fourth, Republican Susan Collins, defeated a Democratic woman. All four women had gender gaps within the same general range as occurred in races where men won US Senate seats in 2020, suggesting that the gender of these women probably did not have a great influence on their election outcomes.

TABLE 5.2 A gender gap in voting was evident in four races where women were elected to the US Senate in 2020 in states where exit polls were conducted

	Women voting for winner (%)	Men voting for winner (%)	Gender gap (in percentage points)
US Senate winners			
Tina Smith (D-MN)	55	43	12
Jeanne Shaheen (D-NH)	63	50	13
Joni Ernst (R-IA)	46	57	11
Susan Collins (R-ME)	49	55	6

Note: Three of the seven women who were elected to the Senate in 2020 – Cindy Hyde-Smith (R-MS), Shelley Moore Capito (R-WV), and Cynthia Lummis (R-WY) – do not appear in this table because exit polls were not conducted in their states.
Source: Edison Research National Exit Poll, 2020.

[28] Elizabeth Adell Cook, Voter Reaction to Women Candidates, in *Women and Elective Office: Past, Present, and Future*, ed. Sue Thomas and Clyde Wilcox (New York: Oxford University Press, 1998), pp. 56–72.

EXPLANATIONS FOR THE GENDER GAP

One observation can be made with a high degree of certainty: the gender gap is not limited to one or even a few demographic subgroups. In an attempt to undermine women's voting power, political commentators have sometimes claimed that the gender gap is not a broad-based phenomenon, but rather one that can be fully explained by the voting behavior of a particular subgroup of women in the electorate – for example, women of color or unmarried voters. Table 5.3 reveals the obvious problem with such claims. When compared with men who shared their demographic characteristics, women of different races and ethnicities, marital statuses, and ages more often voted for Joe Biden in 2020 (and less often voted for Donald Trump). In fact, voting differences between women and men are found in almost all subgroups. Consequently, no single demographic category of voters can be designated as responsible for the gender gap. Rather, the gender gap is clearly a phenomenon evident across most of the various subgroups that comprise the American electorate.

TABLE 5.3 A gender gap in voting was evident across a range of demographic groups in the 2020 presidential election

Demographic group	Women voting for Biden (%)	Men voting for Biden (%)	Gender gap (in percentage points)
Race or ethnicity			
White	44	38	6
College graduate	54	48	6
Not college graduate	36	28	8
African American	90	79	11
Latina/o/x	69	59	10
Marital status			
Married	47	44	3
Unmarried	63	52	11
Age			
18–29	67	52	15
30–44	56	48	8
45–64	56	42	14
65 or older	52	41	11

Source: Edison Research National Exit Poll, 2020.

Beyond the fact that the gender gap is widespread across the electorate and not limited to one particular subgroup, definitive statements about the gender gap are difficult to make. Indeed, the gender gap appears to be a rather complex phenomenon. Nevertheless, a number of different explanations have been put forward to account for the gender gap in voting. None of these explanations seems sufficient by itself. Moreover, the explanations are not mutually exclusive; in fact, they are somewhat overlapping. However, several of the explanations offered by academic and political analysts do seem to have some validity and are useful in helping to account for the fact that women and men make somewhat different voting choices. Four of the most common explanations – compassion, feminism, economics, and the role of government – are reviewed briefly here.

The compassion explanation most often focuses on women's roles as mothers and caregivers. Despite recent changes in gender roles, women still bear disproportionate responsibility for the care of children and the elderly in their families and also in society more widely. Mothers are still called more often than fathers when children become ill at school, and women are still a large majority of health care workers, teachers, childcare providers, and social workers. Women's roles as caregivers may lead them to be more sympathetic toward those in need and more concerned with the safety and security of others. Women's caregiving responsibilities may also lead them to put greater emphasis than men on issues such as education and health care. In short, different life experiences may have created a values gap between women and men when it comes to concern and caring for other people, and that values gap may have political consequences.[29]

As a historical example consistent with this compassion explanation, education and health care were two of the top issues in the 2000 presidential election, which focused largely on domestic politics rather than foreign affairs. Polls showed that these issues were of greater concern to women voters in the election than they were to men, and both presidential candidates spent a great deal of time talking about them. In an obvious attempt to appeal to women voters, the George W. Bush campaign suggested that their candidate was not an old-style conservative, but rather a "compassionate conservative" who genuinely cared about the well-being of Americans.

---

[29] Mary-Kate Lizotte, *Gender Differences in Public Opinion: Values and Political Consequences* (Philadelphia, PA: Temple University Press, 2020).

Although in 2020 women and men were similar in seeing the economy as one of the most important issues in the election, women voters in 2020, like women voters two decades earlier in 2000, continued to express more concern over health care than did men. For example, a poll conducted in October 2020 by the Pew Research Center found that 71 percent of women registered voters, compared with 59 percent of men, said that health care was very important to their vote in the 2020 election. Similarly, more women, 59 percent, than men, 51 percent, reported that the coronavirus outbreak was very important to their vote.[30]

The greater reluctance of women than men to approve of the use of military force to resolve foreign conflicts is also consistent with the compassion explanation. In 1980, when the gender gap first became apparent, Americans were being held hostage in Iran, tensions with the Soviet Union were running high, and foreign policy had become a central issue in the presidential campaign. Women reacted more negatively than men to Ronald Reagan's tough posture in dealing with other nations, and women feared more than men that Ronald Reagan might involve the country in a war. These gender differences were important in explaining why Reagan received stronger support from men than from women.[31] Similarly, in the 2004 and 2008 elections in the aftermath of the 9/11 terrorist attack, gender differences were evident in women's and men's attitudes toward the war in Iraq. For example, a Rasmussen Reports survey released in June 2008 found that just 26 percent of women, compared with 45 percent of men, believed that troops should stay in Iraq until the mission was finished.[32] More recently, a Pew Research Center survey in January 2020 found that 52 percent of women, compared with 34 percent of men, disapproved of the US decision to conduct an air strike that killed the Iranian general Qasem Soleimani earlier that month. The same poll found that 62 percent of women, compared with 47 percent of men, worried that the Trump administration's approach had raised the likelihood of a major military conflict with Iran.[33]

---

[30] Amina Dunn, Only 24% of Trump Voters View the Coronavirus Outbreak as a "Very Important" Voting Issue, Pew Research Center, October 21, 2020, https://pewrsr.ch/2TZRpU2

[31] Kathleen A. Frankovic, Sex and Politics: New Alignments, Old Issues, *PS* 15(Summer 1982): 439–48.

[32] 59% of Adults Want Troops Home from Iraq within the Year, Rasmussen Reports, June 3, 2008, https://bit.ly/3xtebkL

[33] Majority of US Public Says Trump's Approach on Iran Has Raised Chances of a Major Conflict, Pew Research Center, January 15, 2020, https://pewrsr.ch/3yxSq4H

Polls have consistently shown gender gaps on questions such as these, with women having more reservations than men about US involvement in the Middle East and other international conflicts.[34] In fact, one of the most persistent and long-standing political differences between women and men is in their attitudes toward the use of military force. For as far back as we have public opinion polling data, women have been significantly more likely than men to oppose the use of force to resolve international disputes.

As a second explanation for the gender gap, some observers have suggested the influence of the feminist movement. The discovery of the contemporary gender gap in voting in the aftermath of the 1980 presidential election coincided with intensive efforts by women's organizations, especially the National Organization for Women (NOW), to have the Equal Rights Amendment (ERA) ratified in the necessary thirty-eight states before the June 30, 1982 deadline. In addition, NOW undertook an intensive effort to publicize the gender gap and women's lesser support for Ronald Reagan relative to men's. As a result, the ERA and the gender gap became associated in many people's minds, and there was speculation that women were less supportive than men of Ronald Reagan because he opposed the ERA. However, scholarly analyses of voting and public opinion data have consistently shown that so-called women's issues – those issues most closely associated with the organized women's movement, such as the ERA and abortion – do not appear to be central to the gender gap. In part, this may be because women and men in the general electorate have very similar attitudes on these issues, and in part, this may be because most candidates for president and other offices do not put these issues front and center in their campaigns.

However, even if women's issues such as the ERA or abortion are not central to the gender gap, feminism may still play a role. As explained earlier in this chapter, the contemporary women's movement has altered the way most women in the United States see themselves and their life options. The movement has provided women with more awareness about their political interests and greater self-confidence about expressing their differences from men. Compelling empirical evidence suggests that women who identify with feminism are more distinctive from men in their political values than are other women, and that for women, a

---

[34] Michael A. Hansen, Jennifer L. Clemens, and Kathleen Dolan, Gender Gaps, Partisan Gaps, and Cross-Pressures: An Examination of American Attitudes toward the Use of Force, *Politics & Gender* 16(1) (2020): 1–23, doi.org/10.1017/S1743923X20000690

feminist identity may, in fact, foster the expression of the compassion differences described previously. Women influenced by feminism appear more likely than either men or other women to express attitudes sympathetic to those of people who are disadvantaged and in need, and consequently more predisposed to support the Democratic Party.[35]

Other explanations for the gender gap have focused on economic factors. More women than men live below the poverty line, and women earn only about eighty-one cents for every dollar men earn. Because women on average are poorer than men, they are more dependent on government social services and more vulnerable to cuts in these services. Similarly, women are disproportionately employed in jobs that involve the delivery of human services (health, education, and welfare). Although most women in human services jobs are not directly employed by the government, their employers often receive substantial government funding, and thus their jobs are, to varying degrees, dependent on the continuation of government subsidies. As the principal providers of social welfare services, women are more likely than men to suffer loss of employment when these programs are cut.

Beginning with Ronald Reagan and continuing through the 1990s with the Republican Congress' Contract with America, Republicans at the national level have argued that government (with the exception of defense) has grown too large and that cutbacks in domestic spending are necessary. When candidates and politicians propose to cut back on big government or the welfare state, the cuts they propose fall heavily on women, who are disproportionately both the providers and the recipients of government-funded services. Consequently, economic self-interest could lead women to favor the Democrats more than the Republicans.

However, women's economic concerns do not appear to be merely self-interested. Evidence shows that women are less likely than men to vote on the basis of economic considerations, but when they do, they are less likely than men to vote on the basis of their own self-interest and more likely to vote on the basis of how well off they perceive the country to be financially.[36] Thus, women are more likely than men to think not just of their own financial situation but also of the economic situation that others are facing.

---

[35] Pamela Johnston Conover, Feminists and the Gender Gap, *Journal of Politics* 50(3) (1988): 985–1010.

[36] Susan J. Welch and John Hibbing, Financial Conditions, Gender, and Voting in American National Elections, *Journal of Politics* 54(1) (1992): 197–213.

The final explanation for the gender gap, focusing on the role of government, is clearly related to the economic explanation but extends beyond economic considerations. In recent years, some of the most consistent and important gender differences in public opinion have shown up on questions about the role that government should play in Americans' lives. Both women and men agree that government, especially the federal government, does not always work as effectively as they would like. Beyond that, however, their attitudes are quite different. Men are more likely than women to see government as the problem rather than the solution, and they are considerably more likely than women to favor serious cutbacks in federal government programs and federal spending on non-defense-related projects. Men, more than women, prefer private sector solutions to societal problems. In contrast, women are more likely to see a positive role for government in solving social problems and more likely to want to fix government rather than abandon it. Women are more worried than men that government cutbacks may go too far; they are more concerned than men about preserving the social safety net for the people who are most in need in the United States. As an example of this gender difference in perspective, the Pew Research Center found in a March 2019 poll that 58 percent of women, but only 37 percent of men, favored a bigger government providing more services.[37] The Republican Party, which receives greater support from men, is commonly perceived as the party that wants to scale back the size of government, whereas the Democratic Party, which has more women among its supporters, is more commonly perceived as the party that defends or expands government programs and works to preserve the social safety net.

POLITICAL STRATEGIES FOR DEALING WITH THE GENDER GAP AND APPEALING TO WOMEN VOTERS

Given the above explanations for the gender gap, it would appear that the best way for candidates and parties to appeal to women voters is by talking very specifically, concretely, and frequently about issues, whether they be compassion issues (e.g. health care and education), economic concerns, or foreign policy. However, presidential candidates and campaigns often use symbolic appeals in addition to, and sometimes in lieu of, issue-based appeals to win support from women voters.

---

[37] Hannah Hartig, Gender Gap Widens in Views of Government's Role – and of Trump, Pew Research Center, April 11, 2019, https://pewrsr.ch/37o0Rnr

One of the ways candidates and campaigns have attempted to appeal to women voters symbolically is by showcasing prominent women. Joe Biden and, to a lesser extent, Donald Trump tried to win over women voters by having widely admired and accomplished women campaign for them. On the Democratic side, the convention and much of the campaigning were virtual. The Democrats had each of four prominent actresses – Julia Louis Dreyfus, Eva Longoria, Tracee Ellis Ross, and Kerry Washington – emcee one night of their virtual convention. Several well-known political women spoke at the convention; for example, former Congresswoman Gabby Giffords, former presidential candidate Hillary Clinton, House Minority Leader Nancy Pelosi, Senator Elizabeth Warren, and New Mexico Governor Michelle Lujan Grisham all spoke on the third night of the convention preceding Kamala Harris' acceptance of the vice-presidential nomination. Numerous women also appeared at virtual or live events later in the campaign. The Republican convention featured women who were connected to the Trump family or his administration, including First Lady Melania Trump; daughter Ivanka Trump; daughter-in-law Lara Trump; Kimberly Guilfoyle, former Fox News host and girlfriend of Donald Trump Jr.; former UN Ambassador Nikki Haley; and Counselor to the President Kellyanne Conway. Several of these and other women also appeared at Trump campaign events.

Beyond the use of well-known women, presidential campaigns have sometimes used symbolic strategies to appeal to women voters. The presidential campaign of George W. Bush, in particular, was very clever in its use of symbolic appeals to woo women voters. For example, in the 2004 campaign and especially the 2000 campaign, the Bush campaign employed a new term, describing their candidate as a "compassionate conservative." Bush himself suggested, "I am a compassionate conservative, because I know my philosophy is full of hope for every American."[38] Although vague as to what concrete policy proposals might flow from this philosophy, the use of the term "compassionate conservative" clearly invoked the image of a candidate who cared about people, and the term undoubtedly was coined, entirely or in part, as a strategy to appeal to women voters.

Another use of symbolic appeals in campaigns has focused on the targeting of specific groups of women to the exclusion of large numbers of other women voters. Two examples are the targeting of so-called soccer moms in the 1996 and, to a lesser extent, the 2000 elections, and so-called

[38] Joe Conason, Where's the Compassion?, *The Nation*, September 15, 2003, www.thenation.com/doc/20030915/conason

security moms in the 2004 elections. Both soccer moms and security moms were social constructions – a combination of demographic characteristics, assigned a catchy name by political consultants, with no connection to any existing self-identified group or organizational base. When consultants and the media first started referring to soccer moms in 1996, women did not identify themselves as such, but the term subsequently entered into popular usage and some women now refer to themselves this way. Similarly, women did not self-identify as security moms before the term was introduced in the context of the 2004 elections.

Although the definition of a soccer mom varied somewhat, she was generally perceived as a white, married woman with children (presumably of soccer-playing age), living in the suburbs. The soccer mom was considered important politically because she was viewed as a swing voter – a voter whose demographics had traditionally led her to vote Republican but who could be persuaded to vote Democratic. One of the most important characteristics of the soccer mom was that she was not primarily concerned about her own self-interest, but about her family and, most important, her children. As Kellyanne Fitzpatrick, a Republican pollster, noted, "If you are a soccer mom, the world according to you is seen through the needs of your children."[39]

The security mom, who became a focus of attention during the last several weeks of the 2004 presidential campaign, shared many of the demographic characteristics of the soccer mom. Like the soccer mom, she was considered white and married, with young children. Also like the soccer mom, the security mom did not put her own needs first, but rather those of her family and children. She was repeatedly described as preoccupied with keeping her family safe from terrorism. The Republican presidential campaign, in particular, openly campaigned for the votes of these women in 2004. For example, on October 10, 2004, on CNN's *Late Edition with Wolf Blitzer*, Vice President Dick Cheney's daughter, Liz Cheney, urged women to vote for the Republican ticket, explaining, "You know, I'm a security mom. I've got four little kids. And what I care about in this election cycle is electing a guy who is going to be a commander-in-chief, who will do whatever it takes to keep those kids safe."[40]

The intensive campaign and media attention devoted to soccer moms in 1996 and 2000 and to security moms in 2004 deflected attention away from the concerns of many other subgroups of women, including women

---

[39] Neil MacFarquhar, Don't Forget Soccer Dads; What's a Soccer Mom Anyway?, *New York Times*, October 20, 1996, https://nyti.ms/3jvaSop
[40] *Late Edition with Wolf Blitzer*, CNN, October 10, 2004, https://cnn.it/3irPq4e

of color, feminists, college-age women, older women, women on welfare, and professional women. As a result, Bill Clinton was reelected in 1996 and George W. Bush was twice elected to the presidency in 2000 and 2004 without campaigning aggressively on (or, in some cases, even seriously addressing) some of the issues of greatest importance to the majority of women in this country.

Donald Trump's explicit appeals to suburban women in 2020, which stressed law and order and claimed that he had saved their neighborhoods, had much in common with the appeals to soccer moms and security moms in earlier elections. Although Trump did not explicitly mention race, his appeals were clearly racially coded and targeted to white women who believed that the safety of their families was somehow threatened, a narrow slice of the female electorate at best. Not only did Trump's appeals to suburban women leave out all women who live outside the suburbs, but also, as many commentators pointed out, they failed to recognize the increasing diversity that now exists within America's suburbs.

Despite this 2020 example, for the most part recent presidential campaigns have relied less on symbolic appeals to women than on issue-based appeals. The top four issues for women voters in the 2020 campaign were the economy, health care, Supreme Court appointments, and the coronavirus outbreak.[41] These were also among the top issues for men, although women were much more likely than men to say that health care (71 percent to 59 percent) and somewhat more likely to say that the coronavirus outbreak (59 percent to 51 percent) was very important to their vote in the presidential election. Through the debates and the presidential campaigns, the presidential candidates did address these issues of major concern to women voters, although Biden much more than Trump emphasized health care and the coronavirus. Biden also focused on racial/ethnic inequality and climate change, issues of concern to many women among his base voters, while Trump gave more attention to law and order, an issue of concern to voters in his base.

CONCLUSION: WHY THE GENDER GAP MATTERS AND A LOOK TOWARD 2024

The gender gap has increased the political influence wielded by women voters. Most candidates now must pay attention to women voters to win elections. As Susan A. MacManus and Amy Benner observe in Chapter 4

---

[41] Dunn, Only 24% of Trump Supporters.

of this volume, women vote at slightly higher rates than men. Women also are a greater proportion of the population. These two facts combined mean that there have been many more female than male voters in recent elections. In the 2020 election, for example, about 9.7 million more women than men voted.[42] The fact that there are so many more female voters than male voters gives power to the so-called women's vote, and clearly the more women who turn out to vote, the more clout women are likely to have. Women voters in all their diversity received considerable attention in the 2020 presidential election, and the presidential campaigns, especially the Biden campaign, used not only symbolic appeals but also substantive policy-based appeals in an attempt to win women's votes. Joe Biden was able to emerge victorious in large part because he won women voters overall by a large margin – and by a larger margin than Hillary Clinton did in 2016.

Looking forward to 2024, both President Biden and President Trump will be eligible to run for second terms. Will we see a rematch of 2020? Or will we have younger and perhaps more diverse presidential candidates? Might we see a woman presidential candidate on either ticket? Will the Republican candidate make greater attempts than Trump did in 2020 to win the support of women voters? Or will he or she feel that the presidency can be won while losing a majority of women's votes? Will the Democratic candidate, whoever that might be, try to win by maximizing his or her appeal to the subgroups of women (African Americans, Latinas, Asian Americans, college-educated whites) who supported Biden in 2016? And will the Democratic candidate try to do more to increase the turnout of young voters, especially young women? We will have to wait and see. But whatever happens in 2024, women voters will likely be an important part of the story.

---

[42] United States Census Bureau, Voting and Registration in the Election of November 2020, April 2021, https://bit.ly/2VxRYVW

6 *Presente!*: Latinas Mobilizing for Political Change across Candidates, Races, and Voters in 2020

On January 6, 2021, almost two months after winning her ninth reelection to Congress, Representative Linda Sánchez from California was forced to evacuate the floor of the House of Representatives by armed capitol police who feared for the safety of all the congressional members who had gathered that day to certify the 2020 electoral college election results. Those results, which clearly indicated Democrat Joe Biden's presidential victory, were being contested by President Donald Trump, who incited a violent mob animated by calls for white supremacy and toxic masculinity to storm the capital and prevent the peaceful transition of power. Calling into an interview on MSNBC from an undisclosed location while rioters continued to occupy parts of the capitol, Sánchez was both defiant and devastated when recalling the violence:

> Our work will continue. We will get this work of certifying the electoral college votes completed. We are bound and determined to do our constitutional duty and to get that job done. But, it's just – it's really jarring to come into work on a Wednesday to do something that is normally a very procedural thing that is the hallmark of our democracy, the peaceful transfer of power, and to have the events unfold in this way.
>
> It's astonishing. It disheartening. It's dangerous.
>
> I called my husband last night and told him that I was coming into work today but that should anything happen … I let him know … where my will and last testament was located … in the event that we needed it. It's a sad day in America when you are trying to come in and do your job in a democracy and you have to think about things like that. I have an eleven-year-old son who I want to be around to raise.

People who are breaking down barriers and bursting into the capitol and that are armed make it really hard to do that.[1]

Sánchez joined the other members of both the House of Representatives and the Senate later that night to complete the certification, but her chilling interview – recalling how she feared for her life, and feared she may never see her child again simply for doing her job – underscored the price Latinas and other women of color pay in a political context where race and gender violence have become far too commonplace. Her interview made clear the costs – political, emotional, social, and even physical – that women of color bear as they confront entrenched systems of inequality that target them, their families, and their communities. Finally, the interview highlighted the chaotic nature of work that Latinas and other women of color elected to national office encounter as they attempt to legislate in a political environment inflamed by years of racism, sexism, misogyny, transphobia, immigrant bashing, and xenophobia.

Overall, Latinas figured prominently in the 2020 elections as candidates for national office, as political organizers, as campaign strategists, and ultimately as a key portion of the electorate. Latina leaders such as

---

The terms "Latino" and "Hispanic" are used interchangeably by the federal government. Within the US census, the population is defined to include any person of "Mexican, Puerto Rican, Cuban, South or Central American or other Spanish culture or origin, regardless of race" and to reflect "self-identification by individuals according to the group or groups with which they most closely identify" (American Community Survey 2006, American Community Survey Reports 2007).

However, the inability of these designations to properly account for the complexity of persons whose ancestry stems from Latin America but who are living in the US has generated considerable debate and dissension. Central to this discourse is whether the population constitutes its own separate racial group, a coherent ethnic group, or something else. Moreover, long-standing concern about the imprecision of pan-ethnic labels has led many to gravitate to specific national origin references (i.e. Mexican American, Cuban American). Critical gender scholarship has also called into question the privileging of men and masculinity in the common use of Latino, including the inability of a dichotomous Latina/o label to account for more fluid and nonconforming manifestations of gendered identity and expression.

For the purposes of this chapter, I use the term "Latina" when describing persons with ancestral, genealogical, or cultural origins in Latin America, currently residing primarily in the United States who self-identify as women. While admittedly imperfect, in describing the population at large, I opt to use the inclusive term "Latina/o/x," as opposed to the default masculine "o" or "x" that both erase specific reference to a gendered identity and feminist history embodied in the "a." On occasions where the data are reported using the label "Hispanic" or specific national origin identifiers, I duplicate the same terms here for consistency.

[1] CA Dem Rep.: Last Night I Told My Husband Where My Will Was, MSNBC, January 6, 2021, www.msnbc.com/msnbc/watch/ca-dem-rep-last-night-i-told-my-husband-where-my-will-was-98969157961

Marisa Franco and Tania Unzueta Carrasco of Mijente bridged immigrant rights movements with citizenship and voting drives to empower entire Latina/o/x communities, while campaign organizers such as Stephanie Valencia and Julia Chávez Rodriquez led voter outreach and mobilization efforts for high-profile presidential contenders. Latina US House candidates from Democrats Alexandria Ocasio-Cortez to Debbie Mucarsel-Powell confronted misinformation efforts designed to disenfranchise voters in their districts. In the meantime, Latina voters joined Black women and college-educated white women to form a key demographic coalition central to the defeat of Donald Trump and the election of Joe Biden and Kamala Harris.

Despite these gains, and the significance of Latinas to the success of both political parties, Latinas continue to be politically underrepresented in the highest political offices and institutions of power. In 2021, Latinas constitute only 2 percent of the voting body of US congressional representatives, including 3 percent of the House of Representatives, and 1 percent of the US Senate. Senator Catherine Cortez Masto from Nevada stands out as the lone Latina *ever* elected to the US Senate, despite the fact that with over 60 million people Latinas/os/xs constitute the largest racial/ethnic minority population in the United States. Similarly, despite the important legal issues surrounding immigration, pay equity, voting rights, and racial disparities addressed by the federal courts, Latinas constitute only 2 percent of all sitting federal judges, and Justice Sonia Sotomayor stands alone as the only woman of color ever appointed to the US Supreme Court.[2] Finally, despite promises to appoint the "most diverse presidential cabinet in US history," President Biden overlooked Latinas (nominating only one subcabinet appointee – Isabel Guzman – to head the Small Business Administration) while advancing three Latino men to high-profile appointments (Miguel Cardona as Secretary of Education, Alejandro Mayorkas as Secretary of Homeland Security, and Xavier Becerra as Secretary of Health and Human Services). In short, Latinas have consistently shown up and been present for political candidates, parties, and movements, but without a reciprocal investment in their representation. Much like Representative Sánchez, Latinas have gone to work, only to confront entrenched systems of racism, sexism, and inequality without being recognized and honored for that work. The 2020 election season

---

[2] Danielle Root, Jake Faleschini, and Grace Oyenubi. Building a More Inclusive Federal Judiciary, Center for American Progress, October 3, 2019, www.americanprogress.org/issues/courts/reports/2019/10/03/475359/building-inclusive-federal-judiciary/.

brought important recognition of those disparities as well as growth and gains in racial justice as it also revealed shortcomings and enduring forms of racial and gendered discrimination yet to be addressed.

Using an intersectional lens attentive to the raced and gendered context of contemporary politics, this chapter examines the wave of Latina political engagement through the 2018 and 2020 elections, highlighting Latina candidates for national office, the impact of Latina voters along with the enduring gender gap, and the strength of Latina organizers. It concludes with an eye to obstacles and opportunities in the future of Latina politics and racial and gendered justice in the United States.

LATINA CANDIDATES BREAK RECORDS IN 2018 AND 2020

Latinas figured prominently in the 2018 general election as candidates for national and statewide office, as political organizers, and as a key portion of the electorate in states with competitive races for Congress and governor's office.[3] More Latinas ran for national office and won in 2018 than in any prior general election, and their success proved significant to the shift in political power, particularly Democratic control over the House of Representatives.[4] For Latinas, 2018 was a groundbreaking election where candidates such as Michelle Lujan Grisham of New Mexico became the first Democratic Latina (and Democratic woman of color) elected governor in the United States, Debbie Mucarsel-Powell of Florida (26th congressional district) flipped a traditionally Republican seat and became the first South American Latina elected to Congress, and Veronica Escobar (16th congressional district) and Sylvia Garcia (29th congressional district) became the first Latina representatives from Texas, joining nine other Latinas in the House. Finally, it was an election where record numbers of Latinas became part of the electoral process as advocates, fundraisers, donors, campaign staff, commentators, canvassers, organizers, and voters.

While 2018 proved to be a defining election year for women of color generally and Latinas specifically, the volume and diversity of Latina candidates running for national office in 2020 surpassed the records set

---

[3] Jens Manuel Krogstad, Antonio Flores, and Mark Hugo Lopez, Key Takeaways about Latino Voters in the 2018 Midterm Elections, Pew Research Center, November 9, 2018, www.pewresearch.org/fact-tank/2018/11/09/how-latinos-voted-in-2018-midterms/; Anna Sampaio, Latinas Deliver in the 2018 Midterms, Gender Watch 2018, November 21, 2018, https://genderwatch2018.org/latinas-deliver-2018-midterms/

[4] Latina Candidates in 2020, Center for American Women and Politics (hereafter CAWP), August 5, 2020, https://cawp.rutgers.edu/election-analysis/latina-candidates-2020

in 2018. By July 2020, seventy-five Latinas had filed as candidates for national office compared with fifty-one in 2018.[5] This included seventy-two Latina candidates running for the US House with thirty-nine running as Democrats and thirty-three running as Republicans. This also included a record of three Latina candidates vying for the US Senate – two running as Democrats in Texas (Cristina Tzintzún Ramirez and Sema Hernandez), and one running as a Republican (Elisa Martinez from New Mexico). As grassroots candidates operating without the support of political elites and the dominant political parties in their states, all three Latina Senate candidates lost in their respective primary races. However, as Andrea Silva and Carrie Skulley noted in their study of women of color candidates, even when women of color run and lose, their presence on the ballot and their candidacies lay the foundation for other women of color to follow and often result in more women of color candidates running in subsequent election cycles.[6] Consequently, Elisa Martinez has already declared her candidacy for the 2022 House race in New Mexico's 1st congressional district, and several Latinas are considering Senate runs in states with a large Latina/o/x electorate and competitive US House races in Arizona, California, and Florida.

Latina Republicans Challenge Democratic Dominance and Republican Leadership

In addition to breaking previous records, Latina candidates running for national office in 2020 represented an even more diverse field than in 2018 with almost half (45%) running as Republicans, far surpassing the 35 percent of Latinas who ran as Republicans for a congressional office in the 2018 midterm election. Put another way, in 2018, 14 percent of all Democratic women candidates who filed to run for national office were Latinas compared with only 8.7 percent of all Republican women candidates. This reflected a sizable difference in the two major parties' willingness to invest in Latina candidates with the Democratic Congressional Campaign Committee investing more than $30 million. However, by 2020, some Republicans had clearly shifted toward Latina candidate recruitment as the proportion of Latinas among all Republican women candidates grew from 8.7 percent to 10.4 percent while the proportion of Latinas among Democratic women candidates stayed the same.

---

[5] Ibid.
[6] Andrea Silva and Carrie Skulley, Always Running: Candidate Emergence among Women of Color Over Time, *Political Research Quarterly* 72(2) (2019): 342–59.

Among the field of Republican Latinas, Nicole Malliotakis in New York and Maria Elvira Salazar in Florida stood out in 2020 for their successful campaigns in competitive districts. In fact, both defeated incumbent Democrats in districts that were gained by the Democratic Party in the 2018 midterm elections and were central to Democrats taking control of the House. Campaigning in the 11th congressional district in New York, Malliotakis, who identifies as Greek and Latina/o/x and who previously served in the New York State Assembly, defeated Democrat incumbent Max Rose, in a part of the state that is disproportionately white and where Latinas/os/xs constitute less than 20 percent of the population.[7] By contrast, Maria Elvira Salazar defeated Democratic incumbent Donna Shalala in Florida's 27th congressional district, an area comprised overwhelmingly of Latina/o/x voters, where conservative Cuban American politics have dominated for decades and where Ileana Ros-Lehtinen, the first Latina congressional representative, was elected to office in 1989.[8] Salazar, who identifies as Cuban American, ran on a mixed platform spanning a range of traditional conservative issues such as strengthening national security, restricting access to abortion, and reforming the Affordable Care Act, and more traditionally liberal issues such as gun control and humane immigration reform.

Other high-profile Latina Republican candidates in 2020 included incumbent Jaime Herrera Beutler, who won her sixth reelection to the 3rd congressional district in Washington state, and Michelle Garcia Holmes, former chief of staff to New Mexico's attorney general who won the primary in New Mexico's 1st congressional district and unsuccessfully challenged Democratic incumbent Debra Haaland in the general election. To underscore how much the presence of Latina representation (from both parties) matters in Congress, shortly after her election, Herrera Beutler joined only ten other Republicans in defying her party leadership by voting to impeach former President Donald Trump in proceedings that followed the January 6 insurrection. Knowing she would undoubtedly face a backlash, Herrera Beutler issued a public statement revealing details of a phone call she'd overheard between Trump and House minority leader Kevin McCarthy where the former president ignored pleas to "call off the riot" telling McCarthy: 'Well, Kevin, I guess these people are

[7] New York's 11th Congressional District Election, 2020, Ballotpedia, https://ballotpedia .org/New_York%27s_11th_Congressional_District_election,_2020
[8] Florida's 27th Congressional District, Ballotpedia, https://ballotpedia.org/Florida%27s_ 27th_Congressional_District

more upset about the election than you are." In a subsequent interview, Herrera Beutler said that the quote showed that "either [Trump] didn't care, which is impeachable, because you cannot allow an attack on your soil, or he wanted it to happen and was OK with it, which makes me so angry."[9] She also called out her Republican colleagues saying, "and to the patriots who were standing next to the former president as these conversations were happening, or even to the former vice president: if you have something to add here, now would be the time."[10] In response to her standing up to the Republican leadership, Herrera Beutler was formally rebuked by the Washington State Republican Party and received numerous calls for her own impeachment, while the Clark County Republican Party (located in her district) voted overwhelmingly to censure her for the impeachment vote. She also became a target of the former president, who began soliciting candidates to challenge her in the next Republican primary in her district, highlighting the precarity and vulnerability that even a seasoned Latina faces doing her job in a deeply charged political context.

CALIFORNIA AND TEXAS REMAIN EPICENTERS OF LATINA ELECTORAL POWER

In addition to greater party diversity, Latina candidates also made inroads in states and individual districts where the Latina/o/x population is small or nascent. Nearly a quarter (24%) of Latina candidates emerged from nontraditional states with a Latina/o/x electorate that fell below the 30 percent critical mass threshold. These included states that since the early 2000s had seen significant growth in the Latina/o/x population owing to secondary migration patterns, such as Georgia, Indiana, Kansas, Maryland, Michigan, Missouri, North Carolina, Oregon, Tennessee, and Washington.[11] Among the field of Latina candidates vying for office in nontraditional states, one of the stand-out candidates was Christina Hale, former member of the Indiana House of Representatives, who won the Democratic

---

9 Jordan Williams, Trump Told McCarthy That Rioters "More Upset about the Election Than You Are": Report, *The Hill*, February 12, 2021, https://bit.ly/3xy1zZU

10 Joseph O'Sullivan, Washington's GOP Rep. Jaime Herrera Beutler Stepped into the Spotlight in Trump Impeachment Trial. What Happens Now?, *Seattle Times*, February 14, 2021, https://bit.ly/

11 Renee Stepler and Mark Hugo Lopez, Latino Population Growth and Dispersion in US Slows since the Recession, Pew Research Center, September 8, 2016, https://pewrsr .ch/2VAHzZE

primary race in Indiana's 5th congressional district but narrowly lost in the general election to Republican Victoria Spartz. Hale is a single mother who advanced legislation in the Indiana House on a range of important issues from transgender rights and police reform to protections against human trafficking and sexual assault prevention. She also ran for lieutenant governor of Indiana in the 2016 election and lost. While the losses of Latina candidates in these states and districts where white voters still dominate are often devastating, their presence raises both the prospects for change and important questions about the intersections of race, gender, and partisan affiliation in both candidates and the electorate at a time when attention to racial justice and campaigns for racial reckoning are reaching national attention.

Overall, California and Texas continued to serve as the epicenters of Latina electoral politics in 2020, with more than 47 percent of all Latina congressional candidates emerging from the two states. Not surprisingly, over 25 percent of the entire Latina/o/x population in the United States is concentrated in California and Texas, and Latinas/os/xs comprise approximately 40 percent of each state's residents. However, the two states represent vastly different political landscapes with regard to Latina political development, participation, and empowerment. With five Latina incumbents and thirteen Latina candidates in total running for national office in 2020, California is unmatched in the concentration of Latinas elected to national office. Reflecting the dominance of the Democratic Party in the state since the mid 1990s, all Latina congressional incumbents from California ran as Democrats.[12] Similarly, all but one of the Latina candidates who ran for national office in the state in 2020 was a Democrat. Republican Beatrice Cardenas, who ran in California's 27th congressional district in Los Angeles and San Bernardino counties, was the lone Republican Latina candidate in the state in 2020. She lost that race during the primaries, but her filing as a challenger to another women of color, Democratic Congresswoman Judy Chu, an Asian American, reflected a growing trend among Republican Latinas who ran against

---

[12] In 2010, California created a single nonpartisan blanket primary for all state and federal elections (with the exception of the president and vice president). The primary system consolidated separate party primaries for a selected office into one primary election where every voter received the same ballot. In this system, the top two primary challengers advanced to the general election, regardless of their party affiliation. In the heavily Democratic state of California, this system has advantaged Democratic candidates for most state offices.

other Democratic Latinas or other Democratic women of color. I discuss this dynamic in greater detail below.

A different history of Latina/o/x leadership exists in Texas, with Latinas successfully running and winning election to local and statewide offices for decades.[13] However, despite the success of Latinas in winning local and state races in Texas, no Latina had successfully run for national office until 2018 when Veronica Escobar (16th congressional district) and Sylvia Garcia (29th congressional district) became the first Latina representatives from the state. The prospects for Latina congressional candidates from Texas changed significantly in 2020, as twenty-two Latinas ran for national office – including fourteen Republicans. For the first time in history, Texas eclipsed California in Latina candidate emergence for national office. Moreover, with a growing Latina/o/x electorate coupled with the expanded organizing efforts of groups such as Voto Latino and Mi Familia Vota and the inroads to Latina/o/x mobilization made by candidates such as Julián Castro and Beto O'Rourke, Texas became an important battleground state in 2020 for both parties, despite its long history as a Republican stronghold.

Ultimately, investments in the Latina/o/x electorate by the Republican Party paid off, especially in the southern Rio Grande Valley where turn-out and support for Republicans, and specifically Trump, increased over 2016. Polling by Latino Decisions indicated Trump garnered 29 percent of the Latina/o/x vote across the state of Texas (compared to 27 percent of the Latina/o/x vote nationwide) and won areas like Zapata County, dom-inated by Latina/o/x voters, for the first time in a hundred years.[14] While Trump lost the statewide Latina/o/x vote by double digits, the gains he made in the Rio Grande Valley helped Republicans to eventually win the state's electoral votes and prevented Texas from turning blue in a com-petitive election year.

However, these gains for Trump and the Republican Party did not extend to the Latinas running for office as all fourteen Latina Republicans

13 Christina E. Bejarano, *The Latina Advantage Gender, Race, and Political Success* (Austin, TX: University of Texas Press, 2013); Sonia R. García, Valerie Martinez-Ebers, Irasema Coronado, Sharon A. Navarro, and Patricia A. Jaramillo, *Políticas Latina Public Officials in Texas* (Austin, TX: University of Texas Press, 2008); Sharon A. Navarro, Samantha L. Hernandez, and Leslie A. Navarro, *Latinas in American Politics: Changing and Embracing Political Tradition* (Lanham, MD: Lexington Books, 2016).
14 Latino Decisions, American Election Eve Poll 2020; Jack Herrera, Trump Didn't Win the Latino Vote in Texas. He Won the Tejano Vote, *Politico*, November 17, 2020, 6:55 p.m., www.politico.com/news/magazine/2020/11/17/trump-latinos-south-texas-tejanos-437027

lost, with the preponderance of those losses happening in primary races. Only three Latina Republican candidates (Candace Valenzuela in the 24th congressional district, Irene Armendariz in the 16th congressional district, and Monica De La Cruz Hernandez in the 15th congressional district) advanced to the general election, where all three lost.

INTERSECTIONAL CHALLENGES BETWEEN WOMEN OF COLOR

Adding to the complexity of these races, as the number of Latina Republican candidates running for national office grew in 2020, so too did the number of Latinas running against *other* Latinas and Latinos and against other women of color, raising a number of questions about how the parties viewed gender and race in their candidate evaluation and how both parties deployed intersectionality as part of their electoral strategies. Outside of California, several of the Latina Democratic incumbents faced challenges by another man or women of color – most running as Republicans and others running as more conservative Democrats (in districts where Republicans were not competitive).

These included challenges faced by Latina Democratic incumbents such as Alexandria Ocasio-Cortez, who was challenged by Democrat Micelle Caruso-Cabrera in the 14th congressional district of New York, as well as Sylvia Garcia and Veronica Escobar of Texas, who were challenged by Latina Republicans Jaimy Blanco and Irene Armendariz-Jackson respectively. Ocasio-Cortez herself received criticism as part of the group of Progressive Justice Democrats for advancing Black and Latina challengers such as Jamaal Bowman and Jessica Cisneros in an attempt to unseat members of the Congressional Black Caucus and the Congressional Hispanic Caucus.[15] These intersectional challenges were also at the center of two significant losses among Latina incumbents: Democrat Debbie Mucarsel-Powell of Florida, who narrowly lost her reelection bid to a Republican Party mainstay and Cuban American, Carlos Jimenez; and Democrat Xochitl Torres Small, who lost to Republican Yvette Herrell, who became the second Native woman from New Mexico elected to the US House.

Each of these cases highlights unique questions about how intersectionality is invoked and even weaponized by parties and groups seeking

---

[15] Scott Wong, CBC Lawmakers Rip Justice Democrats for Targeting Black Lawmakers for Primaries, *The Hill*, July 12, 2019, 5:00 a.m., https://thehill.com/homenews/campaign/452701-cbc-members-accuse-aoc-linked-justice-democrats-of-targeting-black

electoral advantage in unseating challengers. In particular, why did the Republican Party make such a significant investment in women of color as candidates for national office, especially after so many in the Republican National Committee (RNC) spent four years enabling Trump and his campaign of white supremacy? Most of the Republican Latinas who ran for national office lacked prior experience, making them long-shot contenders, which begs the question, if the Republican Party was trying to increase Latina representation in these national offices, why not advance more competitive candidates? Was the selection of conservative women of color a way for the Republican Party to expand its base or simply undermine Democratic women of color while evading the party's historic enabling of racism and sexism? And what about the Republican Latinas themselves? To what degree were they enabled or empowered in the process? Or were these women simply saddled with thousands of dollars of debt in a failed campaign that was driven by high-price consultants and media buys designed to generate lucrative pay-outs for Republican political operatives without any real opportunity for these women to advance their own political careers? As the number of women of color in national office continues to grow, these intersectional dynamics will undoubtedly become more complex and more pressing for both parties, and will require intersectional analyses to thoroughly unpack their meaning and significance.

LATINA VOTERS PARALLEL LATINA CANDIDATES IN GROWTH AND DIVERSITY

The expansion and diversity of Latina candidates was mirrored in the Latina/o/x electorate, with over 16.6 million Latina/o/x voters casting a ballot in 2020 – an increase of more than 30 percent over Latina/o/x ballots cast in the 2016 election.[16] As a result, Latina/o/x voters became the largest racial minority voting population and once again underscored their significance to the parties, candidates, and campaigns for national office across the country. The record-breaking turnout among Latina/o/x voters included more than 2.4 million first-time voters, many of them young voters.[17] This also included as many as 10 million early voters and

---

[16] Rodrigo Domínguez-Villegas et al., Vote Choice of Latino Voters in the 2020 Presidential Election, Latino Policy & Politics Initiative, UCLA, 2021, https://latino.ucla.edu/research/latino-voters-in-2020-election/

[17] Nicole Acevedo, Young Latinos Mobilized, Voted and Were Pivotal in 2020. Organizers Want to Keep it Going, *NBC News*, November 27, 2020, www.nbcnews.com/news/latino/young-latinos-mobilized-voted-were-pivotal-2020-organizers-want-keep-n1246853

another 6 million who cast their ballots on Election Day – an especially notable feat given the proliferation of voter suppression tactics, such as voter ID laws across states with a high concentration of Latina/o/x voters, and the threats posed by the pandemic, which disproportionately impacted Latina/o/x communities.

Much as they had done in 2008 and 2012, during the 2020 election cycle Latina/o/x voters overwhelmingly supported the Democratic presidential candidate, Joe Biden, even as Republicans made gains among Latina/o/x voters in targeted sites such as Miami-Dade County and the Lower Rio Grande Valley in Texas. According to Latino Decisions, well over 70 percent of Latina/o/x voters supported Biden in the presidential race, while Trump garnered 27 percent of the Latina/o/x vote. Similarly, Latina/o/x voters strongly favored both Democratic House candidates over Republican candidates, 69 percent to 27 percent, and Democratic Senate candidates over Republican candidates, 63 percent to 26 percent.[18] Ultimately, Latina/o/x voters proved significant to a number of races, but especially to Democratic victories in the presidential race and key US House and Senate races in Arizona, California, Colorado, Georgia, Illinois, New Mexico, Nevada, New York, Pennsylvania, Washington, and Wisconsin. They also were critical to Republican state wins in Florida and Texas as well as key House and Senate victories in both states.

The Latina Gender Gap Continues through 2020

Much as they had done over the last two decades, Latina voters outpaced Latinos in voting and support for Democratic candidates and issues. These gender differences in candidate support proved particularly important to the success of the Democratic presidential candidate, as well as key House and Senate candidates in down-ticket races. These victories were vital to the party's ability to retain control of the House and to win a battleground Senate seat and electoral votes in Arizona.[19]

Following the pattern found in national elections since the mid 1990s, the differences in Latina and Latino voting in 2020 resulted in a gender gap reflecting a difference between Latinas and Latinos on the depth of their support for Democratic candidates and issues. In other words, when compared with their Latino counterparts, Latinas consistently vote more

[18]   Latino Decisions, American Election Eve Poll 2020.
[19]   Latino Decisions, NALEO Educational Fund 9-Wave, Weekly Tracking Poll, September–November 2020, https://latinodecisions.com/polls-and-research/naleo-educational-fund-9-wave-weekly-tracking-poll-sept-nov-2020/

Democratic and support more progressive candidates and issues – a pattern that continued in the 2020 election cycle. Data from across a range of polling firms including Edison Research, Vote Cast, Cooperative Election Study (CES), and Latino Decisions underscore this trend, pointing to a difference of between six and eleven points on Latina support for Biden over Latinos and a similar gap ranging from six to eleven points in Latino support for Trump over Latinas. While there were differences in results across the polls conducted by these different firms that indicate substantive differences in sampling and reliability, there is strong evidence to support a smaller gender gap between Latinas and Latinos in 2020 than occurred in 2016.[20]

Table 6.1 highlights the persistence of a gender gap in voting behavior between Latinas and Latinos, drawing on polling data from Latino Decisions during the 2020, 2016, and 2012 presidential election cycles. Data from the 2012 presidential race indicated a relatively small gender gap of four percentage points between Latinas and Latinos and their respective support for President Obama over Republican Senator Mitt Romney. Both Latinas and Latinos overwhelmingly supported the Democratic candidate (Obama), with a slightly larger percentage of Latinas voting for him than Latinos. This difference grew significantly in 2016, as Democrat Hillary Clinton's support among Latina voters surged to 86 percent. In that year, the Latina/o gender gap grew to a fifteen-

TABLE 6.1 The gender gap between Latinas and Latinos was smaller in 2020 than in 2016 but still persists

	2020		2016		2012	
	Biden (%)	Trump (%)	Clinton (%)	Trump (%)	Obama (%)	Romney (%)
Latinas	73	23	86	12	77	21
Latinos	67	31	71	24	73	25
Gap	6	8	15	12	4	4

Source: Latino Decisions, Election Eve Poll 2020; Latino Decisions, Election Eve Poll 2016; Latino Decisions, Latino National Election Eve Poll 2016; ImpreMedia/Latino Decisions, Latino Election Eve Poll 2012.

[20] Anna Sampaio, Trumpeando Latinas/os: Race, Gender, Immigration and the Role of Latinas/os in the 2016 Election, in *Gender and Elections: Shaping the Future of American Politics*, ed. Susan J. Carroll and Richard L. Fox (New York and London: Cambridge University Press, 2018).

point difference between Latinas and Latinos in their support for Clinton and a twelve-point difference in their support for the Republican challenger Donald Trump. Once again, the vast preponderance of both Latinas and Latinos supported the Democratic candidate. In 2020, the data once again points to a difference in Latina and Latino voting as 6 percent more Latinas voted for Democratic candidate Joe Biden and 8 percent more Latinos supported Donald Trump. Even with the modest gains made by Trump among select portions of the Latina/o/x electorate, analysis of 2020 election returns underscores that Biden's support among Latina/o/x voters was consistent with margins won by Obama in 2008 and 2012.[21] Collectively, the data indicate that Latinas once again served as a key cornerstone of the Democratic electorate, with over two-thirds of Latinas supporting Biden and other Democratic candidates in down ballot races.[22]

Gendered and Racialized Messaging Targeting Latinas among Candidates and Campaigns

Recognition of these gender differences among Latinas and Latinos (along with other important differences around age, national origin, region, and history) played out in targeted mobilization campaigns, as both parties employed gendered messaging and outreach. Among Democratic primary candidates, Senator Elizabeth Warren's campaign launched a targeted outreach effort entitled "Latinas Fight, Latinas Win" aimed at highlighting the work of Latina "legislators, activists, and organizers at the forefront of the fight for political, economic, social, and racial justice."[23] The outreach campaign invoked gender, race, and class inequality among Latinas to promote solidarity and affinity with Warren, noting: "Latinas are the driving force behind Latino voter participation, registration, and turnout, and they are the decision-makers in their households and in their communities. Latinas are key to unlocking the full potential of the entire community. And as president, I'm committed to being a real partner with the Latino community."[24]

Warren's campaign employed rallies, social media, phone banking, and traditional canvassing methods directed at Latina voters in advance of

---

[21] Domínguez-Villegas et al., *Vote Choice of Latino Voters.*
[22] Latino Decisions, NALEO Educational Fund 9-Wave.
[23] Latinas Fight, Latinas Win, Elizabeth Warren (website), https://2020.elizabethwarren
.com/latinas
[24] Ibid.

the Democratic primary while also supporting Latina candidates such as Candace Valenzuela and Jessica Cisneros running in competitive districts.

In addition, Julián Castro, who was the lone Latino candidate among a broad field of Democratic presidential contenders in the 2020 election, frequently invoked race and gender in the course of his campaign. These gendered and racialized messages were designed to reach Latina voters and included frequent references to the iconic Mexican figure of La Virgen de Guadalupe and Castro's grandmother, as well as lessons on social justice culled from his mother, Maria "Rosie" Castro, a Chicana political activist who, in addition to running for office herself, was a founding member of the La Raza Unida party.[25] Castro weaved these raced and gendered messages throughout his campaign speeches and debates as well as key policy platforms. His well-developed positions on immigration reform were grounded in an intersectional framework that highlighted the costs of restrictive immigration to women, children, and families. However, it was Castro's vocal support for reproductive justice that most clearly articulated a policy position tethered to the lives of women of color, including trans women:

> I don't believe only in reproductive freedom. I believe in reproductive justice. And, you know, what that means is that just because a woman – or let's also not forget someone in the trans community, a trans female – is poor, doesn't mean they shouldn't have the right to exercise that right to choose. And so, I absolutely would cover the right to have an abortion.[26]

Ultimately, among the Democratic field of presidential contenders it was Senator Bernie Sanders who developed the most extensive Latina/o/x outreach and mobilization effort, which included the hiring of seasoned Latina/o/x staff, integrating grassroots groups into the campaign, staffing field offices with experienced Latina/o/x advocates, and developing meaningful messages responsive to Latina/o/x interests.[27] During his failed 2016 presidential campaign, Sanders lost to his Democratic opponent Hillary Clinton in ten of eleven Democratic primary states where Latinas/os/xs constituted a significant share of the voting electorate. These

---

[25] Jack Jenkins, Democrat Julián Castro Makes His Catholicism Central to His Presidential Campaign, *Washington Post*, February 15, 2019, https://wapo.st/2U0qfwg

[26] Nolan D. McCaskill, What Castro Meant When He Said Trans Women Need Access to Abortions, *Politico*, June 27, 2019, www.politico.com/story/2019/06/27/julian-castro-debate-abortion-1385950

[27] Chuck Rocha, *Tío Bernie: The Inside Story of How Bernie Sanders Brought Latinos into the Political* (Washington, DC: Strong Arm Press, 2020).

states included Arizona, California, Nevada, and Texas. At the time, Clinton's Latina/o/x outreach campaign was unmatched, with prominent Latina political professionals such as Amanda Renteria, Emmy Ruiz, and Lorella Praeli playing key roles throughout.[28] Moreover, the support Clinton received from Latina/o/x voters in 2016 proved decisive to her primary victory over Sanders. While Sanders made outreach and mobilization of Latinas/os/xs a more significant feature of his campaign by the end of the 2016 primaries, his campaign staff was dominated by men, in contrast to the significant number of Latina professionals operating in Clinton's campaign, and his campaign lacked the messaging and meaning Clinton had developed in Latina/o/x communities.[29]

That changed significantly during the next presidential election cycle. By 2020, Sanders had completely retooled and expanded his Latina/o/x outreach, hiring over 200 Latina and Latino staffers, including a number of high-profile Latina political professionals and activists such as Stephanie Valencia, a former senior aide to Barack Obama, and lobbyist Cristina Antelo. His campaign was equally mindful of bringing Latina leaders with community organizing and grassroots experience into the campaign structure, including Analilia Mejia, former director of the New Jersey Working Families Alliance and organizer with SEIU and UNITE HERE, who eventually became Sanders' national political director. His campaign also included Latina activists such as DACA organizer Maria Belén Sisa, who became Sanders' deputy Latino press secretary, and founding member of Mijente, Neidi Dominguez, who was appointed deputy national states director.

The Sanders campaign also dramatically expanded their Latina/o/x outreach, establishing field offices in predominately Latina/o/x communities early in the campaign season, hiring local organizers to staff and lead outreach in their areas, and expanding the Sanders campaign

[28] Katie Glueck. The Power Players Behind Hillary Clinton's Campaign: A Guide to Some of the Most Influential Players in Her 2016 Presidential Bid, *Politico*, June 30, 2015, www .politico.com/story/2015/04/hillary-clintons-power-players-116874; Sandra Lilley, Hillary Clinton Taps DREAMer Lorella Praeli as Latino Outreach Director, *NBC News*, May 20, 2015, www.nbcnews.com/news/latino/hillary-clinton-taps-dreamer-activist-lorella-praeli-latina-outreach-director-n361721

[29] Suzanne Gamboa, Sanders Hires Arturo Carmona of Presente.org for Latino Outreach, *NBC News*, October 2, 2015, www.nbcnews.com/news/latino/sanders-hires-arturo-carmona-presente-org-latino-outreach-n437836; Adrian Carrasquillo, Bernie Sanders Hires High-Profile DREAMer Activist for Latino Outreach, *BuzzFeed*, October 22, 2015, www .buzzfeed.com/adriancarrasquillo/bernie-sanders-hires-high-profile-dreamer-activist-for-latin

platform toward a more comprehensive and inclusive agenda on issues such as immigration and racial inequality in education. In contrast to those of the other Democratic primary contenders, the Sanders campaign invested heavily and early on in Latina/o/x voters, with a significant presence of Bernie supporters and surrogates spread across Latina/o/x communities. Alexandria Ocasio-Cortez was one of the prominent Latina endorsers who also bestowed on Sanders the affectionate moniker – *tío* Bernie – signaling solidarity and familiarity with Latinas/os/xs. Ocasio-Cortez explained her endorsement of Sanders at a rally in October 2019: "Bernie Sanders proved you can run a grassroots campaign and win in an America where we almost thought that was impossible. And with that, I would like to introduce the man, the ally, I call him *tío* Bernie, to my goddaughter he's *abuelo*, but he's my *tío* Bernie Sanders."[30]

Ultimately, the Sanders campaign built such a strong ground game in the early primary states of Iowa, Nevada, Texas, and California, with significant turnout and support from Latinas/os/xs, that it was initially able to withstand a series of dramatic losses to Joe Biden during the Super Tuesday primaries. However, by April 2020 it became clear that Sanders had no realistic path to the nomination, and he dropped out of the presidential race. Unfortunately, Joe Biden's presidential campaign lacked a comparable early investment in Latina/o/x outreach and even lost its most senior Latina staffer, Vanessa Cárdenas, in late 2019 owing to its lack of investment. As a result, by May 2020 polls showed a clear enthusiasm gap among Latina/o/x voters for both Biden and the 2020 election itself, with only 49 percent of registered Latinas/os/xs committed to supporting Biden over Trump, and six in ten committed to voting in November. Moreover, support for Biden was deeply gendered, with 54 percent of Latino men saying they would vote for Biden as compared to 64 percent of Latinas.[31]

Worried about Latina/o/x turnout, the Biden campaign took a number of steps to expand support among this sector of the electorate, including an initial plan to invest $55 million in outreach and mobilization aimed at Latino men. This plan was scrapped in favor of broader Latina/o/x outreach

[30] Benjamin Fearnow, Alexandria Ocasio-Cortez Praises "My Tio Bernie Sanders" during NYC 2020 Campaign Endorsement, *Newsweek*, October 19, 2020, www.newsweek.com/alexandria-ocasio-cortez-endorse-bernie-sanders-queens-tio-ally-2020-democratic-campaign-1466482

[31] Latinos/SOMOS COVID-19 Crisis National Latino Survey, Latino Decisions, 2020, https://latinodecisions.com/polls-and-research/somos-covid-19-crisis-national-latino-survey-april-2020/

in states with significant Latina/o/x voters, such as Florida, Arizona, Colorado, Nevada, and Texas, as well as targeted investments aimed at smaller communities in the Midwest states of Michigan, Wisconsin, and Pennsylvania. Biden also brought in Julie Chávez Rodríguez, granddaughter of the late farmworker union leader César Chávez, as a senior advisor to the campaign. She joined Cristóbal Alex, former president of the Latino Victory Fund, and Latinx outreach director Laura Jiménez. Biden also sought support from national groups (such as Latino Victory, Voto Latino, and CASA en Action) as well as from a broad band of Latina/o/x surrogates (such as famed civil rights and labor leader Dolores Huerta) to make his case among Latina/o/x communities.

Among Republicans, there were also several important outreach campaigns aimed at Latina/o/x voters, but they were far more limited in scope, and focused on producing incremental increases among targeted groups of Latinas/os/xs as opposed to winning the majority of the Latina/o/x electorate. This was especially the case in South Florida, Texas, and parts of Arizona where Trump saw increases in support among Latina/o/x voters over 2016. Despite the relentless demonizing of Latina/o/x communities in his tweets, rallies, and discourse used throughout his administration, during his reelection campaign Trump, along with the RNC, understood the need to increase their margins of support in Latina/o/x strongholds – or they would face significant losses across the ballot. As a result, "Latinos for Trump" was launched in Miami, Florida, in 2019 led by two Latinas – Lieutenant Governor Jeanette Nuñez and Republican Party fundraiser Maggie Paláu-Hernandez. Members of the Trump extended family, especially Kimberly Guilfoyle – Puerto Rican girlfriend of Donald Trump Jr. – figured prominently as surrogates in rallies, online chats, and social media. Trump also targeted Latino evangelical leaders with gendered messaging that advanced restrictions on abortion and reproductive health care and scaled back protections for trans persons and same-sex marriage.[32]

To be clear, the existence of Latina/o/x voters who supported a conservative Republican presidential candidate was neither new nor particularly striking in 2020. Republican presidential candidates such as Ronald Reagan had long realized the potential for mobilizing more politically conservative Latina/o/x voters, such as Cubans in South Florida. Drawing

---

[32] Geraldo Cadava, The Deep Origins of Latino Support for Trump, *The New Yorker*, December 29, 2020, www.newyorker.com/news/the-political-scene/the-deep-origins-of-latino-support-for-trump

on his long-term support from conservative Latinos in Texas, George W. Bush famously received 40 percent of the Latina/o/x vote during his 2000 presidential campaign. Similarly, since 2011, conservative fundraisers such as the Koch brothers had invested millions in outreach and mobilization of Latina/o/x voters through efforts such as the Libre Initiative. All of these campaigns regularly produce modest gains among the Latina/o/x electorate, underscoring the fundamental principles long established by scholars of racial and ethnic politics that Latina/o/x voters are not a monolith group, that they retain some fluidity in their voting behavior, and that outreach matters.

Voter Suppression Tactics Met with Renewed Organizing among Latinas

Finally, no examination of the Latina electorate would be complete without understanding the unprecedented forms of voter suppression aimed at Black and Latina/o/x communities that proliferated in the past decade and produced serious impediments throughout the 2020 election cycle. Following the historic Supreme Court decision in *Shelby v. Holder* (2013) gutting the preclearance provisions of the 1965 Voting Rights Act, states and jurisdictions with a history of discriminatory voting practices that were previously subject to federal supervision were free to create new restrictions with a disproportionate number of changes disenfranchising Black, Latina/o/x, younger voters, and lower-income voters. These voter suppression tactics took several different forms from excessive voter purges, new voter ID laws, limits on early voting, and cutbacks on polling locations, through restrictions on ballot counting, limits on provisional balloting, broken machines, inadequate or nonexistent staffing, an absence of qualified and available bilingual staff and ballots, long lines and waiting periods, voter intimidation, and gerrymandering. According to a 2019 report from the Leadership Conference on Civil and Human Rights, states and jurisdictions whose voting practices had previously been subject to review under the preclearance provisions shut down 1,688 polling locations between 2012 and 2018.[33]

For many Latinas/os/xs pursuing naturalized citizenship in advance of voting, these voter suppression tactics were compounded by dramatic increases in citizenship filing fees, processing wait times that extended

---

[33] Democracy Diverted: Polling Place Closures and the Right to Vote, Leadership Conference on Civil and Human Rights, September 10, 2019, https://civilrights.org/resource/democracy-diverted-polling-place-closures-and-the-right-to-vote/

beyond two years, and revisions to the citizenship exam intent on making the process more difficult and costly. All of these barriers were further aggravated by the spread of COVID-19, which strained local resources, disproportionately impacted Latina/o/x and Black communities, and prompted the creation of new standards for in-person voting that often failed to meet demand and produced confusing results.

The impact of these changes was felt early in the election season with long wait times in heavily minority and heavily Democratic cities during primary elections in both Texas and California. In the Texas Democratic primary, the longest wait times were in Harris County, home to Houston, Texas – a majority/minority county comprised of 43 percent Latinas/os/xs and 19 percent African Americans where the last voter of the night waited six and a half hours to cast his ballot. Moreover, as the *Guardian* reported, in Texas "the 50 counties that gained the most Black and Latinx residents between 2012 and 2018 closed 542 polling sites, compared to just 34 closures in the 50 counties that have gained the fewest Black and Latinx residents."[34]

Significantly, the results of these voter suppression tactics were also gendered. As polling from the National Association of Latina and Latino Elected and Appointed Officials (NALEO) along with Latino Decisions indicates, Latinas were far more likely than Latinos to report experiencing voter intimidation, discouragement, harassment, lines lasting more than one hour, difficulty with finding parking at a polling location, poll workers who could not locate their names on the registration list, lack of Spanish-language voting materials or Spanish-speaking poll workers, and polling locations that failed to follow COVID-19 safety measures, creating significant impediments to deter their voting.[35]

While national parties and candidates engaged in targeted voter outreach, these efforts were not sufficient to overcome the systematic forms of disenfranchisement. Moreover, tracking polling from Latino Decisions throughout the 2020 election cycle suggests that within a month of the general election, when early voting efforts are typically in full swing, about half of Latina/o/x voters (48%) reported they had not been contacted by a political party or a campaign.[36] These outcomes paralleled

---

[34] Richard Salame, Texas Closes Hundreds of Polling Sites, Making it Harder for Minorities to Vote, *The Guardian*, March 2, 2020, www.theguardian.com/us-news/2020/mar/02/texas-polling-sites-closures-voting

[35] Latino Decisions, NALEO Educational Fund 9-Wave.

[36] Ibid.

problems in outreach and mobilization during both the 2016 and 2018 elections, when more than half the Latina/o/x electorate reported receiving no contact. Again, Latinas were more likely than Latinos to report receiving no contact from a political party, campaign, or any other organization (including by phone, text, email, or even in person).

Stepping into this gap in outreach were several nonpartisan, grassroots, community-based, and civic organizations led by women of color, which targeted the interests and needs of women of color. In particular, the 2020 election cycle saw an unprecedented range of civic engagement activities organized by nonpartisan community groups aimed at historically marginalized and low propensity voters, including women of color. Owing to their intersectional foundations, many of these groups engaged women of color well beyond the ballot box, having advanced social justice mobilization on a range of topics including immigrant rights, reproductive justice, police reform, health care, worker rights, and environmental justice long before the election.

Latinas played significant roles as leaders and organizers in these outreach and mobilization efforts through progressive, liberal, conservative, and even religious groups operating nationally and in targeted races. The power of political organizing and activism among women of color advancing racial, ethnic, gender, and immigrant justice during the last four years cannot be understated, and the Latina-led efforts of organizations such as Voto Latino, Mi Familia Vota, Mijente, Florida Rising, New Florida Majority Education Fund, United We Dream, and UNITE HERE were central to this work. Long before candidate filing dates or registration deadlines, Latinas such as Lorella Praeli and Erika Andiola were responding to relentless racialized attacks from a presidential administration that embraced white supremacy and targeted Latina/o/x immigrants with over 400 policy initiatives aimed at marginalizing Latina/o/x communities across the country. Latina organizers and activists seeded the political ground through citizenship drives, education initiatives, and community-based outreach efforts. Even Latinas in organizations such as the National Hispanic Christian Leadership Conference proved instrumental to advancing conservative outreach, in places such as Miami Dade County, and mobilizing voters in support of Latina/x Republican candidates such as Maria Elvira Salazar, who successfully defeated Democratic incumbent Donna Shalala in Florida's 27th congressional district.

These organizations frequently built upon the relationships, social networks, spheres of influence, and survival strategies that Latinas and other women of color had cultivated over the course of their lives to expand voter education, registration efforts, and turnout. Moreover, the organizations helped to manage the myriad of obstacles and new challenges women of color encountered in the course of voting, from complicated identification requirements to long lines and shuttered polling locations. Finally, drawing on the lived experiences of women of color, they often adopted intersectional frameworks that facilitated a greater understanding of and connections with political issues. These intersectional perspectives were also central to their organizing work. As Silvia Henriquez, codirector of All Above All, an organization focused on advancing reproductive justice, noted: "Because we are women of color doing this work, we show up with our entire selves. That allows us to make connections around economic justice, immigrant justice when we are still talking about the issue of abortion."[37]

In the end, Latina/x-led organizing in grassroots organizations, political movements, and nonpartisan voter mobilization efforts expanded and amplified the work done within official campaigns in important ways, and was a key part of the overall picture of Latina political participation in the 2020 election cycle. The work of these nonpartisan organizations did not begin with Trump, as many of the organizing efforts had been in the works for decades. However, their efforts were amplified and took on new urgency because of a political climate that relentlessly undermined Latina/o/x communities and specifically made targeting Latina/o/x immigrants part of a national narrative of belonging. In short, with an administration that consistently advanced white nationalism, masculinity, and xenophobia, Latinas found themselves persistently on the front lines, organizing, defending, strategizing for change, and using the existing social and political networks – both formal political spaces and informal social networks – to effect change and advance racial justice. The results were evidenced in the 2018 midterms, with the election of Biden–Harris, and the successful election of a new cohort of women of color to national office in 2020.

CONCLUSION

From get-out-the-vote efforts at national level to targeted voter mobilization in competitive districts, Latinas have consistently served as important community builders between the political parties and Latina/o/x communities.

---

[37] Ahead of the Majority: Foregrounding Women of Color, AAPI Civic Engagement Fund and Groundswell Fund, 2019, https://aapifund.org/wp-content/uploads/2019/08/WOC_REPORT_8.13.2019_FINAL_web.pdf

For Democrats especially, they have consistently organized, mobilized, and delivered for the party's candidates and causes, establishing an important track record, along with Black women, as fundamental to the party's success. This proved to be no different in 2020, when Latina political engagement broke previous records set in 2018 and even more Latinas engaged in the electoral process as advocates, fundraisers, donors, campaign staff, commentators, canvassers, organizers, voters, and, most importantly, candidates and officeholders. They won a record number of congressional seats around the country and contributed to the Democrats' majority in the US House of Representatives.

In the end, despite the gains made in 2018 and 2020, there is still a great deal of work to be done to address enduring forms of race and gender inequality that disproportionately impact Latinas and other women of color. This will inevitably take more than a single election cycle or even a single administration to properly address. Moreover, while representation within the highest political offices is vitally important to advancing Latina interests, the work of attending to Latina political inclusion and the social and economic well-being of Latinas needs to happen all year long.

Finally, the events of January 6, 2020 underscore that the gains made in the 2018 and 2020 election cycles among Latinas and other women of color cannot be taken for granted. Organized groups intent on disenfranchising people of color, advancing sexist, racist, homophobic, and xenophobic restrictions, and further marginalizing women of color persist. Latina political leadership is needed now more than ever to combat those efforts and advance progressive political changes that will protect and expand democracy for everyone.

7 Elevating African American Women's Political Leadership amid Pandemic Politics

For many, the 2020 presidential election is most linked to the global COVID-19 pandemic, and indeed, this shaped every aspect of the election year, including the emphasis on health and health care policy issues, how campaigning occurred, and where, when and how voters cast their ballots. In reality, we navigated the 2020 election year amid twin pandemics in that the COVID-19 pandemic collided with the nation's racial reckoning in response to the police killings of George Floyd by Minneapolis police officer Derek Chauvin and the police killing of Breonna Taylor during a raid of her Louisville, Kentucky home as she was in bed sleeping. Both the public health crisis and the protests that ensued from more police killings of unarmed African Americans created the unprecedented conditions of "pandemic politics" that centered race from multiple vantage points. Navigating pandemic politics prompted obvious changes to the methods many Americans used to cast their ballots, and unexpectedly created political opportunities that elevated African American women's political leadership on the national stage as elected leaders and political activists. Yet while 2020 saw heightened attention on African American women in formal politics, this election year is only part of the long history of African American women's leadership and political activism.

In this chapter, I examine the 2020 elections from the perspective of African American women as voters, political operatives, and elected leaders, while placing their exercise of and access to political power within historical context. I outline the key role that African American women have played historically, and continued to play in election 2020, in protecting and expanding access to the ballot and turning out as the most reliable Democratic voters. There is growing recognition of their hard work and energies on behalf of progressive politics. Towards the close of his second term as president, in 2015, Barack Obama called out the contributions of African American women to progressive politics and marked their centrality in building a more inclusive democracy for all Americans and helping America fulfill its promise.[1] In response to a letter from African American women leaders calling for recognition of their contributions and greater support of the party, former national Democratic Party chairman Tom Perez engaged the politics of recognition, referring to African American women as the "backbone of the party" and noting that their steadfast support had not always been recognized by party leaders. Despite these sentiments of acknowledgment and recognition, there is still the need to close the gap between African American women's voting heft and their representation as elected officials. I ask: With African American women increasingly moving into the national spotlight as political actors, how will they translate their political power as voters into political strength as candidates for elected office at all levels of government? I explore African American women's advancement as candidates and elected officeholders, with particular attention to progress – or the lack thereof – for African American women's representation across levels of office.

The growing influence of African American women as political leaders – both operatives and elected officials – in and as a result of election 2020 shows that their political power is increasing and coming closer to aligning with their power as voters to decide election outcomes. The historic win of Vice President Kamala Harris as the first African American, first South Asian, and first woman to hold this level of office is the clearest example of the growing political power of African American women. While Harris' election is the first, there is much work to do to assure she is not the last nor the last of a generation of African American women succeeding in winning elected office across national, state, and local levels. Even with this historic election of Madam Vice President, the significant gap between African American women's voting power and political representation remains. When that gap narrows, we will know they are not only acknowledged for fostering progressive politics ideals, but they will also be positioned to bring policy issues to fruition that benefit their communities and improve the lives of women and girls of color. While appreciating the historic electoral firsts that Harris and other African American women represent, evidence of the persistent barriers and

---

[1] Wendy Smooth, Obama African American Women, and the Limitations of Recognition, in *After Obama: African American Politics in a Post-Obama Era*, ed. Todd Shaw, Joseph McCormick, and Robert Brown (New York: New York University Press, 2020), pp. 149–69.

challenges they encounter highlight that African American women's journey from the shadows to the spotlight in American politics is not yet complete. African American women are organizing and exploring new strategies to ensure their future leadership in American politics. By focusing on their experiences, we can examine the extent of America's progress toward political inclusiveness along both race and gender lines and toward a society in which race and gender are less significant as determinants of electoral success.

AFRICAN AMERICAN WOMEN AND THE PARADOX OF PARTICIPATION

Traditional measures and indicators of political participation suggest that African American women would be among the least likely to participate in politics, yet they are heavily engaged in a range of political activities. This contradiction, which I term the *paradox of participation*, has undergirded African American women's political participation since they gained access to formal participation in this democracy. African American women have consistently participated in American politics despite formidable barriers to their participation in formal electoral roles as voters and candidates. At its inception in 1787, the US Constitution limited the citizenship rights of African Americans, both women and men, regarding each one as only three-fifths of a person. Later, as Mamie Locke argues, African American women would move from three-fifths of a person under the Constitution to total exclusion from constitutional protections with the passage in 1870 of the Fifteenth Amendment, which extended the right to vote to African American men only.[2] When women earned the right to vote in 1920 with the passage of the Nineteenth Amendment, large numbers of African American women remained restricted from the franchise through the cultural norms of the Jim Crow South. African Americans were disenfranchised through literacy tests, poll taxes, grandfather clauses, and all-white primaries. It was not until the passage of the Voting Rights Act of 1965 that African American women secured the right to freely practice the franchise. The impact of the Voting Rights Act was keenly apparent in the states of the Deep South; African American voter registration in Mississippi, for example, increased from 6.7 percent in

---

[2] Mamie Locke, From Three Fifths to Zero, in *Women Transforming Politics*, ed. Cathy Cohen, Kathleen B. Jones, and Joan Tronto (New York: New York University Press, 1997), pp. 377–86.

1964 to 64 percent in 1980.[3] The Voting Rights Act (VRA) of 1965 was arguably the single most important piece of legislation in securing the franchise for African American voters and realizing political empowerment. The rapid growth in the numbers of African American elected officials is further evidence of the VRA's impact.

Studies of American politics often define political participation narrowly in terms of electoral participation. As Cathy Cohen argues, such a limited definition of political participation has hindered the development of research on African American women's political activism because their political participation tends to extend beyond electoral politics to community organizing and civic engagement.[4] Because African American women were excluded from participation in formal politics until the passage of the Voting Rights Act of 1965, first by the condition of their enslavement and then by equally oppressive systems of exclusion, their nontraditional political activism developed outside the electoral system and was informed by their political, economic, and social conditions.[5]

Defining political participation beyond the narrow framework of voting and holding elected office allows us to see the consistent levels of African American women's political participation across history. By asking new questions and examining the nontraditional spaces of women's activism, such as churches, private women's clubs, and volunteer organizations, feminist historians have uncovered countless activities of women of color involved in social movements. African American women have been central to every effort toward greater political empowerment for both African Americans and women. As the historian Paula Giddings attests, African American women were the linchpin in struggles against racism and sexism. They understood that the fates of women's rights and Black rights were inextricably linked and that one would be meaningless without the other.[6]

---

[3] Frank R. Parker, *Black Votes: Count Political Empowerment in Mississippi after 1965* (Chapel Hill, NC: University of North Carolina Press, 1990).

[4] Cathy J. Cohen, A Portrait of Continuing Marginality: The Study of Women of Color in American Politics, in *Women and American Politics: New Questions, New Directions*, ed. Susan J. Carroll (New York: Oxford University Press, 2003), pp. 190–213.

[5] See Paula Giddings, *When and Where I Enter: The Impact of Black Women on Race and Sex in America* (New York: Bantam Books, 1984); Darlene Clark Hine and Kathleen Thompson, *A Shining Thread of Hope: The History of Black Women in America* (New York: Broadway Books, 1998); Dorothy Sterling, *We Are Your Sisters: Black Women in the Nineteenth Century* (New York: W. W. Norton, 1997).

[6] Giddings, *When and Where I Enter*.

In spite of this rich legacy of activism, African American women's political participation represents a puzzle of sorts. African American women appear to be overrepresented in elective office while simultaneously holding the characteristics that would make them least likely to be politically engaged. African American women account for a greater proportion of Black elected officials than white women do of white elected officials.[7] For example, as of spring 2021, African American women were over 40 percent of African Americans in the US House of Representatives, while white women were less than a quarter of white House members.

Scholars who study the intersection of race and gender argue that African American women suffer from a "double disadvantage" in politics, in that they are forced to overcome the ills of both sexism and racism.[8] Robert Darcy and Charles Hadley, however, conclude that African American women defied expectations, proving more politically ambitious than their white counterparts and enjoying greater success in election to mayoral, state legislative, and congressional office in comparison with white women throughout the 1970s and 1980s. These authors link the puzzle of African American women's achievement to their activism in the civil rights movement and the skills developed during the movement, which African American women quickly translated into formal politics once passage of the Voting Rights Act opened opportunities.[9] With greater attention to the racialized and gendered dimensions of political ambition, Pearl Ford Dowe argues that African American women's ambition in politics is partially explained by their participation in social movements and is greatly informed by their political socialization, which often occurs within independent African American civic and social organizations. The motivation to serve as elected officials is fostered and nurtured through their membership in organizations and networks steeped in commitments to service.[10] We see this narrative play out in the political lives of many of the notable African American women who garnered national attention in

---

[7] Linda Faye Williams, The Civil Rights-Black Power Legacy, in *Sisters in the Struggle, African-American Women in the Civil Rights-Black Power Movement*, ed. Bettye Collier-Thomas and V. P. Franklin (New York: New York University Press, 2001), pp. 306–332.

[8] See Robert Darcy and Charles Hadley, Black Women in Politics: The Puzzle of Success, *Social Science Quarterly* 69 (September) (1988): 629–45; Gary Moncrief, Joel Thompson and Robert Schuhmann, Gender, Race and the Double Disadvantage Hypothesis, *Social Science Journal* 28 (1991): 481–87.

[9] Darcy and Hadley, Black Women in Politics.

[10] Pearl Ford Dowe, Resisting Marginalization: Black Women's Political Ambition and Agency, *Political Science & Politics* 53(4) (2020): 697–702.

the 2020 election cycle, including Vice President Harris and voting rights activist Stacey Abrams.

Studies of political participation have consistently concluded that the affluent and the educated are more likely to participate in politics at higher rates.[11] However, for African American women, the usual determinants of political participation – education and income – are not strong predictors of participation.[12] African American women's high level of officeholding contrasts with their material conditions, which suggest that they would be far less politically active. Regardless of their socioeconomic status, African American women are far more likely than African American men to engage in both traditional forms of political participation (including voting and holding office) and nontraditional forms of participation (such as belonging to organizations and clubs, attending church, and talking to people about politics). Social scientists do not fully understand these inconsistencies in African American women's political participation.[13] African American women's higher than expected participation rates also mean that they are active in unsuspecting places in politics, and without attentiveness to disaggregating the histories of "women" in politics or "African Americans" in politics, we easily overlook the contributions of African American women at the intersection of these groups.

PANDEMIC POLITICS AND AFRICAN AMERICAN WOMEN VOTING RIGHTS ACTIVISTS

Consistent with more than a century of activism to secure voting rights, African American women were at the forefront of efforts to protect and expand access to voting in election 2020. The safety protocols of the pandemic mandated election officials to shift away from an emphasis on a singular Election Day and toward promoting early or mail-in voting. Prior to the 2020 election, voting rights advocates celebrated early and mail-in voting as a means of creating more inclusive elections that maximize

---

[11] See Andrea Y. Simpson, Taking Over or Taking a Back Seat? Political Activism of African American Women, paper delivered at the annual meeting of the American Political Science Association, Atlanta, Georgia, September 1–5, 1999. For an extensive discussion of political participation, see Sidney Verba, Kay Lehman Scholzman and Henry E. Brady, *Voice and Equality: Civic Volunteerism in American Politics* (Cambridge, MA: Harvard University Press, 1995).

[12] Sandra Baxter and Marjorie Lansing, *Women and Politics: The Invisible Majority* (Ann Arbor, MI: University of Michigan Press, 1980).

[13] Simpson, Taking Over or Taking a Back Seat?

opportunities for voters to cast their ballots. Election officials concerned about minimizing virus spread sought to both expand and promote methods to reduce pressures on Election Day turnout, including early and mail-in voting, the use of drop box voting, and extending both the number of early polling places and the time periods during which early voting was allowed. Despite being utilized by voters in previous elections, election officials faced challenges and lawsuits aimed at questioning the security of these measures, particularly from those supporting President Trump. These challenges echoed the Trump administration's insistence that voter fraud was rampant and that election officials sought to "steal the election." Such lawsuits and accusations of election officials' nefarious activities were especially common in battleground states and in districts with high proportions of voters of color. Moreover, the strong rhetoric of the president sought to sow confusion and distrust of the voting system.

From the onset, African American women voting rights activists responded to attempts to confuse voters, cast doubt on the legitimacy of the election, and reduce voter access by organizing stealth voter education campaigns and voter mobilization efforts to get out the vote, especially among communities of color. Pandemic politics thrust African American women voting rights activists such as Stacey Abrams of Fair Fight and Latosha Brown of Black Voters Matter into the national spotlight as they sought to protect citizens' access to the ballot and protect citizens' rights to vote. Stacey Abrams became a national leader among progressives after losing a hard-fought governor's race in 2018 by just 55,000 votes to Brian Kemp. Abrams famously turned her loss into a formidable organization, Fair Fight, that successfully increased Democratic Party voter turnout in the state by registering new voters and those "left behind" in rural areas of the state. She is celebrated as the critical actor who delivered Georgia for Joe Biden and Kamala Harris in the presidential election, marking the first time since Bill Clinton's election in 1992 that the state voted for a Democrat for president. Further, Abrams is credited with completing Georgia's blue conversion by Democrats winning both senate races in a hotly contested runoff election, sending Georgia's first African American Raphael Warnock and the state's first Jewish American Jon Ossoff to the US Senate.

In addition to the power of Abrams in Georgia, Latosha Brown emerged as another powerhouse shaping African American voter turnout across states. In 2013, Brown cofounded Black Voters Matter and began work focused on voter inclusion in the Deep South. She inaugurated a bus tour across the South and registered voters, making the case that if rural Blacks registered and voted, it would change the electoral landscape of the region. Her message resonated and, by the start of the 2020 election, she had extended the organization's work far beyond the South to tackle voter suppression across the country.

Though much of the media's focus on voter mobilization and protecting voting rights centered on the charismatic and iconic leadership of Abrams, she herself has rightly pointed out that her work in Georgia was bolstered by African American women activists and organizers across the state. Long-established grassroots groups such as the Black Women's Roundtable, a national group led by Melanie L. Campbell with local chapter affiliates across the country, were among those who advocated for voting rights. They were joined by newly formed groups motivated by Senator Kamala Harris' selection as the Democratic vice-presidential nominee, such as #KHive, Mamas for Kamala, and Chucks and Pearls (a network of social media organizing groups who drew their name from Harris' affinity for wearing the practical Converse sports shoes and her signature pearl necklaces). Harris' affiliation with the national organization Alpha Kappa Alpha Sorority, Incorporated signified by her pearls, fueled the group's own voter mobilization efforts. Alpha Kappa Alpha Sorority, Incorporated, a civic-minded group of college-educated African American women to which Harris pledged as a college student at Howard University, mobilized their membership base alongside similar efforts of other African American sororities and fraternities known as the Divine Nine. Beyond these organizations, African American voter mobilization was also driven by alums of other historically Black colleges and universities (HBCUs).

African American women activists led many of the mobilizations in Georgia and across the nation credited with expanding the 2020 electorate and protecting voter access for communities of color. Much research is needed to fully capture the impact of African American women's organizing, particularly their roles as get-out-the-vote (GOTV) operatives. For example, the group #WinWithBlackWomen capitalized on the social distancing and limited travel of the pandemic to convene intergenerational gatherings of hundreds of African American women on weekly Sunday evening Zoom platform calls. Participants at the meetings included executives across major sectors from technology and media to banking and commerce, as well as political strategists, writers, academics, artists, and social media giants. They gathered to discuss strategies to expand the electorate, share best practices to mobilize voters from across states, elevate campaigns of African American women in down-ballot races, and pray for the progress of the nation. These sisterhood spaces were made both necessary and possible by the pandemic. Through their shared networks, African American women convened women at minimal costs, reaching out to African American women across the country to vote, mobilize, and bring their sisters, family members and friends along as well. The conditions of pandemic politics meant that via new networks and organizing platforms, African American women could use their existing and growing social media networks to host virtual phone banking drives, help voters locate early voting drop boxes, educate communities on early voting, and rally people to remain in long early voting lines. Pandemic politics also created spaces for African American women voting rights activists to push back against both rhetoric and policy designed to suppress voting. They built on earlier campaigns across the country to utilize church communities to bring "souls to the polls." In 2020, they brought "soul" to the polls with musical acts, DJs, and food trucks, making coming out to vote a socially engaging and entertaining civic activity, and also a much needed reprieve from the social isolation of the pandemic.

The activism, ingenuity, and creativity of African American women – as individuals, in networks, and as organization leaders – constituted the leveraging power behind activists like Abrams. African American women's efforts and those of others resulted in the 2020 election making history by reaching a new high record in voter turnout, with 66.8 percent of Americans reporting they had voted. According to the US Census, African Americans increased their participation in 2020, with 63 percent reporting voting, a slight increase from the 2016 presidential cycle.[14] Many argue that African American women's success in turning out voters of color in Georgia and other battleground states was the impetus for the increase in voter restriction bills that sprang up quickly after the 2020 elections.

In addition to mobilizing voter turnout among others, African American women continued to lead in casting ballots themselves; according to the US Census, 66.3 percent of African American women compared to 58.3 percent of African American men voted in election 2020. Their high participation rates as voters are part of a broader tradition of political engagement. In 2020, as in previous elections, African American women delivered votes for the Democratic Party across levels of office. At the presidential level, they experienced the historic first of voting for a woman of African American and South Asian descent for vice president of the United States.

---

[14] United States Census Bureau, Voting and Registration in the Election of 2020, tables, https://bit.ly/3jeLRO4

AFRICAN AMERICAN WOMEN AND THE PRESIDENCY

African American women have a long-established history of seeking political inclusion via the highest office in the land, the presidency. The initial excitement of Senator Kamala Harris' campaign for the presidency in the 2020 election was that it linked to the historic runs of other African American women like Shirley Chisholm, the first African American woman to run for nomination on a major party ticket. That Harris would do so in the year that women commemorated the 100th anniversary of the Nineteenth Amendment was especially significant to many of her supporters. However, the excitement over Harris' run for the presidency waned when early evaluations that she was not a "viable" candidate hampered her fundraising. Her strong performance in the first Democratic primary debate in June 2019 yielded significant, but temporary, bumps in attention and support. But they were not enough. Citing fundraising as one of the most significant reasons, Harris dropped out of the Democratic primary campaign in December 2019 before the first votes were cast.

Harris' story is familiar to other African American women presidential hopefuls. Across history, at least six African American women have had their names on the general election ballot for the presidency (see Table 7.1).[15] Most of these candidates represented fringe or third parties. Prior to Harris' campaign, two African American women had run for the presidency seeking to represent the Democratic Party. Shirley Chisholm ran in 1972, and more than thirty years later, Carol Moseley Braun ran in 2004. The candidacies of Chisholm and Braun resemble Harris' 2020 bid in that they were deemed nonviable from the onset. But Chisholm, Braun, and Harris all offered serious challenges to the status quo that suggests that presidential politics is not the domain of women of color. As Kelly Dittmar illustrates in Chapter 2 of this volume, each woman's bid for the White House alters the political landscape and further challenges presidential norms, and each woman's candidacy increases political participation and interest among women across the country. While these women ran very different campaigns indicative of the times in which they found themselves, each campaign shows the challenges that African American women face in seeking the presidency.

---

[15] The Women Who Ran for President, Jo Freeman (website), January 15, 2009, http:// jofreeman.com

TABLE 7.1 Six African American women have appeared on general election ballots for president

Candidate	Political party	Year
Charlene Mitchell	Communist Party	1968
Lenora Fulani	New Alliance Party	1988 and 1992
Margaret Wright	People's Party	1976
Isabel Masters	Looking Back Party	1992 and 1996
Monica Moorehead	Workers World Party	1996 and 2000
Cynthia McKinney	Green Party	2008

Source: Compiled by author using data from the Jo Freeman website www.jofreeman.com

In 1972, Congresswoman Shirley Chisholm broke barriers as the first African American woman to make a serious bid for the presidency.[16] Chisholm was well positioned to run for president, with political experience at community, state, and national levels. She served in the New York General Assembly before becoming the first African American woman elected to Congress. As the lone African American woman in Congress, she joined her twelve African American male colleagues in founding the Congressional Black Caucus (CBC).[17]

After two terms in the House of Representatives, Chisholm decided to run for president. Her run came at a point when civil rights leaders were calling for greater political engagement and the women's movement was at its height. In running for president, Chisholm hoped to bring the concerns of these communities to the forefront of national politics. She spoke out for the rights of African Americans, women, and gays. She was quickly dismissed, perceived as not a serious candidate.

Chisholm faced a 1970s America that was just becoming accustomed to women in the workforce and in politics. She challenged notions of women's proper place. On the campaign trail, she routinely encountered hecklers who were happy to tell her the proper place for a woman. She told the story of a man at a campaign stop who questioned whether she

---

[16] Although Shirley Chisholm's 1972 run for the White House is most often cited, there is a long legacy of African Americans running for the presidency, largely as third-party candidates. For a full discussion, see Hanes Walton Jr., Black Female Presidential Candidates: Bass, Mitchell, Chisholm, Wright, Reid, Davis and Fulani, in *Black Politics and Black Political Behavior: A Linkage Analysis*, ed. Hanes Walton Jr. (Westport, CT: Praeger, 1994), pp. 251–76.

[17] Katherine Tate, *Black Faces in the Mirror: African Americans and Their Representatives in the US Congress* (Princeton, NJ: Princeton University Press, 2003).

had "cleaned her house" and "cared for her husband" before coming there.[18] Chisholm often faced such blatant sexism and, in other encounters, racism in her campaign, but she continued to press toward the Democratic National Convention (DNC).

Although Chisholm fashioned herself as both the "Black candidate" and the "woman candidate," she found herself shunned by both Black leaders in Congress and the feminist community. Far from supporting her, members of the CBC, an organization she had helped to found, charged that her run was detrimental to the Black community, dividing it along gender lines at a time when the Black community could not afford such divisive politics. Chisholm, a founder of the National Organization for Women (NOW), was dealt an equally devastating blow when prominent feminists such as the cofounder of the National Women's Political Caucus (NWPC), Gloria Steinem, and fellow US Congresswoman Bella Abzug decided not to endorse her candidacy publicly. Instead, they opted to protect their political leverage by supporting Senator George McGovern, who was considered at that time the more viable candidate of the Democratic contenders and the candidate most capable of defeating then President Nixon.[19]

Deserted by both the leaders of the CBC and the feminist community, Chisholm survived the primaries and remained a candidate at the outset of the DNC. She received 151 delegate votes on the first ballot, far short of the roughly 2,000 needed to secure the nomination. In the end, Chisholm acknowledged that her bid for the White House was less about winning and more about demanding full inclusion for African Americans and women. By waging a national presidential campaign, her candidacy had shown the world what was possible for women and men of color with increased access to political empowerment in a more democratized America. Indeed, Chisholm blazed the trail that would eventually lead to the election of Barack Obama.

More than three decades later, there was no doubt that Carol Moseley Braun benefited from Chisholm's pioneering candidacy, as Harris did. The differences between the two experiences signify some progress for African American women as high-profile candidates, even as they bring to light enduring problems African American women face in achieving greater political empowerment.

[18] Shirley Chisholm, *The Good Fight* (New York: Harper & Row, 1973).
[19] For a more elaborate discussion of Chisholm's supporters and detractors during the 1972 presidential campaign, see *Chisholm '72 Unbought and Unbossed*, a documentary by the filmmaker Shola Lynch.

Carol Moseley Braun's treatment in the 2004 election cycle symbolizes some progress from the blatant, overt sexism and racism that Shirley Chisholm encountered in 1972. Moseley Braun experienced more subversive, structurally embedded sexism and racism, which are more difficult to recognize. Her experiences reflect the extent to which the office of the president is consistently associated with white men, a pattern that Melanye Price and Kelly Dittmar document in Chapter 1 of this volume. Because Moseley Braun was neither a man nor white, she struggled constantly to convince the public that her candidacy was, in fact, viable. The doubts surrounding the feasibility of her candidacy affected all aspects of her campaign, but were most devastating to her fundraising efforts. The negligible and trivializing media coverage she received reinforced doubts and further stymied her campaign. Such struggles are reflective of the institutional racism and sexism that continue to impede qualified candidates who differ from societal expectations about who should serve as president. Moseley Braun campaigned promising to "take the 'men only' sign off the White House door," but this seemed to be a challenge America was not ready to accept.

By objective measures, Moseley Braun was well positioned to run for the presidency. Once questioned as to why she was running, she quickly responded, "Why not?" adding, "If I were not a woman – if I were a guy – with my credentials and my experience and what I bring to the table, there would be no reason why I wouldn't think about running for president."[20] In the field of Democratic contenders, Moseley Braun's political record was among the most stellar. She was the only candidate to have experience at local, state, national, and international levels of government.

Despite the energetic responses Moseley Braun drew from crowds at campaign stops, political pundits remained dismissive of her campaign. According to her, this was nothing new: "Nobody ever expected me to get elected to anything. For one thing, I'm Black, I'm a woman and I'm out of the working class. So the notion that someone from my background would have anything to say about the leadership of this country is challenging to some."[21] Like Shirley Chisholm, she also faced charges of running a purely symbolic campaign to establish that women are capable of running for the country's top executive office.

---

[20] Monica Davey, In Seeking Presidency, Braun Could Win Back Reputation, *New York Times*, December 18, 2003, https://nyti.ms/3A51kaa

[21] Nedra Pickler, Washington Today: Braun Appears with the Presidential Candidates, but Isn't Running Like One, Associated Press State and Local Wire, May 2, 2003.

Weak campaign fundraising plagued Moseley Braun's campaign from the outset, and her fundraising efforts continuously lagged behind those of most other candidates, even after she gained impressive endorsements from the NWPC and NOW, two of the leading feminist organizations. Notable white feminists, including the legendary Gloria Steinem and Marie Wilson, director of the White House Project, a nonprofit organization dedicated to getting a woman into the White House, publicly supported her campaign. Black women's organizations, including the National Political Congress of Black Women, invested, and Moseley Braun enjoyed public endorsements from legendary African American women such as Coretta Scott King and Dr. Dorothy Height, president emerita of the National Council of Negro Women. Receiving such ardent support from the women's community and Black women's organizations, Braun's candidacy represented progress following the struggles faced by Shirley Chisholm's campaign.

Garnering media attention proved to be an equally challenging problem for Moseley Braun's campaign, creating a circular effect; without media visibility, her ability to raise funds was limited, and with minimal funding, her campaign drew less media attention. She had extreme difficulty getting her message to the voters. When she received any coverage at all, it most often referred to her as "improbable," "nonviable," a "long-shot" candidate, or at worst an "also-ran."

Whatever its challenges, Moseley Braun's campaign was certainly not confronted with the overt sexism and racism that Chisholm had experienced. Instead, a much more subtle, indirect brand of racism and sexism plagued it, characterized by the outright dismissal of her candidacy as a serious bid for the White House. Consistent slights affected all facets of her campaign. The failure to garner media attention, along with fundraising challenges, forced Carol Moseley Braun to pull out of the race in January 2004, even before the first primary.

Political scientist Paula McClain argues that Moseley Braun was disadvantaged from the onset in crafting a name for herself in this campaign, given the Democratic Party leadership's preference that candidates forgo more leftist politics. As she argues, Moseley Braun's identity as an African American woman positioned her clearly as a "left-of-center candidate" and subsequently constrained her ability to establish an alternative identity as a candidate in the minds of voters.[22]

---

[22] Paula McClain, Gender and Black Presidential Politics: From Chisholm to Moseley Braun Revisited, comments made at Roundtable on Black and Presidential Politics, American Political Science Association meeting, Chicago, September 1–5, 2004.

While both Chisholm and Braun were fashioned as too far to the left, Harris' background as a prosecutor and as California's attorney general precluded her from being regarded in this way. In fact, leftist progressives found much to critique in Harris' background, raising concerns that she was not progressive *enough* to win the Democratic nomination. While this ensured that she could not be dismissed with a simplistic too-far-left analysis in the primary election, claims that Harris was "radical" and a "socialist" were central to critiques against the Biden–Harris ticket by Republican opponents. Despite a strong initial debate performance, Harris did not receive the financial influx to sustain her campaign to the Iowa caucuses, causing her to exit the race.

While her political experience surpassed many of her opponents in the Democratic Party primary, Harris never carved a unique space in the field that could sustain her. Among the field of 2020 presidential hopefuls, she was certainly one with a stronger record of public service, which prepared her in significant ways to seek the presidency. It was also precisely her prior experiences in public service that became one of her greatest liabilities. Criticisms against her from the left were stronger and offered more traction than those leveraged by the Trump campaign. Her background as a prosecutor, district attorney, and attorney general were particularly out of step with the many progressives who rallied in protests to reform, defund or even abolish the police and prisons. While some progressives ruled Harris as one who could partner to work on criminal justice issues, for many her connections to law and order stood in too great an opposition to their political interests. Historical research and continuous examinations of polling data and media accounts will help us fully answer the question of the driving forces behind her nonviable moniker. Drawing on intersectionality as a tool of analysis, understanding the interplay between her record of public service and the types of offices she held cannot be separated from the context of racial pandemic politics that shaped election 2020. These factors shaped the ways race and gender operated in this election. All these aspects informed whether Americans regarded the complexity of her identity as a political asset, of no consequence, or as a liability.

Harris' story forever shifts the narrative of African American women in politics, and her story is still evolving. Though she did not win in her own right, she delivered for the Democratic ticket as the vice-presidential nominee. In that capacity, she attracted new donors to the party, and delivered on fundraising – the very pitfall that derailed her own presidential bid. Now we know that an African American woman can raise the money critical to a presidential campaign, which was a hurdle that lingered over every previous woman's race. Over the next four years of the Biden–Harris administration, America will experience Harris' leadership and further dissolve concerns over electing a woman president. The next four years for Harris serve as an extended job interview for her presidential readiness. The roles and level of responsibility she assumes as vice president will tie her to the successes and failures of the administration. Her ability to claim her own successes will shape what a future run for the presidency will look like for Harris. She has already redefined the political opportunity structure for African American women. Her political successes to date show African American women that despite formidable challenges, their political aspirations are no longer a long shot.

AFRICAN AMERICAN WOMEN: ON THE PATH TO HIGHER OFFICE?

The presidential candidacies of Chisholm, Braun, Harris, and the other African American women who have sought the office across history compel us to ask whether there are African American women poised to run for the presidency in future elections. Women and politics scholars and activists discuss increasing the numbers of women elected to public office at lower levels as the first step toward moving women into higher offices.[23] Feeding the political pipeline has become a critical strategy in preparing women to successfully seek the highest offices, including the presidency. Are African American women moving through that pipeline? Are they securing offices at local, state, and national levels in preparation for the highest political offices? Are they poised to run for the presidency in future elections? In light of the contributions of African American women in making up the new American electorate, are they also contributing to diversifying elected offices from national to local levels? Are they seeking political office in step with their participation as voters?

To date, African American women's engagement in electoral politics as a means of securing greater political empowerment and placing their concerns on the political agenda has produced mixed results. On the one hand, they are gaining increased access to political offices, often outpacing

---

[23] For a full discussion on getting women into the political pipeline, see Jennifer Lawless and Richard L. Fox, *It Takes a Candidate* (New York: Cambridge University Press, 2005).

African American men in winning elections. On the other hand, they continue to face considerable obstacles in securing high-profile offices at both state and national levels.

AFRICAN AMERICAN WOMEN IN STATE AND LOCAL POLITICS

Of the more than 3,000 African American women elected officials, most are elected to substate-level offices such as regional offices, county boards, city councils, judicial offices, and local school boards. African American women have gained increasing access to leadership positions at the local level. In 2020, African American women mayors led some of the most populated cities in the United States (see Table 7.2). The numbers of African American women in these roles grew from two in 2014 to the eight currently holding office. The high-profile nature of these executive roles warrants greater scholarly attention since these offices offer a glimpse into the experiences African American women might expect when elected to other executive leadership positions. Though African American women have held these significant leadership posts, few scholars have devoted attention to women of color in substate-level offices, largely because variations among localities make comparisons difficult.

As African American women move beyond the local level, they face greater challenges in winning office. In many ways, statewide offices are more difficult for African American candidates to secure, especially for African American women. No state has ever elected an African American woman as governor, only six African American women currently hold

TABLE 7.2 African American women are mayors of some of the largest US cities in 2021

Mayor	City	Year elected
Keisha Lance Bottoms	Atlanta, GA	2017
Muriel Bowser	Washington, DC	2015
London Breed	San Francisco, CA	2018
Sharon Weston-Broome	Baton Rouge, LA	2016
LaToya Cantrell	New Orleans, LA	2018
Lori Lightfoot	Chicago, IL	2019
Vi Alexander Lyles	Charlotte, NC	2017
Tishaura O. Jones	St. Louis, MO	2021

Source: CAWP, Women of Color in Elective Office Fact Sheet, 2021.

statewide offices, and only sixteen have ever held such positions.[24] In the 2018 election, New York Attorney General Letitia "Tish" James became the first African American woman elected statewide in New York and Illinois Lieutenant Governor Julianna Stratton became the first African American woman elected to statewide executive office in her state. While no African American women were elected to statewide executive office in the 2020 election, Shirley Weber was appointed as California's secretary of state to fill the vacancy created by Alex Padilla's move to the US Senate; she is just the second African American woman to hold statewide office in California.

In running for statewide offices, African American candidates do not have the benefit of African American majority electorates, as they often do when they run in district-level races. As a result, they must depend on the support of white majorities for election. Because African Americans are generally significantly more supportive of African American candidates than whites are, attracting white voters is a significant challenge. Depending on racially tolerant whites to win,[25] African American candidates[26] face the dual challenge of offering strong crossover appeal for white voters while maintaining a connection to communities of color to ensure their high voter turnout.

In state legislatures, African American women are steadily increasing their numbers, but remain significantly underrepresented among all available legislative seats. As of 2021, there were 7,383 state legislators, of whom only about 600 were women of color. As of spring 2021, African American women held 352 state legislative seats nationwide with the vast majority of them representing the Democratic Party (349D, 3R).[27] Although the number of women of color in state legislatures remains small, this figure has increased steadily. Women of color overall and African American women specifically reached new record levels for state legislative representation as a result of the 2020 elections.

[24] Women of Color in Elective Office 2021, Center for American Women and Politics (hereafter CAWP), 2021, https://cawp.rutgers.edu/women-color-elective-office-2021
[25] See Lee Sigelman and Susan Welch, Race, Gender, and Opinion toward Black and Female Candidates, *Public Opinion Quarterly* 48 (1984): 467–75; and Ruth Ann Strickland and Marcia Lynn Whicker, Comparing the Wilder and Gantt Campaigns: A Model of Black Candidate Success in Statewide Elections, *PS: Political Science and Politics* 25 (1992): 204–12.
[26] Sigelman and Welch, Race, Gender, and Opinion; Strickland and Whicker, Comparing the Wilder and Gantt Campaigns.
[27] Women of Color in Elective Office 2021, CAWP.

AFRICAN AMERICAN WOMEN MAYORS AND PANDEMIC POLITICS

The pandemic politics of 2020 placed African American women's leadership as mayors of major cities in the national spotlight as they negotiated between issuing contested and debated public health-centered lockdowns and mediating clashes between protesters against police violence and the law enforcement establishment they sought to change. In 2021, African American women lead eight major cities in the country with populations exceeding 100,000 (see Table 7.2). African American women mayors such as Atlanta's Keisha Lance Bottoms, Chicago's Lori Lightfoot, and Washington, DC's Muriel Bowser were thrust into the national spotlight as their cities became the sites of contentious pandemic politics that often publicly questioned their authorities as elected leaders. Their leadership through the twin pandemics placed a spotlight on African American women elected leaders in action and began normalizing their power as executive leaders in charge of decision-making for their cities while at the same time it shed light on how normal it is to question and challenge their authority.

Stay-at-home orders and lockdown measures initiated a public battle between Atlanta's Mayor Bottoms and the state's governor, Brian Kemp. Bottoms, the mayor of the state's largest city with a majority African American population, issued mask, lockdown, and other executive orders in the hope of slowing the spread of COVID-19, as African Americans experienced more deadly outcomes with the virus. Immediately, Governor Kemp began enacting measures to rescind the mayor's orders to align with President Trump's insistence on keeping the economy open. Kemp and Bottoms faced off in a national debate which called into question the mayor's use of her executive powers. In fact, Governor Kemp sued Bottoms over her implementation of a mask mandate in the city of Atlanta, arguing that he alone as governor was responsible for the management of the virus and he had the right to suspend municipal orders. This challenge to her power as mayor also had the effect of questioning her leadership decision to govern with the realities of her constituents, who were being hospitalized and dying from the virus at higher rates, in mind. In Kemp's challenge to her authority, he also called into question the validity of Bottoms' decision-making. In legal filings, Kemp asserted that Bottoms made unenforceable pandemic rules and that, "As the Mayor of the City of Atlanta, Mayor Bottoms does not have the legal authority to modify, change or ignore executive orders." Though other municipalities implemented similar mask mandates, the governor only named and sued Atlanta alone.

While embroiled in debates over mask mandates and stay-at-home orders, the additional pressures of pandemic politics thrust Mayor Bottoms into the spotlight as she attempted to calm her city in the wake of protests in response to George Floyd's killing. She spoke to residents as an African American mother of an 18-year-old son and with a connectedness to the city's anger and frustration. After many frustrated Atlantans took to the streets, Bottoms took to the microphone with a personal plea to the city's residents that aligned their frustrations, concerns, and grief with her own, stating, "I am a mother to four Black children in America, one of whom is 18 years old. And when I saw the murder of George Floyd, I hurt like a mother would hurt." She continued: "And yesterday when I heard there were rumors about violent protests in Atlanta, I did what a mother would do, I called my son and I said, 'Where are you?' I said, 'I cannot protect you and Black boys shouldn't be out today.'" Her protectionist stance acknowledged the fragility of Black lives and her inabilities even as a mayor to fully protect her son and others who looked like him. She further positioned her decision-making as grounded in an ethics of care that was beyond reproach. "So, you're not going to out-concern me and out-care about where we are in America," Bottoms said. "I wear this each and every day, and I pray over my children, each and every day." She would later call for the resignation of the police chief over handling and mistreatment of protesters, rather than encouraging calm. The mandates to keep people safe as outrage flooded the city meant the mayor squared off against competing authorities at multiple junctures.

Just as Bottoms' experiences highlight the competing pressures of pandemic politics, Lori Lightfoot – Chicago's first African American woman and LGBTQ mayor – also found herself embroiled in battles with the police union during protests in her city. She also became the symbol for the Trump reelection campaign's charges that cities led by Democrats were lawless places of violence and evidenced the need for his brand of "law and order." Lightfoot blasted Chicago police for what she called the negligent, harmful, and disrespectful behavior of officers, who were caught on surveillance cameras resting and snacking during citywide protests while violence and rioting engulfed parts of the city. The damage and loss of property just feet from the officers' resting place included the vandalization of Congressman Bobby Rush's offices. Rush, a former Black Panther Party member, took extreme insult from the officers' camp-out in his district office while his district went underprotected. Lightfoot called out the corrupt behavior and vowed no officer would hide behind the protection of the badge while she was mayor. Her vow to prosecute the police officers involved coupled with her broader call to require licensing and certification of police officers landed her in the center of debates between those who want to defund and those who continue to defend the police. Lightfoot's governance became a centerpiece of President Trump's reelection campaign; he repeatedly cited Chicago, and specifically the violence in the city, as evidence of both Lightfoot's and the Democrats' failed leadership in American cities. As part of Trump's pro-safety, pro-police, and anti-crime stance, he singled out gun violence in Chicago during a law enforcement event at the White House, pledging to "bring down shooting numbers in Chicago and other American cities even if we have to go in and take over." These comments followed earlier statements by the president in which he compared the city's conditions to violence in Afghanistan. Lightfoot and Trump squared off on Twitter after the president referenced Chicago's gun violence as a prime example of what was going wrong in American cities under the Democrats' leadership. Trump pushed a tough-on-crime law and order agenda and continued to paint the picture that he alone would fix Chicago, which drew equally confrontational retorts from Lightfoot on Twitter.

While Lightfoot did direct battle with the president with a series of cut-throat, tough talk exchanges on Twitter, her tone with Chicagoans was more akin to Bottoms' response to Atlanta's residents. She offered Chicagoans compassion, clearly expressing a sense of linked fate and shared experiences of the perils of anti-Blackness in policing. "I feel angry, I feel sickened and a range of other emotions all at once," she said in the wake of city protests. "Being Black in America should not be a death sentence. We should not fear for the lives of our young ones, and mothers shouldn't fear when their young men and women go out into the world that they're gonna get that fateful call." Her sense of empathy with the frustrations Chicago protesters expressed across the city is emblematic of African American women mayors' leadership through the twin pandemics.

The policies and politics of the Trump administration contributed in some respects to elevating all these African American women mayors and others like them into the national spotlight. As they took aggressive action to slow the spread of the coronavirus and maintain calm in their cities amid protests, President Trump and his administration criticized their leadership, and African American women mayors received increased personal violent threats to them and their families. As Lightfoot noted, the president had an affinity for attacking women of color leaders: "And it's an issue that many of us as mayors have, and he seems to have a particular obsession with female and particularly mayors of color." However, none of these power contests with the president was more direct than Trump's challenges to Washington, DC Mayor Muriel Bowser over the Black Lives Matter protests in the city following the police killings of Floyd and Taylor. Because Washington, DC is a territory, it does not have the powers that other cities and states have, and so the relationship between the federal government and the local DC government is a carefully orchestrated balance, with each relying on the other for some aspects of public safety. This was a contributing factor to the limited protection of the United States Capitol during the January 6 insurrection and riot. In summer 2020, Mayor Bowser called upon the federal government to allow Washington, DC police to lead the protest response and requested that the federal government remove the National Guard presence and other militaristic enforcement from the city. She specifically called on the president to not amplify the chaos among peaceful protesters through the use of intimidation and force. Instead, the president took to Twitter to ridicule Bowser's request and levy personalized insults on her and DC residents. One June 5, 2020, he tweeted that Bowser was "incompetent." He continued to promote a forceful response to protesters, consistent with the focus of his reelection bid on a strong law-and-order platform.

The standoff between city and federal jurisdictions intensified on June 1, 2020 when law enforcement used pepper spray and force to clear protesters from Lafayette Square (adjacent to the White House) immediately before President Trust walked from the White House to St. John's Episcopal Church. Once there, he famously held a photo-op holding an upside-down Bible. The use of force against the largely peaceful protesters sparked yet another national spectacle when Mayor Bowser utilized discursive and symbolic power to rename the plaza in the backyard of the White House "Black Lives Matter Way." She used the city's mural project funds to paint the new name in large golden yellow letters on the plaza's main road, making it easily visible from the White House and to the president as he flew over the area when approaching and leaving the White House. Bowser operated in the unmarked spaces of power that were not explicitly held by either side to make an indelible imprint on the city's landscape but also to communicate the power of the largely African American residents she represents.

Bottoms', Lightfoot's, and Bowser's leadership styles through the pandemic embodied their identities as African American women, as mothers, and as executives. They leveraged their experiences to offer more nuanced understandings of the urgency for public health orders to protect the most vulnerable in their communities, especially as African Americans and

Latinos/as were disproportionately hospitalized and dying as a result of COVID-19. They were able to speak authentically to the frustrations and pain African Americans experienced, that gave way to nightly protests amid COVID-19 concerns. In their roles as executive leaders, African American women mayors governed by establishing new norms that valued Black lives and asserted that African Americans must be protected both by and from the state. Their abilities to provide such complex representation of their cities proved highly effective in representing their cities through such unprecedented crises. Through its intense attention to them and their roles as elected leaders, the media paid homage to the steady growth we are seeing in the numbers of African American women serving in elected office. The experiences of these women also showed the racialized and gendered challenges African American women continue to experience in politics. Their exercise of power was met with public attempts to question and usurp their executive powers by governors and even the president of the United States. Yet, these African American women mayors stood as elected leaders and acted on behalf of their cities informed by their own lived experiences with racism.

AFRICAN AMERICAN WOMEN IN CONGRESSIONAL POLITICS

The diversity of Congress in terms of gender, ethnicity, race, religion, and sexual orientation continues to grow with each election cycle, though Congress continues to lag behind the nation's overall diversity.[28] This diversity is especially evident within the Democratic caucus, which is likely to spur more robust debate on the issues before the body. Though we saw an increase in the numbers of Republican women elected to the House, there has only been one African American woman elected to Congress as a Republican, and that representative, Mia Love of Utah, lost her seat to a challenger in 2018, an unusual occurrence for an incumbent but one that speaks to the fragility of her role as one of a few high-profile African American Republican women.

A record number of African American women were major party candidates and nominees for the US House in election 2020.[29] In the 117th Congress (2021–23), twenty-four African American women – all

---

[28] Katherine Schaffer, Racial, Ethnic Diversity Increases Yet again with the 117th Congress, Pew Research Center, January 28, 2021, https://pewrsr.ch/3ih3OMM

[29] Kelly Dittmar, Measuring Success: Women in 2020 Legislative Elections, CAWP, 2021, https://womenrun.rutgers.edu/2020-report/

Democrats – are serving as voting members of the US House, with two more African American women serving as Democratic non-voting delegates (see Table 7.3). This is a slight increase from the 116th Congress, when twenty-two African American women served in the House. Three nonincumbent African American women were elected to the House in election 2020: Representative Cori Bush became the first African American

TABLE 7.3 Twenty-six African American women were serving in the US House of Representatives in 2021

Congresswoman	Party	District	Year first elected to Congress
Rep. Alma Adams	D	NC 12th	2014
Rep. Karen Bass	D	CA 37th	2010
Rep. Joyce Beatty	D	OH 3rd	2012
Rep. Corrine Brown	D	FL 3rd	1992
Rep. Cori Bush	D	MO 1st	2020
Rep. Yvette Clark	D	NY 11th	2006
Rep. Val Demings	D	FL 10th	2016
Rep. Jahanna Hayes	D	CT 5th	2018
Rep. Eddie Bernice Johnson	D	TX 30th	1992
Rep. Robin Kelly	D	IL 2nd	2016
Rep. Brenda Lawrence	D	MI 14th	2015
Rep. Barbara Lee	D	CA 9th	1997
Rep. Sheila Jackson Lee	D	TX 18th	1994
Rep. Lucy McBath	D	GA 6th	2018
Rep. Gwen Moore	D	WI 4th	2004
Del. Eleanor Holmes Norton[a]	D	Washington, DC	1991
Rep. Stacey Plaskett[b]	D	VI	2016
Rep. Ayanna Pressley	D	MA 7th	2018
Rep. Ilhan Omar	D	MN 5th	2018
Rep. Lisa Blunt Rochester	D	DE at large	2016
Rep. Terri Sewell	D	AL 7th	2010
Rep. Marilyn Strickland[c]	D	WA 10th	2020
Rep. Maxine Waters	D	CA 35th	1990
Rep. Frederica Wilson	D	FL 17th/24th	2010
Rep. Laura Underwood	D	IL 14th	2018
Rep. Nikema Williams	D	GA 5th	2020

[a] Eleanor Holmes Norton is a nonvoting delegate representing the District of Columbia
[b] Stacey Plaskett is the nonvoting delegate representing the US Virgin Islands
[c] Strickland identifies as Korean and African American
Source: Compiled by author from CAWP 2021 fact sheets and representatives' websites.

woman to represent Missouri in Congress; Representative Marilyn Strickland became the first African American and first Korean American to represent Washington state; and Representative Nikema Williams won the Georgia House seat of civil rights icon John Lewis. These three women joined the historic group of women of color elected in 2018 who helped to shift control of the House of Representatives to the Democratic Party.

Representative Cori Bush of Missouri's 1st congressional district cut her political teeth as a Black Lives Matter organizer following the killing of Michael Brown. She campaigned with that identity front and center, illustrating that the divisions between protest and politics are less clear cut. Bush's road to Congress also is a tale of perseverance. She won her current seat after two previous losses. In her third bid, she successfully challenged an incumbent legislator to win her seat. Bush has gained notoriety in the House as an outspoken advocate of defunding the police. She maintains that her mission in gaining election is to disrupt politics as usual and bring the protest of the people to the people's governing body.

Nikema Williams won Georgia's 5th congressional district, which is comprised largely of Atlanta. The district was represented by long-term civil rights icon John Lewis, who passed away in 2019 after a long bout with cancer. Williams is a former state senator and was the first African American woman to lead the state Democratic Party. She made her way in Georgia politics and broke into the leadership ranks without generational ties to the African American Atlanta elite political machine. She garnered the attention of Lewis and studied and worked under his leadership as his protégé. Williams went to Washington as part of the dynamic team of African American women in Georgia who are credited, along with Stacey Abrams, for turning the state for the Democrats. Upon her election, Williams pledged to continue the "good trouble" politics that Lewis was noted to elevate.

Marilyn Strickland's campaign to win the 10th congressional district in Washington state was unusual in that the open-seat race was between two Democrat Party candidates. Strickland centered her campaign on her role as a fiscally astute former mayor. Credited with leading the city of Tacoma through an economic recession, she campaigned on emphasizing her proven abilities to bring jobs to the district and generate a stable economy. Strickland's experience as a mayor was a strong asset, and she benefited from the name recognition as a former officeholder. Above all, in deciding to run in an open-seat race as opposed to challenging an incumbent, Strickland used a tried-and-tested approach for women running for office. Her candidacy followed all the best practices. However, Strickland's decision to run and her win in a majority-white district breaks with traditional knowledge of race, gender, and congressional campaigns. Her win in the 10th district builds on a rising trend of African American women finding success beyond the traditional majority-minority districts that are widely credited with ushering in sizable numbers of African Americans to Congress.

The conventional wisdom is that majority-minority districts are the primary means of electing African American women to Congress, though recent elections spur hopefulness that these districts are not the lone path to election for African American women. Majority-minority districts resulted from provisions in the Voting Rights Act of 1965 and its subsequent extensions, which allowed for the formation of new districts where African Americans constituted a plurality or majority of the electorate. In these new districts, African Americans could run for open seats, which not only alleviated the incumbency advantage but also freed them from dependence on white voters. Many scholars concede that, historically, it has been nearly impossible for African American candidates to win in districts without African American majorities, as some whites continue to resist voting for African American candidates.

The number of African American women serving in Congress today is largely a result of the presence of majority-minority districts. Although 1992 was widely proclaimed the Year of the Woman in politics, reflecting the phenomenal success of women candidates for Congress, for African American women 1992 was also the "Year of Redistricting." A number of open seats were created nationally as a result of redistricting following the 1990 Census, and most were majority-minority districts. African American women claimed five additional seats in the US House of Representatives in 1992, more than doubling their numbers. Four of the five African American women won in newly created majority-minority districts, including Corrine Brown, whose Florida district was contested in a subsequent redistricting plan. The fifth African American woman elected in 1992, Eva Clayton of North Carolina, won a special election for a seat that was vacant because of the death of the incumbent, also in a majority-minority district. In the 117th Congress, eighteen of twenty-four Black women House members are serving in majority-minority districts.

While majority-minority districts have helped to secure African American women's place in Congress, these districts have been challenged in the courts as a means of increasing Black representation. As a result of a string of cases in the 1990s from Georgia, Louisiana, North Carolina, and Texas, the future of majority-minority districts is now in question. Many scholars insist that African Americans' continued success in winning elective office, particularly congressional seats, is dependent on the preservation of majority-minority districts. Because of the precarious future of such districts, many raise doubts regarding the continued effectiveness of this strategy to increase African American representation in Congress overall. Recent wins like that of Marilyn Strickland and other African American women offer evidence that African American women are viable candidates and can win in majority-white districts under the right conditions. Four of the five nonincumbent African American women winners in 2018 and one of three nonincumbent African American women winners in 2020 won in majority-white districts, which suggests that we can expand the districts in which African American women are considered viable using the evidence of recent electoral successes.

With the election of Senator Kamala Harris to the vice presidency and her resignation from the US Senate in January 2021, there are once again no African American women in the US Senate. Only two African American women – Harris and Carol Moseley Braun – have *ever* served in the US Senate. African American women political operatives lobbied California Governor Gavin Newsom to appointment an African American woman to fill Harris' seat. Instead, Newsom made history by appointing Alex Padilla as the first Latino to represent California in the US Senate. In election 2020, just one African American woman was a major party Senate nominee; Democrat Marquita Bradshaw lost an open-seat bid for one of Tennessee's Senate seats by a 27-point margin. Some have argued that African American women's representation in the Senate will come from growing the strength of the Democratic Party in southern states where the population aligns with such representation possibilities. A renewed commitment to fortifying the political party's strength would have to predate the success of such an attempt to restore African Americans' representation in the Senate.

THE FUTURE OF AFRICAN AMERICAN WOMEN IN POLITICS

African American female elected officials are enduring symbols of the long fight for political inclusion in US electoral politics. Although legal barriers preventing their participation in politics have been removed, African American women continue to confront considerable barriers when seeking political office. The higher profile the office, the more formidable barriers they face to being considered viable candidates.

In light of the formidable challenges African American women confront as they seek higher-profile offices, they are not leaving their political futures to chance. They are forming political action committees and designing and organizing political trainings and outreach and recruitment initiatives to address the serious barriers they face. Nearly twenty years ago, we began to see a rise in African American women investing in their own political futures by founding groups like Women Building for the Future (Future PAC), which started as a group to capitalize on the growing voting power of African American women. As that group's sun set, many others have followed in that tradition of funding African American women candidates and building national platforms for African American women running in local races. Today, groups like the Collective PAC develop slates of African American women candidates on a shared fundraising ticket, allowing donors to support candidates across the country who shared similar political views, but represented vastly different districts across states and localities.

This type of organizing is essential if African American women are to continue increasing their representation. Such organizing efforts hold the promise of translating African American women's high voting rates into increased officeholding. Other national groups, such as the Black Women's Roundtable, established by the National Coalition on Black Civic Participation, are also working to increase political participation by mobilizing African American organizations, including Greek-letter fraternities and sororities, around voter education and civic empowerment.[30] While pandemic politics shaped election 2020 and increased efforts to suppress and limit access to the ballot, African American women were already well equipped to respond. They had been at the forefront of challenging voter suppression in previous high-stakes elections like election 2012, when efforts to suppress voter participation surfaced in minority communities across the country and particularly in the battleground states of Florida, Ohio, Michigan, and Virginia. African American women have come to understand that voter protection is a critical component of voter mobilization, and the right to vote is understood as an ongoing fight among African American women voting rights organizers. These groups are invested in the important work of empowering citizens, mobilizing voters, and identifying likely candidates. Their mobilization efforts have focused on maintaining

[30] See the Black Women's Roundtable (BWR), a part of the National Coalition on Black Civic Participation, www.ncbcp.org/programs/bwr/

and fully realizing the potential of African American women as voters. The challenge remains to translate African American women's power as voters into increased numbers of officeholders at local and national levels.

The number of groups has increased since 2002, capitalizing on Black women's increased political engagement. Groups such as Higher Heights for Women, a national organization focused on harnessing African American women's political power and encouraging Black women to not only vote but also to run for political office, and the New American Leaders Project, which focuses attention on first- and second-generation new immigrants running for elected office, conduct training that prepares African American women to run for office. Such training programs focus on the hard and soft skills of running for office, including fundraising, building donor networks, refining communication messaging, and cultivating the confidence to execute a run for office. These groups have become particularly critical to identifying and recruiting African American women candidates, doing the work that political parties are assumed to do yet don't undertake when it comes to African American women.[31] The most difficult work for these groups remains transforming American society to fully embrace African American women as political leaders. This issue must be addressed both inside the African American community and throughout American society more widely. The public's willingness to regard these well-prepared women as viable, appropriate political leaders is essential.

African American women elected leaders like the mayors who are effectively negotiating their cities through the perils of pandemic politics are already doing this barrier-breaking work. Their executive leadership is sustaining their cities through turbulent times and, should the economy continue to grow with the Biden–Harris administration's pledges to invest in infrastructure, these African American women mayors will be fully equipped to take their cities further. Since most of these women were elected to office for the first time in the last five years, their futures as political leaders are still undetermined. However, if this presidential election cycle is any indicator, we are likely to see these women's names in consideration for higher offices, as was the case for Keisha Lance Bottoms of Atlanta, who appeared on Biden's list of potential running mates.

While no African American woman has served as governor in the nation's history, all eyes are on the political next steps of Georgia powerhouse Stacey Abrams. Though Abrams lost her first bid for governor to Brian

---

[31] Kira Sanbonmatsu, Electing Women of Color: The Role of Campaign Trainings, *Journal of Women, Politics, & Policy* 36(2) (2015): 137–60.

Kemp, her next dance landed her on a bigger stage as a global phenomenon fighting against voter suppression. Since her first run for governor, Abrams has written books on her experiences in politics, launched the organization Fair Fight to expand voting rights, starred in a documentary on fair elections, and appeared as a celebrity guest on every late-night talk show – not to mention boasts a host of memes, which is the key to stardom in the social media world. What could be next for Abrams? Without question, she has political affinities with a multitude of African American women politicos and their networks, who have refined their activism and elevated ways of connecting to other African American women across the country through a global pandemic. African American women set their political aspirations on becoming historic firsts with two African American women who sought to run for governor Virginia – state Representative Jennifer Carroll Foy and state Senator Jennifer McClellan. In Florida, Congresswoman Val Demings is to challenge the sitting senator in 2022. The prospects for more African American women running in statewide races are high and will mean we are amidst a major shift in the American political landscape.

By all accounts, African American women are positioning themselves to advance in politics and are not awaiting the political parties to lead. The political parties, in particular the Democratic Party, with which most African American women are affiliated, must stop assuming that African American women are left of center by virtue of their intersecting identities as both African Americans and women. Many African American women elected officials prioritize both women's issues and minority issues and build on their ties to multiple communities. In this way, their intersectional identities represent a strength that results in greater representation across underrepresented groups. Not until such core cultural issues are addressed will we see women of color reach their full potential in politics, with well-qualified women of color successfully moving through the political pipeline to hold elected offices at local, state, and federal levels.

RICHARD L. FOX

8 Congressional Elections: Women's Candidacies and the Road to Gender Parity

The 2018 and 2020 congressional elections were filled with dramatic developments for women candidates. But in very different ways. The 2018 election set a record, with a total of 126 women elected to serve in the US House and Senate, far surpassing the 110 who served in the prior Congress. There has not been a single election year jump this large since the historic "year of the woman" elections in 1992. But in 2018, the success of women candidates was entirely on the Democratic side of the aisle. In fact, as these historic numbers were being achieved, the number of Republican women serving in the House fell to its lowest number in several decades.

The election of 2018 was perhaps marked by the stunning victory of Alexandria Ocasio-Cortez, the 29-year-old political organizer and activist who in the June primary defeated incumbent Democrat Joe Crowley, the fourth-ranking Democrat in the House of Representatives. When she won the general election in New York's strongly Democratic 14th district, she became the youngest woman ever to win a seat in Congress. She almost instantly became a household name and a favorite among young progressives. Her victory was one of many firsts as the Democrats retook the House Representatives in 2018, once again making Nancy Pelosi Speaker of the House. Deb Haaland and Sharice Davids were the first Native American women ever elected to Congress. Rashida Tlaib and Ilhan Omar were the first Muslim women ever elected to Congress. And Ayanna Pressley (Massachusetts) and Jahana Hayes (Connecticut) became the first Black women to win seats in New England. In Texas, a state composed of almost 40 percent Latino citizens, voters finally sent their first Latinas to Congress with wins by Veronica Escobar and Sylvia Garcia.

I would like to thank Zoe McGough for assistance in data collection and analysis.

While the Democrats were celebrating historic gains among women and people of color in Congress, something else was happening on the Republican side of the aisle: a dramatic decrease in the number of women being elected to Congress. In fact, the total number of Republican women holding seats in the US House of Representatives fell from twenty-three to thirteen, the lowest number in three decades. In an open letter to her party leaders after the election, Republican Representative Elise Stefanik from New York's 21st district asked that the party take stock and learn from the Democrats' successes.[1] And the Republicans did appear to take some notice. Through increased recruitment efforts and a desire perhaps for many to change the narrative that the Republican Party is not a place for women candidates, a record number of Republican women ran for Congress in 2020.[2] After all of the dust had settled on the 2020 elections, Republicans were sending thirty-eight women to serve in the House and Senate, surpassing the record of thirty from the 2006 congressional elections. And while the types of candidates were not as diverse as in the Democratic candidates elected in 2018, there were some notable firsts. Republicans Young Kim and Michelle Steel both won districts in California's Orange County to become two of the three first Korean American women members of Congress; Democrat Marilyn Strickland, who is both Black and Korean American, joined them. Yvette Harrell, who won New Mexico's 2nd district, will serve as the only female Native American Republican member of Congress. The Republicans also elected two women who touted especially conservative views; both Lauren Boebert (Colorado) and Marjorie Taylor Greene (Georgia) are staunch gun advocates and have flirted with more radical views, supporting the right-wing Q-anon conspiracy theory. To some analysts, Boebert's and Greene's victories showed that women were running and winning as all types of Republican candidates.[3]

Despite these historic elections that set records in the total number of women serving in Congress, an overview of the 2018 and 2020 congressional elections shows that women continue to encounter many obstacles

[1] Tyler Pager, After Big Losses, a N.Y. House Republican Clashes With Her Party, *New York Times*, December 20, 2018, www.nytimes.com/2018/12/20/nyregion/elise-stefanik-republican-women.html

[2] Kelly Dittmar, Measuring Success: Women in 2020 Legislative Elections, Center for the American Women and Politics (hereafter CAWP), 2021, https://womenrun.rutgers.edu/2020-report.

[3] Danielle Kurtzleben, How a Record Number of Republican Women Got Elected to Congress, NPR.org, November 13, 2020, https://n.pr/2X6UNh3

in running for office. After the 2020 elections, women only made up less than 15 percent of all the Republicans in Congress. The total number of women serving in the Senate actually decreased across the two elections. These two elections continue to illustrate how the success of women running for Congress is increasingly tied to the successes of the political parties. More specifically, women have been steadily increasing their numbers within the Democrat Party candidate pipeline, and when Democrats have a good year, such as in 2018, they bring with them a lot of victories for women. This has not been the case with Republicans, at least not prior to 2020. So while the 117th Congress starts off with 105 Democratic women and only 38 Republican women, there are many trends to consider to determine when and whether women will achieve parity in representation in Congress.

This chapter examines the evolution of women's candidacies for Congress and the role gender continues to play in congressional elections. Ultimately, I focus on one fundamental question: Why are there still so few women serving in the House and Senate? I explore the persistence of gender as a factor in congressional elections in three sections. In the first, I offer a brief historical overview of the role of gender in congressional elections, noting how the presidency of Donald Trump may have even sparked a new generation of women political leaders. The second section compares male and female candidates' electoral performance and success in House and Senate races through the 2020 elections. The results of this analysis confirm that, when considered in the aggregate, the electoral playing field in general elections has become largely level for women and men. But if that is the case, why are there still so few women in Congress? In the final section of the chapter, I provide some answers, examining some of the subtler ways that gender continues to affect congressional elections. The combination of gendered geographic trends, women's presence in different types of congressional races, the scarcity of women running as Republicans, and the gender gap in political ambition suggests that gender continues to play an important role in congressional elections.

THE HISTORICAL EVOLUTION OF WOMEN'S CANDIDACIES FOR CONGRESS

Throughout the 1990s, women made significant strides competing for and winning seats in the US Congress. The 1992 elections, often referred to as the "Year of the Woman," resulted not only in a historic increase in the numbers of women in both the House and the Senate, but also in the promise of movement toward some semblance of gender parity in our political institutions (see Table 8.1). After all, in the history of the US Congress, more than 12,000 men but less than 400 women have served. Only fifty-eight women have ever served in the US Senate, nineteen of whom either were appointed or won special elections.

Currently, 76 percent of the members of the US Senate and 73 percent of the members of the US House are male. This puts the United States in sixty-sixth place worldwide in terms of the proportion of women serving in the national legislature, a ranking far behind that of many other democratic governments.[4] Further, despite the notable advances identified in the introduction to the chapter, the majority of women elected to Congress have been white. Of the 119 (out of 435) women elected to the US House in the 2020 election, there were 48 women of color: 24 African Americans, 12 Latinas, 7 Asian Americans/Pacific Islanders, 1 Middle East/North African woman, 2 Native American women, and 2 women who identify as multiracial; Nicole Malliotakis identifies as both white and Latina, and Marilyn Strickland identifies as both Black and Korean American. There are three women of color among the twenty-four women currently serving in the US Senate.

The continued dearth of women in Congress suggests that a masculine ethos, ever present across the history of Congress, is still present in the congressional electoral environment. A host of interrelated factors – money, familiarity with power brokers, political experience, and support from the political parties – contributes to a winning campaign. Traditional candidates are members of the political or economic elite. Most emerge from lower-level elected offices or work in their communities, typically in law or business. They tend to receive encouragement to run for office from influential members of the community, party officials, or outgoing incumbents. And these same elites who encourage candidacies also contribute money to campaigns and hold fundraisers. This process has been in place for most of the recent history of congressional candidacies and, for obvious reasons, has served men well and women very poorly. Though recent elections, especially the 2018 and 2020 elections, suggest this is starting to change.

Because they have been excluded from their communities' economic and political elites throughout much of the twentieth century, women

---

[4] Monthly Ranking of Women in Parliaments, Inter-Parliamentary Union, May 1, 2021, https://data.ipu.org/women-ranking?month=4&year=2021

often take different paths to Congress. Widows of congressmen who died in office dominated the first wave of successful female candidates. Between 1916 and 1964, twenty-eight of the thirty-two widows nominated to fill their husbands' seats won their elections, for a victory rate of 88 percent. Across the same time period, only 32 of the 199 non-widows who garnered their parties' nominations were elected (a 14 percent victory rate).[5] Overall, roughly half the women who served in the House during this period were widows. Congressional widows were the one type of woman candidate that was readily acceptable to party leaders at this time.

The 1960s and 1970s marked the emergence of a second type of woman candidate – one who turned her attention from civic volunteerism to politics. Several women involved in grassroots community politics rode their activism to Washington. Notable figures (all Democrats) who pursued this path include Patsy Mink in Hawaii, elected in 1964; Shirley Chisholm in New York, elected in 1968; Bella Abzug in New York, elected in 1970; and Pat Schroeder in Colorado and Barbara Jordan in Texas, both elected in 1972.

We are currently in the third and possibly final stage of the evolution of women's candidacies. The prevailing model of running for Congress has become far less rigid. The combination of decreased political party power and growing media influence facilitates the emergence of a more diverse array of candidates competing successfully for their parties' nominations. In the first and second wave, the idea of a candidate like Alexandria Ocasio-Cortez knocking off a revered incumbent in the primary or Lauren Boebert becoming an Internet sensation by challenging a Democratic presidential candidate on gun rights would have been unthinkable. The system is far more open. Converging with this less rigid path is an increase in the number of women who now fit the profile of a "traditional" candidate. Women's presence in fields such as business and law, from which candidates have often emerged, has increased dramatically. Further, the number of women serving in state legislatures, often a springboard to Congress, has roughly quadrupled since 1975 (for a thorough analysis of women's fluctuating success in running for state-level office, see Kira Sanbonmatsu and Maria Wilson, Chapter 9 in this volume). Together, these developments help to explain why the eligibility pool of prospective women candidates grew substantially since the 1990s.[6]

---

[5] Irwin Gertzog, *Congressional Women* (New York: Praeger, 1984), p. 18.
[6] Danielle Thomsen and Aaron A. King, Women's Representation and the Gendered Pipeline to Power, *American Political Science Review* 114(4) (2020): 989–1000.

Despite growth in the number of eligible women who could run for Congress, women's progress has continued only in fits and starts in the most recent congressional election cycles. The 2016 elections marked the third time since 1990 that women did not increase their presence in the House. In the Senate, the growth in the number of women has been just as slow with elections alternating between stagnation and modest increases. But these patterns accelerated dramatically with major increases in 2018 on the Democratic side and 2020 on the Republican side.

Table 8.1 presents the numbers of women candidates who won their party nominations and ran in House general elections from 1970 through 2020. As mentioned above, the 2018 and 2020 elections set records. In 2020, the total number of women running as general election candidates was 298, more than doubling the number from a mere ten years earlier. But to put this number into perspective, it is helpful to recognize that more than 500 male candidates garnered their parties' nominations to run as general election candidates. It is also important to recognize that even though 2020 saw record gains by Republican women, these record numbers continue to be driven by Democratic women running for office.

TABLE 8.1 Over time, more Democratic women than Republican women have emerged as general election House candidates and winners

	1970	1980	1990	2000	2010	2018	2020
General election candidates							
Democratic women candidates	15	27	40	81	91	182	204
Republican women candidates	10	25	29	42	47	52	94
Total women	25	52	69	123	138	234	298
General election winners							
Democratic women winners	10	11	20	41	48	89	89
Percentage of all Democrats in the House	3.9	4.5	7.1	19.4	29.0	38.0	40.3
Republican women winners	3	10	8	18	24	13	30
Percentage of all Republicans in the House	1.7	5.2	5.4	8.1	7.0	6.5	14.2

Note: Except where noted, entries represent the raw number of women candidates and winners for each year.
Source: CAWP, https://cawp.rutgers.edu/facts/elections/past_candidates, and *New York Times* listing of election results. For 2020 these represent the number of women as of February 1, 2021.

Despite Republican women's historic gains in 2020, Table 8.1 illustrates the divergent paths of the Democratic and Republican parties. The Democrats have been on a steady path, continually increasing the number of women who run for Congress and eventual winners. The Republicans, in contrast, have put forward only slightly more women over the past two decades, until the 2020 election (more on this later). Despite gains for Republican women in 2020, we are now at a point where there are almost three times as many female Democrats as Republicans serving in Congress.

In the evolution of women's candidacies for Congress, the surprising election of Donald Trump as president in 2016 may have caused a chain reaction that propelled many women to run for Congress. After Donald Trump shockingly defeated Hillary Clinton, the first female major party presidential candidate to make it to the general election, millions took to the streets for the Women's March shortly after his inauguration in 2017, and thousands looked into running for office. To many women (and men), Donald Trump's election was a setback to the cause of gender equality. After all, he was accused of sexual harassment and assault by more than a dozen women and had a history of making derogatory remarks about women. And this was all before the release of the famed "Access Hollywood" tape where Trump boasted of being able to grab women wherever he wanted. And he won despite all of this. While there was some question as to whether Trump's presidency would actually motivate more women to seek office, the results of the 2018 were clear: more than twice as many Democratic women filed to run for Congress than had ever done so before.

Interviews of Democratic women candidates prior to the 2018 revealed how the election of Donald Trump served as a motivator. Mikie Sherill, a navy veteran and lawyer, who decided to run for New Jersey's 11th district, put it this way: "I knew after the election, after I saw the attacks on things I spent my entire life supporting and defending, I felt very deeply that I was being called upon to serve."[7] Veronica Escobar, a county judge in the border district near El Paso Texas, who ran in Texas' 16th district, says she never thought about running for office before Trump was elected.[8] Others saw Republicans' efforts, led by President Trump, to

---

[7] Jacob Pramuk, The Number of Women Running for Office is Rising: 7 First-Time House Candidates Explain Why They're Running in the Age of Trump, CNBC, April 4, 2018, https://cnb.cx/3iAxhBz

[8] Margaret Talbot, The Women Running in the Midterms during the Trump Era, *The New Yorker*, April 18, 2018, https://bit.ly/3xDwyU9

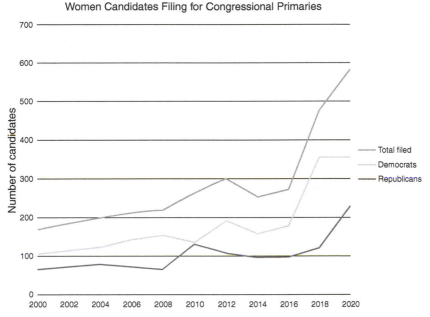

Figure 8.1 After years of no or slow growth, the 2018 and 2020 congressional elections saw a dramatic increase in the number of women filing to run for Congress.
Source: Women Primary Candidates for US Congress – Total Filed 1992–2020, CAWP, 2020, https://cawp.rutgers.edu/sites/default/files/resources/canwincong_histsum.pdf

dismantle the Affordable Care Act as the motivator. Lauren Underwood, a registered nurse, challenged the incumbent in her Illinois district because of his health care policy.[9] In the end, as Figure 8.1 illustrates, roughly twice as many Democratic women filed to run for office in 2018 than did in 2016.

But this was not a one-time blip. The record number of Democratic women filing to run in 2018 was repeated in 2020. The Democrats equaled their 2018 performance with the same number of women stepping up to run in 2020. While Trump may have motivated a number of women to finally jump into the ring and run for office, the 2018 election may have set off a chain reaction. In response to Democratic women's historic gains, after decades of stagnation, the Republicans set a new record for candidates in 2020 roughly doubling their previous high in candidates filing to run for Congress.

[9] Ibid.

Overall, the historical evolution of women's candidacies demonstrates that we are in a period of increasing opportunity for women candidates. However, even with the increases of women in 2018 and 2020, progress remains slow and uncertain. Next, we turn our attention to the performance of women candidates, always focusing on the question of why there continue to be so few women elected to the US Congress.

MEN AND WOMEN RUNNING FOR CONGRESS: THE GENERAL INDICATORS

In assessing why so few women serve in Congress, many researchers have turned to key election statistics and compared female and male congressional candidates. The research increasingly reveals little or no overt bias against women candidates. In a series of experimental studies in which participants are presented with hypothetical candidate match-ups between men and women, researchers have identified bias against women.[10] But studies that focus on actual vote totals fail to uncover evidence of bias.[11] Barbara Burrell, in an early landmark study of vote totals, concluded that candidates' sex accounts for less than 1 percent of the variation in the vote for House candidates from 1968 to 1992.[12] Kathy Dolan, who in 2004 carried out a comprehensive study of patterns in gender and voting, concluded that candidate sex is a relevant factor only in rare electoral circumstances.[13]

Jennifer Lawless and Kathryn Pearson, in an analysis of congressional primary elections between 1958 and 2004, found that women candidates are more likely to face more crowded and competitive primaries, but they did not find evidence of voter bias.[14] Examinations of more recent

---

[10] For examples of experimental designs that identify voter bias, see Leonie Huddy and Nadya Terkildsen, Gender Stereotypes and the Perception of Male and Female Candidates, *American Journal of Political Science* 37 (1993): 119–47; Leonie Huddy and Nadya Terkildsen, The Consequences of Gender Stereotypes for Women Candidates at Different Levels and Types of Office, *Political Research Quarterly* 46 (1993): 503–25; and Richard L. Fox and Eric R. A. N. Smith, The Role of Candidate Sex in Voter Decision-Making, *Political Psychology* 19 (1998): 405–19.

[11] For a comprehensive examination of vote totals through the mid-1990s, see Richard A. Seltzer, Jody Newman, and M. Voorhees Leighton, *Sex as a Political Variable* (Boulder, CO: Lynne Reinner, 1997).

[12] Barbara C. Burrell, *A Woman's Place Is in the House* (Lansing, MI: University of Michigan Press, 1994).

[13] Kathleen A. Dolan, *Voting for Women* (Boulder, CO: Westview Press, 2004).

[14] Jennifer Lawless and Kathryn Pearson, The Primary Reason for Women's Underrepresentation: Re-evaluating the Conventional Wisdom, *Journal of Politics* 70(1) (2008): 67–82.

elections, though, have not found that women are more likely to compete in crowded primaries. Recent books by Jennifer Lawless and Danny Hayes and Deborah Brooks Jordan that rely on sophisticated survey data find little evidence that voters choose or oppose a candidate based on sex.[15] The previous edition of this chapter, focusing on the 2014 and 2016 elections, also found no systematic evidence of voter bias in the results of the general elections.

If we look at the performance of men and women in general election House races in 2018 and 2020, we arrive at a similar conclusion. The data presented in Table 8.2 confirm that there is no widespread voter bias against women candidates. Voters still may use gender stereotypes to assess women candidates, but when it comes to casting ballots, candidate sex appears to matter little. In the most recent House races, women and men fared similarly in terms of mean vote share. In fact, Democratic women running as incumbents, challengers, and open-seat candidates in 2018 and 2020 performed better than their Democratic male counterparts. In 2018, female Democratic incumbent and open-seat candidates even showed a slight advantage over their male Democratic peers. Conversely, on the Republican side in 2018, female congressional candidates tended to fare less well than their male counterparts. In 2020, female and male Republican candidates performed similarly across all three categories. In fact, among Republicans, women running for the House in the general election actually had higher win rates than their male counterparts. In the Senate, with a smaller number of races to consider, it is difficult to assess the vote totals meaningfully. Ultimately, though, general trends reveal no general bias for or against women Senate candidates in 2018 or 2020.

Turning to the second most important indicator of electoral success – fundraising – we see similar results. In the 1970s and 1980s, because so few women ran for office, many scholars assumed that women in electoral politics simply could not raise the amount of money necessary to mount competitive campaigns. Indeed, older research that focused on the few women candidates who did run, concluded that women ran campaigns with lower levels of funding than did men. More systematic examinations of campaign receipts, however, have uncovered few sex differences in

---

[15] Danny Hayes and Jennifer Lawless, *Women on the Run: Gender, Media, and Political Campaigns in a Polarized Era* (New York: Cambridge University Press, 2016); Deborah Brooks Jordan, *He Runs, She Runs: Why Gender Stereotypes Do Not Harm Women Candidates* (Princeton, NJ: Princeton University Press, 2013).

TABLE 8.2 Women and men general election House candidates have similar vote shares for 2018 and 2020

	2018		2020	
	Women (%)	Men (%)	Women (%)	Men (%)
Democrats				
Incumbents	74.5	67.4	65.2	64.3
	(51)	(114)	(85)	(134)
Challengers	40.6	38.4	37.3	33.5
	(93)	(101)	(91)	(67)
Open seats	55.8	48.2	45.7	44.5
	(30)	(28)	(27)	(22)
Republicans				
Incumbents	56.7	59.2	62.5	64.5
	(16)	(179)	(11)	(151)
Challengers	27.9	30.4	37.3	34.6
	(24)	(114)	(69)	(132)
Open seats	42.9	48.9	52.1	53.5
	(13)	(43)	(13)	(35)

Notes: Candidates running unopposed are omitted from these results. Entries indicate mean vote share won. Parentheses indicate the total number of candidates for each category.
Source: Compiled from *New York Times* listing of election results.

fundraising for similarly situated general election candidates. An early study of congressional candidates from 1972 to 1982 found only a "very weak" relationship between gender and the ability to raise campaign funds.[16] More recent research indicates that by the 1988 House elections, the disparity between men and women in campaign fundraising had completely disappeared.[17] In cases where women raised less money than men, the differences were accounted for by incumbency status: male incumbents generally held positions of greater political power and thus attracted

---

[16] Barbara Burrell, Women and Men's Campaigns for the US House of Representatives, 1972–1982: A Finance Gap?, *American Political Quarterly* 13(3) (1985): 251–72.
[17] Barbara Burrell, *A Woman's Place Is in the House* (Ann Arbor, MI: University of Michigan Press, 1994), p. 105.

larger contributions.[18] Since 1992, political action committees such as EMILY's List have worked to make certain that viable general election women candidates suffer no disadvantage in fundraising. (See Chapter 10, by Rosalyn Cooperman, in this volume for a discussion of EMILY's List.)

If we examine fundraising totals of male and female general election House candidates in 2018 and 2020, we see few gender differences (see Table 8.3). In fact, the discrepancies that do exist are often to the advantage of women candidates. Women challengers in both parties, for instance, substantially outraised their male counterparts in 2020. One would be hard pressed to look at general election fundraising totals and conclude that women candidates are universally disadvantaged.

TABLE 8.3 Women and men general election House candidates have similar fundraising patterns for 2018 and 2020

	2018		2020	
	Women	**Men**	**Women**	**Men**
Democrats				
Incumbents	$1,357,873	$1,828,765	$3,449,468	$2,420,677
	(52)	(115)	(85)	(135)
Challengers	$1,930,696	$1,779,751	$1,408,022	$574,075
	(93)	(101)	(91)	(67)
Open seats	$2,562,750	$2,421,281	$2,690,357	$1,739,961
	(30)	(27)	(27)	(22)
Republicans				
Incumbents	$3,405,587	$2,147,230	$3,851,892	$2,622,239
	(16)	(181)	(11)	(153)
Challengers	$238,581	$185,684	$1,293,509	$930,670
	(24)	(114)	(70)	(133)
Open seats	$1,284,617	$1,372,534	$1,625,707	$2,077,830
	(13)	(43)	(13)	(35)

Notes: Candidates running unopposed are omitted from these results. Entries indicate total money raised. Parentheses indicate the total number of candidates in each category.
Source: Compiled from Federal Election Commission (FEC) reports and *New York Times* listing of election results.

[18]   Carole Jean Uhlaner and Kay Lehman Schlozman, Candidate Gender and Congressional Campaign Receipts, *Journal of Politics* 52(1) (1986): 391–409.

For Senate races, the number of candidates is too small for statistical comparisons between women and men. But the 2020 US elections saw a ferocious battle to determine which party would control the US Senate. And it came down to ten key races, four of which featured women candidates. All four of the races featured incumbent women Republicans running in swing states – Martha McSally in Arizona, Kelly Loeffler in Georgia, Joni Ernst in Iowa, and Susan Collins in Maine. Two of the senators were being challenged by Democratic women, Sarah Gideon in Maine and Theresa Greenfield in Iowa. With control of the Senate at stake, the amount of money flooding into these and other contests was eye-popping. More than $200 million in Kelly Loeffler's reelection bid and more than $170 million in Martha McSally's. Even in the tiny state of Maine, more than $100 million poured into the race. In each of these cases, the Democratic challengers raised substantially more money than their Republican opponent. But this was true for each of the top ten Senate races. In the end, two of the incumbent women – Loeffler and McSally – were defeated. In the two races that featured two women squaring off, the Republican incumbents prevailed. Ultimately, once again, there appears to be no widespread bias in contribution patterns to women and men general election Senate candidates.

With all of this mounting evidence that women fare just as well as men in general elections, we do not want to be too quick to completely dismiss the role of gender. Focusing only on general outcomes can sometimes obscure some of the challenges women still face in making it to the general election. While it is fair to say that once women get to the general election they are at least as likely as their male counterparts to raise money and win, the reality remains that for many women candidates, the journey is more difficult. Recent research that has taken a more nuanced approach has found that women in the general election are often more "qualified" than their male counterparts – meaning that they are more likely to have experience holding elective office. This "performance premium" may help explain why women and men perform at equal rates when running for office.[19] The conclusion drawn by this research is that for women to do just as well as men, they need to be better candidates. A 2018 analysis of Democratic US Senate candidates found that women were about three times more likely to have held prior office than men seeking Democratic nominations for the Senate.[20] While one could

[19] Kelly Dittmar, Unfinished Business: Women Running in 2018 and Beyond, CAWP, 2019, https://womenrun.rutgers.edu/

[20] Sarah Fulton and Kostanca Dhima, The Gendered Politics of Congressional Elections, Political Behavior, 2020, https://doi.org/10.1007/s11109-020-09604-7

certainly debate the notion of what makes someone qualified for elective office, it is clear that women candidates for high elective office are more likely to follow the traditional path or in fact might believe they are required to follow the traditional path, while all types of male candidates feel the freedom to throw their hats into the ring.

In terms of fundraising, there are some challenges remaining that a comparison of general election funding totals might not reveal. Women candidates perceive a much greater challenge in raising funds than their male counterparts.[21] So they may feel that they have to work harder to achieve the same results. Also, most of the support networks set up to assure that women have equal funding with male colleagues are on the Democratic side of the ledger, meaning there is less support for female Republican candidates. And studies of women of color running for Congress have found that they have not always been able to raise funds at levels similar to white women.[22] All of this is to say that certainly fundraising differences by gender and race can still be an impediment on the path to becoming a general election candidate.

Nevertheless, on the basis of vote and fundraising tallies in general elections, presented above, we see what appears to be a relatively gender-neutral playing field in general elections. Women are slowly increasing their numbers in Congress, with substantial gains in the most recent elections. The data certainly suggest that men have lost their stranglehold over the congressional election process and that women can now find excellent political opportunities. But these broad statistical comparisons tell only part of the story.

ARE WOMEN MAKING GAINS EVERYWHERE? STATE AND REGIONAL VARIATION

Women have not been equally successful running for elective office in all parts of the United States. Some regions and states have been far more amenable to the election of women than others.

Consider the example of New Mexico. Prior to the 2018 election the state had never been represented by more than one woman in the House

---

[21] Susan J. Carroll and Kira Sanbonmatsu, *More Women Can Run: Gender and Pathways to the State Legislatures* (New York: Oxford University Press, 2013).

[22] Philip Chen and Ashley Sorenson, Intersectionality in Campaign Finance and Elections, paper presented at the annual meeting of the Southern Political Science Association, Austin, Texas, January 17–19, 2019.

of Representatives. After the 2018 election, all three of the state's US House seats were held by Democratic women. And when one of the three, Democrat Xochitl Small Torres, was defeated in her 2020 reelection bid, she was replaced by a Republican woman, Yvette Harrell. Or take a look at Washington state. In the 2000 election, Maria Cantwell defeated incumbent Senator Slade Gorton, joining Senator Patti Murray, making Washington only the second state ever to be represented by two women in the US Senate. At the time, only one of Washington's nine US House seats was held by a woman. By 2021, six of Washington's House members were women – making Washington the only medium-sized or large state to have a majority of their House delegation composed of women. The norm of women running for and winning seats in Congress is now well established in places like New Mexico and Washington.

While some states were solidifying the practice of electing women to Congress, other states maintained their poor records of electing women. Only one state, Vermont, has never sent a woman to Congress. Two other states sent their first women to the US House only recently: Iowa in 2018 with the election of Representatives Abby Finkenauer and Cindy Axne and Delaware in 2016 with election of Congresswoman Lisa Blunt Rochester. Mississippi has a female senator, Cindy Hyde-Smith, but has never sent a woman to serve in the House of Representatives. And Maryland, an early stronghold for congresswomen in the 1980 and 1990s, currently does not have a single female member of Congress.

As the results of recent elections in places like Mississippi and Maryland suggest, though, women may face disadvantages when running for office in some parts of the United States. If we examine the prevalence of male and female House candidates by region and state (Tables 8.4 and 8.5), we see that the broader inclusion of women in high-level politics has not been maintained or extended equally to all regions of the country. Table 8.4 tracks women's electoral success in House races since 1970, breaking the data down by four geographic regions. Data are shown in ten-year increments since 1970, but also include the pivotal 1992 "Year of the Woman" elections.

Before 1990, the Northeast had two and three times as many women candidates as any other region in the country. The situation changed dramatically in 1992. The geographic breakdown in Table 8.4 puts the 1992 elections, as well as the modest increases in women's numbers in Congress since that time, into perspective. The 1992 Year of the Woman gains were largely in the West and the South. The number of women winning election to Congress from western states more than doubled, and in the South

TABLE 8.4 The proportion of US representatives who are women varies sharply by region

	West (%)	South (%)	Midwest (%)	Northeast (%)
1970	3.9	0.0	2.5	4.9
1980	2.6	1.6	3.3	8.1
1990	8.2	2.3	6.2	9.6
1992	17.2	7.9	6.7	12.4
2000	21.4	9.0	13.0	10.8
2010	27.4	9.9	18.0	15.3
2020	35.3	18.7	29.8	28.2
Net percentage change (1970 to 2020)	**+31.4**	**+18.7**	**+27.3**	**+23.3**

Notes: Percentages reflect the proportion of House members who are women.
Source: Compiled by author from CAWP fact sheets and *New York Times* listing of election results.

the number more than tripled. Gains were much more modest in the Midwest and the Northeast.

Since the late 1990s, the West is the one region that has led the way in electing women candidates and continues to show clear gains for women. A lot of the gains in the West can be attributed to the high number of women from California holding House seats, but women also have strong records of success in other western states such as Wyoming, Nevada, and Washington. While all of the regions have started to make more substantial gains, the South has the weakest record in electing women to Congress and continues to lag well behind the other regions. Looking beyond regional variation, there are also several striking differences among individual states. Consider, for example, that after the 2020 elections, fourteen states had no women representatives in the US House and ten states had no women representatives in either the House or Senate. Further, eighteen states have never been represented by a woman in the US Senate.

Table 8.5 identifies those states with no women in the US House, those on their way to gender parity, and those achieving gender parity following the 2020 elections. Since the 2016 elections, women made breakthroughs in large states that had no women serving in the House. Pennsylvania, with eighteen seats, elected four women representatives in 2020, and Georgia, with fourteen House seats, also elected four.

Table 8.5 also demonstrates that women congressional candidates have succeeded in a number of high-population states, like California and New York. Why have women done well in these states and not others? California and New York are among the states with the biggest delegations, so perhaps we can assume that more political opportunities for women drive the candidacies. But this would not explain women's lack of success in populous states like Texas, Ohio, and New Jersey. Moreover, what explains women's success in states like Missouri, where, for much of the 1990s and again in 2020, three of the state's eight House members were women? Missouri borders Kansas, which has never elected more than one woman at a time to the House. By the same token, why has Connecticut historically elected so many more women than neighboring Massachusetts? And things can change quickly in some places, once the political glass ceiling is shattered. Iowa had never sent a woman to Congress until Joni Ernst's US Senate victory in 2014. By 2020, three of

TABLE 8.5 Roughly 20 percent of the states had no women serving in the US House of Representatives after the 2020 elections

States with no women in the House of Representatives	States on the way to parity in the House of Representatives (between 33% and 49%)	States currently achieving gender parity in the House of Representatives (at least 50%)
Alaska (1)	California (53) – 36%	Delaware (1) – 100%
Arkansas (4)	Connecticut (5) – 40%	Iowa (4) – 75%
Hawaii (2)	Illinois (18) – 33%	Maine (2) – 50%
Idaho (2)	Massachusetts (9) – 33%	Minnesota (8) – 50%
Louisiana (6)	Michigan (14) – 43%	Nevada (4) – 50%
Maryland (8)	Missouri (8) – 38%	New Hampshire (2) – 50%
Mississippi (4)	New York (27) – 33%	New Mexico (3) – 100%
Montana (1)	West Virginia (3) – 33%	Washington (10) – 60%
Nebraska (3)		Wyoming (1) – 100%
North Dakota (1)		
Rhode Island (2)		
South Dakota (1)		
Utah (4)		
Vermont (1)		

Notes: Number in parentheses is the number of House seats in the state as of 2021.
Source: Compiled by author from CAWP 2021 fact sheets and *New York Times* listing of election results.

four House members were women. In the matter of a few years Iowa has transformed from a state that never elected women to Congress to one with a congressional delegation dominated by women.

Some political scientists argue that state political culture serves as an important determinant of women's ability to win elective office. The researchers Barbara Norrander and Clyde Wilcox have found considerable disparities in the progress of women's election to state legislatures across various states and regions. They explain the disparities by pointing to differences in state ideology and state culture.[23] States with conservative ideologies and "traditionalist or moralist" cultures are less likely to elect women.[24] Percentages of women in a state's legislature and its congressional delegation, however, are not always correlated. Massachusetts and New Jersey, for example, are better than average in terms of the proportions of women serving in their state legislatures, yet each has a very poor record of electing women to the House of Representatives.

Barbara Palmer and Dennis Simon, in their book *Breaking the Political Glass Ceiling: Women and Congressional Elections*, propose specific causes of regional and state differences in electing women US House members. Examining all congressional elections between 1972 and 2006, they introduce the idea of women-friendly districts. They find that several district characteristics are important predictors of the emergence and success of women candidates. For example, US House districts that are not heavily conservative, are urban, and are not in the South have higher levels of racial minorities, higher levels of education, and are much more likely to have a record of electing women candidates. Palmer and Simon's findings suggest that the manner in which gender manifests itself in the political systems and environments of individual states is an important part of the explanation for the paucity of women in Congress.[25] But things are perhaps changing quickly, and the elections of 2018 and 2020 suggest that the number of women-friendly districts is expanding.

[23] Barbara Norrander and Clyde Wilcox, The Geography of Gender Power: Women in State Legislatures, in *Women and Elective Office*, ed. Sue Thomas and Clyde Wilcox (New York: Oxford University Press, 1998).

[24] Kira Sanbonmatsu, Political Parties and the Recruitment of Women to State Legislatures, *Journal of Politics* 64(3) (2002): 791–809.

[25] Barbara Palmer and Dennis Simon, *Breaking the Political Glass Ceiling: Women and Congressional Elections*, 2nd ed. (New York: Routledge, 2008).

ARE WOMEN RUNNING FOR BOTH PARTIES AND UNDER THE BEST CIRCUMSTANCES?

Most congressional elections feature hopeless challengers running against safely entrenched incumbents. Reporters for *Congressional Quarterly* completed an analysis of all 435 US House races in June 2004, five months before the 2004 elections, and concluded that only twenty-one (out of 404) races with incumbents running were competitive.[26] Such numbers are typical. Even in the more tumultuous election years, it is typical for only 10 to 15 percent of House races, or even fewer, to be competitive. In the 2014 House races, an early analysis from Sabato's Crystal Ball identified only thirty-two (out of all 435) as likely being competitive.[27] In 2018, FiveThirtyEight identified thirty-four highly competitive races.[28] A week prior to the 2020 House election, the Cook Political Report identified only twenty-six toss-up House races.[29]

Political scientists often identify the incumbency advantage as one of the leading explanations for women's slow entry into electoral politics. Low turnover, a direct result of incumbency, provides few opportunities for women to increase their numbers in male-dominated legislative bodies. Between 1946 and 2002, only 8 percent of all challengers defeated incumbent members of the US House of Representatives.[30] In 2016 and 2018 combined, only 6 percent of incumbents were defeated. In most races, the incumbent cruised to reelection with well over 60 percent of the vote. Accordingly, as the congressional elections scholars Ronald Keith Gaddie and Charles Bullock state, "Open seats, not the defeat of incumbents, are the portal through which most legislators enter Congress."[31]

To begin to assess whether women are as likely as men to take advantage of the dynamics associated with an open-seat race, we can examine the presence of women in open-seat House contests. Table 8.6 compares

---

[26] Republicans Maintain a Clear Edge in House Contests, *CQ Weekly*, June 4, 2004.

[27] Kyle Kondik, 2014 House Ratings: Democratic Potential, Republican Predictability, Sabato's Crystal Ball, February 7, 2013.

[28] Grace Panetta and Ellen Cranley, These 25 Congressional Races to Watch are Some of the Most Competitive in the 2018 Midterm Elections, *Business Insider*, November 5, 2018, www.businessinsider.com/most-competitive-house-districts-in-2018-midterm-elections-2018-8

[29] Cook Political Report, https://cookpolitical.com/ratings/house-race-ratings

[30] Gary C. Jacobsen, *The Politics of Congressional Elections*, 6th ed. (New York: Longman, 2004), p. 23.

[31] Ronald Keith Gaddie and Charles S. Bullock, *Elections to Open Seats in the US House* (Lanham, MD: Rowman & Littlefield, 2000), p. 1.

TABLE 8.6 Types of general election seat contested by women candidates in the US House vary by year and party

Type of seat	1980	1990	2000	2010	2018	2020
Open seat	6	8	16	12	43	40
Democrats	4	7	11	10	30	27
Republicans	2	1	5	2	13	13
Challengers	31	37	54	57	117	161
Democrats	13	17	32	27	93	91
Republicans	18	20	22	30	24	70
Incumbents	15	24	52	69	68	96
Democrats	10	15	37	54	52	85
Republicans	5	9	15	15	16	11

Note: Entries indicate the raw number of all female candidates for that electoral category.
Source: Compiled by author from CAWP fact sheets.

Democratic and Republican women's presence in general election House races by seat type and over time. As expected, women were significantly more likely to run for office in the later eras, although the increase in women candidates is not constant across parties. In the 1980s, the parties were very similar in terms of the types of races in which women ran. By the year 2000, however, the number of Democratic women running in all types of races had almost tripled, whereas the increases among the Republicans were quite small. The disparities between the parties became even starker in more recent open-seat elections. In the 2010 election, Democrats put up ten women in open seats, the Republicans just two. If open seats are one of the main "portals" to Congress, then Republican women would hardly stand a chance. Across the 2018 and 2020 elections, there was some upward movement for both parties, but Democrats were still more than twice as likely as Republicans to put up women in these critical election opportunities. One of the biggest jumps in candidacies occurred with female Republican challengers in 2020. Republicans almost tripled the number of women running from 2018, and in an election year where Democrats lost a number of seats, the female challengers were poised for success.

Beyond open-seat races and the Republican increases in 2020, the Democrats have been much more likely than the Republicans to nominate women to run for all types of House seat (see also Table 8.1). This carries serious long-term implications for the number of women serving in Congress. For them to achieve full parity in US political institutions, women must be fully represented in both parties and in the most advantageous electoral opportunities.

ARE MEN AND WOMEN EQUALLY AMBITIOUS TO RUN FOR CONGRESS?

The decision to run for office, particularly at the congressional level, is a critical area of inquiry for those interested in the role of gender in electoral politics. Examples abound of political women who report that they had some difficulty taking the plunge. Wisconsin Congresswoman Gwen Moore never thought of herself as someone who would run for office until she was coaxed to run for a state legislative seat in the 1990s.[32] Even House Speaker Leader Nancy Pelosi claims that she had never thought of running for office until she was encouraged to do so in 1987.[33]

Only in the last twenty years has empirical research emerged that explores the initial decision to run for office. The rationale for focusing on the initial decision to run for office is that if the general election playing field is largely level, then gender differences in the candidate emergence process likely provide a crucial explanation for women's underrepresentation in Congress. In 2001 and 2011, Jennifer Lawless and I conducted separate waves of the Citizen Political Ambition Study. This series of surveys asks women and men working in the four professions most likely to precede a career in Congress (law, business, politics, and education) about their ambition to run for elective office some day. In 2017, we conducted another survey of potential candidates, this time defined as adults with at least a four-year college degree and full-time employment – the baseline typical profile for someone who runs for office. Table 8.7 shows some results of the surveys, focusing on whether women and men have ever thought about running for office and whether they have taken steps that usually precede a candidacy, such as speaking with party officials and community leaders. On the critical question of interest in running for office, the results of the study highlighted a substantial gender gap in political ambition. The results of the most recent survey in 2017 reveal that there has been almost no change in the gap across the past sixteen years. In 2001, there was a sixteen percentage point gap, with men more

---

[32] Reluctant to Take the Plunge, *USA Today*, May 29, 2008, p. 10A.
[33] Dana Wilkey, From Political Roots to Political Leader, Pelosi Is the Real Thing, Copley News Service, November 13, 2002.

TABLE 8.7 Among potential candidates, women are less interested than men in seeking elective office

	2001		2011		2017	
	Women (%)	Men (%)	Women (%)	Men (%)	Women (%)	Men (%)
Has thought about running for office	43	59	46	62	23	38
Discussed running with party leaders	4	8	25	32	2	5
Discussed running with friends and family	17	29	27	38	6	12
Investigated how to place your name on the ballot	4	10	13	21	n/a	n/a
Sample size	1,248	1,454	1,796	1,969	1,001	1,061

Notes: Sample is composed of lawyers, business leaders and executives, and educators. Entries indicate percentage responding "yes." All differences between women and men are significant at $p < .05$. The question about putting your name on the ballot was not asked in 2017.

Sources: Adapted from the 2017 Citizen Political Ambition Study and report. For 2001, see Richard L. Fox and Jennifer L. Lawless, Entering the Arena: Gender and the Decision to Run for Office, *American Journal of Political Science* 48(2) (2004): 264–80. For 2011, see Jennifer L. Lawless and Richard L. Fox, Men Rule: The Continued 'Under-Representation' in published title of Women in US Politics, report, School of Public Affairs, American University, Washington, DC, 2011. For 2017, see Jennifer L. Lawless and Richard L. Fox, The Trump Effect, report, School of Public Affairs, American University, Washington, DC, 2017.

likely than women to have thought about running for office. In 2011, the gap again stood at sixteen percentage points, virtually unchanged. And in the 2017 survey, the gap was fifteen points. The gender gaps in terms of the actual steps that a potential candidate might take before running for office were roughly unchanged across the time period as well. Even though the empirical evidence shows that women who run for office are just as likely as men to be victorious, a much smaller number of women than men are likely to emerge as candidates because women are far less likely than men to consider running for office.

Further, when we consider male and female potential candidates' interest in running for Congress specifically, the gender gap in political ambition is amplified. Table 8.8 shows the interest of potential candidates in running for the US Congress in all three years. Potential candidates were asked to identify which offices they might ever be interested in seeking. Men were significantly more likely than women to express interest in running for Congress. Again, the gender gap in interest in congressional office persisted across both time periods. The one notable change between 2001 and 2011, and 2017 was that both women and men expressed less interest in running for Congress overall, likely a result of the increasingly negative and partisan view of politics in Washington.

Three critical factors uncovered in the surveys of potential candidates explain the gender gap in ambition. First, women are significantly less likely than men to receive encouragement to run for office. This difference

TABLE 8.8 Among potential candidates, women are less interested than men in running for the US House or Senate

	2001		2011		2017	
	Women (%)	Men (%)	Women (%)	Men (%)	Women (%)	Men (%)
Interested in someday running for ...						
US House of Representatives	15	27	9	19	6	15
US Senate	13	20	6	11	n/a	n/a
Sample size	816	1,022	1,766	1,848	1,001	1,061

Notes: Sample is composed of lawyers, business leaders and executives, and educators. Entries indicate percentage responding "yes." All differences between women and men are significant at $p < .05$. In 2017, potential candidates were only asked about interest in Congress, not the House and Senate individually.

Sources: Adapted from the 2017 Citizen Political Ambition Study. For 2001, see Richard L. Fox and Jennifer L. Lawless, Entering the Arena: Gender and the Decision to Run for Office, *American Journal of Political Science* 48(2) (2004): 264–80. For 2011, see Jennifer L. Lawless and Richard L. Fox, Men Rule: The Continued Under-Representation of Women in US Politics, report, School of Public Affairs, American University, Washington, DC, 2011. For 2017, see Jennifer L. Lawless and Richard L. Fox, The Trump Effect, report, School of Public Affairs, American University, Washington, DC, 2017.

is very important, because potential candidates are twice as likely to think about running for office when a party leader, elected official, or political activist attempts to recruit them as candidates. Second, women are significantly less likely than men to view themselves as qualified to run for office. In other words, even women in the top tier of professional accomplishment tend not to consider themselves qualified to run for political office, even when they have the same objective credentials and experiences as men. Third, even among this group of professionals, women were much more likely to state that they were responsible for the majority of childcare and household duties. Although many of the women in the study had blazed trails in the formerly male professions of law and business, they were still serving as the primary caretakers in their households. Although family roles and responsibilities were not significant predictors of political ambition, interviews with potential women candidates suggested that traditional family roles are still an impediment.[34]

The 2018 and 2020 elections suggest some possible shifts in the dynamics of gender and political ambition. The Trump presidency certainly motivated a group of progressive women to run for office and Republican recruitment efforts may also help close the ambition gap in 2020. Future research focusing on the decision to run for office will uncover if there have been fundamental shifts.

CONCLUSION AND DISCUSSION

When researchers and political scientists in the late 1970s and early 1980s began to study the role of gender in electoral politics, concerns about basic fairness and political representation motivated many of their investigations. For many, the notion of governing bodies overwhelmingly dominated by men offends a sense of simple justice. In this vein, some researchers argue that the reality of a male-dominated government suggests to women citizens that the political system is not fully open to them. These concerns are as pertinent today as they were in the past. As Susan J. Carroll, Kelly Dittmar, and I noted in the Introduction to this volume, a large body of empirical research finds that a political system that does not allow for women's full inclusion in positions of political power increases the possibility that gender-salient issues will be overlooked. Ample research has shown that women are more likely than men to promote

---

[34] Jennifer L. Lawless and Richard L. Fox, *It Still Takes a Candidate: Why Women Don't Run for Office* (New York: Cambridge University Press, 2010).

legislation geared toward ameliorating women's economic and social status, especially concerning issues of health care, poverty, education, and gender equity. Despite the substantive and symbolic importance of women's full inclusion in the electoral arena, the number of women serving in elected bodies remains relatively low. This chapter's overview of women's performance in congressional elections makes it clear that we need to adopt a more nuanced approach if we are to understand – and address – gender's evolving role in the electoral arena.

As to answering this chapter's central question – why there are still so few women in Congress – two broad findings emerge from the analysis.

First, on a more optimistic note, women now compete in US House and Senate races more successfully than at any previous time in history. The last two election cycles saw record numbers of women candidates seeking and winning major party nominations. The key to increasing women's representation is to get more women to run for office. As the broad empirical indicators show, female general election candidates are not impeded by the major indicators of electoral success: vote totals and fundraising. The evidence presented in this chapter continues to show that women and men perform similarly as general election candidates. On the basis of recent congressional election results, the findings presented in this chapter confirm, as a number of other studies have found, that there is no evidence of widespread gender bias among voters and financial contributors.

The second broad finding to emerge from this chapter, however, is that gender continues to play an important role in the electoral arena, and in some cases works to keep the number of women running for Congress low. Notably, there are sharp state and regional differences in electing men and women to Congress. Women cannot emerge in greater numbers until the candidacies of women are embraced throughout the entire United States and by both parties.

Additionally, women's full inclusion will not be possible if the overwhelming majority of women candidates continue to identify with the Democratic Party. The 2020 elections suggest change might be on the horizon in this regard, but prior to 2020 Republicans made very little progress in promoting and facilitating the election of women congressional candidates. If the fortunes of women candidates are tied so heavily to one political party, women's movement toward parity in officeholding will prove illusory. But things might be changing. Republican House Leaders Kevin McCarthy and Steve Scalise recruited more women and minority candidates than prior leaders, and appear to want to continue the trend after the successful 2020 election.[35]

Finally, gender differences in political ambition – particularly in the ambition to run for the US Congress – suggest that gender is exerting a strong impact at the earliest stages of the electoral process. Many women who would make ideal candidates never actually consider running for office. The notion of entering politics still appears not to be a socialized norm for women. A recent study of full-time college students aged 18 to 25 reveals that women continue to show far less interest than their male counterparts in ever running for office. These results highlight some of the long-term challenges in creating an environment where women and men are equally likely to be interested in pursuing a seat in the US Congress.

As these findings suggest, gender permeates the electoral environment in congressional elections in subtle and nuanced ways. Broad empirical analyses often tend to overlook these dynamics. Yet the reality is that these dynamics help explain why the road to parity is a slow one to travel.

---

[35] John Bresnahan and Melanie Zanona, McCarthy Heads into Next Congress with Eye on Speaker's Gavel, *Politico*, November 17, 2020, www.politico.com/news/2020/11/17/kevin-mccarthy-house-speaker-436907

9 Women's Election to Office in the Fifty States: Changes and Challenges

For nearly two decades, the percentage of women serving in state legislatures hovered between 20 percent and 25 percent – far below their share of the population. But in 2018, a record number of women sought and won state legislative office. And in one state – Nevada – women became a majority of state legislators after the election, marking the first time in US history that women constituted a majority of a state legislature. In statewide executive offices, as well, new records for women candidates and officeholders were set in 2018. And in 2020, women expanded their presence as state candidates and officeholders albeit less dramatically than in 2018.

State politics and elections are underappreciated and usually attract less public interest and media attention than politics and elections at the federal level. But states are fundamental to public policy making and therefore central to the daily lives of their citizens. This importance was driven home during the COVID-19 pandemic as the Trump administration left major policy choices, including vaccination decisions, to individual states. And many critical policy areas including contentious debates on voting rights and abortion policy are centered in the states.

Decades of research into state legislators reveal that women usually take the lead on policies important to women; women legislators feel an obligation to represent women as a group and work on legislation aimed at helping women, children, and families.[1] Research studies are embarking on more complex analyses of the interaction of race/ethnicity with women's legislative activities, recognizing that women are a large group and gender intersects with other identities. As the two major parties continue to offer distinct policy agendas, understanding differences

---

[1] Kelly Dittmar, Kira Sanbonmatsu, and Susan J. Carroll, *A Seat at the Table: Congresswomen's Perspectives on Why Their Presence Matters* (New York: Oxford University Press, 2018).

between Democratic and Republican women comes to the fore. Meanwhile, pathbreaking LGBTQ candidates are widening opportunities for more women to follow in their footsteps.

The state perspective offers a remarkable window into the relationship between gender and elections, offering fifty different election systems for investigation. Whereas 144 women serve in Congress in 2021, there are 2,279 women state legislators available for analysis.[2] Women have come far from the late 1800s – when they first sought state legislative office – and the 1920s – when the first women governors held the office as widows following the deaths of their husbands.

In the coming pages, we assess the status of women in state elections. We analyze the tremendous progress accomplished in recent elections while identifying remaining challenges. The election of women of color to statewide executive offices and opportunities for LGBTQ candidates, in particular, are areas of slow and uneven progress. And while more Republican women won office than in the past, women as a share of Republican officials is stagnant. We also examine a public policy that may facilitate the election of more women in the future: state policies related to candidates' childcare expenses.

STATE LEGISLATIVE ELECTIONS

As a result of the 2018 election, the Nevada Assembly included twenty-three women and the Senate nine women, giving women a majority and making Nevada the first state legislature in the country in which women held over 50 percent of seats (see Text Box 9.1). In 2020, women grew their majority to twenty-eight in the Assembly and ten in the Senate, making their majority even stronger. No state has caught up to Nevada, but Colorado inched closer in the 2018 and 2020 elections. In 2021 women held thirty-four of the sixty-five House of Representatives seats, helping make Colorado second nationally for the most women in the state legislature. Colorado also had eleven House committees chaired by women. In addition to the majority Colorado House chamber, in 2021 Arizona, New Mexico, Oregon, and Rhode Island each had one chamber that was composed of a majority of women or had equal numbers of women and men.

---

[2] All data on women officeholders and candidates in this chapter are from the Center for American Women and Politics (hereafter CAWP). Our focus on even-year elections captures the vast majority of states' elections. However, four states – Alabama, Mississippi, New Jersey, and Virginia – hold their regular elections for state legislature in off years.

TEXT BOX 9.1 Women Making Change in Nevada

While the women newly elected to the Nevada legislature in 2018 and 2020 had much to celebrate, they did not waste time getting to work. Since holding a majority, women legislators have introduced several key pieces of legislation and have brought attention to the needs of women and other minority groups in the state.

Advancing Reproductive Health Care Rights The Trust Nevada Women Act, introduced by first-time senator Yvanna Cancela, was signed into law in 2019. This bill rewrote state law so that doctors are no longer required to tell women about the emotional implications of abortion, nor would they have to certify in writing a pregnant woman's marital status, age, and written consent before the procedure.

Expanding Firefighter Cancer Compensation Existing Nevada law compensates firefighters who develop certain cancers from exposure on the job; however, until now, breast, uterine, and ovarian cancers were not covered by the law. Senate majority leader Nicole Cannizzaro said, "it had never been something that people thought of – but we have a lot of women serving as firefighters now."

Sources: A First: Women Take the Majority in Nevada Legislature and Colorado House, *NPR*, February 4, 2019, www.npr.org/2019/02/04/691198416/a-first-women-take-the-majority-in-nevada-legislature-and-colorado-house; Did First Female-Majority Legislature in US Make a Difference?, *BBC World News*, March 4, 2020, www.bbc.com/news/world-us-canada-51623420; Nevada Passes Bill to No Longer Require Doctors to Tell Women the "Emotional Implications" of an Abortion, *CNN*, May 22, 2019, www.cnn.com/2019/05/22/politics/nevada-bill-emotional-implications-abortion/index.html

In the early 1990s, political scientists tracking the progress of women in state legislative office predicted that women would achieve parity in officeholding with the passage of time. But new elections did not automatically bring gains for women and they remained far from equal in the state legislatures despite educational and economic advances.

Women seized on the changed electoral landscape of 2018 and finally brought a period of stagnation to a halt. The record 3,418 women who ran in general elections for the forty-four state legislatures with elections that year far outpaced the previous high of 2,649 women in 2016 – an increase of about 30 percent in one cycle. More women candidates would step forward in 2020, establishing another record, albeit a less dramatic one (in 2020, 3,446 women ran in general election contests). Women's presence in state legislatures crossed the 30 percent threshold in 2021, a record high (see Figure 9.1). These gains were long overdue, and confirm that there are more than enough talented women potential candidates to achieve parity in the state legislatures; in a fifty-state study of legislators' pathways to office in 1981 and 2008, Susan J. Carroll and Kira Sanbonmatsu had concluded: "Recognizing that women legislators continue to emerge from a range of occupations and vary in age, education, and political experience, we conclude that the pool of eligible women to run is both wider than commonly perceived and more than sufficient for women to achieve parity in state legislatures."[3]

More women from both major parties ran in 2018 for the legislature, but the rise in women general election candidates was largely a Democratic

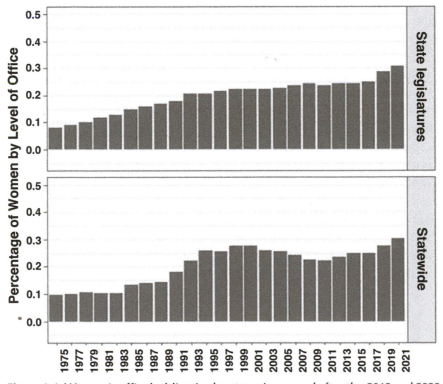

Figure 9.1 Women's officeholding in the states increased after the 2018 and 2020 elections.
Source: CAWP.

[3] Susan J. Carroll and Kira Sanbonmatsu, *More Women Can Run: Gender and Pathways to the State Legislatures* (New York: Oxford University Press, 2013).

phenomenon: while 1,727 Democratic women ran for the legislatures in 2016, 2,402 did so in 2018 – an increase of 40 percent. Republican women expanded from 900 to 993 candidates between 2016 and 2018, yielding an increase of 10 percent.

Just as state legislatures have seen an increase in women running for and winning office, openly LGBTQ candidates saw a "rainbow wave" in both the 2018 and 2020 elections. In 2018 alone, there were at least 283 LGBTQ candidates running for state legislative seats.[4] After the 2020 election, the number of LGBTQ state legislators stands at 150 – a record high, and at least forty LGBTQ people of color were elected to the state legislature.[5]

Among these include several victories for LGBTQ women of color. Kim Jackson (D-GA) won her 2020 election, making her the first Black lesbian elected to the state's senate. Tiara Mack (D-RI), who won her seat during the 2020 election cycle, is the first openly LGBTQ Black person elected to the Rhode Island state senate.[6]

Several transgender state legislators have also accomplished many "firsts" (see Text Box 9.2). In 2017, Danica Roem (D-VA) was elected to the Virginia House of Delegates, making her the first transgender person elected to any state legislature.[7] By 2020, several other transgender candidates followed in Delegate Roem's footsteps, making history in their respective states. In 2020, Sarah McBride (D-DE) became the first transgender state senator elected to a state legislature.[8] Stephanie Byers (D-KS), a member of the Chickasaw Nation, was elected to the Kansas House in 2020, making her the first transgender legislator elected in the Midwest, and the first transgender Native American to hold office in the United States.[9] And Mauree Turner (D-OK) became the first nonbinary state legislator in the United States, as well as the first Muslim lawmaker in Oklahoma.[10]

---

[4]   Donald P. Haider-Markel et al., LGBTQ State Legislative Candidates in an Era of Backlash, *PS: Political Science & Politics* 53(3) (2020): 453–59.

[5]   LGBT People Keep Breaking Election Barriers and it "Feels Amazing," *NBC News*, November 10, 2020, https://nbcnews.to/3s3mu5X

[6]   "Unapologetically Black and Queer" Tiara Mack is Headed to the Rhode Island Senate, *NBC News*, November 18, 2020, https://nbcnews.to/2X51lNa

[7]   Maggie Astor, Danica Roem Wins Virginia Race, Breaking a Barrier for Transgender People, *New York Times*, November 7, 2017, https://nyti.ms/3iG0Mlz

[8]   Delaware Elects Country's First Transgender State Senator, Associated Press, November 3, 2020, https://bit.ly/3xFet8m

[9]   *NBC News*, November 10, 2020.

[10]   Mauree Turner is the First Nonbinary State legislator and First Muslim Oklahoma Lawmaker, *CNN*, November 5, 2020, https://cnn.it/2U4EDDJ

TEXT BOX 9.2 What Running and Winning Means to LGBTQ Candidates

Some of the candidates shared their views on what their candidacies meant for them personally and for the future of politics:

> You have every right to bring your ideas to the table and to champion them, not just sit in the back, not just donate to candidates because you personally would never be able to do it. If we can do this, so can you. Go run. Danica Roem (D-VA)

> I ran on a campaign really calling on my strong history of advocating for people whose voices have often gone unheard and for people who have often been left on the margins and so I will serve in that capacity of really advocating on behalf of all Georgians to make sure that we have access and equity. Kim Jackson (D-GA)

> For a lot of folks, if Kansas, the big red Republican state, can elect a trans person to a state legislature, the doors open up in a lot of other places for people. And it helps those people who are transgender to reinforce that they are people who matter, they are people who are important and they're people who can be successful in their lives. Stephanie Byers (D-KS)

> It has never been a more important time for the next generation to see themselves in our government. It has never been a more important time for those closest to our state's problems to be structuring the solutions. Mauree Turner (D-OK)

Sources: You Can't Just Say "I Hate Trump, Vote for Me": Danica Roem on Her Historic Win, *Vox*, November 22, 2017, https://bit.ly/3s3KDJF; Kim Jackson Reflects on Being Georgia's First Openly Gay State Senator, WABE Georgia Public Radio, January 22, 2021, www.wabe.org/kim-jackson-reflects-on-being-georgias-first-openly-gay-state-senator/; Kansas Makes History, Elects Retired Wichita Teacher as its First Transgender Legislator, *Wichita Eagle*, November 3, 2020, www.kansas.com/news/politics-government/election/article246927272.html; Mauree Turner, campaign press release, www.maureeturner.com/press/announcement-release (accessed 3/6/21)

The 2018 election cycle also saw an increase in state legislative office-holding by Black women, Asian Pacific Islander women, Latinas, and Native American women. In 2019, along with Middle Eastern/North African women and women who identify as multiracial, women of color constituted 25.2 percent of all women legislators. The largest raw number increase in officeholding by women of color occurred with Black women, who grew from 275 state legislators in 2018 to 307 in 2019. Black women are the single largest group of women of color state legislators; they remain underrepresented as a share of state legislators compared with their presence in the population, but fare better than other groups of women of color. The 2020 election cycle saw negligible changes for other groups of women of color.

Because Democratic women drove the uptick in women's state legislative candidacies, the stark partisan imbalance among women state legislators continued. As a result of the 2018 election, in 2019 women composed 42 percent of Democratic state legislators compared with only 17 percent of Republican state legislators (see Figure 9.2). After the 2020 elections, women would constitute 49 percent of all Democratic legislators and 19 percent of all Republican legislators. Whereas the 2021 presence of women as Democratic state legislators is an all-time high, the same is not the case for women as a share of Republican state legislators. In short, dramatic increases in women's state legislative candidacies have largely occurred on the Democratic side of the aisle. This partisan difference has

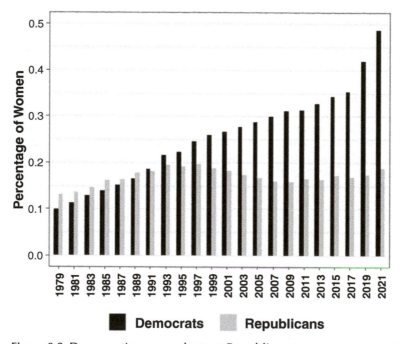

Figure 9.2 Democratic women, but not Republican women, are a growing share of their party's state legislators.
Source: Council of State Governments, and National Conference of State Legislatures, CAWP.

implications for how much influence women wield within their respective parties and ultimately, state policy choices. For example, all seven women serving as speakers of the house in 2020 were Democrats and Democratic women were thirteen of the seventeen women leading state senates.

Despite historic changes for women's state legislative representation, the balance of power between the two parties at the state level changed little in 2018 or 2020. Incumbents, including women, are much more likely to win their races than challengers or open-seat candidates, as shown in Table 9.1. Because most incumbents are men, gains in women's office-holding is likely to result from open-seat contests without incumbents.

Party differences are evident in these statistics about the share of women candidates who won their general election races: Democratic women incumbents had higher reelection rates in 2018 than Republican women incumbents, with a similar pattern for challenger and open-seat contests. These differences reflect the national Democratic tide of that election.

Republicans gained ground in some respects in the 2020 elections despite losing the presidency and control of the US Senate. This reversal of fortunes is reflected in the win rates for 2020 women state legislative candidates, with Republican women outperforming Democratic women on average (see Table 9.1). In 2018, Democrats flipped control of seven

TABLE 9.1 Women state legislative candidates are more likely to win their races as incumbents

	2018 (%)*	2020 (%)
Incumbents		
Democrats	98.0 (809)	92.3 (1,032)
Republicans	87.3 (455)	96.9 (447)
Challengers		
Democrats	14.7 (918)	5.0 (795)
Republicans	5.6 (269)	11.2 (420)
Open seats		
Democrats	51.1 (675)	50.0 (488)
Republicans	52.8 (269)	60.9 (238)

*Women candidates who won that race, with N in parentheses.
Source: Women General Election Candidates for State Legislatures: Election Results 1992–2020, CAWP 2020.

state legislative chambers, narrowing the large Republican seat advantage that began in 2010.[11] Republicans regained seats and two state legislative chambers in 2020, though overall there was little change between the two parties.[12]

In 2021, just 20 women of color state legislators identified as Republicans and 531 as Democrats. Both parties could be more welcoming to women of color candidates in a wider range of districts. Studies show that women's emergence as state legislative candidates depends on race/ethnicity and that more women of color could be elected if they were recruited to run in majority-white districts.[13]

Differences across States in Women's Officeholding

Overall statistics on women's officeholding obscure vast differences across the fifty states in women's status. Table 9.2 shows the variation, with Nevada and Colorado leading the country and Alabama and West Virginia at the bottom. Although the average is 30.8 percent, seven states fall below the 20 percent mark, whereas Nevada is approaching 60 percent. While it is now commonplace for women to seek and hold state legislative office in some states, women candidates remain a departure from the norm elsewhere. These differences mean that party leaders, donors, and voters vary by state with respect to familiarity with women as candidates.

Some studies have found that multimember districts rather than single-member districts are beneficial for women's representation. Ten states have systems in which more than one legislator is elected per district. This relationship is not clear, however, since half of states with multimember districts are in the bottom half of states for women's representation. Another electoral feature found in the legislatures – term limits – that could assist new candidates such as women, may not automatically create more favorable conditions for women's representation either: nine states with term limits are in the top half of states for women's representation with six term-limited states found in the bottom half.

---

[11] Tim Storey and Wendy Underhill, Republicans Still Control Most of the Nation's Legislative Seats, but the Gap between the Parties Narrowed Considerably, National Conference of State Legislatures (hereafter NCSL), November 13, 2018, www.ncsl.org/research/elections-and-campaigns/between-a-ripple-and-a-wave.aspx

[12] Postelection Partisan Control, NCSL, 2021, www.ncsl.org/research/elections-and-campaigns/ncsl-state-elections-2020.aspx

[13] Paru Shah, Jamil Scott, and Eric Gonzalez Juenke, Women of Color Candidates: Examining Emergence and Success in State Legislative Elections, *Politics, Groups, and Identities* 7(2) (2019): 429–43.

TABLE 9.2 Women's representation varies across states

50% plus	40–49%	30–39%	20–29%	Under 20%
Nevada	Colorado	Illinois	Kansas	Louisiana
	Rhode Island	Michigan	Pennsylvania	Wyoming
	New Mexico	Minnesota	Iowa	South Carolina
	Maine	New Hampshire	South Dakota	Tennessee
	Arizona	Florida	Kentucky	Mississippi
	Oregon	New York	Nebraska	Alabama
	Vermont	Connecticut	Texas	West Virginia
	Washington	Georgia	Missouri	
	Maryland	Montana	North Carolina	
		California	Indiana	
		Hawaii	Arkansas	
		Ohio	Utah	
		Wisconsin	North Dakota	
		Massachusetts	Oklahoma	
		Delaware		
		Idaho		
		Alaska		
		New Jersey		
		Virginia		

Note: States are listed from high to low in each column for the percentage of women in state legislatures in 2021.
Source: CAWP.

An explanation that appears to be more promising to explaining cross-state variation concerns legislative professionalism. Among the states with the highest levels of women's representation, none has a full-time "professional" legislature. The desirability of the office, as measured by compensation and the length of the legislative session, may create more competition and less favorable conditions for women potential candidates.

States with stronger party organizations tend to make for less favorable climates for women state legislators.[14] Because parties can encourage as well as discourage candidates, the strength of party organizations and the gender of party leaders is consequential. For Republican women, underrepresentation can beget underrepresentation: without women in

[14] Kira Sanbonmatsu, *Where Women Run: Gender and Party in the American States* (Ann Arbor, MI: University of Michigan Press, 2006).

leadership positions, the likelihood that more women will be recruited diminishes due to gender segregation in social and political networks.

Party control can also affect the level of women's representation given that women state legislators are far less likely to be Republicans than Democrats. In 2021, while women's share of Republican state legislators varied from 5 to 42 percent depending on the state, women were 11 to 69 percent of Democratic state legislators. Most of the states at the very bottom of the list for women's state legislative representation in 2021 were Republican-controlled, indicating that Republican Party strength is negatively related to women's representation.[15]

In both Nevada and Colorado, the rise of women in office can be attributed to recruitment efforts, including leadership training programs like Democratic organization Emerge America and nonpartisan VoteRunLead, which offer mentorship and campaigning training for women who are interested in running for office. Women's organizations across the country play a vital role in recruiting and supporting women candidates.[16]

In Colorado, Serena Gonzales-Gutierrez participated in Emerge Colorado's training program before being elected in 2018.[17] In the 2020 election, Colorado women continued to break barriers. Iman Jodeh became the first Muslim and Arab elected to the state legislature, and Naquetta Ricks, the first African immigrant. Ricks explained the significance of her election: "I don't think I set out to be the first [African immigrant], but I definitely set out to be a voice at the table"; "I'm hoping that by breaking the glass ceiling, more people will see that is possible."[18]

In Nevada, 23-year-old high school teacher Selena Torres was elected in 2018 and was inspired to run for office after hearing Trump's anti-immigrant rhetoric. She ran for office after participating in the Emerge Nevada program. Running for office was important for Torres, who explained: "I think growing up you have this idea that politicians aren't us. They don't look like me. They don't have my type of hair. They don't come from our background. They don't have to send money back to El

[15] Laurel Elder, The Partisan Gap Among Women State Legislators, *Journal of Women, Politics & Policy* 33(1) (2012): 65–85, doi.org/10.1080/1554477X.2012.640609

[16] Rebecca Kreitzer and Tracy Osborn, Women Candidate Recruitment Groups in the States, in *Good Reasons to Run: Women and Political Candidacy*, ed. Shauna L. Shames et al. (Philadelphia, PA: Temple University Press, 2020).

[17] Representative Serena Gonzales-Gutierrez, https://leg.colorado.gov/legislators/serena-gonzales-gutierrez (accessed 3/6/21).

[18] First Muslim and Arab Woman Elected to Colorado State Legislature, *The Hill*, November 14, 2020, https://bit.ly/3fLnarC

Salvador to make sure that their family can make ends meet. But then you come to realize: That's the problem."[19] While Nevada has only recently crossed the threshold of 50 percent women holding office, several women have served in the Nevada legislature before and have watched the changing environment as more women enter the state legislature. Assembly Majority Leader Teresa Benitez-Thompson (D) reflected on the substantive efforts of the legislature since more women have been elected, commenting: "I can say with 100 percent certainty that we wouldn't have had these conversations a few years ago … none of these bills would have seen the light of day."[20]

STATEWIDE EXECUTIVE OFFICE ELECTIONS

The Trump administration left major policy choices during COVID-19 to the states, elevating the importance of governors as well as putting governors in conflict with one another as they sought to procure medical equipment and vaccine doses for their citizens. The politicization of the virus raised the temperature on governors as health restrictions led to backlash against those governors who sought to limit the spread of the virus through stay-at-home orders and mask mandates.

It was in this environment that law enforcement officials thwarted an attempted kidnapping plot by extremists directed at Michigan's Governor Gretchen Whitmer (D), who won office in 2018. This planned attack as well as violent rhetoric directed at Whitmer from politicians including President Trump, who called on his supporters to "liberate Michigan," revealed the vulnerability of women in politics as well as the scarcity of women governors. Trump declined to condemn the attempted attack on Governor Whitmer.[21]

In 2021, just eight women served as governors of the fifty states – five Democratic women and three Republican women – short of the previous historic high of nine women simultaneously serving in the role.[22] Because

---

[19] Emily Wax-Thibodeaux, Where Women Call the Shots, *Washington Post*, May 17, 2019, https://wapo.st/3jBhbqu

[20] Ibid.

[21] Mona Lena Krook, *Violence against Women in Politics* (New York: Oxford University Press, 2020); David D. Kirkpatrick and Mike McIntire, "Its Own Domestic Army": How the G.O.P. Allied Itself with Militants, *New York Times*, February 9, 2021, https://nyti .ms/2U8CUgQ

[22] Gina Raimando, governor of Rhode Island, left her position in order to join the Biden cabinet in 2021.

Republicans hold more gubernatorial positions than Democrats, Democratic women are far better represented in this office than their Republican women counterparts: just three of twenty-seven, or 11 percent, of Republican governors are women compared with five of twenty-three, or 22 percent, of Democratic governors.

With women serving as vice president and Speaker of the House of Representatives in 2021, it might be surprising how few women have served as governors in US history: just thirty states have experienced a woman governor. Of the forty-four women who have ever served as governors, only thirty did so by winning election in their own right. More Democratic women (26) than Republican women (18) have ever served as governor. A Black woman, Native American women, or woman of East Asian descent has yet to win the office of governor.

Over time, women have moved into a wider range of statewide executive offices, although they continue to be more likely to be found in some offices than others. Women constitute only one-fifth of all attorneys general but one-third of all secretaries of state. The eight women who simultaneously serve as attorney general of their state in 2021 is not a historic high. As Figure 9.1 illustrates, women's statewide executive officeholding has not always risen with new elections, and saw a decline between 1999 and 2009.

But women did make inroads in the 2018 and 2020 elections. More statewide executive elections are held outside of presidential election years, meaning that more offices were elected in 2018 than in 2020. And similar to the history-making congressional and state legislative elections, 2018 set records: 188 women filed for statewide executive offices, an increase of about one-third from the 2014 elections, which was the previous comparable cycle. And women composed 42 percent of newly elected 2018 officeholders, with Democratic women outpacing Democratic men in turning statewide elective offices from Republican to Democratic hands.[23] Democrats gained seven gubernatorial offices in 2018, with four new Democratic women elected; one new Republican woman was elected as well. In 2020, Republicans flipped one gubernatorial seat and no new women were elected.

In 2018, more women – sixty-one – filed for governors' races than ever before, beating the 1994 record of twenty-four. While Democratic women set a record for gubernatorial nominees, the same was not true

[23] Kelly Dittmar, Unfinished Business: Women Running in 2018 and Beyond, CAWP, 2019, https://womenrun.rutgers.edu/

for Republican women in 2018. Of eight general election nominees for open seats, five won their races and three lost; meanwhile all four incumbent women won and all four challenger women lost. Despite the large uptick in women candidates, and the nine women serving in 2019 as a result of the election, no new record for women simultaneously serving as governor was established. One of the Democratic women losing her gubernatorial bids was Christine Hallquist of Vermont, who was the first openly transgender major party nominee. Because fewer women run for governor with the benefit of incumbency, open-seat contests are especially important for women candidates. Indeed, two of the newly elected women – Janet Mills (D-ME) and Kristi Noem (R-SD) – became the first women to lead their states by winning open-seat contests.

As a result of the 2018 elections, the racial diversity of women in statewide executive positions expanded. One of the major "firsts" achieved in 2018 was the election of Michelle Lujan Grisham (NM) as governor, making her the first Democratic Latina elected to that role in US history. In 2019, women of color constituted 18.7 percent of women in all statewide executive offices.[24] The newly elected women also included the first Black woman to hold statewide executive office in New York, Attorney General Letitia James (D), and Minnesota's Peggy Flanagan (D), who became lieutenant governor and the state's first woman of color elected to statewide executive office. Flanagan was also just the second Native American woman to achieve an executive, statewide office in US history.

The 2020 cycle saw fewer statewide executive offices up for election. But women's presence as candidates and officeholders continued on an upward trajectory. Eleven women filed for governor's races in 2020, up from six in 2016. Sixty-nine women filed for other statewide elective positions in 2020, up slightly from sixty-three in 2016. As a result of the 2021 elections, women would achieve a record 30.3 percent of all elected statewide executive positions.

One of the challenges for women who identify as other than non-Hispanic white is running statewide in majority-white electorates, and nearly all states fit that demographic description. In one of the most closely watched 2018 races, Stacey Abrams (GA-D) narrowly lost her bid to become the nation's first Black woman governor. Abrams, a former minority leader in the Georgia House of Representatives, had significantly enhanced voter registration efforts for people of color. But changes to the state's election rules led by her opponent Brian Kemp, who served as

[24] Ibid.

secretary of state at the same time he ran for governor, sparked litigation and controversy. Although Abrams lost her race, her accomplishments to increase voter mobilization would benefit her party in 2020 with Joe Biden's win and the success of the two Democrats who won their races for the US Senate.

Despite some noteworthy firsts in recent elections, including the first Democratic woman of color to win gubernatorial office, more work is needed for women of color to realize their potential in the fifty states. Of all statewide executive women officeholders in 2021, 18.1 percent were women of color. This statistic is lower than for women of color as a share of women state legislators (25.5%) and women in Congress (35.9%).

It remains difficult for people of color – regardless of gender – to win statewide executive positions. Stereotypes and lack of party and financial support are factors in this deficit. Doubts about the viability of women candidates of color can hinder critical, early informal support. While the vast majority of all women of color identify as Democrats, even the Democratic Party could be more vested in diversifying its statewide officials.[25]

Whereas most research about campaign finance is centered on Congress and reveals parity for women in many respects, especially for Democratic women, much less is known about the financial landscape in the states. A comprehensive study of campaign contributions in governor's races between 2000 and 2018 revealed that women candidates raise comparable amounts to men once factors such as incumbency status and population size are taken into account, although this gender parity occurs with women exceeding men in likelihood of prior officeholding experience (see Text Box 9.3).[26] Gender differences are also apparent in how women and men raise money, with women more likely to raise money through smaller contributions. The report also found that women, and women of color in particular, are underrepresented as gubernatorial candidates – even in open-seat primary contests. Women donors are underrepresented as a share of all donors and as a share of all money contributed, which may yield missed opportunities for women gubernatorial candidates given that women are more likely than men to give to women candidates. Garnering sufficient financial support matters for state legislative contests, as well.

---

[25] Kira Sanbonmatsu, Officeholding in the Fifty States: The Pathways Women of Color Take to Statewide Elective Executive Office, in *Distinct Identities: Minority Women in US Politics*, ed. Nadia E. Brown and Sarah Allen Gershon (New York: Routledge, 2020).

[26] Kira Sanbonmatsu, Kathleen Rogers, and Claire Gothreau, The Money Hurdle in the Race for Governor: A CAWP Women, Money and Politics Report, CAWP, 2020, https://cawp .rutgers.edu/sites/default/files/resources/cawp_money_politics_race-for-governor.pdf

TEXT BOX 9.3 Money Matters in Gubernatorial Races

Money doesn't buy votes. But money does matter in politics. Financial resources help candidates establish viability, advertise, and mobilize voters. And while women outnumber men as voters, the opposite is true when it comes to campaign contributions: men traditionally outnumber women as donors, and men contribute more when they give.

A detailed report by the Center for American Women and Politics (CAWP) in 2020 contains a wealth of information about how women fare as candidates and donors in gubernatorial races from 2000 to 2018. The campaign finance data for the report are from the National Institute on Money in Politics (NIMP). The report showed the following:

* Women gubernatorial candidates were more likely than men gubernatorial candidates to raise money from small contributions.
* There were no gender differences in how much nonincumbent primary candidates raised. But women primary candidates were more likely than men primary candidates to have held prior office. This may mean that women need to be more credentialed to be monetarily competitive.
* No gender differences were found in the money raised by general election candidates. This similarity between women's and men's receipts should be encouraging news for women potential candidates.
* Women of color gubernatorial candidates were outnumbered by non-Hispanic white women candidates. Moreover, women of color raised less than non-Hispanic white women.

It also included the following findings about donors:

* Men outnumbered women as donors to primary and general election gubernatorial candidates.
* Men provided a larger share of contributions than women to primary and general election gubernatorial candidates.
* Women were better represented as contributors to Democratic than Republican gubernatorial candidates. Within both parties, women were usually more likely than men to give to women candidates.

Source: Sanbonmatsu, Rogers, and Gothreau, Money Hurdle in the Race for Governor.

While the report authors did not make a direct connection, they speculated that gender and race inequalities in income and wealth may contribute to the dearth of women gubernatorial candidates.

Statewide executive campaigns, and gubernatorial campaigns especially, are expensive and rising in cost. If party gatekeepers and donors lack confidence in women's fundraising ability, women candidates may be deterred from running. The scarcity of women of color in gubernatorial races and the lower total receipts of women of color candidates compared with non-Hispanic white women point to additional challenges in accomplishing diversity at the gubernatorial level.

CHILDCARE AND CAMPAIGN FINANCE

One of the persistent challenges for women in politics is family responsibilities. Research finds that women state legislators are less likely than their male counterparts to be parents of young children.[27] Women remain the primary caretakers of children and elderly relatives – caregiving responsibilities that can adversely affect women's economic and political opportunities. But recent election cycles have seen renewed interest in this subject, which may pave the way for more women to run for office in the states in the future.

In the spring of 2018, New York congressional candidate Liuba Grechen Shirley petitioned the Federal Election Commission (FEC) to allow for the use of campaign funds raised to pay for childcare costs that she incurred from her time campaigning for a New York congressional seat. The FEC granted her appeal, stating in Federal Election Commission Advisory Opinion AO 2018–06: "Campaign funds may be used to pay for a candidate's childcare expenses that are incurred as a direct result of campaign activity."[28] The 2018 Shirley ruling only applies to federal level elections, but many state-level candidates have since petitioned to use campaign funds on childcare while running for office in their respective states. Since 2018, seventeen states have allowed childcare as a campaign expense. Seven of these states passed laws via the state legislature, and nine states made changes to campaign finance regulations through administrative statutes, most commonly through state election commissions.[29] Four states (Delaware, Rhode Island, West Virginia, and Iowa)

---

[27] Carroll and Sanbonmatsu, *More Women Can Run.*
[28] Federal Election Commission Advisory Opinion, AO 2018–06: Use of Campaign Funds for Childcare Expenses, www.fec.gov/updates/ao-2018-06-use-campaign-funds-childcare-expenses/
[29] State Candidates and the Use of Campaign Funds for Childcare Expenses, CAWP, 2021, https://cawp.rutgers.edu/use-campaign-funds-childcare-expenses

have considered childcare as a campaign expense but denied or voted against reform.

Childcare can be an issue for men and women candidates who have children, but it has been women candidates who have been vocal about how important these reforms are for mothers, specifically. This topic has gained the attention of many women in politics, including Hillary Clinton, who emphasized the importance of childcare for mothers running for office. Caitlin Clarkson Pereira, a 2018 candidate for the Connecticut House of Representatives, detailed the struggles of campaigning with her daughter: "While I tried to bring her along with me to as many events as possible, it was very hot out, and doing things like knocking on doors with her for quite a few hours at a time was just not feasible."[30] While Clarkson Pereira lost her election, her petition to the Connecticut State Elections Enforcement Commission to use funds for childcare spurred a judicial decision ruling in her favor – setting the precedent that childcare is a valid campaign expense in Connecticut elections.

Many Democratic candidates have championed the issue of childcare as a campaign expense, and Liuba Grechen Shirley is now helping Democratic moms with young children run for office after her experience of running for Congress as a mother. Her political action committee (PAC), called Vote Mama, has supported women candidates at both federal and state levels.[31] While many Democratic women have been making headlines on the subject, the idea that childcare is a legitimate campaign expense is gaining traction among Democrats and Republicans alike. For example, Utah's childcare campaign finance bill was co-sponsored by a Republican senator and passed during the 2019 legislative session, which had a Republican majority.

While there is still much work to be done to ensure that childcare is an allowable campaign expense in all fifty states, the future for campaign finance reform seems bright. In October 2020, the New Jersey state legislature passed a childcare campaign finance bill, making it the seventeenth state to allow it and the seventh to codify it into law. As of 2021, a number of states have bills pending in the state legislature.[32] In 2018, the Massachusetts legislature proposed a bill called the Act Supporting Working Parents Who Choose to Run for Public Office, but it was not

---

[30] Following Lawsuit, Conn. Candidates Now Allowed to Use Campaign Funds for Child Care, WSHU Public Radio, August 31, 2020, https://bit.ly/37ueHEP
[31] Vote Mama PAC: Running for Office Is Just What Mamas Do, www.votemama.org/
[32] State Candidates and the Use of Campaign Funds for Childcare Expenses, CAWP, 2021.

voted on before the end of the session. In 2021, Massachusetts is revisiting this legislation with a new bill after the recently created Campaign Funds and Child Care Commission recommended in a report that the state should allow childcare to be considered a campaign expense.[33] The Virginia House of Delegates has introduced legislation that would prohibit campaign funds from being spent for personal use with the exception of childcare. This proposed law (HB 1299) regulates campaign finance more generally, but it explicitly distinguishes childcare as a legitimate campaign expense and not a personal expense.

The inclusion of childcare as an allowable expense in campaign finance law not only benefits moms running for office, but all working parents. It is also a step that can help close the wealth gap between those who can afford to self-finance their campaigns and those who have limited financial resources when running for office. The cost of running for office has been found to be a barrier to working-class candidates, and authors of a recent study found that, among their sample of women interested in running for office, women who had a responsibility for a majority of their household income were less likely to end up running for office, even though they had expressed ambition to run.[34] While this study is generalizable to only one state and one sample of potential candidates, it highlights the fact that researchers should pay more attention to the structural and financial barriers mothers may face when running for office. Shirley, the candidate who first brought this issue to national attention by asking the FEC to use funds for childcare, highlights the importance of these findings. As she articulated, "Having young children shouldn't disqualify me, or any parent, from running for office, and neither should not being able to afford childcare without an income."[35]

CONCLUSION

Women's gains at the state level in 2018 and 2020 were remarkable. Women surpassed the 30 percent threshold for the first time in state legislative and statewide executive positions in 2021. These election cycles

---

[33] Commonwealth of Massachusetts Special Commission on Campaign Funds and Child Care Commission, https://malegislature.gov/Commissions/Detail/507/191/Bills

[34] Rachel Bernhard, Shauna Shames, and Dawn Langan Teele, To Emerge? Breadwinning, Motherhood, and Women's Decisions to Run for Office, *American Political Science Review* 115(2) (2020), doi.org/10.1017/S0003055420000970

[35] Liuba Grechen Shirley, Want Women to Run for Congress? We Need Someone to Watch Our Kids First, *Washington Post*, April 9, 2018, https://wapo.st/2U4ctbY

featured numerous firsts for women of different racial/ethnic and LGBTQ identities. And for the first time, in Nevada, women became the *majority* of a state legislature. The issue of childcare for women candidates has achieved new prominence.

At the same time, women's gains are arguably several decades behind schedule. Meanwhile, the percentage of governors who are women is stagnant and a state has yet to elect a Black woman or Native American woman as governor. Republican women have set new records in some respects but are failing to gain ground as a share of elected officials from their party. Sufficient financial support remains a more challenging issue for women candidates – particularly for women of color and Republican women.

One of the uncertainties about the future of women's officeholding concerns the medium-term and long-term effects of the COVID-19 pandemic, the accompanying economic crisis, and remote schooling. Women's labor-force participation contributes to women candidates' political and financial networks as well as women's status as donors. The direct and indirect consequences of the downturn in women's labor-force participation remains to be seen.

With the 2022 election cycle underway, new opportunities abound for candidates to achieve new firsts. It is worth remembering that Vice President Kamala Harris previously served as California's attorney general. Thus, the states are critical to watch not only for important policy decisions but also for future congressional and presidential candidates.

10 Supporting Women Candidates: The Role of Parties, Women's Organizations, and Political Action Committees

When Shirley Chisholm ran for and won her seat in the 12th congressional district in New York in 1968, she did so without support from the Democratic Party. Undeterred by her party's snub, Representative Chisholm joined the crowded field of Democrats who sought the party's nomination for president in 1972. Though she failed to secure the nomination that eventually went to George McGovern, Chisholm received over 150 delegate votes – about 10 percent of the total votes. Chisholm would serve through seven Congresses, during which she served as a founding member for both the Congressional Black Caucus (1971) and the Congressional Women's Caucus (1977). Like many women who have sought elected office without party support, Chisholm found her own way to political power and drew on her own counsel to other women: "If they don't give you a seat at the table, bring a folding chair."[1] Given the lackluster efforts from both parties to recruit women candidates as well as the candidate-centered nature of campaigns in the United States, women's organizations and political action committees have served as a figurative "folding chair" for women to gain entry to a place at the table of elected office.

This chapter examines the role that political parties, women's organizations, and women's political action committees (PACs) play in the recruitment and support of women to federal office. First, I examine the structure of the national Democratic and Republican parties and what party organizations do to assist candidates to run for office under their party label. I also examine attitudes about women's political participation and office-holding through the lens of Democratic and Republican party activists and how much (or whether) those attitudes have changed over time. Next,

---

[1] Office of the Historian, United States House of Representatives, s.v. "Chisholm, Shirley Anita," https://history.house.gov/People/Listing/C/CHISHOLM,-Shirley-Anita-(C000371)/

I assess the work of many women's organizations that encourage women to run and often provide training for them to do so. Indeed, many women's organizations were created to demand more women's representation from the parties who had consistently proved reluctant to include women. Finally, I identify the contributions of women's PACs and the campaign finance networks available to Democratic and Republican women candidates. Again, women's PACs organized to provide women candidates with a funding source given the lacking or modest (and late) financial support made available by national party organizations to women candidates. After reading this chapter it becomes evident that while both parties have made some improvements in their efforts to recruit, support, and fund promising women candidates, these efforts are relatively recent and not especially impressive. Moreover, the training resources from women's organizations and the campaign finance networks available to women Democrats far exceed those available to women Republicans. Stated another way, if women are underrepresented as candidates and officeholders, Republican women are especially underrepresented because they do not have access to the same training and funding resources provided to Democratic women by women's organizations and PACs. The uneven status of these networks holds important implications for women as parties compete to capture or expand majority party status in the Congress.

Research has identified political parties as having three distinct components: party in the electorate, party organization, and party in government.[2] Party in the electorate refers to voters, who ultimately select a party's candidate in party primaries and determine which candidate emerges victorious in general elections. Party organization refers to the internal structure of the political parties that organize the party apparatus at local, state, and national levels and the people active within those structures that provide a link between candidates for office and the people who vote for them. And, party in government refers to elected and sometimes appointed individuals who run for office under a given party label and occupy that position of power. Even before women earned the right to vote they fought to be included within the parties and their organizational structures. These early efforts were most successful at the party-in-the-electorate level as post-suffrage both the Democratic Party and the Republican Party worked to "bind fast the loyalty of women" to vote for their preferred party and also convince their spouses and fellow women partisans to do the same.[3] In the decades that followed, women were also

[2] V. O. Key, *Politics, Parties, and Pressure Groups* (New York: Thomas Y. Crowell, 1942).

involved in the Democratic and Republican party organizations to promote civic improvement, but were largely absent from leadership positions within the party structures, and even more so as candidates for elected office. Indeed, as will be discussed later in this chapter, women's organizations formed their own groups and fundraising efforts out of a frustration with the gatekeeping by men in both parties and a demand for more women's representation as party leaders and candidates.[4] In the contemporary political era, parties have sought to welcome new members into their fold and keep existing partisans under an inclusive, "big tent" philosophy. Even so, the organizational structure and leadership composition of the Democratic and Republican national parties matter tremendously to the network of policy demanders within each party who compete with one another to determine the issues and candidates the party formally embraces.[5] In this first part of the chapter, I explore two components of the party organization for Democrats and Republicans – women's absence as national party leaders and attitudes from party delegates regarding women's political participation – that shape how or even whether women are seen as viable candidates for elected office.

THE ABSENCE OF WOMEN AS LEADERS IN THE NATIONAL PARTY ORGANIZATIONS

Each party has a national organization, the Democratic National Committee (DNC) and the Republican National Committee (RNC), whose purpose it is to work with party structures in each of the fifty states and also to help elect and raise money for the party's presidential nominee. The DNC is composed of the chairs and vice chairs from each state's Democratic Party Committee and more than 200 members elected by party members in the states and territories. The RNC allots three seats for each state for a total membership body of 150 members as specified in the Republican Party's charter; one man, one woman, and the state party chair. Each party also selects a national party chair, who typically serves through a presidential election cycle and may stay on in that position at the request of the party's standard bearer, its presidential nominee. Following his loss in the 2020 election, Donald Trump requested that the current chair, Ronna McDaniel,

---

[3] Jo Freeman, *A Room at a Time: How Women Entered Party Politics* (Lanham, MD: Rowman & Littlefield, 2000), p. 80.
[4] Rosalyn Cooperman and Melody Crowder-Meyer, Standing on Their Shoulders: Suffragists, Women's PACs, and Demands for Women's Representation, *PS: Political Science & Politics* 53(3) (2020): 470–73.
[5] Seth Masket, *The Inevitable Party* (New York: Oxford University Press, 2016).

stay on as NRC chair through the 2024 election cycle.[6] The national party chair is a position of significant prominence and responsibility. In addition to serving as the face of the party, fundraising, and promoting its candidates, the chair is also tasked with the less enjoyable task of frequently "tamping down squabbles" between internal party factions.[7]

Both the DNC and RNC have "Hill committees" that have a separate organizational and campaign finance structure from their national parties and work to recruit and support party candidates in the House and Senate, respectively. Democrats have the Democratic Congressional Campaign Committee (DCCC) and the Democratic Senatorial Campaign Committee (DSCC), and Republicans have the National Republican Congressional Committee (NRCC) and National Republican Senatorial Committee (NRSC). Each party and chamber's congressional campaign committees have tailored their organizations to best suit the needs of incumbent members and the prospective members in which they invest resources.[8] Each of the party's Hill committees names a chair, a current member of the House or Senate, who serves as the point person for his or her party's efforts to secure, retain, or expand the party's majority status. Chairs assemble a Hill leadership team to assist them with candidate recruitment and fundraising for their respective chambers, particularly for targeted races designed to protect vulnerable incumbents from the party or recruit promising candidates to win competitive open seats or defeat vulnerable incumbents from the opposing party. Hill committees have more influence over House and Senate races than the national party conference, especially when they target races, grant campaigns access to national party voter data, make independent expenditures, direct hard money contributions, and coordinate grassroots outreach in local communities.[9] Hill committee chairs wield tremendous authority over how party resources are allocated in House and Senate races, and are credited or blamed depending on how well or poorly the party fares in an election cycle. Successful Hill chairs – whose party gains seats in an election or whose candidates fare better than what was predicted by pundits – often retain their chair status for another election cycle, whereas unsuccessful Hill chairs – whose party loses seats or its majority status – are dismissed in favor of a new chair.

[6] Max Greenwood, Ronna McDaniel Reelected as RNC Chair, *The Hill*, January 8, 2021, https://bit.ly/3iBVYgR

[7] Marjorie Randon Hershey, *Party Politics in America*, 18th ed. (New York: Routledge, 2021), p. 79.

[8] Robin Kolodny, *Pursuing Majorities: Congressional Campaign Committees in American Politics* (Norman, OK: University of Oklahoma Press, 1998).

[9] Paul Herrnson, Costas Panagopoulos, and Kendall Bailey, *Congressional Elections: Campaigning at Home and in Washington*, 8th ed. (Washington, DC: CQ Press, 2019).

Taken together, national and Hill committee chairs occupy prominent positions within their respective parties and serve as key strategists for the party's electoral fortunes in Congress. Tables 10.1 and 10.2 identify

TABLE 10.1 Few women have led National Democratic Party committees, 1999–2022

Election cycle	DCCC chair	DSCC chair	DNC chair
1999–2000	Rep. Patrick Kennedy, RI	Sen. Bob Torricelli, NJ	Ed Rendell, PA
2001–02	**Rep. Nita Lowey, NY**	**Sen. Patty Murray, WA**	Terry McAuliffe, VA
2003–04	Rep. Bob Matsui, CA	Sen. John Corzine, NJ	Terry McAuliffe, VA
2005–06	Rep. Rahm Emanuel, IL	Sen. Chuck Schumer, NY	Howard Dean, VT
2007–08	Rep. Chris Van Hollen, MD	Sen. Chuck Schumer, NY	Howard Dean, VT
2009–10	Rep. Chris Van Hollen, MD	Sen. Bob Menendez, NJ	Tim Kaine, VA
2011–12	Rep. Steve Israel, NY	**Sen. Patty Murray, WA**	**Debbie Wasserman Schultz,* FL**
2013–14	Rep. Steve Israel, NY	Sen. Michael Bennet, CO	**Debbie Wasserman Schultz, FL**
2015–16	Rep. Ben Ray Luján, NM	Sen. Jon Tester, MT	**Debbie Wasserman Schultz,* FL**
2017–18	Rep. Ben Ray Luján, NM	Sen. Chris Van Hollen, MD	Tom Perez, MD
2019–20	**Rep. Cheri Bustos, IL**	**Sen. Catherine Cortez Masto, NM**	Tom Perez, MD
2021–22	Rep. Sean Patrick Maloney, NY	Sen. Gary Peters, MI	Jaime Harrison, SC
Years party committee led by a woman	*Four of 24*	*Six of 24*	*Six of 24*

***Donna Brazile (LA)** twice served as acting DNC chair – in 2011 and again in 2016–17.
Source: Democratic and Republican national committee chair information compiled by author from party websites.

TABLE 10.2 Even fewer women have led National Republican Party committees, 1999–2022

Election cycle	NRCC chair	NRSC chair	RNC chair
1999–2000	Rep. Tom Davis, VA	Sen. Mitch McConnell, KY	Jim Nicholson, CO
2001–02	Rep. Tom Davis, VA	Sen. Bill Frist, TN	Jim Gilmore, VA
2003–04	Rep. Tom Reynolds, NY	Sen. George Allen, VA	Marc Racicot, MT
2005–06	Rep. Tom Reynolds, NY	**Sen. Elizabeth Dole, NC**	Ed Gillespie, VA
2007–08	Rep. Tom Cole, OK	Sen. John Ensign, NV	Mike Duncan, KY
2009–10	Rep. Pete Sessions, TX	Sen. John Cornyn, TX	Michael Steele, MD
2011–12	Rep. Pete Sessions, TX	Sen. John Cornyn, TX	Reince Priebus, WI
2013–14	Rep. Greg Walden, OR	Sen. Jerry Moran, KS	Reince Priebus, WI
2015–16	Rep. Greg Walden, OR	Sen. Roger Wicker, MS	Reince Priebus, WI
2017–18	Rep. Steve Stivers, OH	Sen. Cory Gardner, CO	**Ronna McDaniel, MI**
2019–20	Rep. Tom Emmer, MN	Sen. Todd Young, IN	**Ronna McDaniel, MI**
2021–22	Rep. Tom Emmer, MN	Sen. Rick Scott, FL	**Ronna McDaniel, MI**
Years party committee led by a woman	*Zero of 24*	*Two of 24*	*Six of 24*

Source: Democratic and Republican national committee chair information compiled by author from party websites.

who served in these leadership roles for the Democratic and Republican parties, respectively, since the 2000 congressional election cycle (1999–2000) and how (in)frequently women and people of color have served in these leadership positions. Even as Richard Fox in Chapter 8 details how the number of women Democratic and Republican congressional candidates has increased significantly in 2018 and 2020, the electoral default for congressional candidates remains a man versus man matchup. Moreover, most of those individuals serving in congressional party leadership have been white men with people of color and/or women significantly underrepresented. That women have not usually served at the helm of *either* party's recruitment efforts provides some additional insight as to why women's representation in federal elective office ticks upward at a modest rate.

Looking at the names of national party and Hill committee chairs for both parties, it is apparent that women partisans are infrequently tapped for these positions. Women have served at least once in each of the three main party leadership roles for the Democratic Party, but men have typically been named to these positions. Interestingly, Representative Debbie Wasserman Schultz (FL) served as DNC chair during Barack Obama's 2012 reelection bid and also in 2016 when Hillary Clinton won the party's nomination for president. Political strategist Donna Brazile, who is African American, twice served as interim DNC chair during Representative Wasserman Schultz's tenure. Rep. Cheri Bustos, DCCC chair in the 2020 election cycle, resigned her leadership position in November 2020 after Democrats lost seats and narrowed their majority party status. Senator Catherine Cortez Masto (NM), the first Latina to serve as DSCC chair, stepped down from this position following the 2020 elections that resulted in Democrats winning majority party control, citing her intention to focus on her own reelection bid in 2022.[10] Cortez Masto is succeeded by Senator Gary Peters (MI), who narrowly won reelection in 2020.

For Republicans, even fewer women have served in these leadership roles. Indeed, there have been more Republican members of Congress named Tom (four of them!) who have served as NRCC chair than *all* of the Republican women who have served in a party leadership capacity. To date, no Republican woman House member has served as NRCC chair. However, it is important to note that since 2018, Republican women have served as NRCC recruitment chair, the person specifically tasked with helping the NRCC chair recruit Republican House candidates. Representative Elise Stefanik (NY) served as recruitment chair in 2018 (the first Republican woman House member to do so), now retired Representative Susan Brooks (IN) served in 2020, and current NRCC chair Tom Emmer (MN) recently named Representative Carol Miller (WV) as recruitment chair for the 2022 cycle.[11] Representative Miller should have cause to work to increase the

[10] Humberto Sanchez, Cortez Masto Launches 2022 Re-election Bid, *Nevada Independent*, February 24, 2021, https://thenevadaindependent.com/article/cortez-masto-launches-2022-re-election-bid

[11] Michael McAdams, NRCC Announces Deputy and Vice Chairs for 2022, NRCC press update, February 11, 2021, www.nrcc.org/2021/02/11/nrcc-announces-deputy-and-vice-chairs-for-2022-cycle/

number of Republican women House candidates running in 2022. After all, Representative Miller was the *only* first-term Republican woman elected to the House in 2018 and joined thirty-five first-term Democratic women House members elected that year.[12]

An examination of party leadership roles in the Democratic and Republican national party organizations makes clear that both parties need to do a much better job of diversifying who serves in these important and visible leadership roles beyond the default white male partisan.[13] The absence of women and minorities from these positions means that they are largely absent as party messengers, fundraisers, and recruiters. And, their absence not only impacts the Democratic and Republican national party organizations but outreach to prospective candidates as the extant research on gender, race, ethnicity, party, and candidate recruitment makes clear that men in the party do not often see women and minorities as viable or attractive candidates.[14]

PARTY ACTIVISTS AND ATTITUDES ABOUT WOMEN'S POLITICAL PARTICIPATION

Having chronicled the general absence of women in party leadership roles within both the Democratic and Republican national party organizations, I turn my attention to another important component of the party politics – its activists. Here I examine the role that party delegates play in the party structure and their attitudes about women's political candidacy and participation more broadly. As a bridge between voters and candidates, party

---

[12] Daniel DeSimone, Results: Women Candidates in the 2018 Election, Center for American Women and Politics (hereafter CAWP), 2018, https://cawp.rutgers.edu/sites/default/files/resources/results_release_5bletterhead5d_1.pdf

[13] A cursory examination of the party organizations designed to elect partisans to state executive positions – the Democratic Governors Association (DGA) and Republican Governors Association (RGA) – reveals similar trends regarding women's relative absence in these leadership roles during this same time period. The DGA had eighteen chairs from 2000 to 2021. Four of them have been women: Gov. Kathleen Sebelius (KS), 2007; Gov. Christine Gregoire (WA) 2009; Gov. Gina Raimondo (RI), 2019; and Gov. Michele Lujan Grisham (NM) 2021. The RGA had twenty-two chairs in 2000–21. One woman, Gov. Susana Martinez (NM), served as RGA chair in 2015–16.

[14] Richard L. Fox and Jennifer Lawless, If Only They'd Ask: Gender, Recruitment, and Political Ambition. *Journal of Politics* 72(2) (2010): 310–26; Susan Carroll and Kira Sanbonmatsu, *More Women Can Run: Gender and Pathways to the State Legislatures* (New York: Oxford University Press, 2013); Melody Crowder-Meyer, Gendered Recruitment without Trying: How Local Party Recruiters Affect Women's Representation, *Politics & Gender* 9(4) (2013): 390–413.

activists help determine the issues a party champions and shape the candidates who run for office under their party's label. Their attitudes toward women's political participation shed light on whether the demands made by party groups include demands for more women's representation.

Every four years the Democratic and Republican parties each host a national convention where thousands of delegates, typically selected by parties in the states, adopt their party's national platform on issues and formally nominate the party's presidential and vice presidential candidates. Since its 1972 convention, the DNC adopted several reforms to the nomination process, and with the goal of making it more inclusive. Of particular relevance to women is the provision that delegates to the convention be equally divided between men and women.[15] As a result, in every national convention, including the most recent one held virtually in 2020, women have comprised at least half of the membership count for Democratic delegates. By contrast, the language in the Republicans' charter on delegate membership is more of a recommendation than a mandate, as "each state shall endeavor to have equal representation of men and women in its delegation to the Republican National Convention."[16] In practice, the membership count for Republican women delegates has fallen far short of that lofty goal. During the virtual roll call at the 2020 Republican convention, where delegates from each state presented votes for the party nominee, three-quarters of the Republican presenters were male, and the overwhelming majority of them were white.[17] Surveys of the gender, racial, and ethnic composition of party delegates from previous years' conventions affirms that since 1972 delegates to the Democratic national conventions are significantly more diverse than their Republican counterparts.

There are additional measures of party delegates that are instructive. The Convention Delegate Study (CDS), a survey of Democratic and Republican convention delegates, has been conducted in nearly every presidential election cycle since 1972. As new delegates are folded into the party framework along with returning delegates, we observe changes in the internal divisions within the parties and the types of demands party

[15] Democratic National Committee, The Charter and the Bylaws of the Democratic Party of the United States, August 25, 2018, https://democrats.org/wp-content/uploads/2018/10/DNC-Charter-Bylaws-8.25.18-with-Amendments.pdf

[16] Republican National Committee, Call of the 2020 Republican National Convention, November 20, 2019, https://prod-cdn-static.gop.com/media/documents/2020_RNC_Call_of_the_Convention_1575665975.pdf

[17] Philip Bump, Like the Democrats', the Republican Delegate Roll Call Offered a Specific Portrait of the Party, *Washington Post*, August 24, 2020, https://wapo.st/3s8JXmo

coalitions articulate. The CDS surveys delegates about their party-related activities, attitudes about various issues and groups, and preferences for specific candidates. The delegates are also asked a set of questions pertaining to women's political participation. Table 10.3 lists these survey questions and the percentage of Democratic and Republican delegates

TABLE 10.3 Democratic Party delegates have more supportive attitudes toward women's political participation than Republican Party delegates: 1992, 2004, 2012, 2016 (% who strongly and mostly agree)

Question	1992		2004		2012		2016	
	Dems	*GOPs*	Dems	*GOPs*	Dems	*GOPs*	Dems	*GOPs*
Women are underrepresented among political leaders because they have fewer opportunities than men to prepare for leadership positions.	66.3	*28.3*	55.7	*15.9*	58.2	*10.3*	75.6	*8.4*
Most men in the party organization try to keep women out of leadership roles.	35.4	*17.2*	21.8	*8.3*	21.2	*6.6*	32.1	*4.3*
It is almost impossible to be a good wife and mother and hold public office too.	13.8	*23.6*	8.6	*14.9*	7.8	*10.1*	3.6	*4.4*
Most men are better suited emotionally for politics than are most women.	3.8	*11.1*	2.7	*11.9*	1.2	*7.4*	1.1	*4.4*

Note: Values indicate the percentage of Democratic and Republican party delegates who mostly agree or strongly agree with a given statement. Response rates for delegates by party and year during this period range from 17 to 25 percent for Democrats and 15 to 22 percent for Republicans.

Source: 1992, 2004, 2012, and 2016 CDS; averages compiled by the author.

who responded they "strongly agreed" or "mostly agreed" with the specified statements in the four most recent CDS surveys.[18]

Table 10.3 reveals important differences in attitudes among Democratic
and Republican delegates regarding women's political participation. When
asked about women's underrepresentation as political leaders, Democratic
delegates in each of these four time points are significantly more likely
than Republican delegates to agree that women have fewer opportunities.
Interestingly, this sentiment is strongest among Democratic delegates in
the 2016 study, when Hillary Clinton secured the party's nomination for
president over Vermont's Senator Bernie Sanders. In contrast, over this
same time period Republican delegates moved away from agreement and
toward disagreement with the statement about why women are underrepresented among political leaders. In other words, Democratic and
Republican delegates fundamentally differ in their opinions about opportunities available to women to emerge as political leaders.

Next, delegates were asked about efforts to keep women out of leadership roles within the party organization. Again, Democratic and Republican
delegates hold significantly different opinions about whether men in the
party gatekeep women from these leadership roles. Democratic delegates
are more likely to agree that men keep women out of leadership roles
whereas a significantly smaller percentage of Republican delegates agree
with this statement. Taken together, these first two questions speak to
structural questions about party organizations, specifically, how the rules
of the game are structured to encourage or discourage women's leadership. Here Democratic delegates, men and women, believe that the structure of the political system inhibits women's political opportunities,
whereas Republican delegates, men and women, disagree.

The third question asks delegates whether women can fulfill marital
and family responsibilities and hold public office (a question that has
never been asked of men in the CDS). At its essence, this question measures delegates' attitudes about whether women can deviate from traditional caregiving roles. Over time, the percentage of delegates in both
parties who agree with this statement has steadily decreased. One hopes
that the willingness of delegates to reject this statement is a product of the
many examples of women in both parties – wives and mothers – who
serve capably as officeholders.

---

[18] The most recent CDS surveyed Democratic and Republican delegates who attended the
2016 party nominating conventions. There was no CDS in 2008, and the 2000 CDS did
not include the referenced questions on women's political participation.

The last question asks respondents whether men are better suited emotionally for politics than women. This question may seem anachronistic in asking about women's emotional fitness (this question has also never been asked of men in the study), but it addresses a fundamental concern about fitness to serve in an elected or leadership role. Again, delegates from both parties generally disagree with this statement, but Democratic delegates are significantly more likely to disagree compared to Republican delegates.

Taken together, differences between Democratic and Republican party delegates in their attitudes regarding women's political participation and fitness to serve are revealing. Whereas the first two questions ask delegates about the *structure* of the party and political systems, the second two questions ask delegates about the *fitness of women* and their ability to fulfill nontraditional gender roles. Democratic delegates are more likely to blame the system for limiting women's opportunities and reject the idea that women are less well suited to serve. In contrast, Republican delegates reject the idea that the system is to blame for limiting women's opportunities even as they generally reject – although not as strongly as Democrats – the belief that women are less well suited to serve in politics.

Recall that party delegates serve as a bridge between voters and party candidates. Democratic delegates are more likely than Republicans to believe that the problem is the system, not women. Whether Democratic delegates have sought to change the rules of the game to make it easier for women to lead is a fair question, to be sure. At the same time, Republican delegates do not view the structure of the political system as a limiting factor for women. These attitudes among party delegates matter because they impact the types of demands delegates place on their party leaders, who ascends to positions of authority, and what type of candidates win support from the party faithful. Research on political candidacy makes clear that parties can and do influence the willingness of prospective women candidates to throw their hats in the ring. And, this enthusiasm or reluctance registers in party primaries and in campaign financing, which in turn have real implications for the success of women candidates.

In the second part of this chapter I assess the work of many women's organizations that encourage women to run and that train them to build professional campaigns. Women's organizations, created for the very purpose of promoting women's participation in politics, are well suited to channel civic involvement into political candidacy. After all, they evolved separately from political parties as a response to both parties' inattention to women as candidates and party leaders.

WOMEN'S GROUPS AS THE ORIGINAL PEER MENTORS FOR WOMEN CANDIDATES

Women's candidate training groups are especially important as campaigns in the United States are candidate, not party, centered.[19] As we learned in the previous section, party organizations, particularly Hill committees, play an important role in campaigns, especially when they target races and direct resources to party candidates in congressional districts or states. But targeted races comprise a fraction of federal elections in any given cycle, and individual candidates – incumbents, candidates for open seats with no incumbent running, and challengers alike – are expected to assemble their own organizational, communication, and fundraising teams. Moreover, research shows it is candidates, not parties, that bear the majority of start-up costs associated with a campaign.[20] And a number of women's organizations have evolved to stand at the ready to provide women guidance and support. In this regard women's groups are the original peer mentors; they bring women together to share their experiences and expertise to create networks of connection and opportunity. Many women's organizations that dominated during the women's movement of the 1960s and 1970s organized around two central ideas: support for the Equal Rights Amendment (ERA) and reproductive rights for women. To this day several women's groups that provide candidate training expect trainees to affirm support for abortion rights as a precondition for participation in their programs, even as many groups provide training for women that is nonpartisan and/or otherwise issue neutral. The types of groups that offer campaign training to women, and the assumptions that prospective women candidates have about them, is another important component of women's political candidacy.

WOMEN'S CAMPAIGN GROUPS AS "CAPACITY BUILDERS" FOR WOMEN CANDIDATES

A previous edition of this book identified the work of women's organizations as engaged in "capacity-building efforts" to get girls and women to see themselves as political leaders.[21] Women candidate groups (WCGs)

---

[19] Gary Jacobson and Jaime Carson, *The Politics of Congressional Elections*, 10th ed. (Lanham, MD: Rowman & Littlefield, 2020).

[20] Shauna Shames, *Out of the Running: Why Millennials Reject Political Careers and Why It Matters* (New York: New York University Press, 2017).

[21] Barbara Burrell, Political Parties and Women's Organizations, in *Politics & Gender*, ed. Susan Carroll and Richard Fox, 4th ed. (New York: Cambridge University Press, 2018), p. 243.

are an important part of women's paths to public office because they create an opportunity structure, sometimes within, but often outside of the Democratic and Republican parties. WCGs create spaces for women to not just visualize but to build successful political candidacies. They identify and strengthen networks between women, political practitioners, the voters they seek to represent, and, in some instances, donors who will fund them. This section provides a brief overview of women campaign groups and their work to move women to campaign-ready status. I consider the breadth and scope of training groups offer, and why WCGs are particularly likely to serve women who run for office as Democrats. What is demonstrated is that the relationship between women's groups and women's PACs is a close one, and the advantages that accrue to Democratic women by way of candidate training remain in place with the campaign finance networks that fund their candidacies.

In the decades that followed the ratification of the Nineteenth Amendment, women's political participation diversified and focused on bipartisan activism to improve women's economic and political positions.[22] The three main women's groups that emerged in the 1960s – the National Organization for Women (NOW), National Women's Political Caucus (NWPC), and Women's Campaign Fund (WCF) – adopted a pro-ERA stance and worked to bring women into positions of authority and leadership to serve as a counterweight to leaders in the Democratic and Republican parties who ignored them. NWPC cofounder Gloria Steinem laid bare the following goal: "Our aim would be to humanize society by bringing the values of women's culture into it, not simply to put individual women into men's politics."[23] NOW, NWPC, and the WCF recruited and endorsed women who pledged support for issues including the ERA, federally subsidized childcare, and abortion rights. Their candidate recruitment and training efforts were closely tied to the modest financial support they provided to endorsed candidates. The work of these organizations on behalf of women candidates set the stage for the eventual creation of other women's PACs, including the pro-choice, Democratic women's PAC heavyweight, EMILY's List, which endorses and funds progressive women candidates and makes a party-specific demand for more women's representation.

Table 10.4 is a partial listing of national WCGs that offer campaign training programs for women at any stage of the candidacy process. The groups on

---

[22] Annelise Orleck, *Rethinking American Women's Activism* (New York: Routledge, 2014).

[23] David Dismore, Today in Feminist History: The National Women's Political Caucus (July 12, 1971), *Ms. Magazine*, July 12, 2020, https://msmagazine.com/2020/07/12/feminist-history-july-12/

TABLE 10.4 Partial listing of national women candidate groups (WCGs)

WCGs for progressive/ Democratic women	Nonpartisan/issue- neutral WCGs	WCGs for Conservative/ Republican women
Emerge America	Black Girls Vote	Campaign Management
EMILY's List/Run to Win	Courage to Run	School* – National
First Ask	Elect Her Campus	Federation of
Higher Heights	Women Win –	Republican Women
Rise to Run	AAUW and	Catalyst PAC*
	Running Start	Elevate PAC
	IGNITE – Boss Ladies	GOPAC*
	LBJ Women's Campaign	Women's Public
	School	Leadership Network
	NWPC Candidate	
	Training	
	Ready to Run	
	Running Start	
	She Should Run	
	Women's Campaign	
	Fund – 5050x2028	
	Yale Women's Campaign	
	School	
	Vote Run Lead	

*Male candidates are eligible to participate in the training provided by these organizations.

Source: CAWP, Women's Political Power Map, list compiled by the author.

this list are identified by the Center for American Women and Politics (CAWP) and appear on its Women's Political Power Map. I divide them into two main categories, namely WCGs that provide training for partisans – progressive and/or Democrats, and conservatives and/or Republicans – and WCGs that identify themselves as nonpartisan and/or issue neutral in their training programs. I focus on examples from each of these categories to highlight research findings from scholars about WCGs, their impact on women's political candidacy, and why WCGs are more likely to provide candidate training to women seeking elected office as Democrats.

The proliferation of WCGs over the last twenty years has prompted a renewed scholarly focus on their work. A census of these groups – their location, who they serve, and the type of training they provide – and their inclusion in an easily navigable database like the CAWP Women's Political Power Map is a foundational contribution. WCGs exist at both national and state levels. Research on WCGs in the states reveals nearly 400 groups active in forty-eight states, with a majority of those groups providing candidate training that is nonpartisan or issue neutral. Indeed, when looking at the list of national WCGs, we also see that the nonpartisan/issue neutral groups are most abundant. However, at state level the nonpartisan group identification is a nominal one as "nearly three-fourths of active WCGs in our sample have an abortion litmus test for which potential candidates they will support."[24] The national WCGs identified as "nonpartisan or issue neutral" in Table 10.4 do not mention the issue of abortion or reproductive rights on their websites, and instead focus their messaging on themes of women's underrepresentation, demystifying the campaign process, and the importance of giving women tools to become more involved as political and community leaders.

This work of educating prospective candidates about the mechanics of campaigns and the actual work officeholders perform is especially important for women considering a political candidacy. Research shows that women's political ambition increases when the pitch to run is focused on fixing problems and improving communities.[25] Similarly, WCG training sessions increase women's confidence in their leadership skills and boost their interest in running by emphasizing the communal goals associated with public service – that holding office is about helping people, not just attaining power.[26]

In addition to messaging that is tailored to pique women's interest in running for office, WCGs vary widely in the depth and breadth of training they provide to candidates. Pre-COVID, several of these groups had at least some of their programming available online, often with a "go at your own pace" series of self-directed workshops for women who had other part- or full-time work and/or care responsibilities. She Should Run, a nonpartisan training group, sponsors the "Incubator" online project that women complete on their own schedule. Another She Should Run project, "Road to Run," is a four-part series offered over nine months and features training on topics like "fundraising and networking," and "building your brand."[27] Looking at partisan women's training groups, EMILY's

---

[24] Rebecca Kreitzer and Tracy Osborn, Women Candidate Recruitment Groups in the States, in *Good Reasons to Run*, ed. Shauna Shames et al. (Philadelphia, PA: Temple University Press, 2020), p. 185.

[25] Sue Thomas and Catherine Wineinger, Ambition for Office: Women and Policy-making, in *Good Reasons to Run*, ed. Shames et al., p. 78.

[26] Monica Schneider and Jennie Sweet-Cushman, Pieces of Women's Political Ambition Puzzle: Changing Perceptions of a Political Career with Campaign Training, in *Good Reasons to Run*, ed. Shames et al., p. 203.

[27] Consider a Run for Office, She Should Run, https://sheshouldrun.org/

List's "Run to Win" program provides a free, half-day virtual training for Democratic pro-choice women as well as an "Ignite Change Fellowship," an eight-week virtual training program for participants that includes one-on-one meetings with EMILY's List training staff.[28] Higher Heights, an organization designed to "strengthen Black women's leadership capacity," offers a webinar series called #BlackWomenLead.[29] This series is created by Black women political consultants and officeholders and is expressly designed for prospective Black women candidates at any level of office. For conservative women, the Women's Public Leadership Network, a nonpartisan organization that provides training for "center and right-leaning women," offers a free video library with learning modules and worksheets for trainees.[30] During the height of the COVID-19 pandemic, WCGs shifted their training programs wholly online, which has the added benefit of reducing the cost of attending an on-site training session for trainees as well as the host organizations.

The perception of who WCGs are designed to assist is another challenge they face. While the majority of these groups – at both national and state levels – identify as nonpartisan, extant research suggests that these training opportunities may benefit women Democrats more than their Republican counterparts. Perception is definitely a part of the problem. Many Republican women candidates assume that candidate training programs sponsored by women's groups are for progressive women candidates, even when the organizations explicitly indicate they are nonpartisan and issue-neutral.[31] This erroneous assumption likely deters some Republican women candidates who are interested in candidate training programs, which presumably leaves openings for women candidates who are not concerned about the prospect of hearing left or left-of-center messaging that may or may not be a part of the training curriculum.

Another reason that WCGs may advantage Democratic women over Republican women candidates is based on the very practices of WCGs on the right. WCGs for conservative and Republican women invite men to participate in their training programs. The Campaign Management School, sponsored by the National Federation of Republican Women (NFRW), offers

---

[28] The EMILY's List Ignite Change Fellowship – Information and FAQs, EMILY's List, https://emilyslist.org/pages/entry/ignite-change-fellowship

[29] Higher Heights Political Leadership Training Webinar Series, Higher Heights for America, www.higherheightsforamerica.org/webinars/

[30] It's Your Time to Lead, Women's Public Leadership Network, https://training.womenspublicleadership.net/

[31] Malliga Och, Political Ambition, Structural Obstacles, and the Fate of Republican Women, in *Good Reasons to Run*, ed. Shames et al., p. 42.

a nine-part series that covers topics including "creating a campaign budget, strategy and message development, opposition research, and fundraising" and that "All Republicans – both women and men – are welcome to attend."[32] The inclusion of Republican men in the Campaign Management School is in keeping with a central objective of the NFRW to "recruit, train, and elect Republican candidates" instead of a more specific, group-based claim directed to aid Republican women. This strategy is also consistent with the Republican Party's strategy that discourages the intentional recruitment of Republican women candidates more broadly and is summarized by Representative Anne Wagner (R-MO), who "wants a GOP win first and a GOP woman second. If it can get both, it's a two-fer."[33]

Taken together, WCGs provide important services to women. Their messaging is inclusive and designed to normalize the idea of women's political candidacy. Their programming frames officeholding through a communal lens of helping others and solving problems that is appealing to women and rejects the idea that serving in an elected capacity is a power grab. WCGs are abundant at both national and state levels, and increasingly offer training options that are accessible, affordable, and as basic or comprehensive as is desired by the trainee. But the perception of WCGs among some women partisans is that they are geared to women Democrats. The practice of most right-leaning training groups of serving men and women further limits opportunities for Republican women to take part in candidate training that is tailored to them. When looking at the activities of progressive and conservative women's PACs and their strategies of directing funds to women candidates, we see similar trends in play that advantage women Democrats and hurt women Republicans.

WOMEN'S PACS ARE POLICY DEMANDERS FOR MORE WOMEN CANDIDATES

The final way in which parties and women's organizations impact women's candidacy is by providing financial support to endorsed candidates. When thinking about the relationship between political parties, women's organizations, and women candidates, it is important to recall that campaigns are candidate, not party, centered. Essentially, candidates are

---

[32] Campaign Management School, National Federation of Republican Women, www.nfrw .org/cms

[33] Malliga Och, The Grand Old Party of 2016, in *The Right Women: Republican Party Activists, Candidates, and Legislators*, ed. Malliga Och and Shauna Shames (Denver, CO: Praeger Press, 2018), p. 11.

in charge of their own campaigns, and this has traditionally meant that a successful campaign is a well-financed campaign. Thus, a strong funding base for campaigns is the abiding goal. Campaigns are also candidate focused because political parties typically do not endorse candidates in party primaries, particularly when those primaries are contested. The decision of parties to stay out of primaries is costly for women candidates. Research shows that women congressional candidates are more likely than men to run in a race with a contested primary.[34] Because candidates must often first win a primary election to compete in the general election, they must build a strong funding base and build it early. This need creates an ideal opening for women's PACs to take root and flourish, and to demand more women's representation.

In this section a brief history of women's PACs is presented, and we will evaluate the campaign finance networks, now distinctly party specific, they have developed. Using the 2020 congressional elections – a cycle that proved to be very successful for Republican women House candidates – as an example, I detail fundraising activities of the most prolific women's PACs and consider the strategies they employed to boost the campaigns of their preferred candidates. While the breadth of financial support available to women Democratic candidates still far exceeds what is made available to Republican women, some conservative women's PACs have begun to recognize the importance of providing early financial support to Republican women during the primary election phase – a strategy pioneered by EMILY's List to great effect for Democratic women. Here we see that women's PACs have proven to be an essential source of funding for women candidates, particularly Democratic women, as donors who give to progressive women's PACs do so explicitly to demand more progressive women's representation. An additional important consideration here is the willingness of liberal interests to engage in group-specific representation demands of the Democratic Party. This means that in addition to progressive women's PACs there exist even more specialized PACs such as LPAC and Higher Heights for America, which recruit, endorse, and fund LGBTQ women and Black women, respectively. And, since its founding, EMILY's List has frequently endorsed and funded LGBTQ women and women of color. While conservative PACs with group-specific claims, such as the pro-*Roe* Republicans for Choice and the

---

[34] Jennifer Lawless and Kathryn Pearson, The Primary Reason for Women's Underrepresentation? Reevaluating the Conventional Wisdom, *Journal of Politics* 70(1) (2008): 67–82.

LGBTQ-friendly Log Cabin Republicans, have worked to support preferred candidates in previous election cycles, presently there are no conservative interests on the right that make these kinds of group-specific representation demands. As conservative women's PACs continue to grow, they will need to navigate how to demand women's representation while not appearing to make a group-specific demand of their preferred party, which is no small task.

Lackluster efforts by both the Democratic and Republican parties to recruit women candidates for elected office inspired many women's organizations to establish PACs to endorse and fund women candidates. As stated above, NOW, NWPC, and WCF were the original demanders of women's representation. Studies have shown that these groups not only endorsed and funded pro-choice, pro-ERA candidates but also challenged both major parties to back women candidates who supported the ERA and abortion rights.[35] NOW, NWPC, and WCF wanted more progressive women to run for Congress – lose or win – and provided solidarity and financial support to boost their candidacies. The parties had not yet embraced opposing positions on these issues, so these first women's PACs endorsed Democratic and Republican congressional candidates, the majority of whom were women. However, once the Republican Party dropped its support for the ERA and added a pro-life plank to its platform ahead of the 1980 election, the demand for more women's representation evolved into a party-specific demand. Naturally, women's PACs evolved to reflect this changing political context.

The establishment of EMILY's List in 1985, and its plan to recruit, endorse, and fund pro-choice Democratic women candidates, brought with it two important innovations in women's PACs – an emphasis on women's viability as candidates, and a party-specific demand for more women's representation. To earn an EMILY's endorsement, Democratic women candidates had to affirm their support for reproductive rights and abortion, and demonstrate an ability to independently raise funds. It endorsed pro-choice Democratic women ahead of their primaries and bundled together smaller contributions from individual donors to help these women further strengthen and expand their funding bases as their candidacies progressed. This innovation also had the effect of introducing a new group of donors into congressional campaigns – progressive women who had not previously contributed to the Democratic Party and were intentionally demanding

---

[35] Barbara Burrell, *A Woman's Place Is in the House: Campaigning for Congress in the Feminist Era* (Ann Arbor, MI: University of Michigan Press, 1994).

more women's representation by supporting their preferred women candidates.[36] In succeeding elections, EMILY's List has expanded its network to assist viable, pro-choice Democratic women at nearly every stage of their candidacies. Its Run to Win program trains women candidates. Its Political Opportunity Project develops women's candidacies at local and state levels and creates a pipeline of quality Democratic women candidates for Congress. Its traditional. PAC identifies, endorses, and funds Democratic women candidates at the early stages of a campaign ahead of a party's primary, especially when an endorsed candidate faces a contested primary. And, its Women Vote! super PAC raises and spends unlimited amounts of money in independent expenditures that help endorsed candidates facing competitive elections. In summary, EMILY's List has built a resource network that makes it *the* essential women's PAC of progressive women candidates, and an organization that women's organizations and PACs on the right have struggled to replicate with the same degree of success for conservative women candidates.

Noting the success of EMILY's List in both encouraging progressive, diverse women to run for office and building a funding base of donors who will support them, a number of conservative women's groups sought to build their own network to serve as a counterweight for Democratic women. Here I focus on the four most prolific groups – the Susan B. Anthony List, VIEW PAC, Winning for Women, and Elevate PAC (E-PAC) – that recruit and endorse conservative women, the overwhelming majority of whom run as Republicans. These groups vary in their endorsement criteria as well as the resources they provide to preferred candidates.

A key difference between EMILY's List and conservative women's PACs relates to the policy stances that trigger an endorsement from these conservative women's groups. The Susan B. Anthony List, formed in 1992 to "end abortion by electing national leaders and advocating for laws that save lives, with a special calling to promote pro-life women leaders," endorses both male and female pro-life candidates.[37] This criteria also means that pro-life women compete with pro-life men for endorsements and funding. VIEW PAC formed in 1997 to elect "viable Republican women to Congress."[38] Winning for Women formed in 2017 to "support free market conservative women running for federal office." E-PAC was formed

---

[36] Melody Crowder-Meyer and Rosalyn Cooperman, Can't Buy Them Love: How Party Culture Contributes to the Party Gap in Women's Representation, *Journal of Politics* 80(4) (2018): 1211–24.

[37] About page, Susan B. Anthony List, www.sba-list.org/about-susan-b-anthony-list

[38] About page, Value in Electing Women Political Action Committee (VIEW PAC), www.viewpac.org/about

in 2020 by Republican Representative Elise Stefanik (NY), the NRCC's first woman to hold the position of NRCC candidate recruitment chair (in 2018) to "recruit, develop, support, and mentor slates of top tier women Republican candidates who have demonstrated electability and potential for candidate development and growth."[39] The variation in endorsement criteria for conservative women means that some women get endorsed by one or more of these PACs while others do not. For example, Republican US Senator Susan Collins of Maine, who has expressed support for *Roe v. Wade*, which affirms a woman's right to an abortion in the first trimester of a pregnancy, faced a competitive reelection bid in 2020 to serve a fifth term. Senator Collins was endorsed by E-PAC, VIEW PAC, and Winning for Women, but was not endorsed by the Susan B. Anthony List.

Conservative women's PACs also differ from EMILY's List in terms of the timing of when endorsed candidates receive support. The Susan B. Anthony List, VIEW PAC, and Winning for Women have generally been reluctant to endorse or fund women candidates in the primary stage, especially when women run in a contested primary with other fellow partisans. EMILY's List – whose acronym stands for Early Money Is Like Yeast (it makes the dough rise) – is known for its early endorsements. The problem for Republican women, however, is that they typically have more trouble than their Democratic counterparts winning their party primaries, which makes early funding of campaigns even more vital.[40] Indeed, E-PAC founder, Representative Stefanik, retooled her leadership PAC to intentionally fund endorsed Republican women ahead of their party's primaries in 2020. Stefanik's stated intention to "play in primaries" in 2020 was initially met with a rebuke from NRCC chair Tom Emmer (R-MN)[41], however the success of Republican women House candidates in that cycle ultimately proved Stefanik correct about the dividend paid by providing early support to the women she endorsed. Moving forward, it will be interesting to see whether other conservative women's PACs endorse and fund candidates in party primaries more consistently and make a party-specific demand of the Republican Party for more conservative women's representation.

[39] About page, Elevate PAC (E-PAC), https://elevate-pac.com/about/
[40] Shauna Shames, Clearing the Primary Hurdles: Republican Women and the GOP Gender Gap, Political Parity, 2014, www.politicalparity.org/research/primary-hurdles/
[41] Melanie Zanona, Stefanik Fires Back at Incoming NRCC Chairman: "I Wasn't Asking for Permission," *The Hill*, December 18, 2018, https://bit.ly/2VMrKyw

Finally, conservative women's PACs differ from EMILY's List in the breadth and scope of resources available to endorsed candidates. Unlike EMILY's List, which has a development program for pro-choice Democratic women at local and state level thinking about a bid for higher office as well as a candidate training program with different training options for progressive women, none of the four conservative women's PACs profiled here offer candidate training programs for prospective candidates. Conservative women's PACs endorse and fund conservative women but do not train them as candidates. Even though the majority of candidate training programs are nonpartisan or issue-neutral, conservative women often assume these trainings are partisan. That assumption may discourage them from seeking out formal candidate training programs. And, the trainings that are sponsored by Republicans are open to Republican men and women who want to run for office. As such, the training curriculum may not be tailored to include unique challenges that Republican women face. Table 10.5 details information about the five women's PACs included in this inquiry, including their endorsement criteria, the number of women endorsed for the House and Senate, and the money each raised and spent in the 2020 congressional election cycle.

There are two important takeaways from Table 10.5. First, these five women's PACs – one progressive and the other four conservative – vary widely in the number of women House and Senate candidates they endorsed in 2020. This variation in endorsement patterns is relevant since 2020 was a challenging election cycle for many Democratic women freshman incumbents facing competitive reelection bids and a promising election cycle for the largest number of Republican women candidates who filed to run for Congress that year. According to CAWP, 203 of the 356 Democratic women candidates who filed to run for office in 2020 won their party's primaries (85 incumbents, 91 challengers, 27 candidates for open seats), and 94 of the 227 Republican women candidates who filed to run for office won their party's primaries (11 incumbents, 70 challengers, 13 candidates for open seats).[42] EMILY's List endorsed seventy-five Democratic women House candidates, while the number of Republican women House candidates endorsed by the four conservative women's PACs ranged from a high of sixty-two from VIEW PAC to a low of twenty-eight from the Susan B. Anthony List and Winning for Women. And, as the Susan B. Anthony List endorses both men and women pro-life

[42] A Summary of Major Party Primary Candidates for US Senate and US House, 1992–2020, CAWP, 2020, https://cawp.rutgers.edu/sites/default/files/resources/canprimcong_histsum .pdf

TABLE 10.5 Campaign finance activities for selected women's PACs, 2020 elections

Group	Endorsement criteria	Number of women endorsed (House / Senate)	Receipts ($)	Awarded ($)
EMILY's List	Viable, pro-choice Democratic women	75 / 6	80,613,555	79,603,956s
Elevate PAC	Electable Republican female candidates, primary election focus	46 / 4	1,051,719	871,014
Susan B. Anthony List	Pro-life candidates for Congress and high state public office	28 / 4*	1,560,760	1,505,801
VIEW PAC	Qualified, viable Republican women congressional candidates	62 / 8	988,920	972,323
Winning for Women	Free-market conservative women running for federal office	28 / 4	445,509	444,015

*The Susan B. Anthony List also endorsed 29 male Republican House candidates, 1 male Democratic House member, and 12 male Republican Senate candidates.

Source: Expenditure totals and endorsed candidates were compiled by the author from Center for Responsive Politics data and PAC campaign finance reports filed with the Federal Election Commission.

candidates, this PAC actually endorsed more male than female Republican House and Senate candidates that year. Thus, in this election cycle favorable for Republicans, conservative women's PACs actually endorsed fewer Republican women and, in one case, had them compete with Republican men for an endorsement.

The second takeaway from Table 10.5 is the variation in the amount of money raised (receipts) and spent awarded by these women's PACs on behalf of endorsed candidates in 2020. The sheer volume of money raised by EMILY's List, over 80 million dollars, is simply an astonishing figure that speaks to the tremendous support EMILY's List donors are willing to provide to pro-choice Democratic women candidates. Because EMILY's List bundles together small contributions from individual donors to then give to endorsed candidates, it is prohibitively time-consuming to compile a line-item accounting for how much of those receipts went to any given candidate. This remarkable sum does demonstrate the financial power backing the party-specific demand to Democrats for more progressive women's representation. By contrast, the amount of money raised and spent by conservative women's PACs on behalf of endorsed Republican women candidates is not remotely comparable. While the good news for Republicans is that twenty Republican women were newly elected to the House in 2020, conservative women's PACs are still making the financial case for the party-specific demand to the Republican Party for more conservative women's representation.

This disparity in funding available to congressional Democratic and Republican female candidates in 2020 widens even further when examining independent expenditure totals (IEs) for the PACs. Federal campaign finance regulations allow PACs to raise and spend unlimited amounts of money in IEs to support or oppose a given candidate as long as they do not contribute IE funds directly to a candidate's campaign, disclose the source of IE contributions, and do not coordinate messaging or electioneering efforts with a candidate's campaign.[43] PACs use IEs to target campaigns in competitive races in winnable open seats or against vulnerable incumbents. Stated another way, a significant portion of money spent on competitive races comes from independent expenditures, so it is important to consider where this money is directed. Three of the five women's PACs examined here have separate entities that raise and spend IE funds; Women Vote! for EMILY's List, the Women for Women (WFW) Action Fund for Winning for Women, and Women Speak Out for the Susan B. Anthony List. Table 10.6 lists the independent expenditure amounts for these groups and the percentage of those funds that were spent on targeted races in the 2020 congressional elections. I use the Center for Responsive Politics campaign finance data and PAC campaign finance reports filed by these PACs with the Federal Election Commission to disaggregate spending by chamber – whether the money was spent on House or Senate races – to gain a more accurate picture of money flow.

---

[43] Federal Election Commission (FEC), FEC Campaign Guide: Congressional Candidates and Committees, 2014, www.fec.gov/resources/cms-content/documents/candgui/pdf

TABLE 10.6 Independent expenditure (IE) totals and allocation for Women Vote!, Women for Women Action Fund, and Women Speak Out, 2020

Group and affiliation	Total IE raised ($)	% IE spent on House races targeting endorsed female candidates	% IE spent on Senate races targeting endorsed female candidates
Women Vote!? EMILY's List	31,372,168	100	100
WFW Action Fund? Winning for Women	3,353,365	100	100
Women Speak Out? Susan B. Anthony List	8,769,976	48	44

Note: Expenditure totals were compiled by the author from Center for Responsive Politics data and PAC campaign finance reports filed with the FEC.

In 2020, EMILY's List's Women Vote! spent over $31 million on IE funds with about half of that total, $15.3 million, directed to the House and forty-five targeted races featuring Democratic female candidates, the majority of whom were freshman or sophomore members fending off competitive challenges from Republican candidates. The other half of the IE funds, $16 million, was directed at the Senate and ten targeted races. On the Senate side, most of the funds were directed to assist Democratic women challenging Senate Republicans, including Barbara Bollier running for the open Senate seat in Kansas, Sara Gideon running against Senator Susan Collins of Maine, Teresa Greenfield running against Senator Joni Ernst in Iowa, and MJ Hegar running against Senator John Cornyn in Texas. In fact, Women Vote! spent over $1 million in the Iowa Senate Democratic primary to boost Greenfield over her two fellow Democratic male challengers. Greenfield won the primary but lost the general election to Ernst. Women Vote! spent zero IE funds on House or Senate contests in support of male Democratic candidates. Campaign finance reports indicate it did spend over $5 million (in addition to the total reported in Table 10.6) on the presidential election; however, it is important to note that a central message communicated by those funds was the presence of Kamala Harris on the Democratic ticket as the vice presidential nominee and the opportunity for voters to elect the first woman, and woman of color, to that position.

The Winning for Women Action Fund raised and spent over $3.3 million in IE funds and targeted fifteen House races and four Senate races. It spent about $2.2 million – nearly two-thirds of its funds – on targeted House races, with a significant portion of those funds directed to female Republican candidates challenging incumbent Democrats. The group spent the remaining $1.1 million on targeted Senate races, including Susan Collins' reelection bid. While its IE fundraising totals were much more modest than those of EMILY's List, all of those funds were spent on races targeting endorsed female Republican candidates. In other words, the WFW Action Fund spent zero dollars on races targeting male Republican House or Senate candidates.

Susan B. Anthony List's Women Speak Out directed its IE funds differently from both EMILY's List and the WFW Action Fund. As 2020 was shaping up to be a banner year for Republican women House candidates, Women Speak Out spent nearly $9 million total – over $6 million on Senate races alone – targeting its endorsed pro-life candidates. However, the group spent more than half of its IE funds – 56 percent in the Senate and 52 percent in the House – on races with male Republican candidates. Women Speak Out spent zero IE funds on the Senate race in Maine with Susan Collins, whom they oppose given her support for some abortion rights. Interestingly, Women Speak Out directed about $10,000 to support the reelection of one of the few Democratic pro-life candidates they endorse, Representative Dan Lipinski, of Illinois, who lost his primary election to Democratic challenger Marie Newman, who would go on to win the seat in the general election. According to campaign finance reports, Women Speak Out spent an additional $5 million in IEs beyond what it spent on congressional races to support the reelection bid of Donald Trump, whom the group first endorsed in 2016 after Trump won the Republican Party presidential nomination. When looking at the allocation of IE funds by Women Speak Out, it is clear that women Republicans competed with the men in their party for finite funds from this PAC. By contrast, women Democrats have access to significantly larger amounts of IE funds from progressive women's PACs, and do not have to compete with campaigns of male Democrats to have those IE funds directed their way.

CONCLUSION

Forthcoming elections present opportunities and challenges for women's organizations and PACs in their demands of the Democratic and Republican parties for more women's representation. These groups will continue their efforts to bring the "folding chair" for women to take their rightful seat alongside Democratic and Republican men at the national table of political power. Women candidate training groups can point to gains in women's representation on both sides of the aisle as progress in their vital work to encourage and train women to run for office and to normalize the concept of women seeking elected office and leadership positions. While virtual training does not replicate the energy created by in-person training sessions, the focus on delivering this content online has had the unanticipated benefit of lowering the cost and expanding access to training material for women considering or planning a run for office.

Progressive women's groups and PACs are rightfully celebrating the election of the Biden–Harris ticket and the ascension of Kamala Harris, a multiracial woman, to vice president and president of the Senate. These groups are also quick to note that Senator Harris' historic election laid bare the paucity of Democratic women of color in the US Senate, her departure meaning there are now no African American women serving in the body. EMILY's List and Higher Heights, an organization that recruits Black women candidates and mobilizes Black women voters, advocated to California Governor Gavin Newsom for a Black woman to be appointed to serve the remainder of Harris' term (Newsom appointed California Secretary of State Alex Padilla, thereby giving California its first Latino senator).[44] Glynda Carr, cofounder of Higher Heights, noted that the absence of Black women in the Senate points to "a lack of a clear path."[45] In the meanwhile, EMILY's List, Higher Heights, and other progressive women's groups continue the work to demand more women's representation – particularly for women of color – and raise the money needed to support their candidacies.

For conservative women's groups and PACs, the path forward is more complicated. These groups are also celebrating, in this case the election of twenty Republican women serving a first term in the 117th Congress, as well as the reelection of Republican Senators Susan Collins and Joni Ernst. To be sure Representative Stefanik and Elevate PAC will seek to replicate their success in encouraging and funding Republican women to run for Congress, and to provide that support early in their candidacies. The challenge, however, is that the party is still trying to define itself in a post-Trump era that may alienate prospective women Republican candidates.

---

[44] Jeremy White and Carla Marinucci, Newsom Appoints Alex Padilla to Fill Harris' Senate Seat, *Politico*, December 20, 2020, https://politi.co/3AwKGkg
[45] Errin Haines, There Are No Black Women in the Senate. Will Rep. Terri Sewell Run for a Seat?, *The 19th*, February 23, 2021, https://bit.ly/3xCltTp

On January 13, 2021, Representative Liz Cheney (WY), Republican conference chair, the third highest-ranking House Republican, joined nine of her Republican colleagues to vote in favor of impeaching Donald Trump during his second impeachment trial, stating, "There has never been a greater betrayal by a President of the United States of his office and his oath to the Constitution."[46] The reaction by some fellow Republicans to Representative Cheney's vote was swift. Cheney's own state party voted to censure her; her colleague, Representative Matt Gaetz (R-FL), traveled to Wyoming to encourage a primary challenger to run against her in 2022; and 61 of 145 fellow Republican House members voted to strip Cheney of her position as House Republican conference chair.[47] A few months later that effort was successful as Cheney was relieved of her leadership position by a party voice vote with Elise Stefanik, a Trump loyalist, named as her replacement.[48] The very public efforts by fellow party members to call her conservative and party credentials into question will surely have a chilling effect on any Republican woman thinking about a bid for Congress as a means to help her party move on from Donald Trump. Unless and until conservative women's groups and PACs can make a party-specific demand for more conservative women's representation that the Republican Party will not reject as a group-specific claim, Republican women will continue to lag in their efforts to close the gap between them and their Democratic women colleagues in the House and Senate.

[46] Representative Liz Cheney: I Will Vote to Impeach the President, press release, January 12, 2021, https://cheney.house.gov/2021/01/12/cheney-i-will-vote-to-impeach-the-president/

[47] Barbara Sprunt, House Republicans to Keep Rep. Liz Cheney in Leadership Position, *NPR*, February 3, 2021, www.npr.org/2021/02/03/963613720/house-republicans-to-keep-rep-liz-cheney-in-leadership-position

[48] Nicholas Fandos and Catie Edmondson, House Republicans Have Had Enough of Liz Cheney's Truth-Telling, *New York Times*, May 4, 2021, www.nytimes.com/2021/05/04/us/politics/liz-cheney-trump-republicans.html

11 Gender and Candidate Communication: TV Ads, Websites, and Social Media

Just hours after Democratic presidential nominee Joe Biden announced US Senator Kamala Harris of California as his vice-presidential running mate on August 11, 2020, President Donald Trump reacted at a White House press briefing, repeatedly calling her "nasty" and "horrible."

The next day, the Trump campaign sent out a fundraising email with the subject line "Kamala is HORRIBLE," which quoted the president calling Harris "the meanest, most horrible, most disrespectful, MOST LIBERAL of anyone in the US Senate, and I cannot believe that Joe Biden would pick her as his running mate."[1]

Reaction on Twitter was swift, with many recalling that Trump has demeaned women – especially self-confident, powerful women – for decades. Perhaps most notably, Trump referred to his 2016 Democratic opponent Hillary Clinton as "such a nasty woman" during their final presidential debate.[2] He has called Speaker of the US House of Representatives Nancy Pelosi a "nasty, vindictive, horrible person."[3] As many political commentators have noted, Trump's use of the term "nasty" to describe women is not only sexist but, in the case of Harris – the first woman of color, first Black, and first South Asian to be named a major political party vice-presidential nominee – is also rooted in harmful and racist "angry Black woman" tropes. Harris responded to Trump's August 2020 fundraising email with her own message to Biden supporters: "I know that winning this race will be a tougher challenge than any I've faced in my lifetime, but make no

---

[1] Ed Mazza, Trump Campaign's "Desperate" Email Attack on Kamala Harris Mocked on Twitter, *Huffington Post*, August 13, 2020, https://bit.ly/2U5dbWt

[2] Daniella Diaz, Trump Calls Clinton "a Nasty Woman," CNN, October 20, 2016, https://cnn.it/3CuWWDv

[3] Matthew Choi, Trump Calls Pelosi a "Nasty Vindictive, Horrible Person," *Politico*, June 6, 2019, https://politi.co/3scjzbe

mistake: I'm not afraid of Donald Trump. I've been standing up to Trump and people like him for my entire career."[4]

The 2020 political campaign will be remembered not only for the historic nomination and election of the first female vice president of the United States but also for the unprecedented use of candidate-controlled channels – especially political advertising and social media platforms – to communicate with voters during a worldwide pandemic. In addition to the election of Harris as the first woman vice president, the results of the 2020 election saw women increase their presence in the US Congress from 126 to 143, with 24 women in the Senate and 119 in the House, as well as in state legislatures from 28.9 percent in 2019 to 30.9 percent in 2021.[5]

This chapter focuses on three primary means used by female and male political candidates to communicate with voters – television advertising, websites, and Twitter – with a consideration of the gender differences and similarities documented by research. In today's political campaigns, these communication channels are powerful and important sources of information, not necessarily because they influence voting behavior, although there is some evidence that they do, but because they are controlled by the candidate, unlike debates and other media-mediated avenues. Thus, they provide a means to assess how candidates choose to portray themselves in reaching potential voters.

These campaign communication channels became even more important in the 2020 election cycle as the COVID-19 pandemic greatly impacted the ability of political candidates to reach voters through in-person interactions due to social distancing and other safety precautions. Thus, political candidates relied more on television, the Internet, and social media platforms in 2020 to communicate with potential voters. In examining gender and campaign communication in the 2020 election cycle, this chapter provides examples from the ten most competitive US Senate races featuring women candidates – seven Democrats and five Republicans, including two female versus female contests – and eight men, three Democrats and five Republicans. Races included in the sample, ranked in order of margin of victory, are the Georgia special election runoff and the Arizona, Minnesota, Iowa, Maine, Texas, Mississippi, Kansas, New Hampshire, and Kentucky general elections.

---

[4] Caitlin McFall, Kamala Harris Calls Trump "Serial Predator" in Fundraising Email, *Fox News*, August 12, 2020, https://fxn.ws/3lJBCEp

[5] See Kelly Dittmar, Measuring Success: Women in 2020 Legislative Elections, Center for American Women and Politics (hereafter CAWP), 2021, https://womenrun.rutgers.edu/2020-report

By comparing how female and male political candidates navigate the campaign communication environment, we can see how they choose to present themselves to voters and speculate about the effectiveness of their appeals. Ultimately, examining gender differences in political candidate communication reveals that both women and men are using television and online communication strategies to define their issues and images – sometimes to confront, and at other times to capitalize on, gender stereotypes held by voters and the news media.

Studies analyzing gender-based stereotypes in candidate campaign communication strategies have sorted issues and image attributes into categories – often labeled as "feminine" or "masculine" – based on voter expectations regarding the competency of women and men in handling various issues as well as the personality traits they possess.[6] For example, voters expect that female politicians will be more competent at handling education, health care, senior citizen issues, the environment, and so-called "women's issues" such as equal pay; and that men are more competent on defense/military issues, foreign policy, homeland security, jobs/economy, and crime. Voters also view female political candidates as more empathetic, in touch with the people, honest, and caring, while they see male candidates as tough, action-oriented, confident, and possessing leadership qualities.

POLITICAL ADVERTISING IN 2020

With a highly competitive presidential race, some of the most expensive campaigns for the US Senate in history, and the COVID-19 pandemic that cancelled many in-person candidate events, the 2019–20 election cycle was unprecedented in terms of spending on political advertising. Total spending on political advertising reached $8.5 billion across television, radio, and digital media – 108 percent more than spending in the 2017–18 cycle, which was a record at the time.[7] The $8.5 billion spent on political

---

[6] See Mary C. Banwart, Gender and Candidate Communication: Effects of Stereotypes in the 2008 Election, *American Behavioral Scientist* 54(3) (2020): 265–83, doi.org/10.1177/0002764210381702; Dianne G. Bystrom et al., *Gender and Candidate Communication: VideoStyles, WebStyles, NewsStyles* (New York: Routledge, 2004); Kim L. Fridkin and Patrick J. Kenney, *The Changing Face of American Representation: The Gender of US Senators and Constituent Communications* (Ann Arbor, MI: University of Michigan Press, 2014); and Juliana Menasce Horowitz, Ruth Igielnik, and Kim Parker, Women and Leadership 2018, Pew Research Center, September 20, 2018, www.pewresearch.org/social-trends/2018/09/20/women-and-leadership-2018/

[7] Howard Homonoff, 2020 Political Ad Spending Exploded: Did it Work?, *Forbes*, December 8, 2020, https://bit.ly/3iApPGE

advertising from 2019 to 2020 does not include the $486 million spent in the run up to the two Senate runoff elections in Georgia on January 5, 2021.[8]

Of the ten US Senate races highlighted in this chapter, nine were decided on November 3, 2020, Election Day. Women running in six of these races spent more than $95 million on television advertising from January 2020 through November 3, 2020. Democratic challenger Amy McGrath of Kentucky spent $18.6 million followed by Republican incumbent Martha McSally of Arizona, who spent $17.4 million. Democratic challenger Theresa Greenfield of Iowa spent $15.6 million; Democratic challenger Sara Gideon of Maine spent $11.4 million; Democratic challenger MJ Hegar of Texas spent $10.3 million; and Democrat Barbara Bollier of Kansas spent $7.1 million on TV ads in her open-seat race. All six women lost their races. Republican incumbents Susan Collins of Maine and Joni Ernst of Iowa won their 2020 Senate races over their female Democratic challengers, spending $8.8 million and $6.2 million, respectively, on television advertising in 2020.[9] In the two months prior to the January 5, 2021 runoff elections in Georgia, Republican incumbent Kelly Loeffler spent $47 million on political advertising.[10] She also lost.

An analysis of 236 television ads from the 2020 US Senate races highlighted in this chapter offers examples of how women and men portrayed themselves to voters as to their issues, images, relationships, and dress. These examples help underscore some findings of previous research but also point to changes in how female candidates especially are choosing to present themselves in their television ads.

Research on Female versus Male Candidate Political Ads

Since 1985, numerous journal articles and two books have examined the gendered content of female versus male political ads from the 1964 through the 2016 elections, including presidential candidate Hillary Clinton in 2008 and 2016.[11] Results have been somewhat mixed,

8 Simon Dumenco, Out of Control: Georgia's US Senate Runoff Election Ad Spending Hits $440 Million, *AdAge*, December 11, 2020, https://bit.ly/3CzRY8s

9 Presidential Election Ad Spending Tops $1.5 Billion, Wesleyan Media Project, October 29, 2020, https://mediaproject.wesleyan.edu/releases-102920/

10 Dumenco, Out of Control.

11 See Bystrom et al., *Gender and Candidate Communication*; Fridkin and Kenney, *Changing Face of American Representation*; and Kelly L. Winfrey and James M. Schnoebelen, Running as a Woman (or Man): A Review of Research on Political Communicators and Gender Stereotypes, *Review of Communication Research* 7 (2019): 109–38, doi.org/10.12840/ISSN.2255-4165.020

depending on the year of the election – which can affect the issues emphasized by female and male candidates – as well as the level of the races studied. Some studies have focused on mixed-gender races for one level of office – usually the US Senate or House – while others have included gubernatorial contests. Moreover, many studies do not include the intervening influence of political partisanship on the issues emphasized by Democratic versus Republican candidates, female and male, in their television ads. This can underestimate the association of feminine issues with the Democratic Party and masculine issues with the Republican Party. Also, some important changes that are not as well documented in statistical analyses have been nonetheless notable in how women candidates have embraced gender and racial identities and experiences, including motherhood, in the 2018 and 2020 election cycles.

Research on the content of female versus male political ads increased as more women ran for political office in the 1980s and, especially, the 1990s and twenty-first century. A 2003 study analyzing the content of television commercials of female and male candidates running for governor and the US Congress from 1964 to 1998 found that the emphasis on "masculine issues" – such as the economy, budget/government spending, and defense/foreign policy – decreased over this time period as the focus on "feminine issues" – including education, health care, sex discrimination, and reproductive rights – rose in prominence beginning with the 1992 election.[12]

Studies analyzing the television ads of women[13] and female and male candidates running for the US Senate,[14] as well as in a combination of statewide and congressional races,[15] in the 1980s found that women were more likely to emphasize social issues such as education and health care, whereas men were more likely to focus on economic issues such as taxes. In highlighting their personal traits, women were more likely to

[12] Shauna L. Shames, The "Un-Candidates": Gender and Outsider Signals in Women's Political Advertising, *Women & Politics Journal* 25(1) (2003): 115–47.

[13] Anne Johnston and Anne Barton White, Communication Styles and Female Candidates: A Study of the Political Advertising during the 1986 Senate Elections, *Journalism & Mass Communication Quarterly* 71(2) (1994): 321–29.

[14] Kim F. Kahn, Gender Differences in Campaign Messages: The Political Advertisements of Men and Women Candidates for US Senate, *Political Research Quarterly* 46(3) (1993): 481–502.

[15] See James. G. Benze and Eugene R. Declercq, Content of Political Spot Ads for Female Candidates, *Journalism & Mass Communication Quarterly* 62(2) (1985): 278–88, doi. org/10.1177/107769908506200208; and Judith Trent and Teresa Sabourin, Sex Still Counts: Women's Use of Televised Advertising during the Decade of the 80s, *Journal of Applied Communication Research* 21(1) (1993): 21–40.

emphasize compassion and men to stress their strength, although sometimes both emphasized stereotypically masculine characteristics such as competence and leadership. Both male and female candidates were likely to dress in business attire, with women preferring "feminized" business suits.

From the 1990s to the present, most research has shown that female and male candidates are increasingly similar in their use of the verbal, nonverbal, and production techniques – or videostyle – that make up the content of their television ads.[16] Candidates in mixed-gender gubernatorial and congressional campaigns tend to discuss mostly the same issues – with some notable exceptions – in comparable election cycles. They are also mostly similar in the image traits emphasized as well as in their use of negative appeals to attack their opponents on the issues. Still, some gender differences in political advertising have remained consistent through election year cycles and levels of office, including a greater emphasis on some "feminine" issues and "masculine" images by women candidates; the strategies used in going negative; and in the nonverbal content of their ads, for example facial expressions, attire, and the inclusion, or not, of family.

For example, women candidates have been more likely than men to discuss such stereotypically feminine issues as health care and education in their television ads in most election cycles. They also have been statistically more likely than men to discuss women's issues, for example equal pay, but this is not among their top concerns. However, female candidates often mention the economy in similar proportions to male candidates in achieving a balance between so-called feminine and masculine issues in their television ads. Male candidates have focused more exclusively on masculine issues – most often the economy, federal budget, or foreign policy – when running against women in their television ads over time.[17] In the 2016 presidential campaign, Clinton balanced such feminine and masculine issues as women's rights, Iraq, education, public safety, and jobs in her television ads. Trump's ads focused on such masculine issues as taxes, terrorism, jobs, unemployment, and Benghazi.[18] Some differences in the issue emphasis of female and male candidates can be attributed to political partisanship as well as gender.

---

[16] Bystrom et al., *Gender and Candidate Communication*; Winfrey and Schnoebelen, Running as a Woman (or Man).
[17] Ibid.
[18] Clinton Crushes Trump 3:1 in Air War, Wesleyan Media Project, November 3, 2016, http://mediaproject.wesleyan.edu/releases/nov-2016/

As for the images emphasized in their ads, both female and male candidates most often portray themselves as possessing attributes commonly considered masculine, such as tough, action-oriented, and experienced. In 2006, women Senate incumbents were four times more likely than their male counterparts to highlight masculine attributes in their television ads.[19] Male candidates were significantly more likely than women to discuss their experience in politics until the 2008 election, when female candidates were significantly more likely than men to emphasize this trait.[20] In 2012, as Congress grew increasingly partisan and polarized, female candidates for the US House were significantly more likely than men to emphasize their ability to work with others.[21]

Although female and male candidates have used negative ads with similar frequency, they have differed in the purpose of their attacks and employ different strategies. Both female and male candidates use negative ads primarily to attack their opponents on the issues, but women are more likely than men to criticize their opponents' personal characteristics and call them names, often using an anonymous announcer. Male candidates, on the other hand, are significantly more likely to attack their opponents' group affiliations or associations and background or qualifications.[22] In the 2016 presidential campaign, Clinton was particularly focused on attacking the character of Trump as unfit for office in her television ads.[23]

Female candidates may have more latitude than male candidates to make personal attacks because voters stereotypically perceive them to be kinder and more caring. Of course, defying stereotypical norms also may backfire for women candidates, if they are labeled as too aggressive by the media. Male candidates, in contrast, may feel more constrained by expectations that they treat their female opponents with some degree of chivalry by refraining from personal attacks. Instead, men may lash out

[19] Fridkin and Kenney, *Changing Face of American Representation*.

[20] Dianne G. Bystrom and Narren J. Brown, Videostyle 2008: A Comparison of Female vs. Male Political Candidate Television Ads, in *Communication in the 2008 Election: Digital Natives Elect a President*, ed. Mitchell S. McKinney and Mary C. Banwart (New York: Peter Lang 2011), pp. 211–40.

[21] Mary C. Banwart and Kelly L. Winfrey, Is it the Message or the Medium? Female and Male Candidate Messages in 2012, paper presented at the annual meeting of the National Communication Association, Washington, DC, November 20–24, 2013.

[22] Bystrom et al., *Gender and Candidate Communication*; Winfrey and Schnoebelen, Running as a Woman (or Man).

[23] John C. Tedesco and Scott W. Dunn, Political Advertising in the 2016 US Presidential Election: Ad Hominem ad Nauseam, *American Behavioral Scientist* 63(7)(2019): 935–47, doi.org/10.1177/0002764218756919

more often at the opponent's group affiliations, since guilt by association may be a more acceptable and indirect way to question an opponent's character.

In the nonverbal content of their television ads, research shows, female candidates were significantly more likely than men to smile and to dress in business attire through the 2016 election[24] (though examples from the 2018 and 2020 election cycles show more women opting for casual dress). Both of these nonverbal characteristics reflect gender-based norms and stereotypical expectations. In everyday life, smiling is regarded as a nonverbal strategy women use to gain acceptance. The choice of business attire reflects the norms that society imposes on women as they seek to portray themselves as serious and legitimate candidates.

Because society's gender stereotypes more often associate women with families and children, it is interesting to note who is pictured in candidate ads. Studies conducted through the 2016 election show that female candidates rarely pictured their families in their ads, while male candidates were more likely to picture their wives and/or children. Researchers concluded that both female and male candidates were confronting societal stereotypes in their decisions over whether or not to include their families in their television ads. A female candidate may want to dismiss any concerns voters may have over her ability to serve in political office because of family obligations. Male candidates may want to round out their images by portraying themselves as loving husbands and/or fathers. Again, the 2018 and 2020 election cycles provide examples that indicate more female candidates are embracing their roles as mothers in their television ads.

In addition to the content of television ads, it is interesting to look at the effects of TV ads on potential voters. At first, researchers speculated that masculine (aggressive, career) strategies rather than feminine (non-aggressive, family) strategies worked best for women candidates in their political ads.[25] However, it now seems that women are most effective with

---

[24] See Bystrom and Brown, Videostyle 2008; Banwart and Winfrey, Is it the Message or the Medium?; and Kelly L. Winfrey and James M. Schnoebelen, Gender and Videostyle in 2016: Advertising in Mixed-Gender Races for the US House, in *An Unprecedented Election: Media, Communication, and the Electorate in the 2016 Election*, ed. Benjamin R. Warner et al. (Santa Barbara, CA: Praeger, 2018), pp. 274–95.

[25] See Lynda Lee Kaid et al., Sex Role Perceptions and Television Advertising: Comparing Male and Female Candidates, *Women & Politics* 4 (1984): 41–53; and Anne Johnston Wadsworth et al., "Masculine" vs. "Feminine" Strategies in Political Ads: Implications for Female Candidates, *Journal of Applied Communication Research* 15 (1987): 77–94.

voters when they are balancing stereotypically masculine and feminine traits, such as being tough and caring.[26] As far as issue emphasis is concerned, some studies have found that viewers find female candidates more competent on education and health care and men more competent on the economy and defense/military. However, evaluations of issue competency also are influenced by political party affiliation, with Democrats perceived to be more competent than Republicans on compassion issues, regardless of gender.[27]

A recent study examining the effectiveness of male versus female voiceovers in televised political ads found that congruency between issue and voice might be a smart campaign strategy. That is, a woman's voice may be more effective in grabbing a voter's attention and inciting learning on feminine issues with a man's voice having a similar effect on voters with masculine issues. However, the same study found little support for the disproportionate use of male voiceovers in political campaign ads in terms of their perceived credibility or effectiveness with voters.[28]

Recent studies also suggest that the use of negative political advertising appeals may backfire with women voters, who have been found to be less tolerant of negative ads and less likely to vote in highly negative and especially uncivil campaigns. On the other hand, male voters are not only more tolerant of negative ads but also more likely to be motivated to vote by negative, even uncivil, campaign messages.[29]

Television Advertising in US Senate Races in 2020

The 2020 election featured not only a woman of color as vice president on the Democratic ticket but also competitive female versus male and female versus female races for the US Senate. According to the Wesleyan Media Project's analysis of campaign advertisements from October 12 to October 25, 2020, the feminine issue of health care was the top concern emphasized by both Democratic and Republican Senate candidates in their

[26] Bystrom et al., *Gender and Candidate Communication*; Winfrey and Schnoebelen, Running as a Woman (or Man).

[27] Mary C. Banwart and Dianne G. Bystrom, Gender and Candidate Communication: An Analysis of Televised Ads in 2020 US Senate Races, *American Behavioral Scientist* (forthcoming).

[28] Kathleen Searles et al., The Effects of Men's and Women's Voices in Political Advertising, *Journal of Political Marketing* 19(3) (2017): 301–29, doi.org/10.1080/15377857.2017.133 0723

[29] See Deborah Jordan Brooks, A Negativity Gap? Voter Gender, Attack Politics, and Participation in American Elections. *Politics & Gender* 6(3) (2010): 319–41; and Fridkin and Kenney, *Changing Face of American Representation*.

advertising during the final weeks of the campaign.[30] Health care was emphasized in 44 percent of Democratic candidate ads and 33 percent of Republican ads, a sign of its importance in the 2020 election cycle. Other top issues for Democratic Senate candidates in their 2020 television ads were business (33%) and infectious diseases/COVID-19 (25%). Republican Senate candidates focused on taxes (31%) and jobs (17%) and mentioned COVID-19 in just 11 percent of their political ads.

Overall, the Wesleyan Media Project found that about 40 percent of television ads aired in the final weeks of 2020 US Senate general election races were negative, which is less than the four previous election cycles dating back to 2012. The most negative US Senate races featuring one or two women candidates in 2020 were the Kansas open-seat race between Democrat Bollier and Republican Roger Marshall (66.7% negative ads), Republican incumbent Collins versus Democratic challenger Gideon in Maine (58.4% negative), Republican incumbent McSally and Democratic challenger Mark Kelly in Arizona (50.3% negative), Republican incumbent Ernst and Democratic challenger Greenfield in Iowa (46.7% negative), and Democratic challenger McGrath and Republican Mitch McConnell in Kentucky (41.7% negative).[31]

A content analysis of 236 television ads from the ten most competitive US Senate races featuring a female candidate in 2020 found that women were more likely to mention health care when running against men (43% of the total issue mentions) than when running against another woman (27% of issue mentions). Women running against another woman were more likely to mention the economy (42% of issue mentions) than female candidates in mixed gender races (29%). Male candidates were almost equally likely to mention the economy (31%) as health care (29%).[32]

This analysis also found that female and male candidates were quite similar in their mention of image traits in their 2020 campaign ads.[33] Masculine traits – especially fighter, leader, and protector – comprised 72 percent of female and 77 percent of male candidate image mentions in mixed-gender races. Feminine traits – such as honest, caring, and especially "for the people" – comprised 28 percent of female and 23 percent of male candidate image mentions in mixed-gender races. In female versus

---

[30] Presidential General Election Ad Spending Tops $1.5 Billion, Wesleyan Media Project, October 29, 2020, https://mediaproject.wesleyan.edu/releases-102920/

[31] Ibid.

[32] Banwart and Bystrom, Gender and Candidate Communication.

[33] Ibid.

female races, masculine traits made up 68 percent of the total image mentions compared to feminine traits, 32 percent.

Examples of television ads from these 2020 Senate races illustrate how candidates highlighted issues and images. In Kansas, Bollier – a state legislator who retired from practicing medicine in 1999 and switched political parties from Republican to Democrat in 2018 – made health care a key issue of her campaign. In her 30-second ad, "Mission," she appears in a business suit standing in front of a window in what appears to be a living room. Looking straight at a camera, Bollier narrates the ad:

> As a doctor, I care deeply about making health care more affordable and I fought for common sense ways to do it, like lowering drug costs and ending surprise medical billing. My opponent, Congressman Roger Marshall [whose photo is shown], isn't a bad guy, but he voted against protections for pre-existing conditions. Just doesn't make sense and it would hurt so many Kansans. I'm Barbara Bollier and I approve this message because in the US Senate, my mission will be to bring down the cost of health care.[34]

In Texas, Republican incumbent John Cornyn aired a television ad stating his commitment to covering preexisting medical conditions. Cornyn's 30-second ad, "Health," includes seven video clips in which he appears dressed casually in three outdoor settings – sitting alone, walking with a man, and speaking to the man and a woman. An attorney, Cornyn speaks on screen in the first video clip and at the end of the ad in a voice-over. An anonymous female announcer narrates most of the ad, which also shows four video clips of doctors, nurses, and patients in medical settings:

CORNYN: You know, preexisting conditions is something we all agree should be covered.

FEMALE ANONYMOUS ANNOUNCER: And with John Cornyn's plan, they will be covered. Cornyn lowers the cost of health care, lets you keep your doctor, and keeps Medicare intact for seniors who have paid for it their entire life. It lowers the cost of prescription drugs and ends surprise billings. John Cornyn: common sense, thoughtful, proven leadership.[35]

---

[34] Barbara Bollier, Mission, YouTube, October 16, 2020, www.youtube.com/watch?v=-M6U8e610nU (accessed August 9, 2021).

[35] Texans for John Cornyn, Health, YouTube, October 16, 2020, www.youtube.com/watch?v=UteeOOA7fA8 (accessed August 9, 2021).

In addition to health care, Democrat Bollier and Republican Cornyn mentioned the related issues of prescription drugs and surprise medical billings. Cornyn also mentions Medicare. All are considered feminine issues. Cornyn uses a female voiceover, which research has found to be more effective when discussing feminine issues. As for the images emphasized in these ads, Bollier notes that she is caring, a feminine trait, with common sense, and that she's a fighter, a masculine trait often used by women candidates. Although Cornyn does not speak about his image attributes, the female narrator says he has common sense, is thoughtful, and that he is a proven leader. Thus, the health care ads of Bollier and Cornyn tend to emphasize both feminine and masculine image attributes.

In keeping with previous research, women Senate candidates – both Democrats and Republicans – often described themselves as tough or as fighters in their 2020 television ads. Democratic challenger Hegar of Texas and Republican incumbent McSally of Arizona were among the 2020 Senate candidates who described themselves in these masculine terms. Both women served in the US Air Force. Hegar was a major whose helicopter was shot down by the Taliban during a rescue mission on one of her three tours in Afghanistan. McSally retired as a colonel after twenty-six years of service, served in the US House of Representatives from 2015 through 2018, and was appointed to fill a vacant seat in the US Senate in January 2019.

In her 2020 ad, "Tough as Texas," Hegar is pictured in casual clothes in a series of fast-paced video clips riding a motorcycle and in her home with her young sons jousting with foam swords. Cornyn is also pictured and attacked in the 30-second ad. Hegar's narration is as follows:

> Six months since the Senate has done anything. Texans out of work and getting sick, small businesses shuttering and John Cornyn, no action, no leadership. But when his party bosses call, he jumps to rush through a Supreme Court nominee. I'm MJ Hegar. I did three tours in Afghanistan, earned a Purple Heart and am raising two kids in the middle of a pandemic. And John thinks I'm going to get pushed around in Washington, like he has? I approved this message, because it's about time Texas had a senator as tough as we are.[36]

---

[36] MJ for Texas, Tough as Texas, YouTube, October 16, 2020, www.youtube.com/watch?v=EweP8WxHP40 (accessed August 9, 2021).

Figure 11.1 In an ad titled "Tough as Texas," MJ Hegar includes "raising two kids in the middle of a pandemic" as a strength in challenging incumbent John Cornyn in their race for the US Senate.
Source: MJ for Texas, October 16, 2020, www.youtube.com/watch?v=EweP8WxHP40

In her 30-second 2020 TV ad, "Your Fighter," McSally is shown in military gear, holding a helmet, walking toward, and climbing aboard a fighter jet. She narrates as follows:

> I'm Martha McSally. At 12, I l lost my dad [photo of dad shown]. At 17, I became a survivor [newspaper article shown]. And, at 18, I was told girls can't be fighter pilots [newspaper article shown]. Then I became the first woman to fly a fighter jet in combat and help lead the air war after 9/11. America faces serious challenges, but we must overcome them. I approve this message because if you want flashy, you've got a guy. But, if you want a fighter, I'm your girl.[37]

In addition to accentuating their military careers and strength, both Hegar and McSally criticize their opponents, with Hegar making a direct attack on Cornyn and McSally with a more subtle reference to "flashy" Kelly. Both refer to the challenges faced by the United States, with Hegar making a direct attack on the lack of leadership in the US Senate with references to job losses, the pandemic, businesses closing, and the quick confirmation of Supreme Court Associate Justice Amy Coney Barrett.

---

[37] Martha McSally, Your Fighter, YouTube, September 21, 2020, www.youtube.com/watch?v=x3W0jKSyEgU (accessed August 9, 2021).

Figure 11.2 US Senator Martha McSally (R-AZ) recounts the harassment and discrimination she faced before becoming the first woman to fly a fighter jet in combat in an ad titled "Your Fighter."
Source: Martha McSally, September 21, 2020, www.youtube.com/watch?v=x3W0jKSyEgU

While displaying a tough persona, it is interesting that McSally ends this ad – and a few others – with "I'm your girl." Several television ads aired by Republican incumbent Collins in 2020 featured constituents calling her a "county girl," to underscore that she, unlike her Democratic woman opponent, was born and raised in Maine.

The content analysis of television ads from the ten most competitive US Senate races featuring a female candidate in 2020 also tested for mentions of relationships, which included families. Among the ads in which the candidates were featured visually on screen, women were more likely to assume a family role as a mom/mother or wife, and/or to include their children in their ads (24%) when compared to male candidates (15%) in mixed-gender races compared to 17 percent of the women candidates in female–female races.[38]

In Iowa, Democratic challenger Greenfield referred to herself as a "farm kid, military mom, and small businesswoman" in several of her 2020 television ads for the US Senate. However, her opponent, Republican

[38] Banwart and Bystrom, Gender and Candidate Communication.

incumbent Ernst, made the most direct appeal as a mom among the 2020 female US Senate candidates. Ernst served in the Iowa National Guard from 1993 to 2015, retiring as a lieutenant colonel, and served in the Iowa state senate from 2011 to 2014. In a campaign ad titled "What a Mom Can Do," she is pictured with her young adult daughter in two out-door video clips, along with a small dog, and inside with an older grand-motherly woman. Dressed casually and pictured in eight video clips in a home setting and outside, including one clip in a farm field with a young man, Ernst narrates the 30-second ad:

> I want my daughter and other young women to understand that this is what a mom can do. A mom can work. A mom can serve in uni-form. A mom can take those risks. A mom can farm, can run for elected office. These are all things that women can do, and I want her and others to understand that there are no limits. I'm Joni Ernst, and I approve this message.[39]

Figure 11.3 In an ad titled "What a Mom Can Do," US Senator Joni Ernst (R-IA) is pictured with her daughter and mother, saying moms can work, serve in uni-form, take risks, and farm.
Source: Joni for Iowa, October 30, 2020, www.youtube.com/watch?v=cMu3k7EGIvY

---

[39] Joni for Iowa, What a Mom Can Do, YouTube, October 30, 2020, www.youtube.com/watch?v=cMu3k7EGIvY (accessed August 9, 2020).

In another of her 2020 ads, "Challenges," Ernst talks about the Violence against Women Act as being "very personal" as a survivor of sexual assault and domestic violence in her marriage. "You can go through challenges in your lifetime, and you don't have to let those challenges define who you are as a person," Ernst says, dressed casually in a living-room setting. "You can overcome, and the next day is going to be a better day." The ad closes with a photograph of Ernst with her arm around her young adult daughter, both with big smiles.[40]

The highlighted television ads aired by Hegar, McSally, Greenfield, and Ernst in 2020 provide support for Kelly Dittmar's observation that women political candidates are increasingly embracing their gender identities as electoral assets rather than hurdles to overcome. Recent examples of women political candidates discussing gendered barriers date back to the 2016 presidential campaign, when Clinton talked more than she did in 2008 about the hurdles she has overcome as a woman and why those experiences mattered in serving as president. In 2018 and 2020, Dittmar noted that women congressional candidates "found ways to communicate toughness in less stereotypically masculine ways" by "sharing stories of overcoming personal adversity – including gender and racial discrimination – as a sign of strength and resilience." They also leveraged their identities as mothers to communicate "policy perspectives, priorities, and passion" or, in the case of Republican women, an "adherence to traditional roles and values."[41]

In "Tough as Texas," Hegar references raising two young boys as a source and proof of her strength. In "Your Fighter" and "Challenges," McSally and Ernst include their gendered experiences of discrimination, sexual assault, and domestic violence to communicate their toughness and resilience. Hegar, Greenfield, and Ernst equate the various roles performed by mothers with political leadership.

Although the Wesleyan Media Project found that television ads aired in the 2020 US Senate races were less negative overall than the four previous election cycles, attacks still made up a large percentage of the messages aired in several of the races highlighted in this chapter. The special election runoff in Georgia demonstrates how candidates can both launch and respond to negative attacks in high-profile political campaigns.

---

[40] Joni for Iowa, Challenges, YouTube, August 26, 2020, www.youtube.com/watch?v=LmY45V3-mCk (accessed August 9, 2021).

[41] See Kelly Dittmar, Unfinished Business: Women Running in 2018 and Beyond, CAWP, 2019, https://womenrun.rutgers.edu/; and Dittmar, Measuring Success.

Republican incumbent Loeffler – a multimillionaire businesswoman who was appointed to fill a vacant seat in the Senate in December 2019 – ran several attack ads against her Democratic, African American opponent, Reverend Raphael Warnock, and he responded.

Loeffler's 30-second ad, "Saving the Senate," is a series of ten color and black-and-white video clips beginning with elementary school students with hands over hearts saying the Pledge of Allegiance and then turning to riots in the streets, Fidel Castro, Warnock in clergy attire, more riot footage, defund the police signs, and Warnock again, before ending with a US flag flying over the countryside and Loeffler in the final frame. With ominous music playing in the background, an anonymous male announcer narrates the ad until Loeffler verbally endorses it at the end:

> MALE ANONYMOUS ANNOUNCER: This is America, but will it still be if the radical left controls the Senate? Raphael Warnock called police thugs, gangsters, hosted a rally for communist dictator, Fidel Castro, and praised Marxism in speeches and writings. Raphael Warnock will give the radicals total control. Saving the Senate is about saving America from that.
> KELLY LOEFFLER: I'm Kelly Loeffler. I approve this message.[42]

Anticipating the negative attacks, Warnock – the senior pastor at Ebenezer Baptist Church in Atlanta – ran two ads featuring his beagle to respond with humor and sarcasm. In "Walk," Warnock dresses casually as he walks his beagle through a neighborhood, smiling and pausing just before the end to drop a bag of dog poop in a trash bin. He narrates the 30-second ad:

> We told them the smear ads were coming and that's exactly what happened. You would think that Kelly Loeffler might have something good to say about herself if she really wanted to represent Georgia. Instead, she's trying to scare people by taking things I've said out of context, from over twenty-five years of being a pastor. But I think Georgians will see her ads for what they are [drops bag of dog poop in trash bin]. Don't you? I'm Raphael Warnock, and we approve this message [dog barks].[43]

[42] Kelly Loeffler, Saving the Senate, YouTube, November 12, 2020, www.youtube.com/watch?v=sUTe8yemoJM (accessed August 9, 2021).
[43] Reverend Raphael Warnock, Walk, November 24, 2020, Facebook, www.facebook.com/watch/?v=824528165070688 (accessed August 9, 2021).

Figure 11.4 US Senate candidate Raphael Warnock counters attacks made by his opponent in the Georgia special election runoff with humor in an ad titled "Walk."
Source: Reverend Raphael Warnock, November 24, 2020, www.facebook.com/watch/?v=824528165070688

Loeffler's use of an anonymous male announcer in her "Saving the Senate" ad aligns with research that shows male voiceovers are most effective when discussing masculine issues – such as crime and violence – in political ads. Television advertising in the Loeffler–Warnock race also illustrates its racial dynamics. Loeffler was criticized for playing the "race card" in her campaign ads by "targeting known pressure points of white conservative voters' fears and grievances about the distribution of power, social change and the tone or content of Black political demands."[44] Her ads called Warnock radical, dangerous, and anti-American. Warnock contended with such racialized stereotypes with preemptive tongue-in-cheek ads where he jokingly brushes off Loeffler's attempts to demonize him, a strategy that acknowledges that a "Black candidate, particularly a Black man, can't afford to be seen as angry, aggressive or defensive when running against a white candidate – particularly a white woman."[45]

[44] Janelle Ross, For Black Pastors, Calling out Racism is Standard. It's Become a Weapon for Warnock's Opponent, *NBC News*, December 14, 2020, https://nbcnews.to/3lNgT2l
[45] Mark Caputo and Maya King, Why Warnock Talks Puppies Instead of Race, *Politico*, January 3, 2021, https://politi.co/3AGf2kr

Finally, as noted in most of the advertising examples provided, many of the 2020 female candidates for the US Senate tended to dress casually in their TV ads, breaking with previous research findings that women preferred to be shown in formal attire. Among the ads in which the candidates were featured visually on screen, women were as likely to be in casual (50%) as formal attire (47%), with 3 percent dressed in clothing for a profession (e.g. military, health professional). Male candidates were dressed formally in 58 percent of their ads, casually in 35 percent, and in clothing for a profession in 7 percent.[46] Of the twelve women candidates in the ten races featured in this chapter, nine – McSally, Loeffler, Ernst, Greenfield, McGrath, Collins, Gideon, Hegar, and Democratic incumbent Tina Smith of Minnesota – dressed casually when appearing in some or even most of their television ads. Only Bollier, Republican incumbent Cindy Hyde-Smith of Mississippi, and Democratic incumbent Jeanne Shaheen of New Hampshire tended to dress more formally in their television ads. Thus, women running in more recent election cycles seem to be breaking away from another stereotypical constraint when it comes to the clothes they choose to wear in their campaign commercials.

Next, gender research on online candidate communication channels is summarized with examples from the 2020 mixed-gender and female versus female US Senate races provided.

ONLINE CAMPAIGN COMMUNICATION CHANNELS

In recent years, the Internet has provided political candidates and officeholders with important online means of communicating with voters and constituents while giving researchers another way to look at political communication. Websites and social media platforms represent other forms of political communication controlled by the politician. Although all have interactivity functions, Facebook and Twitter are particularly effective in engaging citizens in dialogues about political candidates and their campaigns. Since the 2016 presidential campaign, with Clinton and Trump often bypassing the media to tweet news and opinions directly to voters, Twitter has taken on an even larger role as a candidate communication resource.

[46] Banwart and Bystrom, Gender and Candidate Communication.

Gender and Candidate Websites

Researchers have studied candidate websites for gender differences and similarities for more than twenty years. Similar to gender research on political ads, studies of candidate websites have focused on issue and image emphasis, tone, and how the candidate is dressed and pictured. In examining the content of candidate websites, researchers have used gender-based stereotypes and voter expectations as well as the construct of webstyle, which is an adaptation of videostyle used in many studies of political advertising.

Research shows that female and male politicians present themselves similarly on their websites, but with some differences in election cycles. For example, female and male congressional candidates emphasized mostly similar issues on their campaign websites in 2000 and 2002, including the feminine issues of health care, education, and Social Security/Medicare and the masculine issue of the economy/jobs.[47] Similarly, female and male candidates for the US Senate and governor in 2000, 2002, and 2004 were equally likely to discuss the feminine issues of education and health care as well as the masculine issue of taxes.[48]

However, a study of the campaign websites of incumbent US senators running for reelection in 2006 found more adherence to gender-based expectations for both female and male candidates. Women senators were more likely to focus on communal, or feminine, issues on their campaign websites whereas male candidates highlighted competitive, or masculine, concerns. Almost 60 percent of the issue content on the female senators' biography pages emphasized such communal issues as protecting the environment and helping the elderly. Almost 67 percent of the issue discussion by male senators on their website biography pages focused on such competitive issues as the economy and homeland security.[49]

In 2012, both female and male congressional candidates discussed the economy, budget deficit, and unemployment on their websites. Male candidates in 2012 were more likely than women to discuss the masculine issue of taxes and the feminine issue of health care. Female candidates in 2012 were more likely than men to discuss the feminine issues of education and senior citizen concerns.[50] A study of congressional candidates

47 Kathleen Dolan, Do Women Candidates Play to Gender Stereotypes? Do Men Candidates Play to Women? Candidate Sex and Issues Priorities on Campaign Websites, *Political Research Quarterly* 58(1) (2005): 31–44, doi.org/10.2307/3595593

48 Bystrom et al., *Gender and Candidate Communication*.

49 Fridkin and Kenney, *Changing Face of American Representation*.

50 Mary C. Banwart and Kelly L. Winfrey, Running on the Web: Online Self-Presentation Strategies in Mixed-Gender Races, *Social Science Computer Review* 31(5) (2013): 614–24.

running in primary elections in 2018 found Democratic women were more likely to discuss health care and Republican women more likely to talk about taxes/spending in their website biographies – demonstrating, once again, that political party "ownership" of such issues also affects candidate communication.[51]

As for image characteristics, both female and male candidates running for the US Senate and governor in 2000, 2002, and 2004 focused primarily on masculine traits – such as past performance, experience, and leadership – on their websites.[52] A study of the websites of candidates in all US Senate races and a stratified sample of US House races in the 2002, 2004, 2006, and 2008 election cycles found that both female candidates (35%) and male candidates (31%) were more likely to emphasize empathetic images, such as being "of the people," over leadership.[53] Both female and male candidates running for the House in 2012 most frequently mentioned past performance, their qualifications and experience, and being "of the people." However, male candidates more frequently discussed the masculine trait of being action-oriented, whereas female candidates were more likely to discuss the masculine trait of competency.[54]

In addition to analyzing the issue and image content of campaign websites for gender differences, a few studies have assessed their tone as well as how the candidate appears.[55] Studies have found that candidates have been more likely to launch attacks on their websites than in their television ads. They have also shown that women candidates are most likely to appear in business attire on their websites and male candidates are more likely than female candidates to include photos of their families. A recent study analyzing the campaign websites of congressional candidates in 2008 and 2010 found that women still tended to deemphasize their children whereas men were more likely to showcase their families, most notably in photos.[56]

51 Maura McDonald, Rachel Porter, and Sarah A. Treul, Running as a Woman? Candidate Presentation in the 2018 Midterms, *Political Research Quarterly* 73(4) (2020): 967–87.
52 Bystrom et al., *Gender and Candidate Communication*.
53 Monica C. Schneider, Gender-Based Strategies on Candidate Websites, *Journal of Political Marketing* 13(4) (2014): 264–90.
54 Banwart and Winfrey, Running on the Web.
55 See Bystrom et al., *Gender and Candidate Communication*; and Mary C. Banwart, Webstyles in 2004: The Gendering of Candidates on Campaign Websites?, in *The Internet Election: Perspectives on the Web in Campaign 2004*, ed. Andrew. P. Williams and John C. Tedesco (Lanham, MD: Rowman & Littlefield, 2006), pp. 37–56.
56 Brittany L. Stalsburg and Mona S. Kleinberg, "A Mom First and a Candidate Second": Gender Differences in Candidates' Self-Presentation of Family, *Journal of Political Marketing* 15(4) (2015): 285–310, doi.org/10.1080/15377857.2014.959684

In summary, most gender-related studies of campaign websites to date have found mostly similarities in the issue and image emphasis of female and male candidates. Both women and men often offer a similar mix of feminine and masculine issues on their websites. This suggests, once again, that issue emphasis is more related to the context of the election year than to the sex of the candidate. Still, as with their television advertising, female congressional candidates are more likely to discuss the feminine issues of education and senior citizen concerns on their websites. As for the traits they emphasize on their websites, both female and male candidates tend to focus on the masculine characteristics often associated with winning political office.

Studies of election cycles from 2000 through 2010 have found that male candidates are more likely to include photos of their families than female candidates on their websites. These earlier studies also found that candidates are more likely to go negative on their campaign websites than in their television ads, underscoring the difference between these mediums. As websites are most often accessed by people already supporting the candidate, it is safer to include attacks. Television ads, in contrast, have the potential to reach all voters, some of whom may be turned off by attacks.

Examples from the websites of the ten 2020 US Senate races highlighted in this chapter are consistent with the findings of previous research. Both female and male candidates balanced feminine and masculine issues on their campaign websites in the races examined. However, women were more likely to list more feminine issues (62%) than masculine ones (38%) whereas men were more balanced between masculine (53%) and feminine (47%) issues. The feminine issue of health care and the masculine issue of economy/jobs were each mentioned on 94 percent of the websites in the sample, 100 percent of women's websites and 86 percent of the male candidates'.

Although the feminine issue of education comprised just 4.4 percent overall (3.3% of women and 6.7% of men) of the issue mentions in the television ads[57] of the ten 2020 US Senate races analyzed for this chapter, it was listed on 81 percent of these candidates' websites – 89 percent of women and 71 percent of men. Women were more than twice as likely as men, 100 percent to 43 percent, to include veterans among the issues listed on their websites. Four Democratic candidates in the sample – Greenfield of Iowa, Smith of Minnesota, Hegar of Texas, and Warnock of

---

[57] Banwart and Bystrom, Gender and Candidate Communication.

Georgia – included LGBTQ+ rights among the issues highlighted on their websites. Four Republican candidates in the sample – McSally of Arizona, Ernst of Iowa, Marshall of Kansas, and Hyde-Smith of Mississippi – listed their pro-life stances on their websites.

Consistent with previous research, female and male 2020 Senate candidates in the races sampled emphasized masculine over feminine traits on their websites. Masculine traits comprised 71 percent of the image characteristics highlighted by female candidates on their websites and 69 percent of those mentioned by men. Female candidates most often mentioned their leadership, strength, and accomplishments. Male candidates most often mentioned their leadership, experience, and accomplishments. Seven candidates in the sample – Republicans Ernst of Iowa, Collins of Maine, and Cornyn of Texas, and Democrats Kelly of Arizona, Smith of Minnesota, Shaheen of New Hampshire, and Hegar of Texas – mentioned that they were bipartisan, collaborative, or independent. On their home pages, most of the women in the sample (67%) were dressed in casual clothes, contrary to previous research showing that women preferred formal attire.

Gender and Social Media Messages

In addition to using websites as an online communication channel, political candidates are increasingly turning to social media platforms to reach voters. In recent years, research on the gender differences in the use of such social media platforms, especially Twitter, by female and male candidates has grown. Studies have focused not only on the comparative number of posts and tweets by female and male candidates but also on the intent of their messages (e.g. to communicate policy positions, attack their opponents, or mobilize voters) as well as their use of personalization and interactivity. Some researchers have noted the potential of social media platforms to disrupt gender biases in political campaign communication.

Studies of the Twitter use of congressional candidates in 2010 and 2012 found that women not only tended to tweet more often than men but also were more negative, perhaps to counteract stereotypes that they were weaker.[58] In 2012, women congressional candidates also were more

---

[58] See Heather K. Evans and Jennifer H. Clark, "You Tweet Like a Girl!" How Female Candidates Campaign on Twitter, *American Politics Research* 44(2) (2016): 326–52, doi. org/10.1177/1532673X15597747; Heather K. Evans, Victoria Cordova, and Savannah Sipole, Twitter Style: An Analysis of How House Candidates Used Twitter in Their 2012 Campaigns, *PS: Political Science & Politics* 47(2) (2014): 454–62; and Kevin M. Wagner, Jason Gainous, and Mirya R. Holman, I Am Woman, Hear Me Tweet! Gender Differences in Twitter Use among Congressional Candidates, *Journal of Women, Politics & Policy* 38(4) (2017): 430–55, doi.org/10.1080/1554477X.2016.1268871

likely than men to use policy issues – especially such feminine issues as health care, education, equality, and the environment – and attempt to mobilize voters with their tweets.[59]

Studies of the tweets of Senate candidates in 2012 and gubernatorial candidates in 2014 focused on gender differences in personalization. Male Senate candidates in 2012 were more likely than women (17% to 11%) to use personalization in their tweets. Male gubernatorial candidates in 2014 were twice as likely as women (11% to 5%) to use personalization in their tweets. In 2012, women Senate candidates were more likely to emphasize their gender, uniqueness, and religion in their personalized tweets, whereas men were more likely to focus on family and include personal photos featuring family and friends.[60] In 2014, women gubernatorial candidates engaged in a "particularly gendered form of personalizing" by portraying themselves explicitly as caregivers to their children with images of them cooking, cleaning, and doing homework.[61]

The study of the tweets of US Senate candidates in 2012 also examined interactivity, finding that women were more interactive than men (75% to 61%). Women candidates were three times more likely than men to include @replies, retweets, and retweet pluses (posting a retweet or modified tweet and adding some of their own content) to communicate directly with other Twitter users or promote their voices in their feeds. Male candidates were more likely than women to include @mentions and photos to integrate the presence of others in their feeds. Similar to the findings of researchers who have studied gender differences in the use of family images by candidates in their political ads and websites, Lindsey Meeks concludes that the inclusion of more personal photos by men in their Twitter feeds is "particularly interesting because it is possible that women hedged their use of such photos so as to avoid familial associations that may put them at odds with masculinized politics."[62]

A few studies assessed the social media use of Clinton and Trump in the 2016 presidential campaign. Some differences were found. For

---

[59] Evans and Clark, "You Tweet Like a Girl!"

[60] Lindsey L. Meeks, Gendered Styles, Gendered Differences: Candidates' Use of Personalization and Interactivity on Twitter, *Journal of Information Technology & Politics* 13(4) (2016): 295–310, doi.org/10.1080/19331681.2016.1160268

[61] Shannon C. McGregor, Regina G. Lawrence, and Arielle Cardona, Personalization, Gender, and Social Media: Gubernatorial Candidates' Social Media Strategies, *Information, Communication & Society* 20(2) (2016): 264–83, doi.org/10.1080/1369118X.2016.1167228

[62] Meeks, Gendered Styles, 303.

example, a content analysis focusing on two weeks of the 2015 prepri-
mary phase found that Clinton was much more likely to mention feminine issues (144 times/66%) than masculine issues (75/34%) in her tweets.
Trump mentioned masculine issues thirty-five times (67%) and feminine
issues seventeen times (32%) in his tweets. Of the ninety-one gendered
trait words mentioned by Clinton in her tweets, fifty-nine (65%) were
masculine and thirty-two (35%) were feminine. Of the thirty-eight gendered trait words used by Trump, twenty-three (60.5%) were masculine
and fifteen (39.5%) were feminine. Trump was almost four times more
likely than Clinton to mock or criticize other candidates, the media, or the
government in his tweets, 25 percent to 6.5 percent, which was viewed by
the researchers as an aggressive presentation of his masculine character.[63]

During the 2016 general election, Clinton discussed feminized issues –
including education, the environment, LGBTQ+ equality, equal pay, paid
family leave, and affordable childcare – four times more often (16% to
4%) than Trump in her tweets. Trump was more likely than Clinton to
discuss masculinized issues in his tweets, 21 percent versus 17 percent. As
for values, Clinton discussed feminist values in 4 percent of her tweets,
compared to 0.6 percent for Trump. Clinton also discussed women and
girls in her tweets significantly more often than Trump did, 7 percent to 2
percent, often varying between inspiration and attacks on Trump for his
treatment of women. She was also more likely than Trump to discuss children and families in her tweets, 6 percent to 0.8 percent. Clinton mentioned women's representation (in 2% of her tweets) and her own gender
(3.5% of her tweets) significantly more often than Trump, who never
mentioned women's representation in his tweets and his own gender in
just 1 percent of his tweets.[64]

A few studies have examined the gendered effects of candidate websites and social media messages on voters. One study shows that male
candidates can benefit just as much as female candidates by focusing on
so-called feminine issues such as health care and domestic violence on
their websites in terms of perceived competence as well as the likelihood

[63] Jayeon Lee and Young-shin Lee, Gendered Campaign Tweets: The Cases of Hillary
    Clinton and Donald Trump, *Public Relations Review* 42(5) (2016): 849–55, doi.org/
    10.1016/j.pubrev.2016.07.004
[64] Lindsey L. Meeks, Appealing to the 52%: Exploring Clinton's and Trump's Appeals to
    Women Voters during the 2016 US Presidential Election, *International Journal of
    Communication* 12 (2018): 2527–45, https://ijoc.org/index.php/ijoc/article/view/8763/
    2377

of women to vote for them.[65] Another study indicates the potential of Twitter for women's candidate communication, in that they were more central to the conversations of Twitter users and received more replies when they ran against men. However, the greater levels of interactivity with women candidates could indicate that Twitter users may feel "more comfortable talking to women candidates due to stereotypes of communal traits" or that the "male-skewed population of Twitter encourages men to 'talk back at' female candidates online."[66]

All candidates in the 2020 US Senate races sampled for this chapter had an active presence on Twitter. Examples from their Twitter feeds show how women candidates used this social media platform to communicate their issue concerns and character traits, attack their opponent, and mobilize voters. The examples also show how Twitter users engage with women candidates on the platform, both to support and criticize them.

In a November 2, 2020 tweet, Democratic challenger Gideon of Maine emphasized that several women's issues were on the ballot in encouraging voters to support her: "Health care is on the ballot. Civil rights are on the ballot. The environment is on the ballot. We have one more day to win this race. Let's leave it all on the field, Maine. #mepolitics." The tweet received 1,505 likes, 411 retweets, 46 quote tweets, and 18 comments, including @chuck2cc, who said, "Again you left out the most important thing that people need and want, Jobs."

Both Gideon and her opponent, Republican incumbent Collins, emphasized their willingness to work across the aisle in several of their tweets. On October 15, 2020, Collins noted her bipartisanship and leadership while highlighting another feminine issue, schools: "Following a bipartisanship effort that I helped lead, the USDA took action to ensure that students in Maine and across the country continue to have access to free school meals through June 2021, regardless if they are learning in the classroom or virtually." Her tweet received 256 likes, 20 retweets, 46 quote tweets, and 221 comments, mostly negative and many criticizing Collins for her vote to confirm Brett Kavanaugh to the US Supreme Court, "We are going to lose the right to choice because of you," replied @tabruns.

In Iowa, Democratic challenger Greenfield often tweeted about the feminine issue of health care while attacking her opponent, Republican

[65] Mirya R. Holman, Monica C. Schneider, and Kristin Pondel, Gender Targeting in Political Advertisements, *Political Research Quarterly* 68(4) (2015): 816–29, doi.org/10.1177/1065912915605182

[66] Shannon C. McGregor and Rachel R. Mourão, Talking Politics on Twitter: Gender, Elections, and Social Networks, *Social Media + Society* 2(3) (2016): 1–14.

incumbent Ernst, on the issue. On October 26, 2020, Greenfield tweeted: "Health care is on the ballot. In the Senate, I'll fight to enhance the ACA, allow Medicare to negotiate lower prescription drug costs & protect our rural hospitals. @joniernst wants the opposite. If she got her way 1.3 million Iowans with preexisting conditions could lose care." Her tweet had 1,152 likes; 375 retweets; 29 quote tweets; and 21 comments, most of them positive. @Lalaej, who has more than 12,000 followers, quoted Greenfield's tweet with her own message: "@Greenfield will do all she can to keep your healthcare affordable, incl. drug prices. Ernst has voted to overturn the ACA. The choice is clear #wtpSenate #wtpBlue #DemVoice1."

CONCLUSION

An examination of how female and male political candidates are presented in their television advertising and on such online communication channels as their campaign websites and social media platforms, primarily Twitter, suggests ongoing trends as well as directions for future research. While we can draw on the results of nearly forty years of research examining the television advertising of women running for governor and the US Congress, fewer studies analyze the much rarer campaigns of female vice-presidential and presidential candidates. And, although dating back some twenty years, gendered research on candidate websites has not been as robust as studies of television advertising. Researchers are, however, taking more interest in the gendered use of social media platforms, especially Twitter, by political candidates. Nonetheless, several recurring trends help guide our expectations for the future study of gendered campaign communication.

Television commercials, websites, Facebook, and Twitter provide candidates with tremendous opportunities to present themselves directly to voters. This is particularly important for female candidates, who are still subjected to gender stereotypes by voters and the media. Television advertising is the dominant form of candidate communication for most major races. Female candidates are successfully establishing their own competitive styles of campaigning through this medium. They have overcome the stereotypical admonition that they must avoid attacking their opponent. Female candidates also have successfully achieved a television videostyle that emphasizes masculine traits, such as being a fighter and leader, while balancing such feminine issues as health care with such masculine concerns as jobs/economy. And, as examples from 2018 and 2020 indicate, women are gaining more flexibility in how they leverage their identities as mothers, communicate strength in less stereotypically masculine ways, and dress more casually in their television ads.

Campaign websites provide candidates with a platform to offer significant amounts of issue information, if they choose, as well as low-cost opportunities to interact with supporters. Female candidates can develop sophisticated websites that provide more specialized messages to specific groups, use innovative types of interactivity, and generate a more personalized presence with voters. Twitter, Facebook, and other social media platforms provide candidates with efficient and timely opportunities to offer policy positions, attack their opponents, and engage supporters. As one of the newer communication channels gaining popularity with political candidates, Twitter offers both rewards and risks – especially for women candidates. It can help level the playing field when candidates' tweets go viral and receive positive replay in the media. And, although Twitter has the potential to disrupt deeply rooted gender biases about female candidates, it also can open up women to sexist and even abusive comments.

As researchers continue to study how candidates present themselves to voters through their television ads, websites, and social media platforms, we will learn more about the evolving role of gender in political campaign communication.

Index

Page numbers in **bold** refer to content in tables;
page numbers in *italics* refer to content in figures.

CPSIA information can be obtained
at www.ICGtesting.com
Printed in the USA
LVHW051537241221
707138LV00019B/1775